P9-CBM-444

DODGERLAND

Decadent Los Angeles and the 1977–78 Dodgers

MICHAEL FALLON

University of Nebraska Press
Lincoln & London

Library of Congress Cataloging-in-Publication Data
Names: Fallon, Michael, 1966–author.
Title: Dodgerland: decadent Los Angeles
and the 1977–78 Dodgers / Michael Fallon.
Description: Lincoln: University of Nebraska Press, 2016. |
Includes bibliographical references and index.
Identifiers: LCCN 2016002293 (print)
LCCN 2016004109 (ebook)
ISBN 9780803249400 (hardback: alk. paper)
ISBN 9780803288317 (epub)
ISBN 9780803288324 (mobi)
ISBN 9780803288331 (pdf)
Subjects: LCSH: Los Angeles Dodgers (Baseball team)—
History—20th century. | Los Angeles (Calif.)—Social
conditions—20th century. | BISAC: SPORTS & RECREATION
/ Baseball / History. | HISTORY / United States / State &
Local / West (AK, CA, CO, HI, ID, MT, NV, UT, WY).
Classification: LCC GV875.L6 F35 2016 (print) | LCC GV875.
L6 (ebook) | DDC 796.357/64097949409047—dc23
LC record available at
http://lccn.loc.gov/2016002293

Set in Minion Pro by M. Scheer.

CONTENTS

PROLOGUE

Tuesday, October 17, 1978

The stout figure on the bench told the story. His face had the hang-dog look of an Italian Boxer. His body, slumped backward, was as distressed as a Renaissance pietà. He was in obvious pain, his spirit deflated, his copious ego crushed. He could only watch as his boys—all his beloved "sons"—were being beaten by a remorseless enemy. As the manager of the Los Angeles Dodgers in 1978, he had no choice but to suffer the indignities of yet another likely loss to the Yankees of New York and to suffer it in front of fifty-five thousand live spectators and an entire TV-watching nation.

To the manager's left, the team's first baseman unconsciously mirrored his manager's posture. To his right, assistant coach Monty Basgall sat more upright, arms locked in a tight fold over his chest. All three men had the look of a kid whose favorite toy had just been taken by the biggest bully on the block. And why wouldn't they look this way? It was the eighth inning of the sixth game of the 1978 World Series, and the Los Angeles Dodgers were losing in the worst possible way, to their hated rivals. Here at home, in Dodgerland. In front of their own fans. For the second year in a row.

Down at the other end of the bench, other players were less openly dismayed. After all, they had come about as close as you could get to a happy ending without actually reaching that peak. Sure, it was frustrating, but most players, most people, never even got a shot at baseball's championship. So they wouldn't win this time. They had no reason to hang their heads. Hell, they were a damn good team of ballplayers, and they were still young. There would be other opportunities.

If anything, the players felt bad for the man at the end of the bench, their manager: old Tom. Tommy Lasorda. They regretted they hadn't lived up to old Tom's confidence. Cocksure, blustery Tommy, ever convinced his boys would prevail. "When you guys get to Dodger Stadium and do something special," they remembered him saying years ago when it seemed they'd never get out of Ogden, or Spokane, or Albuquerque, "look up in the stands for the spirit of a guy who helped you get there, a guy with a tear in his eye. Look up at old Tom."

Now, with just six outs to go in Game Six, and the Dodgers about to lose it all, Lasorda had inwardly collapsed. His normally gregarious and enthusiastic self was gone. Tom Lasorda, who had survived the tough love of his Old World father, who had scrapped with bigger kids on Pennsylvania playgrounds, who had outplayed his physical ability to become a Major League pitcher, was now reduced to a taciturn and insecure shell of himself. He had nothing left to spur his players to win on this horrible Los Angeles night. He was defeated.

As Tom Lasorda languished on the bench at Dodger Stadium, about forty-one miles due east in the small town of Alta Loma another Tom had just settled down to watch the World Series on his patio TV. Just a year into his sixties, Tom had spent a long day on his feet at his hardware store, moving stock here and there, helping befuddled customers, and tousling the hair of their kids. Even though he had missed most of the game, catching the last few innings was still a nice way to spend the lovely evening's remains. At least it wasn't work.

When he saw the score, however, Tom let out a small, pained breath. It was audible enough that his wife of nearly forty years, Catherine, sneaked a look at him from her usual perch in the kitchen. Yes, Tom was still a strong man, having helped to raise six strapping Irish American kids (five of them sons) and having built businesses and kept houses in order, but she was still protective of him. When she saw that he was fine, she went back to the dishes.

Tom Fallon had been following the Dodgers for many years, going all the way back to the uncertain days after leaving the Philadelphia orphanage where he had spent eight years after his mother's death. The orphanage was not a pleasant place in his memory. The nuns were cruel, beating him for his left-handedness and other imagined crimes. He left Philadelphia in 1934 and headed straight for New York, where he would later reunite with his three younger (surviving) siblings, whom he had not much seen since they were all sent to different orphanages. It was while in New York that Tom discovered the Brooklyn team.

The Brooklyn Dodgers of the era were a sloppy squad, but Tom liked their pluck. He especially liked a lippy shortstop who would go on to bigger renown, even infamy. "He was a small guy," Tom remembered, "but quick. And he had great hands. Strong hands, but soft as well. He could pick up anything that came close to him. I never saw a shortstop like him before, or since." Leo Durocher was an All-Star player for the Dodgers twice in the late 1930s. In 1938 he finished in the top ten in league Most Valuable Player (MVP) voting, and the next year he took over as the hapless team's player-manager. The 1939 Dodgers surprised everyone by finishing third with an 84-69 record. It was the team's first winning season in a decade and the first of many to come. No wonder Tom Fallon became such a fan of the Dodgers. In the orphanage he long dreamed of better days. Among devoted Dodger fans whose rallying cry was "Wait till next year," he found his tribe.

In time Tom Fallon's love of baseball grew to encompass the history of the game and the great players of the past, whose life stories often sounded like his own. Across the patio from his easy chair, a bookshelf held one of Tom's favorite books: *The Glory of Their Times*, by Lawrence Ritter. "This is a great book," he would tell a curious grandson who was about the same age as Tom had been when he lost his mother. "It says something about what America used to be. Let me know what you think of it after you finish it."

The grandson borrowed the book from Grandpa Tom and, even though it was thick as an adobe brick, read it in three or four sittings. He too became hooked on baseball's history.

Farther afield, the reactions of other critical figures were less certain. From his Manhattan apartment, a third Tom—this one a distinguished writer and a social critic—might have caught wind of a shifting mood on the radio broadcast on the old RCA tube radio outside his office. He had been working away at his typewriter most of the day, trying to reach his daily quota of three pages, but the sound might have reminded him it was time to quit for the day. If so, Tom Wolfe would have pushed back his leather chair from his circular writing desk of polished teak and gilt trim and walked into the alcove just off his office. Then the crowd on the radio would have roared again.

The World Series. He had lost track of the World Series. *What inning is it? What's the score?* He sat down on a nearby settee and listened for a moment. *7–2 after seven innings.* The Yankees were leading, but Joe Ferguson of the Dodgers had led off the eighth with a sharp double to right-center. Wolfe would have pondered this. He had no great love for the Yankees. *How could anyone love the Yankees? They were like Big Government. No one liked Big Government.* Tom Wolfe was an old Giants (and small-government) man. He still worshipped the great Giants of his youth: Bill Terry, a boyish-faced assassin at the plate; Carl Hubbell, efficient as a clock maker on the mound; and Mel Ott, compact and unassuming, but as natural a hitter as ever played the game and with that crazy, eccentric high leg kick. When Wolfe was in college, editing the sports section of his school newspaper and playing semipro ball on the side, the Giants were the most storied team in the league. After school Tom arranged a tryout with the Giants. He was a pitcher, and an adequate one, but his stuff was nowhere near Major League level. He hung on at camp for three days before getting cut. Now, he liked to say, "If somebody had offered me a Class D professional contract, I would have gladly put off writing for a couple of decades."

But that was years ago, and baseball had changed. The Yankees had long overtaken the Giants as the league's dominant team and now represented all the worst impulses in American society: the burning desire to win, even at the expense of fair play; the poisonous love of wealth and success above all else; the imperial urge to dominate. And though the franchise's fortunes had dimmed for the past ten years or so, now, in the middle of this decadent decade, the team had returned to its old ways. Like most Americans of honest conscience, Tom Wolfe hoped for the toppling of the New York Yankees.

On the other hand, he thought, the Dodgers were the ancient, bitter rival to his Giants. And now they were out in the sun-addled, libertine New Age lotusland of Southern California. *How could he root for the Dodgers, with their pleasure dome of a stadium overlooking palm-treed vistas and smog-choked sunsets and glamorous Hollywood stars filling the field-level seats among the earnest women in their snap-around denim skirts and honest calves and their poor wimp husbands with their round eyeglasses and droopy beards and their babies spitting up natural-food mush onto their work shirts?* Wolfe had seen his fill of the California social experiment, which he was certain would someday implode in a giant frenzy of self-satisfaction and waves of feathered, conditioned perfect hair. He did love that catcher Yeager, though—pugnacious and fearless, just like his cousin Chuck. Wolfe would have loved to throw to a guy like Steve Yeager back in his day . . .

A roar from the radio jarred Tom Wolfe from this imagined reverie. He leaned in to listen. Vic Davalillo from Venezuela, a forty-one-year-old retread with an odd, twitchy slap swing, had beaten out a slow Baltimore chop to second baseman Doyle. There were now men at first and second and no outs, and the top of the Dodgers' order was due up. This could still be a game, Wolfe thought, and he waited to find out what would happen.

A bit more speculation about the last key character: In an office in L.A.'s city hall, just down the hall from the mayor's office, two assistants might have leaned in close to the television as the Dodgers threatened in the eighth. The two, working late on details related to an upcoming ceremony at the White House, likely had been unable to stay away from the game. They wouldn't have resented working late. No one who worked for Mayor Tom Bradley could survive for long if they hated long hours. And this was important work. He was poised to sign, at long last and in the presence of President Carter, an important agreement regarding the 1984 Summer Olympic Games. Mayor Bradley wanted everything to be planned out just right. They understood that.

On TV, though the volume was turned down, a burst of noise erupted. The Dodger Stadium crowd showed life for the first time since the third inning, and the Dodger bench was stirring. Score a few runs here, and a comeback was not impossible. As the next batter, Davey Lopes, stepped to the plate, one assistant would have nodded to the other and quickly left the room.

Down the hall, in his well-lit and comfortable office, Mayor Bradley sat working at his desk. The assistant knocked softly and then quietly stepped inside the office and waited. Behind the mayor, atop a large bookcase each ensconced in protective vitrines, sat the mayor's collection of trophies, relics of track and field accomplishments in high school and college. Mayor Bradley paused and looked up, and the assistant told him what was happening in the game. Bradley looked at the assistant thoughtfully for a moment, then nodded before returning his attention to the papers on his desk.

Back in the TV room Davey Lopes flailed against Rich Gossage, striking out on four pitches, the last a breaking ball well out of the strike zone. Bill Russell followed Lopes, looking cooler, though it was hard to tell with Russell. He always looked this way, like he had ice in his veins. Russell waved his choked-up bat, waiting for something he could slash at. Gossage delivered a fastball, and Russell swung furiously, drilling a screamer down the third base line. Both of Bradley's assistants leaped out of their seats—*this could be extra bases!*—and they could hardly believe what happened next.

Dodgerland

PART 1
1977

ONE

The Days of Bad Baseball

> [I would] change policy, bring back natural grass and nickel beer. Baseball is the bellybutton of our society. Straighten out baseball, and you straighten out the rest of the world.
>
> —Bill Lee, *Los Angeles Times*, February 3, 1977

If people in the early 1970s were unaware that America was becoming something different from what it had been a generation earlier, then June 4, 1974, opened a lot of eyes. That evening in Cleveland, the hometown Indians baseball team held a special promotional event at Cleveland Municipal Stadium for its game against the Texas Rangers. Called 10 Cent Beer Night, the idea was this: sell beer so cheaply that young fans would return in droves to support the team. While many baseball fans have a general sense of the events of that notorious night, a deeper look at the Beer Night riot reveals the forces behind the drastic changes occurring in baseball and American society at the time.

There was no big mystery why the Cleveland team had failed to draw fans over the previous decade. In six of the previous seven years, the Indians had been a miserable franchise, finishing at or near the bottom of its division each year. Its lineups were a rogues' gallery of middling talent (Duke Sims, John Lowenstein, Steve Mingori, Frank Duffy, Tom Timmerman, Jack Brohamer, Bill Gogolewski). And its managers were either uninspiring organization men (Johnny Lipon, Ken Aspromonte) or bitter former stars who had fallen from grace (like Al Dark, late of the San Francisco Giants). For the desperate Indians, the Beer Night promotion worked like a charm, at least at first. At game time the stands of Municipal Stadium held more than twenty-five thousand fans, twice the season average. The fans were young and mostly male. They were in high spirits, and the beer flowed freely on a warm night. By one estimate the stadium moved more than sixty-five thousand units of beer. The trouble started almost immediately.

In the middle of the first inning several young male fans ran onto the field, drawing cheers from the crowd. As the Rangers ran up a 5–1 lead in the early innings, fireworks cracked and popped in the stands. More young men, including a streaker (or several, including possibly a woman, according to varying accounts), dashed onto the field. When the Indians narrowed the Rangers' lead in the sixth inning, fans began throwing bottles and other missiles into the visitors' bullpen in right field. The Rangers' manager, Billy Martin, who was both a throwback to these kids' fathers' era of baseball and a famously pugnacious player prone to arguing with umpires, fighting on and off field, and drinking large amounts of alcohol, removed his players from the pen.[1] In response fans threw firecrackers into the Rangers' dugout. In the ninth inning, after the Indians fought back to tie the game, the levee finally broke. After one fan ran on the field and was rebuffed while trying to grab the cap of Rangers right fielder Jeff Burroughs, hundreds of young men flowed out of the stands. They surrounded Burroughs. "I tried to call time," Burroughs said the next day, "but nobody heard me. I was getting scared because I felt the riot psychology." When fiery Martin saw what was happening, he led his players into right field to save Burroughs. Many of them grabbed bats at Martin's urging. "Jeff was out there all by himself," Martin said. "I saw knives and chairs and other things. We just couldn't let our teammate get beat up."[2] The Indians players also got into the act, and skirmishes between ballplayers and fans broke out all over the field. "It's the closest I've ever seen anybody come to getting killed in my more than twenty-five years in baseball," Martin added.[3]

Police, when they arrived on the scene, arrested eight persons and sent one other to the hospital. Nestor Chylak, the chief umpire on the field, had been hit with a chair and had his hand cut. Chylak waited until the field was cleared and all the players were safe before he declared the game forfeited—the victory going to the Rangers by the traditional fictitious score of 9–0.

Afterward, the Indians' director of stadium operations, Don Zerby, blamed the problem on the beer giveaway. "You had college students, teenagers, high school graduates and older folks drunk," said Zerby. "I don't think they even checked identifications when they sold the beer for 10 cents. They just put their money up on the counter and got their beer. It was just as simple as that." Commentators around the country railed against the rowdiness of the Cleveland fans. One columnist said that the Indian faithful had "overwhelmingly passed the New York Mets' fans as the worst in baseball," and he suggested the city did not deserve a ball team. Bud Harrelson, a player for the New York Mets, suggested the problem was the era's "permissive age." "If the cops belted a few [rowdy fans] on the head," he said, "they wouldn't do it." Nestor Chylak also had little sympathy for the fans. Chylak, a decorated World War II veteran who had become a Major League umpire in 1954, was widely admired around the league for his sense of fairness. After the game Chylak railed against the rioters, calling them "uncontrollable beasts" and saying, "Have I ever seen anything like this before? Yes, in the zoo."[4]

A small number of commentators defended Cleveland's fans, pointing out they might have been provoked by a brawl between the two teams a week prior in Texas. The brawl had been precipitated by Martin's penchant for having his pitchers throw at opposing players. Others pointed out that Martin may have further provoked the home fans during the Beer Night game. "Martin threw gravel at the fans and thumbed his nose at them near the Texas dugout," said Indians vice president Ted Bonda the next day. "Then it just mushroomed and snowballed and you know what happened after that."[5]

Whatever the truth, American League (AL) president Lee MacPhail confirmed the forfeit despite protests by the Indians' general manager, Phil Seghi. MacPhail also declared that the three other 10 Cent Beer Nights that Cleveland had planned were to be canceled.

Though a singular event, the 10 Cent Beer Night riot demonstrated something important about baseball and the times. The nation's pastime, which had captivated the average American sports fan as recently as the 1950s and '60s, seemed by 1975 to be in fast decline. Part of the issue was a generational shift. On that summer night in 1974 many of the fans who spilled onto the field in Cleveland were baby boomers anxiously approaching full adulthood. These were unruly, unsettled young people clinging to their waning days of youthful rebellion. To the seventy million baby boomers, society was defined not by shared sacrifice, C rations, victory gardens, breadlines, and soup kitchens. Boomers defined themselves in opposition to the rules and strictures of their parents' generation. And this opposition often manifested itself in ways that were inexplicable to their elders.

Beyond the 10 Cent Beer Night riot, signs of great boomer unrest were everywhere in the early years of the 1970s—at Altamont, in the burning streets of many American cities, at war-protest rallies, on campus at American universities, even around dinner tables. Writer Tom Wolfe, who chronicled new social trends and transformative events that emerged out of America's postwar prosperity for magazines such as *Esquire*, *New York*, and *Rolling Stone*, famously labeled the 1970s "the Me Decade." In an article that originally appeared in the magazine *New York* in August 1976, Wolfe described the self-centeredness and atomization of the era's young people. Even amid the excess of luxury goods, conveniences, and abundance of 1970s America, Wolfe saw a drove of hucksters and shills selling self-involvement to a generation of naïfs. According to the writer, everywhere ordinary housewives were leaving regular society to fall in with self-help gurus, sex-hungry hippies were going off the grid to find themselves, and lost souls were experimenting with fads like encounter sessions and primal-scream therapies. The author saved his sharpest vitriol for the new religions of the era: the Moonies, followers of Carlos Castaneda and Werner Erhard, the worshippers of the acid trip and the occult and the paranormal. Wolfe fretted that, hidden behind the recurring message of self-focus and self-improvement, the new religions of the 1970s were actually built on a spirit of schism and isolation. "The various movements of the current religious wave," he wrote, "begin with the most delicious look inward; with considerable narcissism, in short. When the believers bind together in religion [now], it is always with a sense of splitting off from the rest of society."[6]

If the country's young people were psychologically and spiritually off track during the Me Decade, they came to their confusion somewhat honestly. Between 1972 and 1975 Americans struggled with several vast and seemingly insoluble crises that shattered their belief in the country's way of life: the slow unraveling of the country's government in the wake of the Watergate crisis, the resignation of Richard Nixon, the country's final capitulation in the long Vietnam War, the energy crisis of 1973, and a long, slow period of economic malaise, weakened productivity, and diminishing quality of life among the country's middle and lower classes.

By 1974 most Americans were certain the country was going in the wrong direction. One could hardly fault the cynics, as the country's economic and political stresses had accelerated a number of problematic social trends. Researchers noted alarming rises in divorce rates, crime rates, and the number of single-parent families as well as declines in the birthrate and overall standard of living. "I keep hearing the 1970s described as a lull, a rest period, following the uproars of the 1960s," Wolfe wrote in his 1980 book *In Our Time*. "I couldn't disagree more. . . . The uproars did not subside in the least. On the contrary, their level remained so constant, they became part of the background noise." Wolfe went on, citing the various "epidemics" of the age—the divorce epidemic, the drug epidemic, and a vast shift in the values that had long sustained the country. As a result, according to Wolfe, "it became perfectly okay, quite the acceptable thing, to cash in on your life. . . . There was no law that said you had to suffer an attack of scruples, and precious few of the boys did. Selling off chunks of one's righteous stuff via television commercials became not merely acceptable but conventional behavior for famous people in the 1970s. In 1969 the first man to set foot on the moon, Neil Armstrong, delivered, via television, a cosmic *symploce* measuring the stride of mankind itself in the new age of exploration. In 1979 Armstrong was on television, in a Sales Rep sack suit delivering Cordobas, Newports, and Le Barons for the Chrysler Corporation."[7]

So difficult was the era that *Time* would eventually, in 1979, offer this hard assessment: "The economy's most disruptive decade since the Great Depression has borne the stagflation contradiction of no growth amid rampaging inflation, the can't do trauma of receding productivity in the nation that was long the world's cornucopia, the reality of an energy shortage in the land of supposedly boundless resources, and the debauch of a dollar that once was 'as good as gold.' . . . 'Things just do not work now as they used to,' says former Federal Reserve Chairman Arthur Burns, and who can contradict him? The U.S. economy, bloated and immobilized, has been turned topsy-turvy."[8]

In light of all this, in light of the degeneration of America's once polite society and of the so-called American way of life, what Cleveland's fans did on the field at Municipal Stadium in June 1974 is unsurprising. In truth baseball was suffering the times as much as the rest of the country. Chief among the modern game's problems was, as with the rest of the country, a distinct lack of class and decorum. Nestor Chylak, a member of the Greatest Generation who had survived the grueling Battle of the Bulge, was witness to the growing unruliness that surrounded the game. In one famous incident in 1968 in Baltimore, Chylak had nearly been brained by an anonymous fan who threw a bottle at him from the stands. The incident had occurred after Chylak, who was the third base umpire at the time, had leaped out of the way of a line drive. He was not very happy about the incident, to say the least. "There were a bunch of guys up there," Chylak said after the game, "near the Baltimore dugout, who were stone drunk. . . . It scares you, I tell you. Maybe people don't think I've got eyes, but I do and I wanna keep 'em."[9] Chylak, like many of his generation, believed in the necessity of strong rules and hard, but fair, judgment. Chylak's bitter denunciation of the rioters in Cleveland was likely influenced by his generation's disillusionment with the changing times.

The 10 Cent Beer Night riot was not the only sign of declining decorum in baseball during the 1970s. Not long after sportswriter Milton Richman predicted that events like the Beer Night riot would likely recur, Shea Stadium in New York closed off its right-field bleachers to deter fans from throwing bottles and other debris at rival players like Pete Rose. In 1976, meanwhile, two people were stopped while trying to burn an American flag at Dodger Stadium during a game against the Chicago Cubs. A few years later, in 1979 in Chicago, another ill-conceived promotion would cause an even more massive fan disruption in the middle of a White Sox doubleheader.

Adding to baseball's problems in the 1970s, at least in the view of traditional-minded fans, was the current crop of baseball players. By the middle of the decade an entire generation of players—rugged, no-nonsense, no-complaint guys of a certain old-school quality—had retired. These were guys who had been born during the Depression, had lived through World War II, and whose outlooks had been defined by the key American values of their time. These were players such as Ted Williams, who served in the prime of his career as a naval aviator during World War II and the Korean War; Willie Mays, a player so admired he received honorary doctorate degrees from Yale and Dartmouth; Bob Feller, who was the first baseball player to enlist in the armed forces after the attack on Pearl Harbor on December 7, 1941; and Joe DiMaggio, who served in the U.S. Army Air Forces during World War II. By the mid-1970s this generation of player had retired, replaced by a completely new brand of player.

The young players of the 1970s often seemed to reflect some of the worst aspects of the culture at large—the indulgences, foibles, lifestyle choices, and indiscretions that older baseball fans found objectionable. Pete Rose of the Cincinnati Reds, for example, approached his play in the field and at the plate like a Paleolithic hunter. Reds fans, of course, loved Rose's troglodytic drive to succeed, dubbing him Charlie Hustle and repeatedly voting him to the All-Star Game, but the darker aspects of Rose's approach to the game—his fights with opposing players, pushing matches with umpires, obsessing over playing statistics, and, famously, a senseless full-body hit at home plate on rookie catcher Ray Fosse during the 1970 All-Star Game—were truly ugly. And Rose was just the tip of the iceberg. Numerous star players in the 1970s were plain unlikable. Dave Kingman once sent a live rat wrapped in a pink box to a sportswriter, just because she was female. Dick Allen was so sullen and flatly dismissive of his own fans, they threw debris at him from the stands. Keith Hernandez was a noted (and unapologetic) misogynist. And so on.

Although it's true that baseball has always had its share of unsavory characters, bad behavior among the nation's sporting heroes had long been, by implicit agreement, swept under the rug or simply tolerated as part of the cost of doing business. What was different in the 1970s, however, was that in an age of crisis, eternal Cold War conflict, and political corruption, the culture no longer seemed able or willing to ignore the raging flaws of ballplayers.

Beyond the obvious failings of many star players of the 1970s, even the ordinary average-Joe players seemed different from the players of old. Beginning with the wild early-1970s Oakland A's teams, an "anything goes" attitude meant players grew wild mustaches, beards, thick sideburns, and long manes of hair. In 1970 the Pittsburgh Pirates adopted a new uniform with pullover shirts, elasticized and beltless pants, and a breathable, knitted cotton-nylon fabric that allowed players to show off their physiques. Soon, nearly every team was developing similar uniforms and adding polyester fabrics and colors as wild as Saturday-morning cartoons. And while one could argue that the players' new fashion sense in the 1970s was a harmless bit of fun, the new personal permissiveness also translated to reckless behavior. Though drugs like "greenies"—a psychostimulant that players used to gain alertness and energy—had long existed in team clubhouses, the 1970s saw a rise in the popularity of recreational drugs like cocaine and, to a lesser extent, marijuana and hallucinogens. Dock Ellis of the Pittsburgh Pirates pitched a no-hitter in 1970 while supposedly under the influence of LSD. Some players in the era gave their dealers an open invitation to visit them in their teams' clubhouses. So rampant was the drug problem in baseball that, by decade's end, sting operations led to two drug cases involving large groups of Major League ballplayers.[10]

Partially as a result of these flaws, baseball's popularity went into decline in the early 1970s. In terms of attendance, TV revenue, and numbers of fans, the old "national pastime" had been surpassed by professional football in the 1960s, but in the 1970s it was being increasingly challenged by professional basketball. Attendance at baseball games had flatlined, stuck at essentially the same levels as in the 1950s, despite a greater than 30 percent increase in the overall population.[11] The stagnant attendance led to league-wide financial pressure. Each year it seemed at least one baseball club struggled to stave off bankruptcy. Between 1966 and 1976 baseball teams bolted—or attempted to bolt but were blocked from doing so—from Milwaukee, Seattle, Kansas City, San Diego, San Francisco, Oakland, and Washington DC.

Adding to baseball's problems was some misguided and counterproductive rule tinkering by the sport. In an attempt to speed up what had always been a languid and pastoral sport, in the early 1960s baseball officials expanded the traditional batter's strike zone, or, more accurately, they began enforcing the literal rule concerning what constituted a strike.[12] By the mid-1960s baseball had become dominated by pitching, and the sluggers who had made the game thrilling since the 1920s were in decline. The league average in runs scored per game fell from about 4.5 in 1961 and 1962 to fewer than 3.5 in 1968, the year that became known widely as the Year of the Pitcher. Fans grew bored, and additional tweaks meant to improve things only made matters worse. Purists bemoaned the arrival of goofily costumed team mascots, novelty "throwback" uniforms and blinding uniform redesigns, bullpen carts shaped like giant baseballs, the designated-hitter rule, and the like, while they fretted that owners resisted real, resonant changes to the game. Charlie Finley, the iconoclastic owner of the Oakland A's, hinted at the depth of the problem in 1975. "I've never seen so many damned idiots as the owners," Finley said. "Baseball's headed for extinction if we don't do something. . . . Only one word explains why baseball hasn't changed: stupidity! The owners don't want to rock the boat."[13]

Whatever the cause, by the mid-1970s it was clear that baseball was less and less how people were choosing to pass their time. And as evidenced in Cleveland in the hot and frustrated summer of 1974, the unrest of baseball fans occasionally made for ugly times at the ballpark.

TWO

Where It Will Always Be 1955

The strongest thing that baseball has
going for it today are its yesterdays.

—Lawrence Ritter, widely quoted

By early 1975, six months or so after the 10 Cent Beer Night fiasco, Americans' spirits seemed as dimmed as at any time since the Great Depression. In an era of growing national malaise, people grasped for any easy way to forget their problems. This meant throughout the decade people constantly pined for a lost golden age, a time when Americans were proud, knew how to get the job done, and made things that worked. Several peculiar cultural phenomena of the 1970s can be traced to this desire.

Throughout the decade people fixated on the musical culture of a more vibrant, optimistic time. "Oldies" radio stations proliferated, playing the music of a supposed "golden" age that roughly spanned the July 1954 release of Elvis Presley's "That's All Right" and the February 1964 release of the Beach Boys' "Don't Worry Baby." Encouraged by the renewed attention, acts like Fats Domino, Little Richard, Chuck Berry, and Jerry Lee Lewis made comebacks in the 1970s. Meanwhile, contemporary groups like the Flamin' Groovies, Dave Edmunds, the New York Dolls, and even the Sex Pistols recorded old rock songs such as "I Hear You Knocking," "Baby I Love You," "Tallahassee Lassie," and "Stranded in the Jungle." Only an era drowning in nostalgia could have enjoyed a band like Sha Na Na, which charted throughout the decade with rehashed doo-wop songs from the 1950s and early '60s. Only in an era bent on ignoring a changing world would a grating track like Bob Seger's "Old Time Rock and Roll" become a hit record (in 1978).

And America didn't just *revisit* the styles and culture of the past; it also used the material to inspire new cultural production. In 1971 the stage musical *Grease* referenced the fads, fashions, and musical styles of the 1950s as part of a story about contemporary sexual mores. In 1973 filmmaker George Lucas—who would become widely known a few years later for another little movie—released *American Graffiti*, which followed a group of teenagers during a long night of cruising and listening to rock and roll in the very early 1960s. In 1974 TV followed Lucas's lead with *Happy Days*, a sitcom that presented an almost surreally idealized 1950s middle-American family, the Cunninghams. The show became so popular it spawned national catchphrases, icons like the "Fonz," and endless cultural detritus (lunch boxes, dolls, play sets, board games, comic books, trading cards, clothing, books, and so on). The 1970s also saw the resurgence of 1950s phenomena like the yo-yo, Ovaltine, and, briefly, Howdy Doody. Even the original 1950s version of the Mickey Mouse Club found enough of an audience in the flood of nostalgia to go into syndicated reruns between January 20, 1975, and January 14, 1977.

The patriarch of the *Happy Days* family, Howard Cunningham, was an American ideal with wide appeal: a hardworking small businessman who ran his own hardware shop. Starting in 1976 Tom Fallon would follow Howard Cunningham's lead. In that year Fallon bought an existing business called Cucamonga Hardware—located, appropriately enough, in Cucamonga, California, a small town located about fifty miles due east of Los Angeles—along with a partner named Nelson Hawley.[1] As in *Happy Days* Tom Fallon was following his vision of an America in which hardworking, independent, average American citizens could go about their business without interference, putting a bounty of daily bread on the table in front of their strapping American families and otherwise living the good life.

Far across the country, meanwhile, a humble and unknown politician—James Earl Carter Jr. of Georgia—cleverly tapped into the national nostalgia when he announced his campaign for presidency late in 1974. "We Americans are a great and diverse people,"

Jimmy Carter said. "Each of you is an individual and different from all the others. Yet we Americans have shared one thing in common: a belief in the greatness of our Country. We have dared to dream great dreams for our Nation. We have taken quite literally the promises of decency, equality, and freedom. . . . Now it is time . . . for American citizens to join in shaping our Nation's future. Now is the time for new leadership and new ideas to make a reality of these dreams."[2] Reality, of course, stood in sharp relief against the country's wistful nostalgia for more golden times. But on TV, in music, and in the deep recesses of the public imagination of the 1970s, Detroit was still ascendant, America was still the undisputed leader of the world, Ozzie Nelson still dispensed golden nuggets of wisdom, and Mickey and Joe and Willie and Teddy Baseball still played the national game.

That the deep and all-consuming nostalgia for the past extended to baseball in the 1970s is clear in how Americans said they viewed the game at the time. Throughout the Me Decade baseball fans remained attached to an older game and its storied stars. This attachment took a number of shapes. For one, there was the popularity of an unlikely baseball book written in 1966 by an unknown economics professor from New York University. Lawrence Ritter was a fan of the work of John and Alan Lomax, ethnomusicologists who recorded, in the 1930s and 1940s, the aging exemplars of the nation's nearly forgotten early folk music. Ritter's own anthropological book on baseball—called *The Glory of Their Times*—was conceived after the author had heard about Ty Cobb's death in 1961 and began wondering what happened to the rest of the great baseball stars of Cobb's era. The idea came not a moment too soon: many of the game's heroes of the early twentieth century were—like the country's folk singers twenty years earlier—fading away in near obscurity. Ritter logged more than seventy-five thousand miles over four years to interview players such as Rube Marquard, Wahoo Sam Crawford, and Smoky Joe Wood where they lived. *The Glory of Their Times* sold more than 350,000 copies. It was so popular in the 1970s that Ritter also released a vinyl album containing some of the actual recordings of the interviews, and Bud Greenspan made a documentary film version of the players' stories in 1977.

The craze for old baseball players spread widely into the culture. One famed baseball player of the 1940s was memorialized in a Grammy Award–winning song in 1969, Simon and Garfunkel's "Mrs. Robinson." In the song's lines "Where have you gone, Joe DiMaggio? The nation turns its lonely eyes to you," Paul Simon perfectly encapsulated the national regret over lost heroes. And DiMaggio was the perfect symbol for such sentiment. Nearly universally admired for his on-field grace and exploits with the bat, DiMaggio was dubbed by journalists in 1969, on the occasion of the game's centennial celebrations, baseball's "greatest living player." Fortunately for nostalgic baseball fans, for a brief, celebrated moment Joltin' Joe returned to baseball. In 1969 he took a position as a coach for the Oakland A's. Almost immediately, however, the elusive DiMaggio struggled with the attention that growing numbers of fans showered on him. "I think he would have really enjoyed [the A's coaching post], if not for his notoriety," said one of his players, Joe Rudi. "He loved coaching, he loved being around the guys and road trips and plane rides. He was a different person than when he was trying to get from the bus to the ballpark, or the bus to the hotel, and people were bugging him. They were just fans wanting his autograph, but he was just overwhelmed." Around the same time, another all-time great—Ted Williams—took over as manager of the Washington Senators to much the same fanfare. And when Williams led the last-place Washington squad to a fourth-place finish in his first year at the post, the fanfare became a hallelujah chorus. "[The Senators' players] started believing in him," said Darold Knowles, an All-Star pitcher for the Senators that year, "because they knew he was Ted Williams."[3] Fans started believing as well, attending games at twice the rate in 1969 as they had the year before. Unfortunately, the Senators tumbled back to earth during the next three years of Williams's tenure. In 1972, having moved to Texas, the team (now called the Rangers) finished in last place with a 54-100 record, and Williams hung up his spikes for good.[4]

After DiMaggio and Williams finally left the game in the mid-1970s, interest in aging stars from baseball's "golden age" remained high. Commercial television regularly trotted out former players like Mickey Mantle, Whitey Ford, Yogi Berra, Willie Mays, and even Joe DiMaggio to pitch products like light beer, video games, athlete's foot spray, bowling equipment, Tab cola, and the Mr. Coffee machine. In 1974 the Baseball Hall of Fame selected Mickey Mantle for induction in his first year of eligibility—only the seventh player to be so chosen—and the Committee on Baseball Veterans, which was particularly active throughout the 1970s, added Jim Bottomley, Sam Thompson, and Negro Leaguer Cool Papa Bell to the hall. For the decade special Hall of Fame committees would select thirty-two old-time players for induction (compared to just seventeen in the 1980s), as well as an additional nine veterans from the Negro Leagues.

Amid all this nostalgia for the baseball of old, nothing quite compared to a game-changing event that occurred in 1972. That summer the New York publishing house Harper and Row released a book by a little-known journalist named Roger Kahn. "This is a book about some young men who learned to play baseball during the 1930s and 1940s," read the book's back-cover copy, "in such places as Reading, Pennsylvania; Anderson, Indiana; Plainfield, New Jersey; Woonsocket, Rhode Island; and then went on to play for one of the most exciting professional teams that the major leagues ever fielded—the Brooklyn Dodgers of the 1950s." In some respects the release of Kahn's *The Boys of Summer* was fortuitous, as it was perfectly timed to capitalize on fan nostalgia. In other ways, though, *The Boys of Summer* was its own phenomenon that encapsulated a generation's love of baseball tradition.

Organized into two sections, *The Boys of Summer* began by recounting Kahn's memories of his Brooklyn youth and of his two years covering the Brooklyn Dodgers as a young reporter for the *New York Herald Tribune*. The second section, which took place in the 1970s present, portrayed where the great players from the 1950s Brooklyn Dodgers had landed in their middle age. Chapters were devoted to each of the players as Kahn rediscovered them: some living quiet lives away from the game, some struggling with tragedy and pain, and some thriving in sports or business. Kahn's book became an instant success and a widely acknowledged classic.[5]

The Dodger teams of the 1950s may well have experienced an explosion of interest in the 1970s even had Roger Kahn not supplied the spark. Not only was the team wildly successful in those years—only its cross-league rivals the New York Yankees had more success—but the basis of the Dodgers' winning ways, indeed the team's essential makeup, reflected two aspects of American culture that were disappearing in the Me Decade. First, as longtime sportswriter Jack Lang put it, the Dodgers were a uniquely homespun baseball team. "There it was family," he said. Owned by the O'Malleys since the early 1950s, the Dodgers managed their business with much the same personal flair and idiosyncrasy as a mom-and-pop hardware store. The Dodgers of the 1950s were often seen as part of the neighborhood fabric of Brooklyn. Duke Snider and a few of his teammates—including Pee Wee Reese and Carl Erskine—lived in the Bay Ridge neighborhood and would carpool together to their home games at Ebbets Field. Additionally, perhaps because of this familial feel, the team had its own particular well-structured, tradition-based system for teaching young players how to play baseball—called the "Dodger Way"—that stressed pitching, defensive fundamentals, and several intangible personal values.

The Dodger Way had not always existed. The franchise, which had been founded in 1884, was, for many years, rather disorganized and bumbling, something of a league doormat. The team's name, for instance, settled on in 1932 after a series of forgettable false starts—Atlantics, Grays, Bridegrooms, Superbas, and Robins—was short for Trolley Dodgers. This was a result of the fact that a confusing tangle of nine trolley lines ran on and around Flatbush Avenue outside of the team's ballpark, Ebbets Field. As if inspired by the Dodgers' chosen sobriquet, the years leading up to the 1940s were haphazard and futile for the Brooklyn team—only two World Series appearances, both losses, in nearly sixty years and many years spent in or near last place in the eight-team National League (NL). Even the Dodgers' own fans—rough and crude, but not unaffectionate, Brooklynites—called the team by their own more descriptive nickname: "Dem Bums."

Notwithstanding the boost that Leo Durocher brought to the Dodgers, the team's ultimate elevation as a franchise was spurred by the 1942 hiring of Branch Rickey to be the team's general manager.[6] Rickey transformed the team's outlook and philosophy. His pronouncements, delivered with the bombast of a proselytizer—his nickname was "the Mahatma"—became legendary around the Dodger organization and around baseball. Above all else he advocated some very midcentury American values: good character, discipline, clean living, dedication, and, especially, willingness to work hard. "Sweat is the greatest solvent there is for most players' problems," Rickey said. "I know of no cure, no soluble way to get rid of a bad technique as quick as 'sweat.' . . . Make a man do it over and over again."[7]

But Rickey wasn't just an aphorist and moralist. He was also a genius innovator. Before coming to the Dodgers Rickey helped make his previous employer the St. Louis Cardinals a perennial powerhouse by inventing the team's "farm system" of affiliate Minor League teams. Rickey came to the Dodgers in 1943 from St. Louis, where he had developed a team that won three World Series in just over a decade. With the Dodgers Rickey would expand on his approach to developing Minor League players, growing the Dodgers' system from four to twelve and eventually eighteen teams, and making other crucial changes. In 1947 Rickey, seeking to expand the farm system at his new club, purchased—through a one-dollar lend-lease agreement—a rapidly decaying abandoned naval air station in the city of Vero Beach, Florida. Rickey liked the site because it was isolated and could allow the team to manage the sticky racial politics of the Deep South.[8] Also, with the vast barracks and nearly unlimited land on the site, Rickey knew he could build a vast spring baseball school—the Dodger Baseball School—that could focus completely on the task of churning out myriad Major League ballplayers versed on a series of principles he was already calling the "Dodger Way."

The first full Dodger spring-training camp in Vero Beach in the winter of 1948 welcomed an unprecedented 660 young players—far more than attended any other team's spring-training camps at the time—and all 660 were allowed to compete for spots on the big-league team. Through the years the team's full spring-training facility became the state-of-the-art Dodgertown, and Rickey continued innovating, encouraging the use of new tools such as batting cages, pitching machines, and batting helmets. Under Rickey's system the Dodgers became known for their play-it-by-the-book, no-nonsense approach to baseball, but they were also among the league's most daring teams.[9] Most significantly, the Dodgers overturned the league's de facto policy of excluding African American ballplayers by fielding a twenty-eight-year-old rookie second baseman named Jackie Robinson in 1947. Again, much credit goes to Rickey for this. With his keen eye for competitive advantage, Rickey was convinced that the African American ballplayers of the age were an untapped pool of talent that would make the Dodgers perennial champions. It was an insight that would pay immense benefits, as players like Robinson, and later Roy Campanella and Don Newcombe—and still later Joe Black, Jim Gilliam, and John Roseboro—added speed, power, and live arms to fuel the Dodger win factory through the 1950s and into the 1960s.

As Tom Fallon could attest after having moved his family from Albany, New York, to suburban Southern California in 1953 and having reacquainted himself with the Los Angeles Dodgers after their 1958 move west, being a Dodger fan in the 1950s and '60s meant you were near the pinnacle of all American sport. In the three decades leading up to 1977, only one other team in the league—the New York Yankees—had won more regular-season games than the Dodgers.[10] Also during this period the Dodgers won four World Series, a record again surpassed only by the Yankees. Even more admirable to many beyond the wins and championships was the fact that the Dodgers won on their own merits, primarily by developing players from within the team's system—as opposed to buying players or bullying and bilking weaker teams out of quality players. Between 1947 and 1977 the Dodgers developed more Rookies of the Year (seven) and more Cy Young Award winners for the league's best pitching (six) than any other team. In fact, the Dodgers had more than double the number of these awards than the next-closest team.

By the 1960s the now Los Angeles Dodgers had the best of everything: a noteworthy and unique historical legacy, a beautiful new home field in Dodger Stadium, a beautiful setting in Chavez Ravine, and plenty of fans and supporters. Moving deeper into the decade, as the country struggled through urban riots, the civil rights movement, political assassinations, and a floundering foreign war, the Dodgers continued their winning ways by constantly updating their roster with homegrown stars such as Don Drysdale, Maury Wills, Willie Davis, Wes Parker, and Sandy Koufax. Pitcher Koufax in particular was a catalyst for Dodger dominance, winning three Cy Young Awards and one MVP Award and leading the league in earned run average (ERA) for five straight seasons and in strikeouts for three. Between 1960 and 1966, during Koufax's heyday, the Dodgers won two World Series, appeared in one other, and narrowly missed appearing in a fourth when they lost a divisional playoff game in 1962 to the San Francisco Giants.

But the success eventually ended. The Dodgers were ill-equipped to cope when Koufax, who had struggled for several years with severe elbow troubles, announced his retirement after the 1966 World Series. In 1967 the Dodgers collapsed. They finished near the bottom of the National League in the next two seasons. It was the first two-year stretch of losing seasons for the team in thirty years.

While the Dodgers recovered enough by the early 1970s to record winning records again, the team seemed somehow out of sync with the times. Some critics blamed the team's struggles to regain its old magic on its dedication to the traditions of yesteryear. Even as the game, and American society, was rapidly changing around them, the Dodgers still preached the value of the Dodger Way and stood firmly by their traditions. To name just one superficial, but highly visible, example of how this dedication to tradition played out, the Dodgers were one of the few teams in the league that did not adopt the new tight-fitting pullover uniforms that became popular in the 1970s. In fact, through the decade the team's uniform essentially remained unchanged from its first LA-era design in 1958.

Dick Allen, a talented but flawed slugger who played one season, 1971, with the Dodgers, blamed the team's poor finish that year specifically on its devotion to tradition. The Dodgers could have won the National League West crown in 1971, Allen suggested, but "the problem was all that Dodger Blue jive. [The organization puts] a lot of pressure on players to sign autographs and have their picture taken. They want you to visit with celebs in the clubhouse before games. Have a laugh with Don Rickles. Eat spaghetti with Sinatra. . . . It distracts from the team's mission to win ballgames."[11] The Dodgers lost the Western Division title by one game in 1971, and Allen was traded to the White Sox in the off-season.[12]

Allen wasn't the only one who questioned the value of the Dodger Way. The great syndicated Los Angeles sports columnist Jim Murray, a longtime follower of the team, wrote about its Dodgertown spring-training facilities in the mid-1970s and found it curious that no picture of any recent Dodgers hung on the walls of the team's clubhouses. "Will any of today's players become streets in Dodgertown?" he wrote. "Or even pictures on a wall?" He noted that among the photos, only three depicted players from the team's years in Los Angeles. And all three of these players—Koufax, Drysdale, and Wills—had retired. "Everything else is newer, shinier, and more efficient at Dodgertown. Gone are the barracks, the leaky roofs, the porous screens, the dripping showers, the 660-man chow lines, the raggedy old bedrooms. . . . But gone, too, are the Koufaxes, Hodgeses, Reeses, Drysdales, Robinsons, Campanellas, Newcombes, Labines, and Sniders. There is no movement afoot yet to take down their pictures for newer, more exciting ones. Dodgertown's walls stay black-and-white. . . . On the walls, it will always be 1955."[13]

Considering the Dodgers' glorious history over the past few decades, the reluctance to eschew traditions even in the new decade of the 1970s was understandable. But seven long seasons of mediocre play after the 1966 World Series had raised questions about the Dodger Way. In this the team had much in common with the country at large, since ordinary Americans were questioning the value of the American way. The conflict between the national desire to hold on to traditional values and a youthful embrace of rapid cultural change was a defining feature of the times. Caught in these muddy, uncertain waters, both in baseball and in the culture at large, the Dodgers were fortunate to have the phlegmatic presence of their tradition-minded manager, Walt Alston.

"Now we could write two or three books on all the ifs, ands, and buts in baseball," the patient Alston said of the seven-year stretch of futility for the team in the late 1960s and early 1970s. "But that wouldn't change the standings in any of those years or any of the scores. . . . In those seven years without a pennant we seemed to have all the ingredients—even in 1967 and 1968—but frustrations pursued us every season."[14] Behind Alston, and with the blessing of the tradition-minded O'Malley family, the Dodgers remained determined to find a winning formula during a confusing new era of baseball. And the result of these efforts would affect the National League pennant races for years to come, even as it would move the Dodgers deep into the swirling maelstrom of change—to baseball, to the times, to sports in America.

THREE

Detours along the Dodger Way

Over my years in baseball I've made a lot of friends among what we now call the media. It used to be the press but now radio and television are so big the name has changed. A lot of them have called me the Quiet Man—a reference I don't totally agree with. Maybe I am to some. Others might not agree. Everyone who knows me well realizes that I'm slow to anger but, once I boil—watch out, it's pretty hard to calm me down.

—Walt Alston in 1976

If I were starting my career again, I'd like to have Tom Lasorda as my manager.

—Tommy Lasorda, *Los Angeles Times*, September 30, 1976

The roots of the Dodger turnaround in the 1970s were actually planted during the team's low point in 1967 and 1968. Chastened by their repeated failure at employing aging veterans to fill roster holes those years, and desperate for any sort of Band-Aid to stop the hemorrhaging, the Dodgers refocused on their own farm system and immediately found some talent there: a young pitcher named Don Sutton, an infielder named Ted Sizemore, and outfielders Bill Russell and Willie Crawford. Sutton became a solid regular starting pitcher for the team in 1966. Second baseman Sizemore won the Rookie of the Year Award in 1969, and, that same year, Russell and Crawford were brought up as quick corner outfielders. Russell eventually established himself as the team's regular shortstop after Maury Wills retired at the end of the 1972 season, and Crawford became the team's regular right fielder around the same time.

The emergence of these players could not have been better timed, reminding Dodger management of their long history of "building from within" and leading them to seek a return to that model. Complicating matters, however, was the fact that, in 1965, Major League Baseball (MLB) had established a new method for teams to choose and sign first-year players. Whereas the effort to sign new players had long been a free-for-all that favored teams with more resources to scour the bushes and pay bonuses to new prospects, baseball's new amateur draft, conducted for the first time in 1965, was meant to give every team an even shot at the prospect pool. As a result, after a few years the team's management decided they had to deal with the new reality. "The Draft was in its infancy," said Bill Schweppe, who was the Dodgers' assistant farm director at the time, "and we didn't have much experience." So, sometime before the 1968 season, Al Campanis, the Dodgers' director of scouting, and general manager (GM) Buzzie Bavasi decided to consult with a coterie of respected talent evaluators from the National Football League (NFL): Dan Reeves, then owner of the Los Angeles Rams; Sid Gillman, coach of the San Diego Chargers; and Al LoCasale, the draft coordinator for the Chargers. The key advice they received? *Numbers*. The NFL draft experts suggested the Dodgers bring in large numbers of prospective players. "The thought was that you didn't know how well you would do signing these players," Schweppe said, "so you better draft as many as you can."[1]

In the two phases of the 1968 draft, the Dodgers made 101 selections in fifty rounds. Campanis, reviewing recent statistics, had noted that the Dodgers were the National League's worst hitting team in 1967—with a team average of .236—and had started out even more ineptly in 1968, held to one run or less in twenty of forty-nine games through May. "In our meeting before the Draft," Campanis recalled, "I remember telling Peter [O'Malley, the owner's son and an executive vice president for the team] that we were going for bats. We couldn't buy a hit. So every time we had a tough choice to make, we went for the better hitter."[2] The team's scouts dug deep, suggesting a number of players, led by standout Bobby Valentine, that the team would develop into future stars. Valentine won the Pioneer League MVP Award in his first year in the Minors, appeared in five games with the Dodgers in 1969, and was brought up to the Majors full-time in 1971. Rounding out the team's picks, meanwhile, were a number of future Major Leaguers—Bill Buckner, Dave Lopes, Joe Ferguson, Steve Garvey, Ron Cey, Tom Paciorek, Doyle Alexander, and Geoff Zahn. They all entered the Dodgers' farm system to gain seasoning.

Dodger scouting notes and approach to developing these players reveal much about how a new team would eventually come together: Buckner was deemed a "hitting machine," and quick, but difficult to place in the field. He rose through the system in much the same way as Valentine, eventually settling in at corner outfield and first base for the Major League team in 1971. Dave Lopes, an outfielder chosen in the second round of the January secondary draft, was called a "handy little guy," who possessed a good attitude, great speed, and a good batting eye. He moved more slowly through the system, eventually making the team as a second baseman in 1973. Joe Ferguson, drafted in the sixth round of the June draft, was a strong-armed catcher with good plate skills and some power; he landed in the Majors in 1971. Steve Garvey, chosen in the first round of the June secondary draft, was a sharp-hitting third baseman who had questionable fielding range and a poor throwing arm, but his bat earned him significant playing time at the Major League level in 1970. Ron Cey, chosen two rounds after Garvey also as a third baseman, had solid power and was expected to rise through the system once he could shore up his fielding. He became the Dodgers' everyday third baseman in 1973. Years later, Bill Schweppe rated the 1968 Dodger draft as outstanding, giving it a rare "nine-plus." One of the players chosen in 1968, Tom Paciorek, concurred: "That might have been the best Draft in the history of baseball, because everyone played a long time in the big leagues." Paciorek stayed with the Dodgers only a few seasons, never establishing himself as a regular, but became an All-Star after being traded and stayed in the Majors for eighteen years. "Some had better careers than others," Paciorek continued, "but they were all tremendous players with good baseball minds. And they were all great people."[3]

While Dodger fans remained disappointed and impatient over

the next several seasons as their team got beat out by rival teams with established stars, the Dodgers' brain trust never panicked—preferring to wait for the team's young new players to develop. They did not have to wait terribly long. The team finished in second place in the 1971, 1972, and 1973 seasons, improving their overall record each year. Fans were still restless for a championship. "But," said Alston, "everything came together in 1974."[4]

The 1974 Dodgers were an intriguing team. Orderly, efficient, no-nonsense, youthful, and relatively "starless," they surprised the league from the start and won 102 regular-season games. The lineup in 1974 was a mishmash of homegrown talent that had blossomed seemingly despite the odds. Steve Garvey, for instance, had almost failed as a Major Leaguer before switching positions in 1973 and emerging as a regular starter at first base halfway through the season. Clean-cut and well spoken, Garvey was a write-in starter of the 1974 All-Star Game, one of only two times that such a thing has ever happened. He would provide a consistent, middle-of-the-lineup bat for many seasons for the Dodgers. On the corner opposite Garvey, at third base, was Ron Cey. Prior to Cey's call-up in 1973, third base had easily been the least stable position for the Dodgers—the team had fielded forty-five different third basemen since their move to Los Angeles just fifteen years earlier. Cey's physique—all torso, with too short legs that gave him a wobbly, awkward running style—had often been questioned by the team as he came up through its farm system. (The Dodgers once tried to trade Cey to Milwaukee, but the Brewers' GM nixed the trade, saying, "I ain't going to trade for no duck.")[5] Yet with his solid fielding and fair amount of slugging power, Cey brought stability to the position for a decade—the longest stint ever for a Dodger third baseman. Converted shortstop Bill Russell, on the other hand, was a quiet, unflashy, lead-by-example sort of player who covered shortstop territory adequately, had a solid arm (one of his nicknames was "Ropes"), and hit slightly better than average for his position. And Dave Lopes, the second baseman, blossomed from a shy speedster to a more vocal leader and capable catalyst of the team's offensive attack. Another adequate fielder, Lopes set the table for the Dodgers in 1974 by stealing fifty-nine bases and scoring ninety-five runs.

In keeping with the Dodger Way, perhaps the biggest key to the team's success in 1974 was its surging pitching staff, led by twenty-eight-year-old Andy Messersmith, who had been picked up in a trade with the California Angels a few years earlier. The hard-throwing Messersmith blossomed on the Dodgers, winning twenty games while losing only six and finishing second in the Cy Young balloting. Reliever Mike Marshall, meanwhile, was the Cy Young Award winner that year, the first time a reliever had ever been so named. Picked up in a trade from the Montreal Expos, Marshall was an eccentric pitcher who espoused the idea that, with the right conditioning and mechanics, a pitcher could throw every day. In 1974 he broke the league record for appearances in a season (the record still stands today) and paved the way for new thinking about the evolving role that a "closer" played in a pitching staff. Marshall's gruff personality and blunt manner of speaking also made him widely reviled among opposing players, opposing fans, even among his own teammates.[6]

Pitcher Don Sutton was the team's longest-tenured player. An occasionally acerbic man who was the son of a sharecropper from Alabama, Sutton saw himself as the face of the team in the years after its post-Koufax decline. Unfortunately, his teammates in the 1970s didn't think quite as highly of him, and Sutton would run into trouble with several of the team's new young players. And finally, there was Tommy John. A good-natured, aging, left-handed sinker baller, John was arguably the team's most effective pitcher in 1974. He posted a team-leading 13-3 record with a 2.59 ERA in July before a severe elbow injury shut him down for the year and likely doomed the Dodgers' hopes in the World Series.

Rounding out the 1974 lineup was an array of young and promising everyday players—the speedy line-drive machine Bill Buckner, cannon-armed defense-specialist catcher Steve Yeager, rangy veteran outfielder Willie Crawford who, though still only twenty-seven, was playing his seventh season as a Dodger regular in 1974—as well as a slew of other Dodger farm products like Von Joshua; Lee Lacy; Joe Ferguson; Tom Paciorek; pitchers Doug Rau, Charlie Hough, and Geoff Zahn; and a few key veterans such as Jimmy Wynn, Manny Mota, Al Downing, and Jim Brewer.

After the team's surprising success in 1974, Dodger manager Walt Alston was awarded his sixth Manager of the Year Award by the Associated Press (AP). In his twenty-first season as the Dodgers' manager, Alston put to rest any doubts, at least for now, about his insight and acuity in the face of the rapidly changing sport of baseball. It was difficult to argue with the sum of Alston's amazing record. Going back to 1954, his first season as the Dodgers' skipper, "Smokey" Alston, as he had been known since his childhood—or the "Quiet Man" as he had been dubbed later by the press—had managed the team through all of its glory years, including all four of its World Series victories and three more National League pennants. He had won more baseball games than all but five (at the time) other managers. Nineteen of his twenty-three seasons had been winning ones, and he had led the National League All-Star team to a record seven victories.

Alston had so long been a fixture in the Dodgers' dugout, sitting somewhat aloof from his players as he took in the game, that it seemed to many that the Quiet Man had always been manager of the Dodgers and always would be. Alston was not particularly old—just sixty-two years of age at the end of the 1974 season. Connie Mack, by comparison, had managed the Philadelphia A's for fifty years, until he was eighty-seven years old. More recently, Leo Durocher managed until he was seventy-one and Casey Stengel until he was seventy-five. Still, as fans knew, there was a world of difference between the era when Alston had started managing—in the 1950s—and the 1970s. The players had changed in significant ways, not least of which was their growing expectation that the game owed them more—more money, more security, and much more personal attention. What's more, unfortunately, there were signs that player expectations in the 1970s had begun to rankle the famously stoic manager.

Prior to the 1970s baseball had long been a small-town sport. Mickey Mantle had come from Spavinaw, Oklahoma, the population of which hovered around 500. Ralph Kiner had come from Santa Rita, New Mexico, a place so small it eventually became a ghost town. Ken and Cletus Boyer had come from Alba, Missouri (pop. 588); Rod Carew from Gatun in the Panama Canal Zone (another ghost town); Catfish Hunter from Hertford, North Carolina (pop. 2,185); and so on. These were places that Walt Alston understood. Born in rural Ohio in 1911 to a town ball–playing farmer and his wife, Alston always remained a small-town ballplayer at heart. For twelve seasons as a Minor League manager in the 1940s and early 1950s, Alston had returned home to Ohio in the off-season to teach at the local high school. (He quit teaching only when his higher-level Minor League managerial jobs became too time-consuming.) Even in 1974, in the off-season away from the lights of Dodger Stadium and L.A., Alston lived in a large brick ranch home in Ohio that he and his father had built to house four generations of the family.

Because of his particular ways, by the 1970s Alston had become something of a cipher to many of his players. Alston proudly called himself a midwesterner, and he was not by habit showy or demonstrative. As a manager his overall approach to the game was studious and analytical. He preferred not to play "hunches." In many ways Alston's managerial style was to strip things down to their barest essence. "I believe in keeping everything simple," he wrote in his autobiography, which he wrote a year after the Dodgers' World Series run in 1974, "allowing a great deal of room for the individual to think on his own and respond within general confines we have set down for the whole Dodger organization." Rival managers like Sparky Anderson admired Alston for his character and his convictions. Alston, said Anderson, managed "by the book all the time" and worked to "force the other team to make plays." Despite his seeming aloofness, however, Alston still cared greatly about winning and had done more of it than all but a handful of men in the game. "On the outside," Sparky Anderson said of his rival, "Alston . . . was the wise old grandfather. You couldn't trick him. He knew everything that was going on. As soon as he stepped onto the field he had so much presence. . . . He was cooler than a professional poker player. I always wondered how he could stay so peaceful. Alston was an excellent strategist. He played chess on the field, but was never fancy." "Walt is an agitator, make no mistake about that," said Red Adams, a longtime Dodgers pitching coach. "But one thing about him is that he never lets little things bother him. He's so damned consistent that you could set your watch by him, and he doesn't miss a thing. He does everything so easy, he gives the impression that he's not doing a lot. But he has a way of getting through to a player, even though he's quiet."[7]

After the team's surprise appearance in the World Series, hopes ran high among the Dodger faithful going into 1975. The youth movement begun by the team six years earlier had finally paid full dividends, and the team's prospects looked good for years to come. But in 1975 these hopes were crushed hard when the Dodgers fell to second place, twenty games behind Sparky Anderson's vaunted world champion Cincinnati Reds. As in the corporate world, and in politics, and in many other fields of endeavor in America, baseball fans are a "What have you done for me lately?" lot, and so, in the off-season after the Dodgers' setback in 1975, rumors swirled that Alston would retire or be fired.

Alston did briefly consider ending his career before deciding to rededicate himself to the 1976 campaign. He held out hope that, with a few key personnel changes, the team would have enough gas in the tank this year to catch the Reds.[8] But it was not to be. In 1976 the Dodgers lost out once more to the Reds, further distressing team followers and, this time, throwing the Dodger clubhouse into a state of turmoil. Most disappointing to fans and management during these two seasons was the fact that the Dodgers had sprinted out in front of their division early on, only to fall apart in the latter part of the summer.

The turmoil around the team was made clear by a few telling episodes. In August 1976, with the season's hopes fading, Allan Malamud, the sports editor for the *Los Angeles Herald-Examiner*, was first to suggest in print what many were thinking—that the Dodgers should finally dismiss Alston. The story was not well received by the manager, and on August 22, before yet another loss—this time to the Pirates at home, 6–1—the Dodgers' manager caught Malamud roaming the halls outside his office at Dodger Stadium and uncharacteristically read him the riot act. Said Malamud afterward: "He called me an overstuffed pig." "Everyone is entitled to his opinion," Alston told reporters about the incident. "He wrote his. I told him face to face, man to man. I have no complaint with the press. I'm not saying this guy isn't a good writer. . . . But how often is he in the clubhouse? Two or three times a year? Does he know what goes on here? Does he know what I say in my meetings? This is my bread and butter, my job. I've got a right to my opinion and that's the end of it."[9]

It was a unique moment in Alston's long career. Not only had he almost never been confrontational with the media, but he had rarely done anything to make media headlines. Unfortunately, the furor around Alston only increased as the disappointing season wore on. By mid-September the Dodgers had fallen ten-plus games behind the Reds when the *L.A. Times* reported that the team's very fabric was fast unraveling. For a story called "If Fired, I Won't Cry," a *Times* reporter surveyed the team's players and found "little clubhouse support for Alston." As one anonymously quoted veteran player told the paper:

> I flatly believe that Walt does not deserve to be rehired. He has made too many mistakes in strategy, and he has become too stereotyped. We're not aggressive, we don't intimidate anyone. We make fundamental mistakes and they're allowed to go uncorrected. . . . There have been times I've sat next to Walt on the bench, and he had to ask me the names of players on the other teams. . . . He's become more hardened and calloused to his own players. We're all just numbers. The other day, before the first game of the series with the Reds, he had a clubhouse meeting and told us we were not as good as Cincinnati, that the Reds were simply the better team. Maybe it's the truth but what point is there in saying it, how does it help our confidence?[10]

Alston was his usual blasé self in his response to the accusations. "There are always frustrations and disappointments," he said, "but I continue to feel I have the best job in the country. . . . I still like my work and yet I don't want to hang on longer than I feel I should." In fairness to Alston in 1976, not everyone blamed the manager for the Dodgers' troubles. "Anyone who criticizes the manager should first look in the mirror," the *Times* quoted another anonymous Dodger veteran. "We have the ability to get the job done and we haven't done it. There is a tendency toward selfishness on this team, a tendency toward thinking of the individual rather than the team." The story also quoted Sparky Anderson, again praising the job that Alston had done, even though his team was about to beat out the Dodgers in the pennant race for the fourth time in five years. "Here's a man who has managed for 23 years and won over 2,000 games. Those totals will never be matched. He doesn't need defending."[11]

The late-summer months of 1976 were an excruciating time all over Los Angeles, as the local baseball team's fortunes were sinking as fast as the local economy. After being swept in a four-game series against the Reds at home on August 8, the Dodgers fell thirteen games off the division lead. Speculation about Walt Alston's future with the Dodgers was so rampant that Dodger president Peter O'Malley felt compelled to put minds at ease, stating clearly, late in the season, that no decision had been made regarding removing Alston as the team's field manager.

As Dodger management deliberated, in August 1976 Tom Fallon found himself facing a set of nerve-racking personal decisions. Tom's middle son—James—was struggling. Having married at a young age, James Fallon had been forced to settle on work after college. Now, ten years later, his job at Allstate Insurance barely brought in enough money to support his family of three growing boys. It didn't help that he hated the job, hated being a corporate cog and having his boss take credit for several innovations he had made at the office. For some time James Fallon had been looking for other work. Earlier that summer, after thinking long and hard on the matter, Tom Fallon called James to present his son a business proposal. It was not an easy call to make, as their business history together had been checkered, at best. But Tom pushed all of that out of his mind. He wanted at least one, if not several, of his sons at his side as a partner in the hardware store. He wanted to share his own success with his family—it was the least he could do.

Things moved quickly once the decision was made. That August James Fallon quit his job at Allstate and quickly shifted to the life of an independent businessman. His young family struggled to adjust to his new schedule: six long days of work each week that lasted well into the evening. It didn't help that the store, located in Cucamonga, was a good forty-five-minute drive, on a good traffic day, from James Fallon's home in Pasadena. So rarely was James home, he had all but ceased listening to radio, or watching the occasional television broadcasts, of Dodger games with his fanatic eldest son. But, James Fallon said to himself, these are the sacrifices one makes to provide for the family.

All through the late summer and into fall, as Tom and James Fallon, and then James's brother Kenneth, worked to bring new business to Cucamonga Hardware, baseball people around the country speculated about manager Alston's future with his longtime family, the Dodgers. Alston himself finally put an end to the speculation on September 27, when he announced his retirement at a press conference at Dodger Stadium. The timing of the announcement, with still four games left to play in the season and coming so close to the *L.A. Times* article in which numerous players criticized him, was revealing. No doubt Alston was stung by the depth of the criticism of his recent leadership of the team. "A manager can't escape it," Alston said to the *Times*, speaking on the day of his retirement announcement. "I'm as disappointed as anyone that we didn't beat the Reds this year. . . . But," he was quick to add, "I'm not retiring because of criticism." Alston also insisted there had been no "communication gap" on the team, though the story reported that the manager had confided to friends that he had become increasingly soured on the game in recent years—mostly because of the attitude of players who needed constant validation and encouragement in order to play to their potential. "I don't blame the players as much as the times," he said in his announcement. "We used to have 24 or 25 farm clubs. It would take six or seven years to reach the majors. A player had to beat out a dozen guys to do it. He was appreciative of what he had. Now they get a free ride through college and a bonus even before they've swung at a major league curve. They expect it to be that easy for them all the way."[12]

After Alston's announcement, players and fans alike expressed their support of the longtime leader. Don Sutton, who had played for Alston since coming up with the Dodgers in 1966, was most vocal in his support of Alston. "I felt it was coming all year and I was hoping against hope that he'd change his mind. I'm very disappointed. . . . Walt is the only guy I've ever known more stubborn than myself. We've disagreed strongly and in most cases he's been right. He's consistent, he's honest, he's upfront." Steve Garvey also expressed disappointment. "It's a sad day. To me, Walt has always represented the standard of his position. He's been a man's manager. Not too many rules, not too many restrictions. All he expects is your honesty, your respect, a full effort. I feel blessed to have played for him." Catcher

Steve Yeager, meanwhile, said, "He'll be missed by fans, by players, and by baseball. . . . It's a shame he didn't have 25 guys working their ass off for him all year long." And outfielder Bill Buckner said, "The thing about Walt is that he's always been fair, he's never carried a grudge . . . . I always felt he was on my side. You could respect him as a man as well as a manager."[13]

In the moments after the press conference at Dodger Stadium, Alston locked the doors of the players' lounge and delivered a brief message to the team. Later, Alston told reporters that he didn't say a lot to his players. "I just tried to impress on them that even though they finished second this year, that with a little help, with everyone contributing, they'll have a good shot next year. I wished them well and told them . . . I'd do everything I could to help."[14]

Reportedly, as Alston the old stoic returned to his office after his speech to his players, his eyes were filled with tears.

Anyone concerned about who would replace the Dodgers' Hall of Fame–bound outgoing manager would not have to worry long. Just twenty-four hours after the press conference announcing Alston's decision to retire, the Dodgers were back at Dodger Stadium's press room, this time introducing their new manager: forty-nine-year-old former Dodger player and current third base coach, Tom Lasorda.

At the press conference Alston put on a gracious face, telling Lasorda he should take over the team immediately and manage for the final four games of the season. "But you better win," Alston smiled, "because the results go on my record."[15] The gesture was perhaps meant to look like a generous baton passing, but in retrospect something about it and its timing was suspect. No one's ever gone on record saying that Alston was pushed out by Dodger management, and everyone involved made every effort to imply that retirement was Alston's idea alone, but then why retire with four games left in the season? Was Alston registering a quiet complaint by not waiting until the off-season's relative calm to step down? Or were the Dodgers forcing him out early so they could start the rebuilding process before the off-season? People around the Dodgers organization remained silent on the subject.

Although the media and fans had speculated furiously in the

immediate aftermath of Alston's announcement—suggesting that Maury Wills and Jim Gilliam were, along with Lasorda, leading candidates—the planned succession of Lasorda had been an open secret within the organization for a number of years. Not that Lasorda wasn't deserving of this chance. As of the end of the 1976 season, Lasorda had spent twenty-eight years in the Dodgers organization, starting first as a journeyman pitcher who lost his shot at a place on the team in the mid-1950s because the team had signed a young prospect named Sandy Koufax. After his playing days Lasorda returned to the Dodgers to work as a scout. By 1965 Lasorda had landed a managerial position in the Dodgers' Minor League system. Like Alston twenty years before, Lasorda moved up through the system for the next eight years. He won the Minor League Manager of the Year Award in 1970 after his Spokane team won the Pacific Coast League flag. In 1972 the Dodgers' front office asked him to coach third base for the Major League team. He was reluctant to take the job at first, but he eventually realized that the third base coaching job would be right up his alley. Third base coaches are field generals. They relay signs to hitters and runners, make split-second decisions, take the heat when things work out badly, and take the credit when they work out well. This fitted the impulsive and effusive Lasorda's personality to a tee.

Beyond his years of service to the Dodgers, Lasorda was the natural choice to manage the Dodgers for another reason. He had been a key component in developing many of the players who were now on the big-league team. Eighteen of the Dodgers' roster players at the start of the 1977 season had played for Lasorda while they were in the Minor Leagues. Further, when he had arrived in Los Angeles to begin his new coaching gig under Alston in 1973, Lasorda, seeing the distance between Alston and his players, decided to start a "111 Percent Club" at spring training. Lasorda's club encouraged nonroster players to show their stuff by taking extra fielding instruction and batting practice. Even as Alston became more and more rigid and remote toward players over the next three years, Lasorda was more and more loose and encouraging. By the 1976 season Lasorda had even taken to giving pregame pep talks that predicted the team's inevitable success. Eventually, players rewarded his long-standing confidence in them by letting it be known—to management and press—how much they liked playing for Lasorda.

Lasorda's unique personality also played a key role in cementing his rise to Dodger manager. During the 1974 World Series, from his third base coaching post, Lasorda's loud encouragement of the young Dodgers, his on-field instructions, his enthusiastic gestures, backslaps, and hugs had provided a constant background soundtrack to the game. After Steve Yeager hit an RBI (run batted in) single in the second game of the Series, for example, Lasorda yelled to the catcher from across the field—"Thatta boy, Stevie!"—then gave him thirty seconds of instructions about the game situation. When Joe Ferguson hit a two-run home run (HR) in the sixth inning of the same game, Lasorda exploded, gesturing wildly: "Oh get on it! Go on, ball! Oh yeah. It's a home run. I told you. Oh yeah! I knew he was due. . . . I called it! Oh yeah. What a shot, what a blast!" So relentless was Lasorda's patter that in Game Three, as the Dodgers threatened the A's one-run lead, third base umpire Ron Luciano looked over at Lasorda, who was in the middle of his ongoing game narrative, and said half-jokingly: "Will you stop talking to yourself?" Lasorda looked over at Luciano, took a nervous step forward and then another step back, and said: "That's not too bad, Ron. It's when I start answering myself that you're really in trouble in this game." While Lasorda's antics didn't make a difference in the Series, which the Dodgers lost in five games, it did raise his national profile. Some even suspected Lasorda was the soul of the surprise champions, and after the 1974 season he received at least two managerial inquiries. The Montreal Expos wanted him to manage their team in 1975. At the time, as third base coach for the Dodgers, Lasorda was earning just $17,000 a year and living in a relatively modest tract home in suburban Fullerton. The offer by the Expos was a multiyear contract worth $250,000. Lasorda very nearly took the bait before he declined, telling the Expos, "I'm sorry, I love the Dodgers, and I want to stay here."[16]

Though Lasorda and Alston could hardly be more different in temperament, in some ways Lasorda was actually quite similar to his predecessor. Like Alston, Lasorda was a failed Major Leaguer. Alston had famously had just one at bat (an out) in the Majors and spent most of his years in the Minors, while Lasorda had been a part-time pitcher for just three seasons in the Majors, recording no wins against four losses. Both Alston's and Lasorda's postplaying careers had been orchestrated by a Dodger general manager—Branch Rickey in Alston's case, Al Campanis in Lasorda's—who seemingly had seen enough character or intelligence in the failed players to put them in charge of a lower Minor League team. And both Alston and Lasorda were so fiercely loyal to the organization that they had become dedicated to the hard work of developing young players and teaching them the proper way to play the game. Perhaps as a consequence, both were very successful in the Minor Leagues.

Despite these similarities between Alston and Lasorda, the Dodgers' change in management at the end of 1976 was a definitive change of direction. Whereas Alston was a quiet schemer, happy to sit in the recesses of the dugout or clubhouse and plot subtle ways to defeat his opponents, Lasorda was a less introspective, more in-your-face type of manager whose larger-than-life personality kept him at the center of the games he managed. It's no stretch to say that while Alston shrank from the spotlight, Lasorda craved it (and he made no apologies for this). He loved to hold court at Dodger Stadium while surrounded by the media and Hollywood celebrities. Whereas Alston never seemed affected by either victory or loss, Lasorda's emotions rose and fell with the team's fortunes. Lasorda was fond of saying he "bled Dodger Blue," almost to the point of annoyance, and that he prayed to the "Great Dodger in the sky."[17] He seemed bemused at the suggestion that anyone might not root for the Dodgers. The local media, quickly picking up on the new manager's own mythologizing, called Lasorda "a fighter," a "man of many words," and a "motivator." One sports columnist who followed the Dodgers suggested that Lasorda made, in his first nineteen minutes as Dodger manager, more appearances around town than Walt Alston had made in nineteen years.

The fact that Lasorda and Alston were so markedly different in personality may have had much to do with why Alston did not stick around for the last four games in the 1976 season. "He never liked me," Lasorda said in his autobiography. "I have no idea why. But it is one of the great disappointments of my life that Walter Alston never liked me." The antipathy between the two went all the way back to the beginning, in 1950, when Lasorda was a junk-balling pitcher moving up through the Dodgers' Minor League system and Alston was manager of the Dodgers' top farm team in Montreal. The gregarious Lasorda first raised Alston's ire by conspiring with several players to pull a few pranks on Alston. It was, Lasorda later said, part of an effort to draw out the reserved manager. "Hey," Lasorda said, "he wanted to be one of the guys, so I made him one of the guys." But Alston was not amused, and afterward, for four seasons in the Minors, Alston had nothing but stern, disapproving looks for Lasorda. Once both made the Majors in 1954—Alston as the Dodgers' manager, Lasorda as a rookie pitcher—Alston got revenge by making it difficult for the pitcher to settle in. He barely used Lasorda. In 1955, during Alston's tense second year as a manager, he stuck with the players he favored. "I won ten games in a row at Montreal [in 1955]," said Lasorda, "and I get called up to the Brooklyn Dodgers, and I only played in one game the entire time I was there. That guy Alston never gave me a chance, and I never forgot it."[18]

Despite the mutual antipathy between the team's outgoing and incoming managers, the Dodgers took care to focus mostly on the positive at the end of 1976. After the season most of the team's players at the time continued praising Lasorda's appointment. Bill Russell, the starting shortstop, said Lasorda had "all the qualifications for the job. He has worked hard, he knows the players and it was a good choice." Pitcher Tommy John, who had just returned in 1976 from reconstructive surgery on his elbow, said, "I don't think you could have picked a better man. He has worked in the organization for a long time and paid his dues. I think he will do a good job." Third baseman Ron Cey agreed that Lasorda was the most qualified man for the job. "He is a tremendous motivator. He believes in hard work. He has meant a great deal in my career as a player. I will try to perform above my capabilities for him." And star first baseman Steve Garvey pointed out that he had been on four championship teams with Lasorda, two in the Minors and two in the Winter Leagues. "I know as well as I know anything that he is the right man. He is a dedicated man and will do a fine job."[19]

Lasorda, for his part, was immediately clear about one thing: he had finally obtained the position he long coveted. "This is the greatest day of my life," Lasorda told the press. "To be selected as manager of an organization I love so deeply, to wake up and learn I had inherited a post being vacated by the greatest manager in baseball, it's like being presented the Hope Diamond." That Lasorda was still nervous despite his bluster is clear in how he deflected a few hard questions by reporters, protesting that he had nothing to prove as Alston's follower. "I just don't look at it like I'm following a legend," he said. "If you start defying the pressures of following someone, you're actually creating pressure within yourself. . . . I don't want people to be looking back at what Walt Alston did but to look at what Tom Lasorda is doing." When Vin Scully, the Dodgers' veteran sportscaster, prodded further, Lasorda was even more defiant: "I'm worried about the guy who is going to replace me."[20]

With Lasorda in charge of the Dodgers in late September, and Jim Gilliam now stepping into the third base coaching job, the Dodgers split their last four games of the 1976 season to finish with a respectable 90-68 win-loss record. Despite this success, however, for the fifth time in the past seven seasons the team ended up in second place behind the seemingly unstoppable Cincinnati Reds, who won their second straight World Series in 1976 by beating the New York Yankees. It was another disappointing season for the Dodgers, and Tom Lasorda was not pleased. Going into the off-season the Dodgers' new manager was more than eager to begin making his mark on his team. "I have this 'weight' problem," Lasorda said during the off-season. "I just can't 'weight' to get started."[21]

Lasorda would make several conspicuous moves during the off-season to distance himself from the past regime. Whereas Walt Alston's office had long been, like the man himself, hard to find, Lasorda immediately moved it, taking over a larger, more centrally located training room. He hung his own personal photos on the cinderblock walls, laid down new carpeting, and brought in new couches that would be used to invite players to postgame buffets. Next, thinking of the hated Reds, Lasorda announced a ban on the color red in the clubhouse. Players could wear no red clothing or accessories anywhere within his sight. This was juvenile stuff, to be sure, but Lasorda brought some humor to the gesture by carrying it to ridiculous extremes. Although he would allow players to continue, should they choose, to chew Red Man Tobacco, he changed the nickname of his pitching coach, the highly regarded Charles Dwight Adams, from "Red" to "Blue."

With his clubhouse situated to his satisfaction, Lasorda began considering the keys to his hopes for a championship in 1977—his players. In early December Lasorda sat down and wrote each member of the Dodgers' presumptive roster a Christmas card, informing them it was a privilege to be their manager. "We have the nucleus of a very fine club," he wrote. "Each of you is gifted with talent and will play a major role in the success of the Dodgers, but there is only one way to win a pennant and that is for 25 players, the coaches and manager to pull and work together. We have to be totally involved and determined to come out of spring training totally prepared."[22]

Throughout his career Lasorda had employed various techniques to motivate his players. He had long treated many of his players like they were his own sons, making sure to know the names of their mothers and the most intimate details of their lives—in order to use them as a spur later. And like any benevolent family patriarch, he demanded, above all else, obedience. In the Minor Leagues Lasorda even trained young players to drop to their knees at his command and shout out their love for the Dodgers. "It was all about getting these guys to visualize the major leagues," Lasorda said later. "What better way to visualize it than to shout about it?"[23] Once the letters were received Lasorda then called each of the players and told them what he expected them to do during the upcoming season. Knowing the team needed to generate more offense, Lasorda called shortstop Bill Russell and told him he wanted him to use his speed to steal more bases. He told first baseman Steve Garvey that he would rely on him to supply the team some extra power. He asked Davey Lopes to become a team leader. He told Dusty Baker he was counting on him to finally establish himself in the outfield. And he told Reggie Smith, a slugging outfielder who had a reputation for being somewhat mercenary, that his leadership was critical. "I really need your superstar talent this year. I need you to help me survive my first year of managing." Smith, who had been an All-Star with the Boston Red Sox and St. Louis Cardinals before coming to the Dodgers in a trade in 1976, said no manager had ever told him he was needed. After the calls were completed some players who had come up in the ranks with him understood what he was trying to do, yet many worried about how distracting it might be to spend an entire big-league season with Lasorda as manager. And at least one player actively opposed Lasorda's antics. Pitcher Don Sutton made a few pointed comments about the incoming manager's style. "I've been able to respond better to a person like him (Alston) than to a guy who licks your boots, who gives you pats on the back," Sutton said. "Walt never second-guessed us, has never competed against us. . . . I just don't believe I can play for a manager who's a headline grabber, who isn't honest."[24]

As Lasorda worked to launch a new team era, Walt Alston quickly faded into the background. On December 7 the Dodgers held a farewell dinner for Alston in Los Angeles, celebrating his accomplishments and career. And even though Alston was slated to continue working with the team as an adviser, the event had a distinct air of finality it. "Walt's new title hasn't really been decided upon yet," explained Dodgers president Peter O'Malley at the function, which was sponsored by the Los Angeles Junior Chamber of Commerce, "but he's certainly going to be doing a great number of things for us."[25]

Gathered at the dinner were many current and former Dodger players, as well as VIP friends of Alston such as Sparky Anderson, Buzzie Bavasi, Al Campanis, Mayor Tom Bradley, and Vin Scully. All stood up to praise the great manager. Don Sutton called him an "honest man" and said he was grateful "for eleven wonderful years." Steve Garvey said Alston was the kind of man all other managers should pattern themselves after, "not necessarily from a baseball stance, but from the standpoint of being a human being." Finally, Vin Scully gave a moving tribute that ended with: "We're so much richer to have known you, and we're so much poorer for letting you get away."[26]

There's no record of Lasorda having attended the event, but the new manager did pause his transition project for the holidays before renewing efforts again after the start of the new year. In early January the headline on the front page of the *L.A. Times* sports section told the story: "Now the Dodgers Know Where They Stand." "I want everyone tugging on the same end of the rope," Lasorda boldly announced to the reporter. "What happened in the past doesn't matter. We're looking ahead. Baseball has to be played with a relaxed and confident attitude. Putting the uniform on should be fun. I want a team that's aggressive, that wants to win. . . . I simply feel that the best team doesn't always win. The team that wants it the most does."

Considering these sentiments, the announcement of a team transaction in mid-January would surprise, and perhaps dismay, a number of Dodger followers. The transaction would somewhat belie the manager's bluster about his loyalty to "his sons" and raise questions about what it mean to be dedicated to "Dodger Blue." At the same time it would show the depth and intensity of Lasorda's, and the Dodger management's, desire to win. And critics couldn't argue with that.

FOUR

Great Expectations, Everybody's Watching You

This job doesn't start and end with the first and last pitch. You have to be a father, teacher, philosopher and disciplinarian. I want the player who's down to know I'm with him. I want them all to go home and say, "I hope our children get a chance to have Tom Lasorda as their manager."

—Tommy Lasorda, January 1977

In many ways Bill Buckner epitomized the Dodger teams of the early to mid-1970s. Drafted at age eighteen by the organization in the second round of the 1968 amateur draft, Buckner was a natural and gifted hitter with good hands and foot speed. In 1968 Buckner hit .344 for the Dodgers' rookie league team in Ogden and swiped twenty-four bases. His manager that year was Tommy Lasorda, who was leading the team to a third straight Pioneer League championship. In 1969 Buckner split time between the Dodgers' AA team in Albuquerque and its AAA team in Spokane. On the Spokane Indians, he was reunited with Lasorda and hit .315, good enough to earn a brief September call-up to the Major Leagues at the age of nineteen. By 1971 Buckner had become a semiregular on the Dodgers. In 1972, as Lasorda was wrapping up his Minor League career by leading the Albuquerque Dukes (now the Dodgers' top AAA team) to a 92-58 record and a Pacific Coast League championship, Buckner batted .319 for the Dodgers, which would have qualified him for a top-five finish in the batting title had he reached the threshold for plate appearances (PAs).[1] On the 1974 World Series team, Buckner was a fixture, batting .314, the fourth-best average in the National League, and stealing thirty-one bases. He also knocked four hits in the Series, including one home run.

Described as a "free spirit" with an "enthusiastic style," Buckner wore a characteristically mid-'70s style of mustache, à la Burt Reynolds in his *Cosmopolitan* centerfold, and he had otherworldly bushy eyebrows. Like many of the 1976 Dodgers, Buckner's star was hitched to Lasorda's. Lasorda loved mentoring players, but Lasorda grew particularly close to the offbeat Buckner. Lasorda had scouted Buckner as a high schooler in Northern California and, while managing him in Ogden and Spokane, had put Buckner up in his home for a time. On the 1976 Dodgers Buckner, now twenty-six, had played fairly well, again batting over .300. But the previous year, in 1975, he had developed ankle problems that required two surgeries. As a result he lost much of his natural speed. With Steve Garvey's emergence at first base in 1974, Buckner was now barred from playing from that position, even as he had lost much of his range in the outfield. Further, he had also shown his limitations as a run producer, hitting just seven home runs and batting in just sixty runs in 1976. It's likely Buckner was the player Alston had in mind when he said the team needed more "sock" in the outfield if they were ever going to catch the Reds.

On January 12 the *L.A. Times* reported the Dodgers had traded Bill Buckner to the Chicago Cubs for the power-hitting left-handed thirty-one-year-old center fielder Rick Monday. As Lasorda told the *Times* on the day after the trade, Monday would make the Dodgers' outfield sounder defensively, and he would provide the power the team desperately needed. "Rick Monday," said Lasorda cheerfully, "is one of the outstanding centerfielders in the game. He won't hit as many homers in Dodger Stadium," a notorious pitcher's park, "as he did in Wrigley Field, but he has good extra base power, the type of power that's needed for doubles and triples in our park."[2]

Buckner was bitterly disappointed, like a son cast aside in favor of an upstart stepchild. "I'm going from a contender to a non-contender, from a city that I love to a city I dislike," Buckner told an L.A. sportswriter. "It's a real drag. I'm very upset about it. . . . I feel like a piece of meat. They use you for what they can and get rid of you in the same way." And Buckner's feelings of frustration and betrayal had been intensified by the fact that his longtime mentor and friend had signed on to the deal. "He's been like a father to me," Buckner said of Lasorda. "Now he becomes the manager and I'm traded. It's hard to understand and it's a real disappointment, especially since he hasn't called me."[3]

There is no record of how Lasorda handled telling Buckner of the trade in the end, but the Dodgers' new manager did express some public regret about losing the offbeat outfielder. "The hard part," Lasorda said, "is giving up Buckner. We came up through the system together and he's been like a son to me. . . . He's a tremendous competitor who should give the Cubs a lot of good years. He's a bona fide .300 hitter."[4] Still, despite Lasorda's regret at losing Buckner, the manager knew where his ultimate loyalty lay. And he knew the move would show he was serious enough about getting the Dodgers to the Series to let one of his "sons" go.

The newest Dodger as of January 13, 1977, Rick Monday had never been part of Lasorda's Minor League "family"—Monday arrived in the Majors too early for that—but he had known the Dodger manager for quite some time. When Monday was a young high school star in nearby Santa Monica in 1963, Lasorda had scouted him for the Dodgers. Lasorda in fact tried to convince Monday to sign with the team (for a bonus of twenty thousand dollars) instead of going to college, but he failed and Monday instead became an All-American outfielder for Arizona State University before the Kansas City A's made him famous for being the first player drafted in baseball's very first amateur draft in 1965.

In contrast to Buckner, Monday was a notably straightlaced "all-American" kind of guy. Softly handsome with feathered hair and a granite jaw that made him look a bit like Adam West of the 1960s TV series *Batman*, he seemed a throwback to the age of heroes. With the A's, who moved to Oakland in 1968, Monday became an All-Star, and by the mid-1970s he'd established himself as a solid Major Leaguer who could run, field, hit for power, and drive in runs. In 1976 in particular, the center fielder hit thirty-two home runs for the Cubs and drove in seventy-seven runs from the leadoff position for a mediocre team. He also had the second-highest fielding percentage among all outfielders in the league.[5]

Beyond Monday's local-boy and all-American qualities, and his solid playing record, the Dodgers were also likely interested in Monday because of his role in an incident that had occurred at Dodger Stadium in 1976. On April 25 Rick Monday and the Cubs had rolled into Dodger Stadium for a Sunday-afternoon game, little aware of the monumental event that would take place that day. As Monday later recounted, it was "between the top and bottom of the fourth inning, [and] I was just getting loose in the outfield, throwing the ball back and forth." Without warning two fans dropped out of the stands beyond the third base line and onto the playing field. "Wait a minute, there's an animal loose," Dodgers announcer Vin Scully said from the radio booth. "Or two of them." Monday, who was the closest player to the two fans, wasn't sure at first if they were drunk or playing a gag. However, after noticing what the first figure had cradled under his arm, the Cubs outfielder quickly realized something was wrong.

The game was not televised, but in a super-8 film clip that would surface in 1984, the fans, both male, are small figures on a wide expanse of grass in left-center field. At first there is only one man in view. Unfurling his bundle on the ground like a picnic blanket, he kneels on one knee and begins to douse it with lighter fluid. Then, from the direction of left field, another figure appears, kneels down, and begins attempting to light a match. "I'm not sure what he's doing out there," Scully continues, in an annoyed voice. "It looks like they're going to burn a flag." On the field Rick Monday had come to the same conclusion. "He got down on his knees and I could tell he wasn't throwing holy water on it," Monday told the *Los Angeles Times* when interviewed after the game. In that moment the outfielder, who was a marine reserve during the off-season, grew incensed. "If he's going to burn a flag, he better do it in front of somebody who doesn't appreciate it. I've visited enough veterans hospitals and seen enough guys with their legs blown off defending that flag."[6]

In the film clip, as the men kneel and struggle with their task, the Cubs' center fielder suddenly comes in view from the direction of right field. Running at full sprint, he dashes past the kneeling man's left shoulder and without slowing scoops up the flag from the ground before the flag burners even know what has happened. As Monday jogs away in the direction of third base, one of the stunned would-be flag burners hauls back and throws his can of lighter fluid at the outfielder's back. But he misses wide to the right, and as several players, the Dodgers' third base coach, and an umpire rush to confront the two would-be flag burners, Monday jogs to the third base foul line and hands the flag to Dodger pitcher Doug Rau. A few moments later the two protesters are escorted from the field by two security guards and the head groundskeeper. The report after the game suggested that fans gave Monday a standing ovation for his heroic gesture, but Monday was modest about his actions, saying he did not feel the cheers were for him. "The way people reacted was fantastic," he said, "but I felt they were cheering for what the flag meant."[7] A photo from the game shows a sign on the Dodgers' scoreboard reading: "RICK MONDAY . . . YOU MADE A GREAT PLAY." Monday himself on more than one occasion has recollected that he recalls a spontaneous version of "God Bless America" breaking out across the stands, though no paper reported at the time that such a thing happened.

Whatever exactly occurred it's certain that fans at the game, and many more who were not at the game—Americans who had had enough of flag burning in recent years, during the height of anti–Vietnam War sentiment and the continued fallout from the Watergate scandal and the ineffectual Ford presidency—were in favor of Monday's spontaneous heroism. One fan for example, thirty-year-old Joe Shaver of Santa Monica, was stopped by police as he tried to reach the Cubs' dugout to shake Monday's hand. In the days following the incident, Monday was interviewed by the media and celebrated all over the country. The National League commended Monday on April 30. When he returned to Chicago in early May, after two weeks of traveling with his team, Monday discovered stacks of mail that had been sent to him by well-wishers and admirers from around the country. Included in the pile were congratulations from senators and congressmen, from former president Richard Nixon, and from Alabama governor George Wallace. The Illinois House of Representatives passed Resolution 747, proclaiming Tuesday, May 3, as Rick Monday

Day in Illinois. Chicago mayor Richard J. Daley named Monday the grand marshal of the Chicago Salute to the American Flag Parade to be held on June 12. And recall, all of this fanfare came despite the fact that almost no one actually *saw* what happened, as this was well before cable game broadcasts, *SportsCenter* highlights, and instantaneous video postings to Facebook and Twitter.

Interestingly, Monday said he never cared to find out the reason these two wanted to burn a flag—it was enough for him to know that they wanted to. But if he had been interested, he would have learned that the brain behind the protest was an unemployed thirty-seven-year-old man from Eldon, Missouri, named William Errol Thomas. His accomplice, meanwhile—the person with the matches—sadly was Thomas's eleven-year-old son. After their arrest and booking, the son was sent to juvenile hall and the father taken to Parker Center, the headquarters at the time for the Los Angeles Police Department, where he was sentenced to pay a fine of sixty dollars or spend three days in jail in addition to twelve months of probation. Thomas pleaded guilty and chose to spend three days in jail in lieu of the fine. After he was released a small item ran in the paper explaining that his attempt to burn the flag was meant to draw attention to what he claims was his wife's "imprisonment" in a Missouri mental institution. How or why he came to Los Angeles to make such a protest, and what he hoped to achieve from the act, or even if his story was true, is not clear. His attorney in the public defender's office said that Thomas was American Indian, a transient living out of the back of his car. The Department of Motor Vehicles yielded no information, nor did the registrar of voters or Veterans Administration. The Bureau of Indian Affairs in Phoenix had no information, nor were there any military records. In the end Thomas simply faded away, and no one followed up with him. There's no record of a story running in the paper once William was released from jail. The fact was, no one cared. They cared only about the flag rescuer.

And, indeed, after the flag incident Rick Monday was forever a hero in Los Angeles, his image cemented in the minds of fans across the region. At a ceremony at Wrigley Field some weeks later, Dodger general manager Al Campanis presented Monday with his trophy—the flag, back from police impound. During the event Campanis admitted that he had for some time been trying to make a trade to the Cubs for Monday and now had "given up hope." "There's no way they'll trade him now," Campanis was quoted as saying. "He's Mr. Red, White and Blue."

So how did the Dodgers finally manage to land Monday in 1977, at the height of his popularity? "Rick was simply asking for more than we were able to pay," Cubs general manager Bob Kennedy told the *L.A. Times*. "We traded him strictly as a matter of dollars and cents."[8] Reportedly, after 1976 Monday had asked the Cubs for a multiyear contract deal, a rarity in those days, and the Cubs, wary of locking in a thirty-one-year-old center fielder, took a pass. To get the heroic player, however, the Dodgers broke their own long-standing policy and offered the center fielder a five-year contract—the longest the team had ever tendered to that point—reportedly for somewhere in the range of one million dollars, making him one of the highest-paid players on the team. It was a signing that would have deep ramifications, but in ways that the Dodgers could never have predicted in January 1977.

With this last major off-season move completed, and with Lasorda in possession of a new tool for his championship quest, all that was left was to wait for the official date for players to report to camp. Spring training for the Los Angeles Dodgers officially opened in Vero Beach, Florida, on an unseasonably cold spring day on March 1, 1977. In mid-January an abnormally cold winter had brought snow, for the first time in recorded history, as far south as Miami. Because of a pressure front known as the Aleutian Low, temperatures remained low in Florida throughout February and into the first part of spring training. Things, of course, could have been much worse—Buffalo, New York, had received so much snow (a total of 181.1 inches between October 1 and March 1) that the city was forced to ship it out of town by rail—but arriving players recoiled from the unexpected cold. As backdrop to the players' arrival, meanwhile, the number-one song on the U.S. *Billboard* charts at the time was by a California-based rock group, the Eagles. The sentiment of the song, "New Kid in Town," was appropriate for the moment.

In 1977 the Dodgers invited fifty-six players to the team's spring-training site, the storied Dodgertown of Vero Beach, Florida, which was immaculately maintained and overrun with an unusual number of amenities and services for the era. Founded in 1948, Dodgertown was a full-service, self-contained training facility, as well as a residency-based resort, created for the purpose of studying baseball.[9] Forty of the invitees were on the team's expanded roster, and sixteen other players were not on the roster but given special invitation to participate in spring training—primarily because the team had special interest in their long-term potential. Although not every one of these players would make the Major League team, all were pretty much guaranteed a job for the season. If they didn't make the team's roster of twenty-five active players who were allowed to travel with the team and "dress" for games, or if they didn't find their way onto the "extended roster" of forty players (which included the twenty-five players on the active roster and anyone just a step away from the big-league club on an "optional assignment" in the Minor Leagues), they knew they would still end up somewhere in the Dodgers' farm system.

At the start of his first full spring training as the Dodgers' manager, Lasorda continued making unusual and unexpected moves. First, Lasorda surprised the team, and the baseball establishment, by announcing that he had already decided on the team's starting lineup. "Never in anybody's memory has the Dodger lineup been set so early," wrote John Hall, sounding somewhat irritated, in the *L.A. Times* on March 18. "Every position secure even before the first day of spring training."[10] Not that any of Lasorda's declared starters were a surprise, as it was essentially the lineup, with a few additions, that had taken the team to the 1974 World Series. The infield remained unchanged, with Steve Garvey, the 1974 MVP, at first base; Davey Lopes at second base; steady Bill Russell at shortstop; and the streaky slugger Ron Cey at third base. The catching spot, meanwhile, was owned by twenty-eight-year-old defensive specialist Steve Yeager, who was starting his sixth season with the Dodgers. Only the outfield lineup was relatively new. Reggie Smith, the team's most consistent power hitter who had come to the team in a trade midway through the 1976 season, would return to his spot in right field; Rick Monday would take over center field from Dusty Baker, whose 1976 season had been shortened by a knee injury; and Baker would attempt a comeback in left field. Still, one couldn't fault the sportswriter for his frustration. Spring training is usually a time of chaotic substitutions, a chance for coaches and managers to experiment with different lineups and team configurations, and an opportunity to observe future prospects (while making sure the regulars are fit and healthy for the season)—all of which provided grist for column inches.

Adding to the writer's troubles was the fact that not only had Lasorda decided who his starters were, but he had declared that these eight players would spend all of spring training playing together. They would be together during workouts and practice drills, at meals and team meetings, and in exhibition game after exhibition game, and they would even sit the bench together. They would remain one indivisible unit throughout spring training. Across the Grapefruit League, those in the know watched the new manager's antics and declared that the Dodgers' projected starters would get tired of playing together so much; they would end up bickering and hating each other by season's end. When Sparky Anderson saw the Dodgers' starters running on the field together before a spring game, he belittled Lasorda's strategy, saying that not only would they be clashing with each other by September, but the team's reserves would not be game ready. But Lasorda would not be deterred by any amount of criticism, and, in fact, there was a clear method to Lasorda's madness. Lasorda did what he did in the spring of 1977 because, having known most of these players for years as their Minor League manager and third base coach, he was well aware this was a team of independent personalities not particularly prone to getting along with each other. He was certain that the key to getting them to pull together toward the greater goal—a World Series victory—was to have them become a single indivisible unit.

Despite Lasorda's focus on his starters in 1977, there were still, as in any year, a number of hopeful young prospects in camp. The top prospects—those included on the Dodgers' forty-man roster—included a variety of types of players from different backgrounds. Lance Rautzhan, for example, was a twenty-four-year-old left-hander out of Pottsville, Pennsylvania. Drafted by the Dodgers out of high school at the age of seventeen in the third round of the 1970 amateur draft, Rautzhan had, in 1977, been in the Dodgers' farm system for seven years without seeing the big lights. In 1976 he reached the Dodgers' Class AAA team in Albuquerque as a relief pitcher. And since one of the Dodgers' two biggest perceived needs going into 1977 was left-handed relief, Rautzhan hoped he was close to his dream. He just had to convince the Dodgers he could get batters out when it counted.

Claude Westmoreland, meanwhile, was a tall and muscular twenty-four-year-old position player who had been drafted out of college by the Dodgers in the first round of the 1974 draft. Originally from Fresno, Westmoreland had played baseball and football at the University of California, averaging 9.2 yards per carry as a running back on the freshman squad and eventually rooming with Steve Bartkowski, the All-American quarterback (and All-American first baseman) at Cal who would be the first overall pick in the 1975 NFL draft. Westmoreland was a gifted athlete, and in 1976 he went on a hitting tear through the Dodgers' farm system—excelling first at the Dodgers' single-A team in Lodi and then in the summer Instructional League in Arizona. All through his Minor League stints Westmoreland showed he had the potential to hit for power, one of the Dodgers' biggest concerns going into 1977.[11] In fact, Westmoreland's only major drawback appeared to be his play in the field. He was too big ultimately to be an effective outfielder, the position he played at the start of his career, and in 1977 he was struggling mightily to find his footing at the position he'd adopted, third base.[12]

Another top young player in the Dodgers' camp in the spring of 1977 was outfielder Glenn Burke. Although he was not completely new to the big-league level, having been called up to the Majors in 1976 as an injury replacement, he was still considered a rookie. Drafted in 1972 out of Berkeley High School, Burke was a rising prospect in the Dodgers' system, said by team scouts to have "all the tools to become a major leaguer in the near future."[13] For four of his five years in the Minors, he batted over .300 and led several leagues in stolen bases. At the same time Burke acquired a reputation for being somewhat unconventional. "His attitude is a question mark," another scouting report read.[14] Among other things Burke had a tendency to be the clubhouse cutup—blasting music, cracking jokes, pulling elaborate pranks. Burke's stated goal was to loosen up any team he played on. Unfortunately, as a big-league call-up Burke had yet to carry this looseness to the plate. He batted .239 over twenty-five games with the Dodgers in 1976 and was used mostly as a defensive and base-running specialist. Still, Burke had a legitimate hope, leading up to 1977, that he'd be given a shot at the Dodgers' starting center-field job on opening day. That hope had, of course, been dimmed in January by the acquisition of Rick Monday. In fact, the Monday trade was doubly bad news for Burke—as during the 1976 season, while on the big-league team, he had befriended the outfielder they'd traded to get Monday. "On the road that first year," Burke said, "Bill Buckner and I would hang out. He's strange. He had those big heavy eyebrows. He was a great player. I really enjoyed his company a lot. Maybe because I was kind of strange too." Burke would not get along with Buckner's replacement. "Rick Monday and I never had a chance," he later said. "He gave me a lot of grief. But I didn't care, because I was after his ass. He would fuck with me. Try to keep me off balance. But that shit of his didn't really bother me."[15]

Young rookies weren't the only players included on the Dodgers' forty-man roster in 1977. A burly right-handed reliever named Mike Garman had also come to the team in the Rick Monday–Bill Buckner trade. Garman was a veteran of six seasons who had been sporadically effective in recent seasons with the Cardinals and Cubs. Dodgers pitching coach Red Adams thought he saw something in the hard-throwing Garman and intended to make a reclamation project of him. On December 6, 1976, meanwhile, the Dodgers had picked up a twenty-nine-year-old utility infielder named Teddy Martinez in the Rule 5 draft. Martinez had been left unprotected in the Cincinnati Reds' farm system, where in 1976 he had batted .255 as a utility player for their AAA team. His last appearance as a Major Leaguer before showing up at the Dodger camp was in 1975, when he hit .172 for the Oakland A's. Wiry and quick, Martinez was originally from the Dominican Republic and lived during the off-season in Santo Domingo, the home of an established Dodger veteran and pinch-hitting specialist, Manny Mota.

Of the players who were nonroster invitees in 1977, a few were highly prized young prospects, but most were a ragtag collection of lesser names, B-level journeymen, and flagging prospects looking for a last chance to fill an emergency need on the team's roster. On February 7, 1977, just a few weeks before spring training, the Dodgers had sent infielder Rick Auerbach to the New York Mets in exchange for a twenty-six-year-old right-hander named Hank Webb. Webb was a tall, rangy pitcher who hid a boyish face behind a scraggly Doobie Brothers–style mustache and a reputation for a blasé attitude. Originally drafted by the New York Mets in 1968, Webb's career highlight had come in 1974, when he'd tossed a no-hitter on the Mets' AAA team in Tidewater and started the International League's All-Star Game. But 1975 didn't work out as Webb hoped: in twenty-nine games—fifteen as a starter—Webb struck out only thirty-eight while walking sixty-two, and he recorded an ERA of 4.07 (compared to the league-wide ERA of 3.36). By 1976 Webb's window of opportunity was closing fast, and he spent most of the year in Tidewater, looking less and less impressive to a frustrated Mets management. The trade to the Dodgers was the New York team's final proverbial washing of the hands.

As a Dodgers nonroster invitee, Webb got lumped in with a batch of mostly forgettable players like Marty Kunkler, Mitch Bobinger, Mike Seberger, and Mark Hance. Of the sixteen total nonroster invitees in Dodgertown in 1977, only five would ever see any playing time in the Majors, and only two would have any sort of sustained career. Ted Power was a twenty-two-year-old right-handed pitching prospect who would play thirteen years in the Major Leagues as a journeyman reliever for the Dodgers, Reds, and a few other teams. The other future Major Leaguer—in fact, a future All-Star—was a young eighteen-year-old Italian kid from Morton, Pennsylvania, who played catcher and had just finished his first season in professional baseball with the lower-A-level team in Bellingham, Mike Scioscia. All of the hopefuls—no matter their background, their prospects, and their burning desire to play—landed at the Vero Beach airstrip in late February, found their way to the Dodger compound, unpacked their suitcases, and readied themselves for the team meeting Tom Lasorda had called for the afternoon of March 1, 1977.

FIVE

The Land of Golden Dreams

> I love your old gray Missions—love your vineyards stretching far.
> I love you, California, with your Golden Gate ajar.
> I love your purple sun-sets, love your skies of azure blue.
> I love you, California; I just can't help loving you.
>
> —F. B. Silverwood and A. F. Frankenstein, "I Love You, California," California's official state song (1913)

On the opposite side of the country from Vero Beach, far from the rising expectations and excitement of the first day of spring training, the bright metropolis of Los Angeles glittered in the sun. From afar, L.A. looked to many ballplayers—who came from all parts of the nation and from several other countries—like a New World Marrakech, a proverbial land of milk and honey that had magically been dropped on the coast of a vast and wealthy nation. That the young men who played baseball for the Dodgers were fond of or, in the case of various rookies and other hopefuls, intensely curious about the "Land of the Lotus" is understandable. Every ballplayer who had spent a life practicing the game and honing his skills at it naturally hoped to reach a final destination like Los Angeles.

Situated in the sprawling suburban-urban region known as Southern California, Los Angeles was a palm tree–laden, sparklingly bright, but relentlessly complex city. Americans throughout much of the twentieth century, and particularly after World War II, saw L.A. as an oasis for people seeking a more exciting and satisfying life. After all, most Americans knew—from a string of movies and television programs, popular music, and everyday folklore—all about the region's reputation for boundless warmth and beauty, open-mindedness and plentiful opportunity, and free love and unencumbered sex on the beach. The peak cultural moment for California occurred in the late 1960s. After the Summer of Love in 1967, young people flooded to California. After all, who wouldn't want to come the place where, according to *Time* in 1969, "the citizens of lotusland seem forever to be lolling around swimming pools, sautéing in the sun, packing across the Sierra, frolicking nude on the beaches, getting taller each year, plucking money off the trees, romping around topless, tramping through the redwoods and—when they stop to catch their breath—preening themselves on-camera before the rest of an envious world"? Because of Hollywood's influence, and because of a confluence of historical and cultural forces, the Los Angeles of the imagination offered all the bounty and possibility of the latter part of the American century. California at the turn of the 1970s, *Time* continued, was the "hothouse" incubator of the latest, most promising fads, fashions, and ideas: "California clothes, architecture, arts, business ventures, topless/bottomless parks, table wines, liberated leisure styles, cults, think tanks and Disneylands seem to be spreading everywhere."[1] By the later 1970s life in California had become synonymous with ocean breezes, swaying palms, fast cars, warm beaches, an endless (and endlessly lucrative) summer, and beautiful young women and boys.

Tom Wolfe had been a frequent visitor to Southern California all through the golden days of the 1960s and early 1970s. His first book, *The Kandy-Kolored Tangerine-Flake Streamline Baby*, was a 1965 collection of essays that had as its titular centerpiece an essay on the wild and eccentric customized hot-rod car culture of Los Angeles. In the essay Wolfe described the aesthetic and styles that California's custom-car fetishists adopted in the era—the baroque curves, a.k.a. the "streamline"; the tail fins and other lurid details; the chrome and the sparkly tangerine-flake paint jobs; and so on. Wolfe also described how California's teenagers would meet and perform esoteric local car rituals on weekends. "Everybody would meet in drive-ins," he wrote, "the most famous of them being the Piccadilly out near Sepulveda Boulevard. It was a hell of a show, all the weird-looking roadsters and custom cars, with very loud varoom-

varoom motors. . . . The real action, though, was the drag racing, which was quite . . . illegal."[2]

Wolfe would return again and again to California throughout the 1960s and '70s, focusing, for instance, on the Bay Area psychedelic drug culture by following Ken Kesey and his Merry Pranksters on a 1968 cross-country road trip for his book *The Electric Kool-Aid Acid Test*; writing about a group of California surfers in an essay that became the title of another book of essays, also released in 1968, *The Pump House Gang*; and writing a story on California's visual landscape (of billboards, neon lights, advertising murals, and "electrographic" signs) for the *Los Angeles Times Magazine* called "I Drove around Los Angeles and It's Crazy! The Art World Is Upside Down."

That the nation's perceptions of Los Angeles in 1977 were mostly faux—created on a flimsy basis, and fostered by no small amount of marketing, public relations, Hollywood fabrication, and wishful thinking—was part of the place's charm to those who loved it. After all, though the landscape of Southern California had few tangible qualities to recommend it, King Charles III of Spain had founded Los Angeles in 1781 as a dusty outpost pueblo that had few natural resources and even fewer geographic advantages.[3] Despite this the Spaniards of the eighteenth century were the first to suggest, in a paroxysm of longing, the near-mythical qualities of California. They concocted the name of the territory from a sixteenth-century Spanish novel that described a fictional island called California that was "very close to a side of the Earthly Paradise."[4]

In 1821 Los Angeles became part of Mexico after that country achieved its independence from Spain. In 1848, as part of the peace treaty that ended the Mexican-American War, Los Angeles and much of the rest of California became part of the United States. The American city of Los Angeles, originally composed of a land grant of just twenty-eight acres, was officially incorporated in 1850, just five months before California, which had rapidly grown since the 1849 Gold Rush, became the country's first state west of Texas. As a vast unexplored outpost far from much of the rest of the country, California, from its origins, came to represent something very specific in the country's collective imagination. California was a place of open opportunity and quick riches. Even after the famous California Gold Rush of 1849 proved overhyped, to people stuck on the cold cornfields of the Midwest or in the drab factory cities of the Northeast, California's reputation as a land of plenty remained. Indeed, California's promise of a better, happier life became so entrenched that it was written into the state's constitution in 1879. The California Constitution's Article 1, Declaration of Rights, reads: "Section 1. All men are by nature *free and independent*, and have certain inalienable rights, which are those of enjoying and defending life and liberty; acquiring, possessing, and protecting property; and pursuing and obtaining safety and *happiness*" (emphases added).

In its early years as an American town, Los Angeles remained a small, dusty, and remote home to five thousand souls, mostly ranchers and farmers. Los Angeles began to grow after the arrival of the railway in 1876 and the discovery of crude oil in 1892. In 1900 its population was 100,000, and by 1910 it had grown to 319,000. In the 1920s Southern California continued to grow, thanks to several new and developing industries—particularly aviation and the Hollywood film industry. By 1930 Los Angeles's population of 1.2 million made it the fifth-largest American city. In 1932 the city was large enough to attract the Olympic Games, hosted in and around the grand new Los Angeles Coliseum. The sense that the city had arrived on the international stage was boosted by the fact that contemporary newspaper accounts suggested these were the first Olympic Games to turn a profit, even though they were being held in the midst of the Great Depression.[5]

As early as 1945 *Life* proclaimed that the California lifestyle was influencing American society, pointing the way to a new form of "modern living." Before the war, as the reach of the American automobile expanded, freeways were seen as key to connecting the disparate communities spreading across the Southern California basin. In fact, Los Angeles constructed one of the country's first urban expressways, the Arroyo Seco Parkway in 1940, and continued building them more ambitiously than anywhere else in the country.[6] In the 1950s California's highway budget was the largest of all states, as roads were increasingly needed to reach the ever-expanding sprawl of shopping malls and housing developments. Many of the newcomers to California in the late 1940s and early 1950s, whose cars filled the new freeways and were parked in the attached garages of new tract homes, were servicemen who had tasted the tempting fruit of California during their military training. Los Angeles had been the nation's most dominant staging location for the war effort in the Pacific, home to numerous war factories and training camps that housed hundreds of thousands of military personnel. Mainly young men away from home for the first time, they marveled at the sunny weather, the openness of the local people, and the openness (and cheapness) of the land. After the war, as the country grew more mobile and more prosperous, countless servicemen returned home, packed up their belongings in a new Edsel or Chevy station wagon, and hopped on the new highways to head west.[7]

The newly arrived postwar Californians eagerly pursued the American Dream of the time by purchasing the trappings of the middle-class Good Life: clapboard house, backyard patio and barbecue, big American car in the garage, maybe a pool, and, on the weekend, the proliferating local popular entertainments. Los Angeles had all of this to offer anyone seeking to live the dream—in fact, it was the dream-making center of the country.[8] In the late 1950s and early 1960s, Gallup polls consistently ranked California number one as a vacation spot, an "ideal place to live," and the most beautiful state with the most beautiful cities. Americans in the mid-1950s mentioned California most frequently as the state where they would most like to relocate, citing the job opportunities and climate as the main attractions.[9] In 1955 Disneyland opened in Anaheim, and people grew ever more curious about the golden magic that increasingly seemed to define Southern California. In 1958 Major League Baseball's Dodgers and Giants shocked the eastern establishment by leaving New York City and moving to Los Angeles and San Francisco, respectively. And, despite the local dismay and anger at the loss of Brooklyn's favorite "bums," in 1960 a *Look* poll revealed that 11 percent of all Americans, if given the opportunity, would choose to move to California, too.

One of the families who had been bedazzled by the idea of California was Tom Fallon's. Since Fallon's marriage to the former Catherine Kolber in the late 1930s, he had raised his family in New York amid a tangle of Irish and German relatives. A few blocks away from their too small two-story clapboard house in Menands (across the river from the state capital, Albany) was Catherine's sister, Helen, who lived with her husband and two children. Tom's two brothers had each made their way—after they each escaped their own stays in separate Pennsylvania orphanages—to live and work for a time in the Albany area before each decided, in turn, to move elsewhere in the state. John Fallon, the second-oldest brother after Tom, moved to Binghamton, about 140 miles southwest of Menands, and Jim, the youngest of four surviving siblings (a younger sister had died in an orphanage), moved to Brooklyn. Their ostensible reason for leaving Albany was to escape being close to their father, a raging Irish alcoholic, and out-of-work coal miner, who had indirectly caused the death of their mother.[10]

Tom Fallon had not been drafted to serve in the armed forces during World War II. Instead, he had been steadily rising through the local police force, gaining the rank of sergeant in the early 1950s. But he was frustrated by the job. Not only did it pay barely enough to keep his family fed, but it did nothing to feed his imagination and sense of doing something big. In the 1940s, when Tom Fallon was a young man, they called it "know-how." American know-how—it was what built the great cities of the country, transforming a new country into a burgeoning nation. To make extra money after hours in those days, Tom Fallon painted houses and did various handyman jobs for families around Albany.[11] He was known for his meticulousness, for covering every square inch of space with tarps so that there was no chance anything could get spoiled by paint drips. Tom wanted to be in a place where his skill, his attention to detail, his imagination would matter.

By the early 1950s, as people increasingly talked of the opportunity and sunshine in California, Fallon began to wonder if life out west wouldn't be more rewarding than life in the East. They had freeways in Southern California. Cars. A vast network of radio stations beaming entertainment across the wide urban basin. They had show business. Jobs and cheap land. When asked many years later why he would leave behind a good civil-servant job with plenty of future opportunity, as well as all of his siblings and extended aunts and uncles and other family in the area, Tom Fallon said without any sentimentality, "I wasn't going to get rich on a policeman's salary."

In the middle of February 1953, the Fallons decided—on the uncertain promise of a well-paying painting job—to pack their six young children and what belongings they could carry into a station wagon and an Airstream trailer that Fallon had assembled by hand. Leaving Menands forever behind, the Fallons joined a long procession of other young families doing the same—traveling part of the time on the first vestiges of President Eisenhower's grand interstate highway system and part of the time on the storied highway of song and lore, Route 66. Tom's youngest child, a boy named Barry, was just a baby. Catherine kept Barry occupied during the entire trip by repeatedly giving him a Kleenex box from which he pulled tissues, one by one by one. The rest of the children spent their time in the novel confines of the trailer, watching the country slowly pass by outside the trailer windows.

Coming to California was not an easy adjustment for the Fallons. During their first year in the state the family lived in modest conditions in a trailer park in Fontana, a city located about nine miles from San Bernardino and noted for its steel mills. Life in Fontana—choked as it was by dust and smog, overrun with tumbleweeds and coyotes and strange varmints—certainly was different from that back home. Tom's middle son, James, or Jimmy as he was known, was nine years old when the family made its move, and for a time he felt like a fish out of water. A fan of cowboy movies, Jimmy noted the dusty heat of the California sun and imagined this was how John Wayne must have felt as he rode the range in movies like *Hondo*. He also was immediately schooled by his schoolmates about how one dealt with local weather conditions. In a rare California rainstorm that first year, Jimmy put on his galoshes and trudged to school just as he had countless times before in Menands. But in the land where the sun always shone and image mattered more than anything, the other kids were put off by his odd fashion choice. "You wear those?" someone asked dismissively. Jimmy never wore galoshes again.

Over time the Fallons slowly adapted to their new life. At thirty-four years of age in 1954, Tom Fallon painted houses, yes, but he held other jobs—security guard, bakery truck driver, night stocker at a supermarket, whatever it took to get by. He was hardly ever home, but eventually he managed to save enough money to buy some property. That spring Fallon bought a house in San Bernardino proper, the eponymous county seat of the largest county in California.[12] Here Tom and Catherine became prolific year-round producers of tomatoes, cucumbers, and all manner of fresh vegetables in their small, but fecund, backyard garden. The entire yard around Tom and Catherine's house would always be well maintained and exceedingly lush. And just beyond the yard, the murky green leaves of several groves of lemons and oranges provided a playground for the Fallon kids to dart and hide and play cowboys and Indians until the sun set beyond the valleys to the west.

It was in the new house in San Bernardino that the California Dream would start to seem finally within reach for Tom Fallon's family. Two particular Californian institutions in those days would provide rich fodder to fatten the yearnings—the great desire to become the kind of "self-made" man that had made California what it was since its earliest history—that had brought Tom Fallon west. First, just down the street from the new house, a small food joint was known for selling a bag of hamburgers for a buck. Run by brothers named Richard and Maurice McDonald since 1940, the place was a modest success. In 1954 the brothers took as a partner a traveling salesman, Ray Kroc. Kroc eventually had a simple idea—Tom Fallon noted—that would transform the McDonald's concept and, eventually, the American food business.

Additionally, in the fall of 1955 during a record-setting heat wave, the family drove nearly fifty miles southwest of their home to Anaheim. Disneyland, the new amusement park that had opened in July of that year, was still so new that many of the drinking fountains were not yet working. In the one-hundred-plus-degree heat that day, park employees passed out free glasses of ice water to keep half-sunstroked park visitors from collapsing. Despite the inconveniences, the family had a memorable enough time that they spoke of it for many years afterward.

To Tom Fallon there were no better examples of the 1970s spirit of California know-how than fellow transplants Ray Kroc and Walt

Disney. Kroc, after serving as an ambulance driver during the First World War, had tried his hand at a succession of temporary trades—salesman, pianist, jazz musician, and radio technician—in his home state of Illinois. His life changed after he came to California and, by chance, met the McDonald brothers in San Bernardino. With them Kroc developed the idea of expanding the McDonald's business through franchises, and he began to do so by establishing the McDonald's Corporation in Illinois in April 1955 and opening a number of restaurants there that year.

Meanwhile, Walt Disney's various midcentury enterprises epitomized the California penchant for turning a pipe dream into reality. Disney, like Kroc, had served in the ambulance corps during the First World War, then returned to his home in the Midwest—in Kansas City—and struggled to establish himself. After failing as a newspaper cartoonist Disney worked on the animation team at the Kansas City Film Ad Company, then formed his own animation company, called Laugh-O-Gram. This company soon went bankrupt, but Disney was undeterred. In 1926 he moved to Hollywood, where he started the Walt Disney Studio. Again Disney nearly failed, as Universal Pictures grabbed the rights to his first popular cartoon character, Oswald Rabbit, and then hired away his team of animators. Rather than give up, however, Disney again risked all on a new staff, a new character named Mickey Mouse, and a bold new animated short, called *Steamboat Willie*, that was the first commercial film to be synchronized with sound.

After producing a number of popular animated features starting in the late 1930s, Disney was at last legitimately successful, but he remained restless for more. In the early 1950s Disney became fixated on another risky idea: a Disney amusement park. Amusement parks were not popular in the early 1950s. People were drawn to the new air-conditioned movie palaces, as these seemed safer from juvenile delinquents and other perceived dangers. Over and over people—especially owners and managers of other amusement parks—advised Disney against pursuing his idea. Even worse, banks and investors shied away from Disney's sales pitch, suggesting the idea was a "fantasy" that offered "too little collateral" for the price. Even Disney's own brother Roy, who was the financial officer for the thriving Disney company, refused to allow company money to be spent on this windmill tilt. But Walt Disney continued pushing, raising eleven million dollars on his own for the park's construction by mortgaging his house, cashing in his life insurance, calling in debts, and establishing a partnership with the local entertainment industry.[13] He built his pipe dream, Disneyland, and the results, of course, were stunning. By the end of the park's first year of operation, three million people had visited, and Disney collected profits of thirty million dollars. Disneyland, which almost no one believed would work, revolutionized an entire industry and changed the local and national cultural landscape forever.

California's association with opportunity, an idea first set down in its constitution and then woven into its social fabric, in fact drew all manner of wild dreamers, risk takers, and adventurers to the state throughout the twentieth century. In addition to Kroc and Disney, Jack LaLanne was born to an immigrant family in San Francisco at the dawn of World War I. Though a temperamental, nervous child, LaLanne later became famous in California, and across the country, as the national "godfather of fitness." Richard Nixon, meanwhile, was born in 1913, just a year before LaLanne, to a family of poor Quaker ranchers in Yorba Linda. After attending Duke Law School on scholarship, Nixon practiced law in California and became a politician of some note (and notoriety). And César Estrada Chávez was born in 1927 and raised by an itinerant farm family in California's Central Valley. As an adult Chavez would become an internationally renowned grassroots organizer, leader, negotiator, and icon to agricultural workers.

The Californian self-made man would increasingly fascinate Tom Fallon in the years after 1955. Over time Tom Fallon would get to know a number of them—including Frisbee inventor Fred Morrison,[14] whom Tom had met while he was working as a carpenter; craftsman Sam Maloof, who had developed his own signature style out of his garage in the years after the war; and an inventor who had innovated the ball-bearing release system on the Craftsman socket wrench. Tom Fallon worshipped these self-made men, identified with them, and dreamed of being one himself.

Another prominent figure at the time who fitted Tom Fallon's criteria of the self-made man—that is, a person from modest circumstances who came to Southern California and rose to the top of his field—was the mayor of Los Angeles in 1977, Tom Bradley. Born in 1917 in Calvert, Texas, Bradley was the son of cotton-field sharecroppers and the grandson of a slave. In 1924 Bradley's parents, seeking to get away from the "oppressive social conditions and out of the no-win economic conditions" of Calvert, moved Tom and his four siblings to Los Angeles.[15] Here Bradley's father worked a number of jobs: waiter, cook, railroad porter, whatever it took to earn a living for the family. Through it all Bradley's parents—neither of whom had completed grade school—emphasized the importance of a good education, and Bradley took the advice to heart and excelled in school. In high school Bradley realized two things. First, he noted that a severe racial problem existed in Southern California, even despite the region's reputation for opportunity and openness. Second, Bradley learned he had a talent for connecting with people despite their differences. Whenever an issue developed between students of different races, for example, the school's principal asked Bradley to help find a resolution.

Despite various obstacles Bradley set his sights on a college education, eventually becoming the first African American in his school to be named to an honor society. In 1937 Bradley entered the University of California at Los Angeles on a track scholarship.[16] After studying and running track at UCLA for a few years, on a whim Bradley took the police officer exam. He scored well enough to be selected for the police force, so he left school after his junior year and served twenty-one years with the Los Angeles Police Department.

During his years on the force Bradley often played a key role in addressing racial issues, just as he did in high school. For instance, Bradley proposed an idea that would eventually end a long-standing racist policy that forbade black and white officers from riding in the same car. He also, while still on the force, continued his education, eventually earning a law degree from Southwestern University Law School. After his retirement from the police department Bradley set his sights on a higher goal: to become the first African American elected to serve on the Los Angeles City Council. The election in 1963 was bitterly contested, with predictably ugly race-baiting by an unpopular and controversial incumbent candidate, but Bradley took the high road, campaigning solely on the issues of the day. He won the seat by a two-to-one margin.

On the Los Angeles City Council Tom Bradley became known for tackling tough issues and for his ability to bring together disparate groups of people. He was also, perhaps most notably, a strong and important voice of criticism regarding the conduct of both the rioters and the local police during the unrest that broke out in the city of Watts in the summer of 1965. Bradley was widely criticized for his views, but he held fast, pushing the city to focus on investigating the root causes of the Watts riots rather than punishing its participants. He was most concerned, he said, in preventing such a tragedy from occurring in the future. When the state governor's commission investigating the Watts riots essentially agreed with Bradley, he was somewhat vindicated; at the same time, though, the majority of the city council, as well as Los Angeles's mayor at the time, Sam Yorty, remained in disagreement with Bradley and did little to change the city government's policies.

After 1965, then, Bradley grew increasingly disillusioned with Mayor Yorty. Although California, and Los Angeles, was at the apex of its reputation as America's presumptive Shangri-la, the anxieties and tensions of 1965 and the tumultuous year of 1968 hit Los Angeles hard. In fact, the hard realities of the times were made clear just after midnight on June 5, 1968, on the night after the California primary election for the Democratic presidential nomination. Bradley had passed up the election-night festivities—scheduled to take place at the Ambassador Hotel in Los Angeles—in order to join his wife, Ethel, a huge baseball fan, for a game at Dodger Stadium. Still, Bradley had announced his support for Robert Kennedy's campaign because he believed, among other things, that the senator would bring a swift end to the war in Vietnam. The city councilman's support worked: at 12:10 a.m. Kennedy gave a victory speech at the Ambassador to his cheering supporters, then ducked away from the crowd to meet with reporters. Kennedy took a shortcut through the hotel's kitchen, where a twenty-four-year-old Palestinian refuge (and resident of suburban L.A.) named Sirhan Sirhan was hiding. As Kennedy passed, Sirhan stepped out from behind a stack of trays and fired a .22 caliber revolver, striking Kennedy in the head and killing him.

Even beyond the violence that increasingly seemed to rule his city, Tom Bradley was concerned in 1968 about the lack of direction and vision he saw coming from the current mayor of Los Angeles, Sam Yorty—a man widely ridiculed for his poor work ethic and for his penchant for using his office as an excuse to make official state visits to places like Europe, the Far East, and Mexico, earning himself the nickname "Travelin' Sam."[17] As problems began to mount in Los Angeles, Yorty was—it became clearer and clearer to Bradley—a major cause. At first Bradley tried to solve the problem by proposing a council resolution to limit the mayor's tenure to just two terms, but the resolution failed to pass. Bradley's next solution, then, was to run for the mayor's office in 1969 as one of thirteen Democratic Party primary candidates challenging the incumbent.

In the lead-up to Election Day, Bradley was, according to most estimates, well ahead of the unpopular incumbent. "Every poll that was run," said Bradley some years later, "showed me running comfortably ahead of the incumbent mayor." Unfortunately, this would change almost overnight. In the last two weeks of that campaign, Bradley explained, "the constant, vicious campaign of fear that was waged by the mayor and his supporters finally began to take hold." Among other things, the desperate Yorty suggested a vote for Bradley would open the door to a city government occupation by black nationalists. "We simply didn't believe that people would be gullible enough to buy that kind of strategy," Bradley said, "but it caught on. By the time we realized it was being an effective approach, it was too late to do anything about it."[18]

The loss was discouraging, but Bradley was undaunted, stating his determination to try to unseat Yorty in four years. "I pledged to myself," Bradley said, "that I would do whatever I needed to, to ensure that the next time I ran, people would know me for my record, for what I could provide for the city." In 1969 Bradley began what would become his regular pattern of work. "I determined that I would work twelve hours a day," Bradley said, "in every section of the city, so that when the next campaign came along, [Yorty] would, if he ran again, not be able to sell the same kind of political strategy. In other words, people were going to get to know me as a person, not as just some name on the ballot. They, therefore, were unlikely to become victims of that kind of campaign strategy again."[19]

In 1973 Bradley ran for mayor again, this time with a far different campaign strategy. "I came out swinging, so to speak," said Bradley, "and it was a much sharper, attacking kind of campaign than in 1969. . . . We had decided that we were just going to take the gloves off." Throughout the campaign Bradley kept on the offensive, attacking the incumbent mayor's record, questioning his ethics and dedication to the city, portraying him as lazy and out of touch. Yorty, meanwhile, returned to the same methods as before, attacking Bradley with vague notions of his attachments to radical black elements. "They couldn't get any dirtier. They were the same, but they didn't work," Bradley said, then laughed. "He was constantly on the defensive, largely because of our strategy of going out on the offensive. I think he never quite got on track in that campaign, and he was not able to generate the kind of credibility for the racial campaign that he attempted in 1973."[20]

This time, on May 20, 1973, Bradley emerged from the Los Angeles mayoral election with 56 percent of the vote (against Yorty's roughly 44 percent), becoming the first African American mayor of the city and the first African American mayor of an American city that was majority white. With his strategy of appealing to all voters across the city, Bradley gained the support of a widespread and diverse coalition of voters—African Americans and other minority groups (especially Hispanics), white liberals, Jews, and, partially as a result of an endorsement by the *Los Angeles Times*, just enough of the local business community. Bradley's win in the election was a triumph at a time when people across the region were starting to give up hope for any semblance of racial harmony. In 1973 the election of Tom Bradley to serve as the mayor of California's biggest city seemed to be not only the fulfillment of the dream of one young man from humble beginnings but also the first step toward realizing the promise of California.

Whatever the reasons that people came west, by the spring of 1977 Los Angeles was closing in on a population of 3 million. Soon it would become the second-largest city in America, knocking Chicago from a position it had held for more than ninety years. In the nearly seventy years since the 1910 census, thanks to all the good press and national interest, Los Angeles had experienced a tenfold increase in population. The same was true of the rest of California, which grew from a population of just under 2.4 million people in 1910 to a population of just under 24 million by 1980. This explosion of population in California gave it an energy and self-assured vibrancy that was unlike any other place in the country at the time.

Among the Dodger veterans there was a marked fondness for their hopeful and lively adopted home. Bill Buckner, after all, made a point of voicing his disappointment at being traded away from a "city that I love," Los Angeles, to a "city that I dislike," Chicago. Other Dodger regulars had settled with their families into nice houses in the region's sunny hillside neighborhoods. In their sharp blue-accented uniforms, the Dodgers were like local nobility in the still new city of Los Angeles, garnering proud attention and adulation. They joined various civic and philanthropic groups and were often in demand. For many of the young Dodger stars, being in Los Angeles meant lucrative endorsement opportunities, appearance fees, and other chances to be entrepreneurs.

On a darker side, however, when family life grew tedious for these young men, the city's proximity to Hollywood gave players an opportunity to occasionally hobnob with movie and television stars. Of course, for any Dodger who was particularly bored, there were the acclaimed "California girls" of song and film lore. That is, there were plenty of adoring and attractive young women willing to show these popular young men a good time. In sum, the virtues of the California way of life—especially in the rollicking, free-and-easy 1970s—was not a tough sell to anyone considering a career with the Dodgers. Any young hopeful rookie trying to break into the Dodgers' lineup in the 1970s knew that if he made the team, he'd be free to pursue any number of personal fantasies. The very thought of L.A. gave hopefuls like Webb, Westmoreland, Rautzhan, and Burke the boost they needed to apply themselves to the drills, exercises, and long, dull practices of spring training in 1977.

SIX

We Were All Rookies Again

I can't believe they're paying me to do this.

—Tommy Lasorda, spring training, 1977

By the start of the spring exhibition season in 1977, the atmosphere in the Dodgers' clubhouse was uncharacteristically electric, and Tom Lasorda was at the center of the buzz. The pace of his commentary, the speed and relentlessness of his chatter, and the range of his subjects were noticed by all. "Thank you, Lord, thank you," he would call out while pitching batting practice to his second baseman, "for blessing Davey Lopes with so much speed—a beautiful and deserving virtue surpassed only by his enthusiasm and love for baseball." Or "Look at Reggie Smith," Lasorda would shout, "he can't wait to hit that ball. Reggie Smith's name is in the book of a lot of great pitchers!" Or "If any of you guys can hit one out off Charlie Hough's knuckleball, I'll buy you a new car! Charlie Hough you've got the best knuckleball in baseball."[1] Lasorda was particularly adept at finding the most sparkling trait, talent, or key characteristic of each and every of his players and driving home awareness of that trait in open view of the team. Additionally, Lasorda made a science of employing player nicknames as shorthand for his hopes and aspirations for, or mischievous sense of irony about, each and every one of his squad. "Hey, Ace," he called veteran pitcher Al Downing, "you're looking good," even though "Ace" Downing wasn't actually looking all that good.[2] "Hondo, take it easy," Lasorda told utility player Lee Lacy, named after the Celtics' highly regarded sixth man, John "Hondo" Havlicek. "You're going to kill somebody. You're hitting the ball too hard. My God, you're hitting it hard." "Harpo, you're sensational," he told backup corner infielder Ed Goodson, named for the silent, and frizzy-haired, Marx brother, "Listen to that wood sing. Look at that drive. Harpo, you are the best hitter in baseball, bar none." Pitcher Burt Hooton was "Happy" Hooton, because of the habitual glumness of his countenance. Rick Rhoden was "Young" because of his age, and Mike Garman was "Pickles" because of his fondness for the food. Johnnie Baker was no longer "Dusty," as most fans knew him, but Johnnie B., seemingly just because Lasorda said so. On and on it went. At one point, during a spring batting practice, Rick Monday got up to take some cuts. "Hey, Rick," Lasorda shouted across the diamond, "we don't have a name for you." To which the outfielder quickly responded, much to Lasorda's delight, "Just call me Betsy Ross."[3]

Despite his back-slappy, loosey-goosey, seemingly boundless, and wholly contagious joviality, make no mistake, almost every word and act of Lasorda's that spring were calculated, intended for the good of the team's overall emotional well-being and balance. The yelling, the ribbing, the nicknames—all of it not only brought the team closer together but also reinforced the idea that the manager was aware of, and cared about, each and every one of his players. In fact, as spring training got fully under way for the Dodgers in 1977, it became increasingly clear to observers how extensive had been Lasorda's efforts to connect members of the team. In addition to the Christmas cards that Lasorda sent to his players, before the start of spring training the manager had made a point of talking directly with each of his projected starting players. As would be revealed over the first weeks of spring camp, Lasorda told each how much he appreciated their talents, what he hoped for them, and, perhaps most important, what he expected them to do in the coming season. Lasorda told Dave Lopes, for example, that he was the team's catalyst. "One of our real keys . . . I expect him to become the leader." The quiet Bill Russell, meanwhile, was, according to Lasorda, underappreciated. He had plenty of speed, and his fielding statistics were as "good or better than any shortstop in the game." Dusty Baker was the "big guy, the key guy," and Lasorda believed in his ability to come back from injury. Reggie Smith had "superstar talent" that just needed to be demonstrated. Ron Cey had the potential, with a little work and extra plate discipline, to become one of the game's "premier hitters." Steve Garvey was capable of more power. Steve Yeager was the "best defensive catcher in baseball" and capable of hitting "50 points more." He ended by telling his pitching staff they were the "best in the National League" and explaining to each exactly what he thought they could achieve.[4]

All through spring Lasorda strove to build up his players' confidence. He told them, over and over and loud enough for anyone to hear, that they could do anything if only they believed hard enough. He told them that he knew, in his heart, that this was a World Series–bound team. When asked during spring training if he felt the Dodgers were hungering for communication and motivation, if he felt the club was handicapped for lack of it in the past, Lasorda brushed aside the question. "What happened in the past doesn't matter," Lasorda said.

> We're looking ahead. Baseball has to be played with a relaxed and confident attitude. Putting the uniform on should be fun. I want a team that's aggressive, that wants to win, but I can't be naive enough to think that as the manager I'm going to win any games. The players do it all and my job is to stay with them and motivate them, know their strengths and weaknesses, make each feel he's a part of it and create a happy attitude by making sure I walk into that clubhouse each day with an enthusiastic and happy face.[5]

While Lasorda saw his motivational skills as key to his inevitable success as a manager, there was more to his approach than was evident at first glance. Lasorda, who knew the names of each of his players' wives and children, was connected and generous. But he was also demanding. "I want everyone tugging on the same end of the rope," he said. "I don't see anything wrong in that. I'm close to my son. I love him. But I'm also capable of disciplining him, of giving him a whack if necessary."[6]

In the main Lasorda said he was content if his players did their job as professionals. "You owe it to yourself and teammates to stay in shape" was how Lasorda explained his expectations to players on the first day of camp. Gathered at those earliest meetings were thirty-six roster players and fifteen nonroster invitees. Only a few veterans were missing—including pitcher Tommy John and outfield John Hale, who each had unresolved contract issues, and outfielder Glenn Burke and veteran catcher Ellie Rodriguez, who were ailing.[7] At the same time Lasorda knew that teams had to have at least *some* rules, and there had to be some sort of limit to all the fun. After one sunny but frigid and windy day of early workouts, Lasorda told the team he had made a decision. Dressed formally in jacket and tie during a team dinner, Lasorda declared that, as a measure of respect to the traditional image of the Dodgers, players should keep their hair cut short. This was no mean request in wild and woolly 1977. Lasorda also imposed a few other cosmetic rules, concerning things such as signing autographs, and he enforced the rules in his own particular and somewhat roundabout and offhand way. Whenever a player inevitably wanted to test Lasorda's resolve by refusing, say, to get a haircut, Lasorda would respond not by fining or suspending the player, as was widely the league norm. "Fine," he would say, "but next time we're on the road, don't ask me if you can fly home on a day off. . . . [I]f you wanted something from me, you had to give something to me."[8]

There were several intriguing by-products to Lasorda's jolly, hands-on approach. On the one hand, a few Dodger players bristled at Lasorda's approach. On the other hand, however, several other players who had been all but given up on, or who were branded as "problem players" or "damaged goods," were suddenly more at ease, more eager to play and contribute, than they had been in some years. Reggie Smith, for example, had been called by his previous team, the St. Louis Cardinals, a "malingerer," who often "jaked it" on the field. But in the spring of 1977, under Lasorda, Smith was suddenly a different player—"quiet," "serious," "reserved," and an "astute student of the game," according to Dodger beat reporters. In a story written two weeks into spring training, at a time when player grievances usually start to bubble to the surface, Smith had nothing but good things to say about his new manager and the new team atmosphere. "I'll say one thing for [Lasorda]," said Smith. "While other managers tell you that with a break here and there we may win, he tells you we are going to win. And he means it. He's even made me believe it. I'm going around saying Dodger blue."[9]

After the distant reserve of Alston, most of the players at the Dodgers' training camp in 1977 found Lasorda's methods refreshing. Spring practice drills—ordinarily a tedious forced march—remained lively throughout camp, mostly thanks to Lasorda's antics. Many veteran players took the extra drills that Lasorda offered. Early in spring training the new manager had announced a special session of instruction he would call "Lasorda University." After regular practice Lasorda would hold up to three hours of extra drills for young players on topics ranging from the squeeze bunt to the double-play exchange and anything else under the sun. "I told all the guys," Lasorda said, "if you enroll in Lasorda University, your tuition will be perspiration, determination, and inspiration. And if you are lucky enough to graduate, you'll make more money than a professor at Harvard or Yale." Sometimes classes ran so late that he had to have the stadium lights turned on. And while the players sometimes looked like they would collapse from sheer exhaustion, the sessions were well attended. At least one of the team's hardened veterans remarked that the team was approaching training with more "enthusiasm" than usual. "It was kind of like we were all rookies again," the player said.[10]

Lasorda never let doubt break into the confidence he expressed in his team's chances in the 1977 season. But, as Lasorda University revealed, the new manager couldn't help but take on projects—small incremental tweaks intended to improve his team's chances over the long season. For instance, he took special interest in catcher Steve Yeager, a strong defensive specialist who had hit an anemic .214 in 1976. The new manager instructed his third base coach, Jim Gilliam, to work on Yeager's swing. Lasorda insisted that, with work, the catcher could hit at least thirty points higher. He also focused on Bill Russell, bringing in specialist coach Maury Wills to work on the shortstop's footwork and loudly suggesting in the press that he could, with effort, raise his steal total from fifteen in 1976 to forty in 1977. Lasorda also instructed Gilliam to work with Russell on hitting to the opposite field, making the shortstop less vulnerable to left-handed pitching. With Steve Garvey, meanwhile, Lasorda offered instruction on making the throw to second base on a bunt. Garvey, an All-Star, Gold Glover, and former MVP whose arm was suspect at best, took Lasorda's suggestion to heart, running the drill fifty times a day through spring. With his outfielders Lasorda worked on hitting the cutoff man. And so on. "I don't call it spring training," Lasorda said to a reporter as spring wore on. "It's a refinement-of-capabilities camp. . . . [And] I'll tell you one thing," Lasorda emphasized with a jab of his finger, "this team is going to be prepared physically and mentally. If you just wanted them to get in good condition, you could hire a gym teacher."[11]

Still, behind the bluster Lasorda must have been nervous, knowing full well the vast expectations that fell on his shoulders and realizing he'd have only one chance to prove himself to demanding fans and media, to the Dodgers' upper management, to his players. He knew he needed his team to reach the World Series or he'd be considered a disappointment. And because of these pressures, Lasorda's mind continued chewing on several burning questions through the spring: What could he do to light a fire under what had been, to that point, an underachieving team? How could he keep pushing his young players to be better than they thought they could be? What more could he do to help the Dodgers reach their full potential? Meanwhile, on a more practical level, Lasorda struggled to decide whom to bat in the number-two spot in the lineup. Would he put Rick Monday in the slot and hope the center fielder would break through, in power-dampening Dodger Stadium, with an endless barrage of line-drive doubles to the power alleys? Or would he bat the speedier contact hitter Bill Russell second, hoping the one-two battery of middle infielders would generate enough early run production to keep the pressure on his pitchers to a minimum? The issue remained an open question, with Lasorda musing about it to anyone who would listen right up until the start of spring-training games, when he finally chose Russell.

Through all of it, with all the pressure and expectation for the team to win, Lasorda seemed to be having the time of his life. "I can't believe they're paying me to do this," he said over and over during spring training to anyone who would listen.

If the early exhibition season revealed something else about Tom Lasorda, it was that he seriously hated to lose, even in the meaningless games of spring training. The Dodgers played their first spring exhibition game of 1977 on March 11, beating the Boston Red Sox, 7–5. It was a typically sloppy Florida League game that went back and forth before being decided on a ninth-inning Reggie Smith home run. Bill Russell batted in the two slot and went two for four. Rick Monday, batting sixth and playing center field, was one for four. On March 12 Lasorda's squad took a close one against the Atlanta Braves in the typical fashion of the Dodgers of old: a 1–0 shutout win. Though Tommy John started the game and pitched three solid scoreless innings, Lasorda also worked several of his younger pitching prospects—Rick Sutcliffe and Rex Hudson. The team lost its first spring game on March 13 against the Braves, 5–3, when right-handed reliever Mike Garman gave up two unearned runs in the ninth inning. On March 14 the team lost to the New York Mets after giving up a first-inning two-run homer to Mets slugger Dave Kingman.

The team's exhibition record was now 2-2, and Lasorda was silent after the game, perhaps fuming to himself about the losses. To make matters worse, in the hometown paper the next day reporter Don Merry wrote of former manager Walt Alston, who had been hanging around Dodgertown in his capacity as a special consultant for the team. It was a presence Lasorda did not relish being reminded of, especially after a loss. Alston, for his part, was noncommittal about the welfare of the team, saying he was keeping busy, even though his duties were not terribly clear. "Sometimes," the paper quoted Alston as saying, "I feel as though I'm not earning my keep."[12] Alston gave a perfunctory assessment of Rick Monday, Yeager's new swing, and some of the younger prospects at camp before he slipped quickly away to the golf course, and the reporter seemed disappointed the old skipper didn't have anything more of note to say. But he shouldn't have been particularly surprised—this dull nonstory about a non-event was on par with the vast majority of reports that had emerged thus far from the Dodgers' spring camp in 1977. As the spring progressed, and Lasorda kept his pledge to play his starting eight for much of the exhibition season, the beat reporters in camp were growing increasingly exasperated. They need not be, though, as the story lull would end soon enough.

On March 17 the Dodgers broke open a tie game versus the New York Yankees in Vero Beach, when the team's thirty-nine-year-old pinch-hitting specialist, Manny Mota, knocked a two-run single in the eighth inning. With the 5–2 victory the Dodgers improved their record overall to four wins and two losses. All seemed to be back on track, and Lasorda was his jovial self again, little aware that a runaway train was about to upset his carefully constructed sense of harmony. That morning back in Los Angeles in the august pages of the *L.A. Times*, a story had broken that flew in the face of Lasorda's rhetoric: the Dodgers' ace pitcher and arguable face of the franchise, Don Sutton, was unhappy as a Dodger.

It came up as such things often do in spring training. Two days earlier, on March 15, a report announced that the Dodgers had come close to trading their thirty-two-year-old ace to the Boston Red Sox for the promising twenty-four-year-old outfielder Jim Rice. Sutton, who'd been saying for two seasons now that he was dissatisfied with his contract, had reportedly asked for a trade, and the Dodgers had been seeking a way to oblige him.[13] When Don Merry, the frustrated reporter who'd spoken a few days earlier to a blasé Alston, asked Sutton directly if he was unhappy as a Dodger, the veteran smiled ironically. "No, I'm not unhappy," he said. "I just shot a 74 [on the Dodgertown golf course], that's only one over par."[14] Whatever the actual circumstances of the trade offer, or whatever the extent of Sutton's unhappiness, the story sent shock waves among many who followed the Dodgers. As a result the team's management quickly sought to contain the damage. Dodger GM Al Campanis, for instance, immediately downplayed the near trade as typical spring exploratory talks. Tom Lasorda, meanwhile, said simply, "I hope and pray that Don, no matter what is said, is loyal enough to himself and the Dodgers to do his best to win. . . . I know he's too much of a pro to give anything less."[15]

In light of the news about Sutton, as well as the continued holdout of Tommy John, many wondered what really was going on with the team. After all, how could the Dodgers' two most veteran starters both be unhappy? This was the Dodgers of Koufax and Drysdale, of Don Newcombe and Carl Erskine, of Johnny Podres and Phil Regan, and an endless array of phenomenal pitchers. Who around the league, they wondered, wouldn't trade place with either of them in a heartbeat? Heck, even Tom Seaver had wanted to be a Dodger. And *Sutton*? He had come up with the Dodgers back in 1966, right at the end of Koufax's career. He had picked up his pregame habits from Koufax, learned how to act like a Dodger pitcher from Don Drysdale. For more than ten seasons he'd pitched his heart out for the team, winning nearly two hundred games in eleven seasons. Sutton in 1977 epitomized one of the game's great ongoing traditions. How could he *not* want to be a Dodger pitcher? It was akin to Roger Staubach wanting to be rid of the Dallas Cowboys. The Dodgers just wouldn't be the same without Don Sutton, nor Sutton without the Dodgers.

As for Tommy John, the veteran left-handed sinker baller, he had brought himself back from the dead with the Dodgers in 1974 by undergoing a radical new surgery to repair his frayed elbow—the type of surgery that was avoided by ballplayers of the time, who were convinced that the moment you went "under the knife" your career was likely over. John had been a journeyman veteran of nine seasons when he came to the Dodgers from the White Sox at age twenty-nine in 1972. With the Dodgers, however, his career blossomed. First, he began to win games—a lot of games, turning his lifetime losing record around to lead the National League in winning percentage in 1973 and 1974. Then, after blowing out his elbow late in the season, John was rescued by Dodger medical consultant Dr. Frank Jobe. The new surgical procedure, called ulner collateral ligament reconstruction but more commonly known as "Tommy John surgery" today, was like something out of science fiction—akin to what had happened to a popular TV character of the time, Steve Austin, a.k.a. the "Six Million Dollar Man," whose body had been reconstructed with cyborg parts after a horrible plane crash. Jobe took a tendon from John's right (nonpitching) forearm and used it to replace a ruined ligament in his left elbow. The idea was not a completely new one, as Jobe had used the technique to repair what he termed "Overuse Syndrome" on damaged wrist and hand ligaments for some time. However, since the type of elbow injury that Tommy John had was something experienced only by baseball pitchers, and since baseball pitchers long avoided any kind of surgery on their elbows, there had as yet been no opportunity to attempt the ligament reconstruction surgery on a patient's elbow. Jobe's idea was certainly radical and innovative, but what's often overlooked in this event is how much credit is due to John for risking the surgery—for overcoming prevailing attitudes and fears of the baseball world—and then working bullheadedly, completely on his own, in the face of the complete unknown and through the pain and partial temporary paralysis and uncertainty to get his arm back in good-enough shape to become a star pitcher again.

In 1976 John returned to the Dodgers to pitch solidly for the team, winning ten games against ten losses and recording a respectable 3.09 ERA. By the spring of 1977 John, knowing that his arm was as strong as ever, that he was poised to help the team return to the World Series, simply wanted some extra assurance from them in the form of a multiyear contract. And Dodger fans certainly hoped there was a resolution to the impasse—the prospect of losing John and Sutton in the same year that the team lost Walt Alston was too frightening for many to imagine.

Despite all of the uncertainty, on March 18 Sutton helped the Dodgers improve their spring record to 5-2 by scattering only three hits and one run over five innings in an eventual 5–3 win over the Montreal Expos. Before the game Sutton would not comment on the *Times* story about the trade. "It's been a smooth, uncomplicated spring," he said cagily, "and I don't want to get involved in any debates."[16] Still, despite taking the high road in the press, Sutton's feelings about the Dodgers remained mixed. Sutton always seemed to feel he was not given his due with the Dodgers. He was not a flashy pitcher, not a big-weapon guy. Sutton simply had his own way of pitching that was good enough for him to finish in the top five in Cy Young Award balloting in each of the previous five seasons.[17]

Now, with blustery Lasorda running things, Sutton's patience had worn thin. (It didn't help that Sutton was jealous of the contract the Dodgers had given Steve Garvey that spring.)[18] Throughout spring training and beyond, then, Sutton waged a solo campaign. He flaunted Lasorda's rules whenever he could, almost daring the new manager to take a stand with his most accomplished single player. Lasorda, bristling, took note of the slights but said nothing. Whenever Sutton made subtle comments or semirude cracks during clubhouse meetings, whenever he raised mild questions about Lasorda's managerial techniques and strategies in the press, whenever he demanded trades, questioned other players' contracts, or cracked jokes at the team's expense, Lasorda said nothing. The manager simply said that he expected Sutton to be a "professional," and Sutton, realizing perhaps he was doing himself little good, eventually simmered down.

Once the furor over Sutton's unhappiness slowly died down, Lasorda faced other critical issues. On March 18 the manager announced that he had a new "number one concern." Dusty Baker, the big twenty-seven-year-old left fielder who had undergone knee surgery during the off-season, had come up lame. The problem was, according to team trainers, that Baker's repaired knee was responding to daily therapy much more slowly than they had hoped. While Baker insisted he felt no pain and pointed out he was swinging the bat well (batting over .400 in spring-training games so far), he continued to run with an obvious limp, and this worried Lasorda. "I don't want to play him," Lasorda said, "unless he is completely well."[19] On March 19, then, against the New York Mets, Lasorda inserted in Baker's spot a twenty-year-old outfielder from the Dominican Republic named Pedro Guerrero. Guerrero was a promising prospect that the Dodgers had received in a trade with the Indians back in April 1974, when he was just seventeen years old. In the game against the Mets, which the Dodgers eventually eked out in twelve innings thanks to a three-hit, two-error rally, Guerrero got a key RBI as Baker watched from the bench.

With Baker's lingering injury leaving his status uncertain, and with Sutton's attitude keeping the pitching staff unsettled, Lasorda and the Dodgers at least came to a kind of agreement with Tommy John. At the start of spring training the thirty-three-year-old John had been looking for at least a three-year contract deal. "Every time I was asked to start," he said, "I started. I'm not asking for the moon. I just want a fair, reasonable salary comparative to Sutton, Hough and Rau—the guys I have to pitch with."[20] In comparison to his cohorts, though, John was actually reasonably well paid, but he had a point.[21] While John acknowledged that the Dodgers feared that his arm would weaken or be injured again, the veteran pitcher also thought that his unprecedented feat—of overcoming, and recovering from, what was considered a career-ending injury—should have earned him some longer-term security.

The Dodgers, however, had a history of strict contract dealings, and an aversion to long-term contracts, even with their most successful veterans. And so the team balked at renegotiating the pitcher's contract. When John finally reported to camp in early March, just a few days after the expected reporting date, he hugged the ebullient Lasorda, saying simply he was ready to pitch. He would not be the gadfly that Sutton was, though later John confided to a reporter that he was determined to leave the team after his current contract expired in 1978.

SEVEN

The Game Has Gotten Worse

Eight hundred thousand a year . . .
and *you* throw to the wrong *base*!

—A baseball fan yelling from the stands in a May 1979 cartoon, "The National Pastime," by Tom Wolfe, one of his *In Our Time* series of cartoon illustrations for *Harper's* that parodied fads and values of the day

If fans fretted at the Dodgers' disgruntled veteran pitchers—good old "Black & Decker" and the team's "Six Million Dollar Man"—they did not have much time to dwell. On March 20 the Dodgers' spring exhibition season continued with a 4–0 victory over the Mets and pitcher Tom Seaver. The Dodgers stood in first place in the Grapefruit League, but not all seemed right. This was because many began to question—especially now that Baker's leg problems had recurred—Lasorda's wisdom in focusing so heavily on playing his regulars during the spring's meaningless games. Injuries were a part of the game, to be sure, but injuries suffered by a team's starting lineup even before the season was under way could be a blow to the upcoming season. *What exactly was Lasorda trying to prove?* they wondered. *Did he think these games actually mattered?* Still, no one could argue with Lasorda's success thus far. The team had a 7-2 record; they were playing like rookies again and winning like a team of top-notch veterans.

While spring training, at its core, has always been a meaningless event, some commenters in 1977 suggested that the practice had, like baseball itself, changed for the worse in recent years. "At best," wrote *L.A. Times* columnist John Hall on March 22, "spring baseball is a hoax. A gentle and harmless hoax. A time to sell tickets and tone a few muscles and enjoy the weather and lack of pressure while making with outrageous gossip. . . . Once, spring was merely a time of innocent promise—managers promising pennants and players promising the moon. Now, one must wonder if this whole mumbling, grumbling double-taking trip was really necessary."[1]

Of course, spring baseball in Florida had never been as innocent and bucolic as Hall suggested in 1977. The first recorded professional baseball team to conduct a full late-winter preseason training camp in the state of Florida was the Washington Senators, whose manager brought the team to stay in Jacksonville in February 1888. The conditions that year were far from genteel, or, as a young catcher on the Senators named Connie Mack put it: "There was a fight every night, and the boys broke a lot of furniture. We played exhibitions during the day and drank most of the night."[2] By 1977, however, fans of a certain mind-set had long forgotten the raw origins of spring baseball and now viewed the Florida baseball camps as a relic of some lost golden era. Followers of the Dodgers, in particular, who cherished the team's adherence to tradition, knew that Dodger spring-training practices had been established by the grand doyen of the team's golden era, Branch Rickey. And they knew that the results of his spring-training experiments through the next three decades had justified Rickey's notions. But now, in 1977, tradition was out of sync with modern times. For traditionalists like Hall, the growing problem was plain: spring training had become a time for whining, for self-absorbed players to eschew the traditions and focus on contract demands. With local mainstays like Sutton and John proving the point in 1977, it was hard to argue with the old-timers like Hall that things were truly better in the heyday of yore.

On March 21, despite his contract frustrations, Tommy John pitched six solid innings against the New York Yankees in a 4–3 loss. Lasorda had given the regular starters a rare day off, and the backups had failed to produce, accounting for just four hits against the Yankees' fourteen. After the game John reiterated that he felt strong and was ready for the season. Of the eight hits against him, "only four were well hit," John said. "I felt very good. This is the best shape I've been in since I've been with the Dodgers."[3]

A day later, on March 22, Don Sutton got knocked around a bit, giving up ten hits in six innings to the Astros and taking a 6–5 loss. The team's spring-training record of 7-4 now put them in second place behind the San Diego Padres. A day earlier Hall had written, somewhat giddily, about the rumors of an "unhappy Don Sutton"; today, however, none of the journalists dwelled on Sutton's loss. Instead, they pointed out that there was at least one bright note from the game: Dusty Baker, quietly inserting himself back in the lineup, had gone one for three and batted in a run.

On March 23 the Dodgers beat the Cincinnati Reds 2–1 on the strength of first-inning RBIs by Reggie Smith and Rick Monday. Cincinnati turned around and got its revenge on March 24, however, pounding fifteen hits—including four home runs and five doubles—to beat the Dodgers 11–9. From here, mindful that March 27 was the day that teams were required to finalize their twenty-five-man rosters for the year, the Dodgers seemed to shift into high gear. Lasorda had made plain that there was little question who the team's eight regular starters would be, but that didn't mean there weren't still questions about who would be on the team's bench and in the bullpen. Rick Sutcliffe, a promising young pitcher, had looked strong when he'd been given a chance to pitch in the spring, and Pedro Guerrero had swung the bat well. Despite their obvious promise, however, consensus around the team was that these players, who were both just twenty years old, needed more seasoning in the Minors. They were assigned to Albuquerque. The management continued to tinker, and, in the lead-up to final roster decisions several additional rumors began to circulate. Seeking at least one more veteran bat to bolster its bench, the Dodgers had sought a trade with Montreal for reserve infielder Jose Morales, a pinch-hitting expert who had batted over .300 in the last two seasons. When Al Campanis was unwilling to part with the pitching prospects that Montreal desired, the deal quietly died. The same was true with a deal he had been trying to reach with the Cleveland Indians for veteran slugger Boog Powell and with the Baltimore Orioles for reserve third baseman Tony Muser. Then on March 28 a news report revealed that the Dodgers had come close to trading left-handed starter Doug Rau to the Twins for a young, emerging star outfielder named Lyman Bostock. As a rookie in 1976 Bostock had batted .323, the fourth-best mark in the American League. Although Bostock would have made an intriguing addition to the Dodgers' outfield, the deal fell through when the team decided it needed to keep as many left-handed pitchers on its roster as possible in order to counter the dangerous left-handed bats in the Cincinnati Reds' lineup.

Between March 25 and 27 the Dodgers won three straight games and moved back into first place in the Grapefruit League by just a half game over the Philadelphia Phillies. After this stretch Lasorda revealed the team's final roster, which reinforced his stated focus for the year: aggressive base running, speed, fielding, and, of course, strong pitching. The team would keep ten pitchers on its roster in 1977, including starters Don Sutton, Tommy John, Doug Rau, Rick Rhoden, and Burt Hooton and relievers Charlie Hough, Al Downing, Stan Wall, Mike Garman, and Elias Sosa. Lance Rautzhan and Hank Webb, not included on the roster, would be packing for the team's AAA affiliate in Albuquerque. In the infield Lasorda would keep the speedy but light-hitting Teddy Martinez, along with twenty-nine-year-old journeyman corner infielder Ed Goodson. Behind the plate he had written in Steve Yeager and the veteran Johnny Oates. And in the outfield he had chosen, in addition to the starters, the young backup outfielder John Hale, utility player Lee Lacy, and veteran pinch-hitter Manny Mota. Glenn Burke and Claude Westmoreland would return to Albuquerque.

John Hall's gripe about spring training in 1977 had of course risen not just out of his frustration with the Dodgers' camp. His concern went much deeper—to baseball itself and to some of the changes occurring at the core of the game. The problem was, as many tradition-minded baseball fans saw it, that America's pastime was moving away from its roots as an old-fashioned gentleman's club, built around backroom handshakes and traditions taught the age-old way, toward something more modern and far less appealing. Baseball was becoming, they believed, a sport that was greedy and petty and far less grand than what they expected from the "grand old game."

In fact, in 1977 more and more voices expressed their discontent over baseball. In February Ray Kroc, the owner of the San Diego Padres, had registered his complaints. Having bought his team just three years before, Kroc, who had made his wealth as chairman of the board of the McDonald's Corporation, was bemused by what the game was becoming. "I certainly didn't envision all the changes," Kroc said in a *Times* interview by Charles Maher. "This free-agent thing," Kroc complained in particular. "In the old days teams were pretty permanent. The Yankees had Ruth and Gehrig and then DiMaggio and they were fixtures. Now you might be an Andy Messersmith fan with the Dodgers and all of a sudden he's gone." And while Kroc acknowledged, ironically enough, that he had bid for many of the new free agents available over the past two years, he explained that he had done it reluctantly, simply because he didn't want his team to fall behind. "I don't like contracts. Nobody in McDonald's has a contract. Buzzie [Bavasi, the Padres' general manager] doesn't have a contract with me. But all of a sudden we're talking about all these five-year contracts for these free agents. It's against the norm. . . . [But] you're stuck."[4]

Sparky Anderson, the Reds' outspoken championship-winning manager, agreed with Kroc. In a separate *Times* article Anderson admitted he was worried about "what is happening to baseball" and about the changes he had seen in his own players. "The next two years in this business are going to be the most critical we've ever seen," Anderson said. "If they don't put a stop to this stuff, no young manager's going to be able to handle it. . . . I think somebody has to, somewhere, make a stand. . . . And we'll have to find out how much it detracts from the players' drive. . . . How do you motivate a guy who's got two more years on his contract and he lets himself get out of condition and he doesn't aspire to work at it?"[5]

In 1977 money was distracting baseball players like almost never before. During spring training John Hall surveyed a number of key players around the league who, like the Dodgers' Don Sutton and Tommy John, were unhappy with their current contracts. His list included such stars as Pete Rose of Sparky Anderson's Reds, Tom Seaver of the Mets, Jim Palmer of the Orioles, Mickey Rivers of the Yankees, Luis Tiant of the Red Sox, and so on. Rose, who was beloved in his own hometown of Cincinnati, told Hall he'd asked the Reds to trade him. "I just can't go on like this," Rose said bitterly. Tom Seaver was so fed up that he said that "the feeling" for his club, the Mets, "was gone." Jim Palmer, meanwhile, said, "It doesn't pay [to be Mr. Nice Guy]. The only way to get anything out of the Orioles is to put a gun to their head." Tiant, a veteran pitcher who had helped lead Boston to the World Series in 1975, said of his team, "I'm tired of all this bull from the Red Sox. I'm mad. My attorney is mad. My wife is mad. She said come home and we'll move to Mexico."[6]

Just about every team had their version (or versions) of this player; no franchise was immune. And why was 1977 so particularly frustrating to certain players? The main reason: 1977 was the first year of full free agency. Established after the 1975 season following a series of court decisions and other legal battles, free agency was essentially the right for a player to sign a contract with any team he chose—something that had not been possible in baseball for nearly one hundred years.[7] After the 1976 season the contracts of thirty-nine veteran players—who, per the new rules, had gained free agency by serving six years in the league—had expired, making them eligible to negotiate with any team. Some of the new free agents—Reggie Jackson, Joe Rudi, Rollie Fingers, Bobby Grich, Doyle Alexander, Don Gullett—had been among the most coveted players in the league, and they cashed in. Reggie Jackson, for example, who famously signed with the New York Yankees in the 1976 off-season, saw his salary jump from $200,000 to $525,000 per year. Joe Rudi's salary leaped from $67,200 in 1976 to $400,000 in 1977 when he left the Oakland A's to sign with the California Angels. And so on.

In 1977, thanks to free agency, the overall average player salary, which had for most of the past decade grown by about 8 or 9 percent per year, jumped by nearly 50 percent in one year.[8] With such a sudden payroll jump, and an attendant sense that this change was accelerating beyond anyone's control, it was no wonder that many traditionalists were nervous. More surprising was the fact that these feelings, as journalists like John Hall discovered, extended to many players. On the surface this inflation might seem like something they would wholeheartedly embrace. Unfortunately, because the transition to the new contractual realities was so sudden in baseball, not every eligible player was reaping the reward in 1977. As Don Sutton and Tommy John (and Pete Rose, and Tom Seaver, and Jim Palmer, and so on) could affirm, baseball teams in 1977 were populated by a small cadre of newly rich haves and a wider, angrier array of have-nots. The fat salaries that some players had drawn through free agency during the off-season in fact were the talk of spring training in 1977, causing heated discussions to break out on the field, in clubhouses and dugouts, and in the press about who was making what money and why (or, more accurately, whether they deserved it). Tension grew so intense in some clubhouses that a few team managers felt the need to take action. "The one thing I don't want to hear in the clubhouse," said decidedly old-school Sparky Anderson at the start of spring training, "is talk about money, contracts, and playing out options. . . . Nobody should refer to a man's salary. It's a personal thing."[9] But very little could soothe the raw nerves. The subject rankled too much for players to avoid it.

To be fair to the traditionalists, especially from our current vantage point—in which free market–based economic self-determination seems such an obvious right for athletes—in 1977 it was impossible to know where free agency would take baseball. The ongoing economic troubles of teams like the Brewers, A's, Padres, Giants, and so on were well known. And as certain free-agent players began to cash in big time, ordinary baseball fans—many of whom were still feeling the effects of an extended economic downturn with lingering high unemployment, runaway inflation, and a rising national debt—felt for the first time their favorite baseball stars moving out of sync with their own lives. So widespread was the anxiety over the changes occurring in baseball during the transition to free agency that it rippled down into the basest forms of popular media. In 1975, as players fought to win the right to free agency through arbitration, Bob Dylan recorded a song about marquee player Catfish Hunter, who was the first player to win freedom (after the 1974 season on an isolated contract technicality) from the "farm" of a greedy Charlie Finley and sign with a new team, the New York Yankees. Then, on March 13, 1976, comic artist and noted baseball fan Charles Schulz made reference to the struggles of the players of the time in his widely syndicated daily comic strip, *Peanuts*. Schulz introduced a story line in which a victory-minded character named Peppermint Patty decides her baseball team is lacking a decent shortstop. Over the phone Patty strong-arms rival manager Charlie Brown to send his shortstop, Snoopy, to her team. Later, Patty is chastised by one of her players, Marcie. "You owners are all alike!" Marcie says. "You think you can trade us players like cattle!" "Moo!" Snoopy adds.

In actuality, the complaints of ballplayers in 1977 were really nothing new. They had been desperately begging for any possible table scrap from team owners, going nearly back to the earliest days of the reserve clause that essentially tied them to one team for their entire careers.[10] A prominent player of the era, John Montgomery Ward, said in an 1887 magazine article, "Like a fugitive slave law, the reserve rule denies him a harbor or a livelihood, and carries him back, bound and shackled, to the club from which he attempted to escape."[11] To fight back against the owners, in 1890 Ward helped create a new baseball league to rival the National League: the Player's League. At first the new league showed promise, siphoning off about half of the National League's regulars and drawing a respectable audience for the first season. Unfortunately, the new league's nervous team owners gave up when large profits did not immediately materialize. Over the next decade or so, a number of other rival leagues either closed down a few years after starting or, in the case of the American League in 1901, were swallowed up by the older league. In the mid-1940s four Mexican brothers tried, and ultimately failed, to create a player-focused alternative major league. And in the early 1950s Branch Rickey, recently let loose by the Dodgers, nearly led several new would-be baseball team owners to found a "third major league," which would have banished the reserve clause. Unfortunately for players, Rickey's Continental League fell apart due to actions undertaken by the Major League owners. This included the co-optation of many of the would-be owners of the Continental League by deciding, in 1961, to expand the number of Major League teams for the first time since 1901.[12]

Beyond these failed attempts to organize against the reserve clause, players' struggles against the rule were conducted piecemeal, mostly by individual players who made futile attempts to hold out for better contract terms. Honus Wagner, the greatest player of his era, held out for more money from his team, the Pittsburgh Pirates, way back in 1908. And twenty-one-year-old Ty Cobb did the same that year with the Detroit Tigers. Edd Roush, who held out nearly every year of his career in an ongoing quest to get better contract terms from his team, the Cincinnati Reds, took the extreme step of holding out for the entire season in 1930. Even widely beloved Yankees slugger Babe Ruth famously held out—seeking money in keeping with his fame and impact on the game and threatening not to play if he did not get it—in 1919 and 1930. (As did Joe DiMaggio in 1938, Ted Williams and Stan Musial in 1948, Mickey Mantle in 1960, and on and on.)

It wasn't until the early 1950s that a journeyman Minor League player, George Toolson, took the unusual step of challenging the reserve clause directly in court. Toolson's battle went all the way to the Supreme Court, where justices, unfortunately, reaffirmed the shaky legal basis for the reserve clause. In the mid-1950s a handful of players made a proposal to the owners that would have allowed a kind of limited free agency to be phased in over six years. As one of these players, Robin Roberts, put it, "For the owners, it would have been a chance to loosen up on control. They didn't give us any satisfaction. It was short-sighted on their part. . . . They were so used to having complete control, they were out of control."[13]

Despite all of these failures, each new step emboldened players who were seeing signs of change throughout the society outside of baseball. By the 1960s—the era of massive public protests in the free speech movement, the civil rights movement, Vietnam War protests, and so on—only the truly out-of-touch baseball fan was unaware that the reserve clause was doomed.

So what happened in 1976 that led, after one hundred years of struggle, to the fall of baseball's loathed reserve clause? Today, many baseball histories point to a single figure, outfielder Curt Flood, as being the key to the reserve clause's demise. Flood was a star outfielder who had been traded against his will from the Cardinals to the Philadelphia Phillies after the 1969 season. Because Flood did not want to leave St. Louis, where he ran several businesses and had built a comfortable life, he took the advice of Marvin Miller, who was in his third year as director of the Major League Baseball Players Association (the fifth, and ultimately successful, attempt at a player's union), and brought an antitrust suit against Major League Baseball. As important a step as this was in communicating to owners how seriously the players, and the fledgling players association, took the reserve clause, the Flood case did not directly kill the rule.[14]

A more complete understanding of how baseball's reserve clause was overturned requires a look at, of all teams, the highly conservative and tradition-minded Los Angeles Dodgers. The Dodger outlook and image in the era leading up to free agency were more fixed and unchanging than almost any team in baseball. Because of this particular character—the focus on tradition, the unwavering commitment to the Dodger Way of playing the game, a rigid approach to the game—the Dodgers became, in the 1960s and '70s, a fulcrum around which rotated an increasing amount of activity intending to change baseball's status quo. Most important were two particular episodes that involved the most traditional aspect of the tradition-minded Dodgers—that is, their pitching. These events, which occurred ten years apart, in fact straddled the Flood case, and each had nearly as crucial an effect on the case against the reserve clause as did Flood's lawsuit. The first event involved two of the greatest pitching stars in the history of the Major Leagues, and the second event involved a more recent Dodger pitcher, whose stance against the reserve clause (and the team) would make him the first true free agent in baseball.

The first episode unfolded this way: In the off-season prior to the 1966 season, as the Dodgers were basking in the glow of another World Series victory in 1965, two of the team's top players—indeed, the two key cogs in the team's ongoing dominance of the National League, pitchers Don Drysdale and Sandy Koufax—had made an accidental, offhand discovery. That winter Koufax had come to the team offices at Dodger Stadium, as usual, to negotiate a new yearly contract with Dodger general manager Buzzie Bavasi. And afterward, as fate would have it, he went to a dinner meeting with his friend Drysdale.

Koufax, the 1965 World Series MVP who had nearly single-handedly beaten their opponent, the Minnesota Twins, by winning Games Five and Seven on just two days' rest, told Drysdale he had been bothered by the meeting. "You walk in there and give them a figure that you want to earn," Koufax said, "and they tell you, 'How come you want that much when Drysdale only wants this much?'" Upon hearing this Drysdale immediately exclaimed, "I'll be damned. I went in to talk to them yesterday for the first time and they told me the same story. Buzzie wondered how I could possibly want as much as I was asking when you were asking for only this."[15] Both pitchers were flabbergasted by the team's dishonesty. And both were well aware that their worth to the team was of far greater value than the money they were earning. They were, after all, the best pitching duo in the Majors. No two-player tandem had as much standing in the league at the time or affected their team as much at these "Big Two" did. Not only had Koufax and Drysdale been responsible for fifty-two victories during the 1965 season and World Series run, they drew fans, a lot of fans, to the ballpark—according to the Dodgers' own estimates an average of ten thousand more fans than average came when Koufax pitched, and three thousand more came when Drysdale was on the mound.[16] It was no wonder the discovery of Dodger deceit was so highly upsetting to the two great Dodger stars.

It was Drysdale's wife of the time, Ginger, who first suggested that her husband join forces with Koufax and meet the Dodgers head-on. "If Buzzie is going to compare the two of you," she reportedly said, "why don't you just walk in there together?" So the two pitchers joined forces to negotiate their contracts, thereby becoming the first collective-bargaining unit ever in baseball. To Bavasi, Koufax and Drysdale said that neither pitcher would sign for the 1966 season unless the Dodgers met their joint contract demands: a three-year, no-cut (that is, guaranteed) contract for each pitcher to be valued at $500,000 apiece (or a total of $167,000 per year, which would have been by far the richest yearly salaries in baseball at the time). Further placing the tandem in no-man's-land was the fact that Koufax's entertainment lawyer, J. William Hayes, had agreed to advise the two on their collective negotiations. "It was a radical step," said Marvin Miller, who had just been elected, in the spring of 1966, to direct the Major League Baseball Players Association, "and it got more radical as it went."[17]

During that year's spring training, as Koufax and Drysdale held out and Miller introduced himself for the first time to players at their various camps, he was asked over and over about the two Dodger pitchers. Miller, wisely, used the opportunity to push the value of collective bargaining, and many players thus became open, for the first time, to the very idea of joining forces with their fellows. This change in player attitude, plus Miller's savvy negotiating and fund-raising skills, would eventually make it possible, at last, for a players union to establish itself.

By policy the Dodgers and O'Malley steadfastly resisted signing multiyear contracts, negotiating with player's agents, or allowing any precedent that could weaken the reserve clause. So the team, predictably, rebuffed Drysdale's and Koufax's requests and began fighting a public opinion battle in the press. All through winter and into spring training, as many in the baseball world noted, the two pitchers held firm in the face of unrelenting pressure. In the end the pitchers did negotiate a compromise deal: a one-year $125,000 contract for Koufax, $110,000 for Drysdale. And though this fell far short of their demands, it was more than the team had originally offered (and more money than either pitcher had ever made). The damage was done. The Koufax-Drysdale holdout had planted an important seed: there was value in collective bargaining.

Flashing forward ten years, past the solitary stand of Curt Flood, it makes sense considering the legacy of Drysdale and Koufax that the first true free agent was a Dodger pitcher, Andy Messersmith. The mechanism by which Marvin Miller and the players association finally broke the reserve clause with Messersmith was through a technicality that came as an unexpected offshoot of the Flood case. During arguments against Flood, perhaps sensing the rising tides against the reserve clause, baseball owners had somewhat desperately argued that baseball's contractual language was not a matter for the courts to decide but instead a collective-bargaining issue best settled by arbitrators.

Miller, seeing the small opening left by this argument, shrewdly waited for the right moment to exploit it. In 1975 Peter Seitz, the chairman of the arbitration panel that baseball's owners had established after the Flood case, voided the contract of Jim "Catfish" Hunter. A pitcher for the Oakland A's at the time, Hunter claimed his contract was invalid because the A's owner had not paid an insurance premium, as had been stipulated in the contract. Seitz declared Hunter a "free agent" as a result of the invalid contract, and Hunter, a top-notch star at the time, signed with the New York Yankees for $3.75 million over five years—by far the richest contract baseball had ever seen. While Hunter's free agency terrified owners and baseball traditionalists alike, the case still did not establish a firm legal precedent against the reserve clause—since it had occurred because of a technicality.

Andy Messersmith, meanwhile, had been an All-Star pitcher for the Dodgers in 1974 but had grown disillusioned with the team after asking that a no-trade clause be placed in his contract in 1975. Like Flood, Messersmith was a proud man, and he was tired of being treated like chattel. While Walter O'Malley offered Messersmith more money and a longer-term deal, he refused—as per Dodger policy—to acquiesce on the subject of a no-trade clause. As a result Messersmith decided to play the 1975 season without a contract, intending, with Marvin Miller's encouragement, to challenge the validity of the reserve clause in front of the arbitration panel after the season.[18] "It was less of an economic issue at the time than a fight for the right to have control over your own destiny," Messersmith told *The Sporting News* a decade later. "It was a matter of being tired of going in to negotiate a contract and hearing the owners say, 'OK, here's what you're getting. Tough luck.'"[19]

In 1975, in advance of the pending arbitration hearing, baseball commissioner Bowie Kuhn nervously proclaimed that widespread free agency would open the door to "potential anarchy" and could conceivably lead to the total destruction of the sport. Frantic owners, meanwhile, argued that baseball's arbitration panel couldn't consider a grievance involving the reserve clause. But Peter Seitz—who had, amazingly enough, been retained by the owners despite ruling in favor of Catfish Hunter—cited the owners' arguments in the Flood lawsuit and prepared to arbitrate the case. On December 23, 1975, Seitz made a monumental ruling, declaring that the reserve clause in the uniform player contract bound a player to his club for only one year, not indefinitely, as previously understood. Because

Messersmith and his coplaintiff, Dave McNally, had played the 1975 season without signing contracts, the ruling granted them immediate free agency.[20] McNally stayed home in Billings, Montana, but Messersmith signed a three-year contract with the Atlanta Braves for $1 million. As a result of the Messersmith-McNally case, the reserve clause was dead. And when owners signed a new basic agreement on July 12, it officially and formally established the terms of free agency in baseball.

The Dodgers ended their 1977 stay in Florida on Wednesday, March 29, recording a 7–6 victory over the St. Louis Cardinals to bring their spring record to 13-6, tops in the Grapefruit League. Don Sutton got the win after a solid seven-inning effort in which he scattered five hits and three runs and at one point retired thirteen in a row. The game was a textbook look at how the Dodgers wanted to play this season. In addition to their traditionally solid pitching, all of the Dodger starting position players, including an improving Dusty Baker, appeared in the game. And several of them—Reggie Smith, Steve Garvey, and Rick Monday—were productive, knocking in the bulk of the team's runs. It was a victory for a team that was learning to work together, to pull on the same rope, just as Lasorda had envisioned.

Before the game against the Cardinals, the Dodgers had announced, to the surprise of none, that Don Sutton would be the team's opening-day starter when the season began on April 7 at home against the San Francisco Giants. It was not a point Lasorda dared leave up to discussion—not with Sutton's notorious prickliness, not with the current contract issues dogging his clubhouse. Even so, it could be argued that Tommy John and the team's reticent right hander Burt Hooton had both pitched better than Sutton during the spring. Even the oft-overlooked knuckleballer, Charlie Hough, whom Lasorda was eyeing as the team's closing reliever this season, had seemed more solid than ol' Black & Decker. But Sutton was the obvious opening-day choice because the pitching-proud, tradition-minded Dodgers always sent their nominal "ace" to the mound on opening day.[21]

After the final game in Florida, on Wednesday evening, the remaining Dodgers left Vero Beach and flew home to Los Angeles, Dodgerland, where skies were mostly sunny and a cool wind blew down from the canyons. The weekend promised seasonable warmth and sunshine across the metro area, as it did almost every year at this time. Just south of L.A., down in Anaheim, the Dodgers' crosstown American League rivals—the California Angels—had just returned from their own spring-training stint in Tempe, Arizona. Having signed a number of free agents during the off-season, California had competed well in the Arizona League, and the team, and its free-spending owner, cowboy-entrepreneur Gene Autry, harbored their own postseason hopes for 1977. Both teams looked forward to their upcoming three-game exhibition showdown known locally as the "Freeway Series," an early test of how the coming season might go.

EIGHT

But You Can Never Leave

> The golden epoch that gave rise to the California dream began when America, disillusioned over the loss of its hero President, looked west for spiritual renewal. On the edge of the horizon it found California. . . . [Here] while think tanks scanned the future, aerospace technicians outfitted adventures to the moon. There was a flourishing journalistic "underground" and an archipelago of multiversities that bristled with post-modern architecture. . . . "Do your own thing" was the golden rule; ambivalence was its only sin. . . . California was the future, and it worked.
>
> —*Time*, July 18, 1977

Even beyond its place-names—Los Angeles, San Diego, Santa Barbara, San Francisco—and the widespread proliferation of clay roof tiles, Spanish culture and history have long influenced the Golden State, California. Early in the state's prehistory, for example, the Spaniards thought of California as their "El Dorado," a mythic desert *espejismo*, or "mirage." This association with El Dorado became something of a wish fulfilled after gold was discovered in the state in the mid-nineteenth century, setting off the frenzy of California's Gold Rush.[1] Still, by 1968, when California adopted "the Golden State" as its official nickname, some might have suggested a more fitting figure from Spanish literature to represent what California had become: Alonso Quijano—better known as the somewhat deluded knight-errand Don Quixote de la Mancha.

There was always an element of fantasy behind the rise of California to the country's richest, most populous state. In 1923, for instance, a downtown financial firm with an obvious vested interest in the economic welfare of the city published an illustrated brochure called *Why Los Angeles Will Become the World's Greatest City.* The publication described the appealing natural beauty of the region—its verdant foothills, lush flora, wide-open skies, and, most important, its sun-drenched valleys. "Los Angeles," the brochure's copy effused, "has touched the imagination of America. She has become an idea . . . A longing in men's breasts. She is the symbol of a new civilization, a new hope, another try. . . . Can there be any doubt but what Los Angeles is to be the world's greatest city . . . greatest in all the annals of history?"[2]

As a result of such efforts people flocked to the state's propaganda like moths to flickering candlelight. "Los Angeles," noted historian David L. Clark in 1977, "grew because people wanted what it had to offer, or because they saw in it the chance to fulfill their dreams and fantasies."[3] Of course, for much of the twentieth century, this wish-fulfilling vision—the California Dream—was also fueled by one primary source: Hollywood. Filmmakers had first scouted then wide-open and sun-drenched Southern California as the location for western films as early as 1909.[4] In 1910 D. W. Griffith filmed a short seventeen-minute film in Hollywood. In 1911 the Nestor Motion Picture Company completed the first full-length Hollywood film, set in the middle of orange groves located just off Hollywood Boulevard. In the next few years four major production companies moved out to Hollywood from back east, drawn by sun and cheap land. By 1915 the majority of American films were being made in Hollywood.

Southern California was a perfect partner to the movie industry, as each added to the other's mythology and appeal. "Hollywood is a particularly American state of mind," Jack Slater wrote in a June 1976 *Los Angeles Times* feature called "Possessed by the Hollywood Dream," "a city that has become a national yearning or a kind of mental landscape devoted exclusively to the manufacture of the American Dream."[5] Profiling a dozen or so souls who had come west to follow their Hollywood dreams, Slater captured the clear sense of ordinary Americans' enduring fascination with the California Dream. These were young ordinary people who were willing to risk a life spent as stagehands, car salesmen, or restaurant servers just for the chance to break in as actors, directors, or screenwriters in Hollywood. Slater described these "perpetually optimistic" California dreamers as "artists and would-be artists [who] still come here not only to become immortalized in celluloid make-believe but to become the Dream itself—to personify it in much the same way that movie stars, America's only real heroes, have personified the dream for the past 50 years."[6] Thanks to these dreamers who flocked to the city, Los Angeles became the City of Lights, the City of Angels, the magical Lotus Land where it was possible to find happiness and contentment within sight of the Hollywood Hills.

Despite the fact that the economic downturn of the 1970s had affected moviemaking, as it had most other industries, the vision of the local movie industry remained a potent lure. The attraction of Hollywood, of course, has always been mostly intangible, mostly wish fulfillment. This fact was acknowledged as far back as 1935, when Harry Carr, an old newsman, wrote: "Hollywood is at once the pot of gold at the end of the rainbow and the struggle between two drowning persons for the last life-belt."[7] As the 1970s progressed, however, more and more commentators came to realize how tenuous was the "Implausible Dream" of Los Angeles. In early 1978 Art Seidenbaum was examining the truth that lay behind the city's gauzy facade. "Los Angeles began without easy overland contact with the rest of America," Seidenbaum wrote. "[The city] was cut off from the United States by harsh deserts and high mountains. We started thirsty from the beginning, without adequate or consistent water supply. . . . We didn't have a natural harbor, unlike almost every major city. . . . [And the] mountains and dry lands constitute the great wall of California. They are the barriers that separate the West Coast industrially from other states. California is an economic island."[8]

The split personality of 1970s California—a land of golden fantasies on one side, and something far less perfect on the other—was no real surprise. After all, from the get-go the driving engine of California's growth was overblown propaganda. After the Spaniards left and America wrested California from Mexico, the prospectors who came to California after the start of the Gold Rush—the so-called forty-niners—were only the first of many groups whose California dreams were unrealistic. Each successive wave of California dreamer, drawn to the West, hoping for a better life, found much the same as the forty-niners had—life in California was not markedly better here than anywhere else, or at least it was not as wonderful as advertised. And this dynamic, of course, caused plenty of problems in California. As Erik Davis noted in his book *Visionary State: A Journey through California's Spiritual Landscape*, because of the successive mad dashes to California of people seeking to capture the fleeting chimeras of wealth and happiness, significant numbers of Californians possessed a warped, out-of-touch, even pathological outlook. "When the United States seized the territory from Mexico in 1848," Davis wrote, "California became the stage for a strange and steady parade of utopian sects, bohemian mystics, cult leaders, psychospiritual healers, holy poets, sex magicians, fringe Christians, and psychedelic warriors."[9] From its earliest history California was home to a continuous stream of fads and gizmos, cults and mysterious secret societies, snake-oil salesmen and proselytizers, and the world's most savvy pitch men and public relations (PR) professionals.[10] Even more strange, as became clear in the early 1970s, the California Dream itself was the very cause for most of California's growing problems. That is, the way that the ever-increasing newcomers pursued the dream led to a number of less than beneficial side effects. Consider, for instance, the state's vaunted status as a car mecca. The many pilgrims who came to California in the 1940s, '50s, and '60s loved the seemingly limitless space in which to move and constantly seek better horizons. By the late 1950s, in fact, only six states had more cars than Los Angeles County. But, over time, the intensely itinerant way of life in California set in motion a death spiral of freeway building and land development. Already by 1960 approximately two-thirds of the land in metropolitan Southern California supported car-related needs: highways, roads, driveways, freeways, parking lots, service stations, and car lots. The constant construction of this auto-based infrastructure swallowed up the former open spaces and farms of California and pushed the growing metropolis outward in all directions. The Southern Californian pattern of development destroyed much of the natural beauty of the region, created a vast and barely sustainable urban megaplex, and even spawned a new concept: "urban sprawl" (sometimes also somewhat disparagingly called Los Angelization). By 1977 the spread of concrete and pavement now called Southern California reached in all directions across vast valley floors from the Pacific Coast inland to the foothills of the Sierra Madre range and out into the Palm and Mojave Deserts.

Southern California's low-density development patterns, once lauded as the American growth-model of the future, contributed to diminishing quality-of-life issues even beyond the destruction of open spaces and natural beauty. Since the city was situated in a low basin surrounded by mountains and was both blessed and cursed with a unique weather pattern of warmth and dryness, a strong atmospheric inversion layer often trapped factory smoke and vehicle emissions. Early on observers noted the bad air of Los Angeles. The word *smog*, a nineteenth-century portmanteau of *smoke* and *fog*, first appeared in a January 19, 1893, *Los Angeles Times* article. And the millions of vehicles that flooded into the region in the twentieth century, which were necessary to traverse the rapidly expanding cityscape, only made the air quality worse. In 1954, for example—only a year before the opening of Disneyland—the smog had grown so intense in Los Angeles that schools and major parts of local industry were shut down for nearly the *entire month* of October.[11] The sprawl of people, highways, parking lots, and low-slung buildings across the semiarid mountain valleys of California also created intractable logistical problems for the area's residents. Sustaining the growing spread of people and concrete across such a harsh and unforgiving landscape was particularly problematic. Yearly, Californians battled harsh desert winds, brush fires, mud slides on the region's raw-earth hills, sudden violent flash floods, dryness from lack of rain, even drought. While the California sunshine was a common reason so many were drawn to the state, its constancy was not terribly accommodating to the needs of human habitation, especially on the scale it had developed across the Southern California basin. "It never rains in Southern California" went the 1972 song by Albert Hammond, which was very nearly accurate—the region drew only about fifteen inches of annual rainfall (comparing, for example, with Marrakech, in Morocco, which had about ten inches of annual precipitation). Water had always been somewhat scarce in semiarid Southern California, and although the city's early water problems had been solved by William Mulholland, a water engineer who was responsible for the construction of a system of dams and aqueducts in the 1910s,[12] it was only a temporary solution. The city's constant growth stressed the water system, leading *Time* to note in 1969, "If someone turned off the irrigation faucet for a week, green Southern California would be a dust bowl."[13]

Another unforeseen result of California's development pattern was the division and isolation of formerly quiet ethnic and culturally vibrant neighborhoods. The massive freeway structures built between the 1940s and 1970s unexpectedly blocked millions of people's access to other parts of the city, trapping them in their own circumstances and causing widespread economic hardship. Mike Davis, in his book *City of Quartz*, described how the dominant cultural driving force in the Los Angeles in these years—its "malevolence" in reshaping the natural landscape—caused systemic problems like crime, unemployment, drug abuse, and general depression, and it ruined many potentially lovely and wholly livable swaths of the city, including newly isolated ethnic neighborhoods like Watts, East Los Angeles, and Compton. The economic and physical isolation brought on by local development patterns is thought to be a root cause of the Watts riots in 1965. Although this event occurred immediately following the arrest, on August 11, 1965, of a young black motorist, behind the arrest lurked the long frustration and malaise among the neighborhood's underemployed, isolated, and unengaged youths. After peace was restored nearly one thousand buildings in the area were damaged, stripped bare, or completely destroyed.

The riots attracted widespread national attention to local inequalities, appearing bleakly on the cover of *Time* and damaging the idea of California as a social paradise. But this wasn't even the worst of it. That would come a few years later, near the end of the Vietnam War, when Californians began to realize that the century-long free and unfettered bacchanalia of construction and development was coming to an end. "During the Vietnam boom," wrote Davis, "developable coastal land—the raw material of the Southern California dream—began to disappear. Resulting land inflation, which went ballistic in the late 1970s . . . profoundly reshaped the distribution of wealth and opportunity."[14]

What happened to Tom Fallon's family after resettling in California in 1953 reveals everything one needs to know about what life was like in Southern California. Despite coming to the state to pursue his dreams of the easy life, once in California Fallon discovered how difficult it was to make money. For the longest time, in the 1950s and 1960s, Fallon got by doing relatively menial work, often holding several such jobs at one time. His children grew up hardly knowing him. Despite his struggles, however, Tom's faith in the California Dream, like that of many locals, remained unshaken. He remained ever optimistic about the possibility of nabbing California gold, even to the point of going to the Mojave Desert to find it.

The story is this: Sometime in the later 1960s Tom Fallon, who always had an ear for wild dreamers, came to know a man who claimed he had invented a machine that could draw gold dust from desert sand. "There's more gold scattered around the deserts of California," this man told him, "than have ever been extracted from all the gold mines in all of history. All you need is an easy way to capture all those riches." The man's name is lost in family lore, but his was enough of a sales pitch to convince Fallon to throw his money into a speculative enterprise being set up in a desert outpost of Barstow. His middle son, Jim, was finishing college and looking for a way to support his wife and two-year-old son. Tom offered him a job, for a salary of $150 a week, toiling away at the hard task of finding gold in the Barstow sands.

Summers in Barstow are blazingly bright and hot, and after a few futile months of hard effort Jim realized that the machine did not work, that it would never work. Jim left Barstow in the fall and found a desk job at Allstate Insurance in Pasadena. But he would never stop dreaming of striking gold. Neither would Tom Fallon. And in Tom and Jim Fallon's defense, it was not their fault that they'd been duped by promises of desert riches. It was, to be sure, a normal, everyday occurrence in Southern California. Almost daily, after all—in local newspapers, on television, around water coolers, on neighborhood corners—came the same message: Dream Big! And weekly, no matter where you were, you would come across a certain kind of person: dreamers selling faddish meditation techniques and diets, hucksters intent on reinventing fashion or language or style, savants mired in idiosyncratic pursuit of an arcane hobby, as well as all manner of entrepreneur, dabbler and tinkerer, snake-oil crackpot, mystical cultist, and sellers of magic beans. For every visionary founder of a future multimillion-dollar company like Intel, Jiffy Lube, Kinko's, and McDonald's—or for every small-time operator with a big idea who was lucky enough to strike it rich—California was home to thousands upon thousands of others who never came close to realizing their dreams. And it was okay. It was the California way.

By the spring of 1977, as the Dodgers gave the city of Los Angeles a dose of much-needed hope going into the new baseball season, most Californians agreed the California Dream was all but dead—though, as *Time* would suggest, "Californians differ[ed] over when the dream fizzled."[15] Some people traced their disappointment back to the previous November, when California failed to register its electoral college vote for the candidate who eventually became president, Jimmy Carter. Some suggested the state had peaked in 1973 and 1974, when gasoline supply shortages and steep fuel price hikes followed the Organization of Petroleum Exporting Countries oil embargo, resulting in a sharp recession. Others blamed the idea that, because it was inevitable that a large earthquake would eventually strike the overgrown city of L.A., mass devastation was inevitable. (In 1971 sixty-five people had died from a magnitude 6.6 earthquake in San Fernando.) And others suggested further reasons: increasing crime rates, the loss of 180,000 jobs by the failure of the state's aeronautical industry, the turmoil and systemic strain being caused by an ongoing drought, the spread of street gangs in Compton and East Los Angeles, the state's rising divorce rates in the 1970s after the passage of the country's first no-fault divorce law,[16] the mass student protests in the later 1960s and into the 1970s, and on and on. Whatever the reason, *Time* concluded, everyone agreed that the California "of the '60s, a mystical land of abundance and affluence, vanished some time in the 1970s."[17]

Having reached the end of his first term in office in 1977, Mayor

Tom Bradley had a markedly different view of his city as he had in 1973. A year before, in 1976, Bradley had worked as the cochair of the Democratic National Convention in New York, during the campaign that elected Jimmy Carter to the presidency. After the election Carter had offered Bradley a position in his cabinet, as the secretary of housing and urban development. Bradley's own messages of hope for the multidimensional, multicultural city of Los Angeles likely influenced Carter's decision to invite Bradley. But Bradley had already promised local business leaders, who were concerned about a number of ongoing issues, that he would run for reelection in 1977, so Bradley declined Carter's offer. "This was in December [1976]," said Bradley, "so by that time I had made a firm decision to run. It would have been unfair to my supporters for me to back off at that point. So it was an easy decision, having made that prior commitment to running for reelection."[18]

Throughout his first term Bradley had set a strong tone that many in the city admired. He continued to work hard—often twelve or more hours a day—to tackle the many challenges and problems, some quite intractable, that his city was facing. This included, among other things, addressing head-on the need for a modern public mass transit system, for which he obtained federal dollars to develop a new rail line downtown (though his tax proposal to finance mass transit failed to win approval from county voters); petitioning the federal government for funds to provide better services to local citizens; setting up an Office of Small Business Assistance to help struggling businesses get through the recession; improving the availability and quality of housing for low- and moderate-income families in the city; encouraging various urban renewal projects in some of the more destitute parts of the city; undertaking a massive revitalization of the city's harbor in order to expand its capacity to handle international shipping; and so on. And he did all of this work quietly, with little regard to gaining accolades. "One of the major differences between Tom Bradley and other politicians," said prominent local businessman Barry Erdos, toward the end of the mayor's first term, "is that he is not always looking for a spotlight for himself."[19]

Even with all the successes, not all was well behind the scenes. Part of the problem was the sense that, no matter what he accomplished as mayor, some things would never change. Back in 1973, after his first election victory, Bradley had expressed his hopes for Los Angeles and Angelenos. "Never did I lose faith that this city could live by the creed of this nation's birth," he said in his July inauguration speech. "Let it be said that here in Los Angeles, we began today to build the kind of government that means what it says and says what it means. Let it be said that we built the kind of government that the decent, hardworking citizens of Los Angeles respected because it respected them." Now, four years later, Bradley was disheartened by a number of setbacks, both personal and political. In 1973, just after taking office, Bradley had received news that his eighty-two-year-old mother, Crenner Hawkins Bradley, had died of a heart attack. Then, about a year into his first term in office, Tom Bradley's twenty-nine-year-old daughter, Phyllis, had the first of what would be many run-ins with the police—a resisting-arrest charge after a minor traffic stop.[20] Even as Bradley racked his brain to come up with a solution for his daughter's problems, in February 1976 he had to accept the resignation of a longtime friend and adviser, and one of the most important members of his cabinet, Deputy Mayor Maury Weiner. Weiner had been found guilty of lewd conduct in a movie theater, a misdemeanor charge, but to minimize the political damage he decided to step down.

Despite these ongoing issues and frustrations, during the lead-up to the election in 1977 Bradley was hopeful that the city had truly turned a corner in its history. In particular, he hoped that this election might avoid much of the ugliness that had characterized the previous two elections. In mid-December a state senator from the San Fernando Valley named Alan Robbins announced his candidacy for the mayor's office, declaring that he would steer clear of the racial overtones of past elections. Robbins's pledge was disingenuous, of course, as he immediately began criticizing Bradley for his stance on the issue of mandatory school busing, for being soft on crime, for kowtowing to downtown business interests, and so on. In all of Robbins's criticisms and campaign themes, there was, as election observers noted, a subtle undertone of racism. "The persistent thrust . . . of much of Bradley's opposition," wrote journalist Kenneth Reich, "[was] that the predominantly white Los Angeles electorate will not believe a black is as safely conservative as a white."[21]

In the end Bradley need hardly have worried about the racial rhetoric. After lining up endorsements from a wide array of political figures—Governor Jerry Brown, Senator Alan Cranston, the American Federation of Labor and Congress of Industrial Organizations, and the majority of city council members, just to name a few—on April 5, 1977, Bradley swept back into office, winning just less than 60 percent of the vote to Robbins's 28 percent. Despite the lingering sense of frustration and malaise that afflicted many in Los Angeles, Bradley's reelection was at least something to crow about. There was still some light to be found behind the clouds of 1977.

NINE
Hollywood Stars and Blue Hard Hats

I bleed Dodger blue.

—Tommy Lasorda, Los Angeles Dodgers' 1977 yearbook

Tell him that blood comes in only one color. Red.

—Sparky Anderson, March 26, 1977, in response to Tommy Lasorda

In Los Angeles at the end of March 1977, the Dodgers' diehard fans were increasingly eager for the team's return. Despite the meaninglessness of spring-training games, fans could see that the lineup was firing on all pistons. Some fans even allowed themselves the tiny hope that *this* might finally be *the year*. On Friday, April 1, the Dodgers played the first game in their annual Freeway Series against the Angels, winning 5–0 in front of nearly thirty thousand fans at Anaheim Stadium. Starting pitcher Doug Rau easily baffled the Angels' vaunted new million-dollar free-agent signees Joe Rudi, Bobby Grich, and Don Baylor, giving up only one hit in six innings. Steve Garvey and Dusty Baker provided all the power the Dodgers needed by each slugging a two-run homer. In the next game on Saturday, also at Anaheim Stadium, Los Angeles got to the Angels' All-Star left-handed starter Frank Tanana quickly and then amassed fifteen hits and ten runs en route to a lopsided 10–3 victory. Finally, on April 3, Tommy John shut out the Angels 3–0 in Los Angeles. The win gave the Dodgers their first Freeway Series sweep of the Angels since the series started in 1962, the Angels' second year in the league.

After the final game of the Freeway Series, both teams attended the annual Southern California Baseball Writers Awards banquet, where local sportswriters vote on the best players on both local teams in certain categories. For instance, Manny Mota, the Dodgers' aged pinch-hitting specialist, won the Most Popular Player Award; Rick Monday won the Civic Award; Steve Garvey won the MVP Award for both the 1976 season and the 1977 Freeway Series; and Don Sutton, who did not attend the event because he was shooting a commercial, won the Dodgers' Best Pitcher Award. (After learning of his award, Sutton suggested that winning the award gave him "a chance to show the writers how *happy* I really am.") Afterward, columnist John Hall, who attended the event, praised the Dodgers despite his lingering distaste for the current spirit of the game. "There was no gloating," Hall wrote of the various Dodger players' conduct at the banquet, "not even a mention of their sweep of the Angels putting them ahead for the first time ever in the rivalry that began in 1962." Various Dodgers had fun at the banquet, poking gentle fun at each other, but beneath the facade was a seriousness of purpose that seemed to thrill Hall. "Maybe the Dodgers' gentlemanly attitude was a bit humiliating to the Angels. Like ho hum, no big deal, they *expected* to whack the daylights out of the ambitious American Leaguers."[1]

Hall's comments after the Freeway Series pointed to two strong character traits that were emerging among the 1977 Dodgers. On the one hand, the team exhibited a businesslike attitude that was different from previous years. The Dodgers were serious about proving their mettle to the rest of the league. On the other hand, the Dodgers were also, as a group, surprisingly loose. After game 2 of the Freeway Series, Bill Russell suggested the key reason for this. "Usually spring gets boring," the ordinarily restrained Russell said, "but it hasn't been that way with Tommy around. Honestly, I think he's got us jacked up."[2] (As if to illustrate his point, Russell had gone three for three in the game and had knocked in four of the team's ten runs.)

Lasorda—who by now had been dubbed, because of his vocally eternal optimism, "Mr. Bubbles" by the local press—had indeed ratcheted up his antics in the final days before opening day. For instance, prior to game 1 of the Freeway Series Lasorda had finally cleared Baker to start the season in left field. But he had made the announcement in his own particular way. "I'm sorry to tell you this, Dusty," the Dodger manager told Baker after calling him into his office, "but you've been traded to the Indians. I don't know how they could have done this to me because I was counting on you to play left." Only when Baker's head dropped into his hands did Lasorda break character, looking at a calendar and saying, "Oh, wait a second. It's April 1st. It's April Fool's day, isn't it?" Lasorda's prank, upsetting as it was, of course served a larger purpose. By poking fun at Baker's deepest concerns—that he might not, after all his work, be part of the Dodgers' long-term plans—Lasorda reinforced how committed Lasorda was to Baker for the 1977 season. It was just Lasorda's way of giving the weak-kneed Baker one more shot of confidence for the season. And in the game that followed Baker smashed a double and a homer. Throughout the season Lasorda used this ironic method of reinforcement and encouragement, making a joke out of a weakness, distracting players with a purposeful prank, and so on. And Lasorda's focused banter and targeted frivolity had already seemed to draw the Dodgers' wide range of strong clubhouse personalities together. Or as John Hall noted, "The Dodgers already are playing like July."[3]

After the Freeway Series, with the start of the regular season now only three days away, Lasorda and his coaches were determined not to let up. They continued working with players on the small parts of their games—Lasorda and coach Monty Basgall riding Ron Cey as he worked on his swing in the batting cage, Maury Wills working with Garvey on a long footwork session, Lasorda taking Bill Russell aside to discuss a mental lapse while running the bases, and on and on. As opening day loomed Lasorda continued to challenge his team of veteran professionals to take their game to the ultimate level, and his players—with perhaps just one or two key exceptions—rose to the challenge without outward complaint. The Dodgers won their next exhibition game on April 4 against the Giants in San Francisco and then ended the exhibition season with a loss against the Chicago Cubs in Arizona. Despite the final loss the Dodgers finished spring training with a 17-7 win-loss record, the best in the Majors by a full game over the Phillies and Brewers. Inspired by the team's spring record and the infectious enthusiasm of Lasorda, team owner Walter O'Malley was overheard boasting at a Chamber of Commerce luncheon before opening day. "I have no apologies at all for our group," O'Malley said. "After 20 years in L.A. this is our best team."[4]

Lasorda's motivation for driving his team in 1977 may have gone deeper than just wanting to prove his own managerial chops, and it may have gone deeper than his desire to prove himself worthy of his predecessor. Lasorda may have been out to return his beloved Dodgers to the heights of success that their owner, staff, fans, and followers expected. As if to explore these lofty team expectations before the 1977 season got under way, the *L.A. Times* published a story called "The Dodger Image," written by Don Merry, which attempted to pinpoint the exact elements that made up the Dodger "brand." The article enumerated the team's unique assets: Dodgertown was considered the cream of spring-training sites in 1977, and Dodger Stadium, overlooking downtown Los Angeles, was widely admired. Plus, the Dodger fan base was enviable—in twelve of the previous nineteen seasons in Los Angeles, two million–plus people had come to see the team play. Part of the reason for the strong fan support, according to the article, was the consistently lively, and mostly positive, coverage of local media, led by the team's television and radio broadcast guru, Vin Scully, who had been with the Dodgers since 1950. "I think that we came close to creating something like a Yankee dynasty in the early 60s," Vin Scully told Merry. "But we didn't have that cold, U.S. Steel approach to winning. There was always something zany happening. The Dodgers just seemed more human." And there was also, continued Merry, the shrewd and able leadership of its longtime owner, Walter O'Malley, and the "family" atmosphere that he engendered. This atmosphere had spread through the entire organization, become part of the institutional culture, and created a unique sense of team loyalty among staff and former players. This, the article pointed out, was perhaps the Dodgers' biggest single asset: Dodgers, both former and current, were known far and wide for buying into the Dodger brand and promoting it. Roy Campanella, Pee Wee Reese, Dixie Walker, and current players like Ron Cey all were spokesmen for the Dodgers at events, civic functions, and throughout the baseball world. "They all created . . . a good public-relations image," said Walter O'Malley. The article's author agreed. "It is doubtful that even a high-powered Madison Ave. firm could have concocted a more favorable public image than the Los Angeles Dodgers enjoy today," wrote Merry. "To spectators at Dodger Stadium, relentlessly billed as the finest of its type in the land, the product they pay to see represents success and excitement. . . . To others in baseball, the Dodgers come across as extremely professional, slightly conservative, authoritarian and dedicated to doing things correctly and in first-class style. They radiate a slight aura of superiority."[5]

Interestingly, the article singled out one particular current player who perfectly personified "the Dodger image," the team's star first baseman, Steve Garvey. Garvey was described by Merry as "talented, good looking, friendly, happily married to a beautiful woman and well-educated." Steve Garvey was, in many ways, the heart and soul of the Dodgers in 1977. Or, more precisely, he was the player that the public saw as the team's heart and soul. Easily the team's most popular player among its fan base, Garvey carefully cultivated a clean, wholesome, and friendly image. He was known for always taking extra time to talk to sportswriters, to stop and sign autographs or acknowledge fans, and to participate in a number of highly visible public charities around Los Angeles. Garvey, with his thick, dark hair parted across his forehead and his square All-American jaw, was nearly as telegenic as a Hollywood star. It helped too that his wife, Cyndy, was tall and blonde and as put together as a shampoo model. (In the late 1970s Cyndy began appearing on local television as a talk show host and would eventually land a regular position on AM Los Angeles, as a cohost opposite a veteran media personality named Regis Philbin.) The Garveys, as they built their presumed dream life together, were featured often in the media as the "Ken and Barbie" of baseball. Mostly this was said with admiration, but not always. At least outwardly, the Garveys were made for Los Angeles and the Dodgers, and the Dodgers and Los Angeles were made for the Garveys.

The team's proximity to Hollywood affected the careers of Steve Garvey and a number of other Dodgers—such as the much less telegenic Don Sutton—heightening their visibility and turning them into fixtures on local, and sometimes national, media. While Garvey, the local media king, signed lucrative deals to endorse Aqua Velva, SegaVision's new big-screen TV, Geritol, and Southern California Chevrolet dealers and made appearances on television shows like *The Gong Show* and *The Celebrity Challenge of the Sexes*, Don Sutton appeared on the game show *Match Game PM*. Several Dodger couples—Ron and Fran Cey, Sally and Tommy John, Steve and Cyndy Garvey—were featured in *Family Circle*. Davey Lopes was a spokesman for the Ronald McDonald House. Ron Cey endorsed Wheaties, hoarsely singing the "Eaties for My Wheaties" jingle, and so on. But this was nothing new; Hollywood had long helped define the team's core identity. In the 1950s key Tinseltown figures had been among the most prominent local voices supporting bringing the Dodgers to town.[6] And from the team's first opening day in Los Angeles, on April 18, 1958, at the jimmy-rigged ball field at the old L.A. Coliseum, Hollywood turned out in force to support the team. Among the nearly eighty thousand fans gathered to watch the Dodgers beat their rivals, the Giants, who had moved to San Francisco, were Edward G. Robinson, Ray Bolger, Jimmy Stewart, Gregory Peck, Danny Kaye, Chuck Connors, Burt Lancaster, Jack Lemmon, Nat Cole, Danny Thomas, and Groucho Marx.[7]

The Hollywood-Dodgers connection lasted beyond just the first season or two. With the demise of the old Pacific Coast League Hollywood Stars after 1958, the Dodgers established an annual "Hollywood Stars" charity event, in which famous old Dodgers and team figures played a slow-pitch game with various Hollywood figures of the day. Among the stars who played the game during the event's heyday were Pat Boone, Phyllis Diller, Milton Berle, Dean Martin, Bobby Darin, Phil Silvers, Nancy Sinatra, Annette Funicello, Mickey Rooney, Frank Sinatra, Walter Matthau, and Jack Lemmon. Even beyond this event the Dodgers' fan base of the 1960s and '70s included such Hollywood figures as Bing Crosby, Danny Kaye, Cary Grant, Frank Sinatra, and Milton Berle.

Several Dodger players took advantage of this connection to Hollywood through the years. Chuck Connors, a former Dodger first baseman, landed a role as the star of television's *The Rifleman* in 1958. Connors had come up through the Dodgers system in the 1940s and would become associated with the team and various Dodger players. In the 1960s Dodger megastars Sandy Koufax and Don Drysdale, both friends of Connors, appeared on numerous TV shows and movies, including *77 Sunset Strip* and Connors's *Rifleman*. In fact, the two Dodger pitching stars used the threat of roles in a film called

Warning Shot as leverage against Dodgers management during their holdout before the 1966 season.[8] In 1977 Wes Parker, the slick-fielding first baseman who had retired from the Dodgers in 1972, was tabbed to appear in a new Norman Lear situation comedy, *All That Glitters*.[9] Parker got the job on a fluke when he was invited to do a walk-in audition after Lear saw him doing play-by-play TV commentary. Parker suggested that his experiences on the Dodgers had been good preparation for acting. "Acting has many things in common with baseball," he said. "Acting has the same excitement and creativity. It lets you be a ham if you've got a little of that in you, which I'm sure I do or I wouldn't be in the business. It has the best aspects of the sports life without some of the things I didn't enjoy, primarily the travel." And when asked where he thought the job would take him, Parker was confident: "Eventually, I'd like to do feature film work. . . . I just want to be a good actor. I'm not in this for a lark. I don't want them to say, 'Yeah, for an athlete he's a pretty good actor.' I want to be a good actor in my own right."[10]

Adding additional fuel to the Hollywoodization of the Dodgers in 1977 was, of course, the arrival of Tom Lasorda, whose outsize, larger-than-life personality fitted perfectly with the local schmooze-and-be-schmoozed Hollywood ethic. The stars of Hollywood, many of whom already appreciated the Dodgers, loved Lasorda because he was, like them, an entertainer. Among Lasorda's particular friends were Gregory Peck, Milton Berle, and comedian Don Rickles, who would serve as an honorary batboy for Lasorda's team throughout the 1977 season. Still, no Hollywood figure connected to Lasorda would be bigger in his first year as manager than one: the Chairman of the Board, Frank Sinatra. This connection added a complex dimension to the new manager's clubhouse pull. Even some of the most jaded of his players—the ones who resisted even the manager's most outlandish antics—would have to pause and consider, if Lasorda was so full of bull, why would the most famous singing star on the planet hang around him so much? "That's why I put up a whole wall of his photos in my office," Lasorda said. "Because nobody would believe it." Throughout 1977 Lasorda would often have dinner with Sinatra in Los Angeles and at Sinatra's Palm Springs estate, and Sinatra would get his baseball fix by coming to hang out in Lasorda's office.

When asked to tell the story, Lasorda would explain he had first met Sinatra years before through former Dodger manager Leo Durocher. Though Lasorda was only a Minor League manager at the time, Sinatra immediately appreciated the manager's sense of humor and appreciated that he did not try to curry the singer's favor. A few years later, when the two were gathered at a back table at a restaurant, Sinatra looked at Lasorda, by then the Dodgers' third base coach, and said, "You know, Tommy, I've been thinking about it. You should be the manager of the Dodgers." Lasorda, stunned by the pronouncement, was for once at a loss for words. "Tell you what," Sinatra continued. "The first day you manage the Dodgers, I will come out and sing the national anthem for you."[11]

And that's how it happened that, for the Dodgers' home opener on April 7, 1977, in the bright afternoon sun before a game against the rival San Francisco Giants, Frank Sinatra stepped up to a microphone that had been placed near the outfield wall in left field. Wearing a Dodger warm-up jacket, Sinatra sang the national anthem for a sold-out crowd, and the crowd erupted in pleasure as hundreds of yellow balloons were released into the air, brightening the already impossibly bright California sky.[12]

The Dodgers' slick Hollywood image was not universally admired around the Major Leagues. Sparky Anderson, for instance, seemed particularly dismissive of the Dodgers before the 1977 season, suggesting the team was not strong enough to thrive over the long season. "They start getting ready in January," said Anderson, whose team had dispatched the Dodgers after trailing them in both 1975 and 1976. "We'll just have to stay within five games by July. If we do that, we'll be all right." And plenty of rival players looked at the Dodgers with disdain simply because of the team's image. "I love to beat the Dodgers," said Giants pitcher John Montefusco, "because I hate them so."[13]

On opening day in 1977 the Dodgers faced Montefusco, who had predicted, after winning the Rookie of the Year Award in 1975 and playing in the All-Star Game in 1976, that he would win twenty games this season and the NL Cy Young Award. This prediction, of course, could come true only if he beat his team's rival multiple times. In

1976, after all, Montefusco had faced the division-rival Dodgers six times, recording a 3-2 record against the team on his way to winning sixteen. The Dodgers fared well against Montefusco in the first game of the season. Taking advantage of a new ball produced by the sporting goods company Rawlings—the first new baseball in the Major Leagues after using one by Spalding for nearly one hundred years—the Dodgers played flawlessly, outhitting the Giants 9–4 and securing an easy 5–1 victory. Lasorda's managerial career had begun with a mark in the win column.

The Dodgers took two of three games in the opening series against the Giants, and then they closed their first home stand by taking two of three from the Atlanta Braves and former teammates Andy Messersmith and Mike Marshall. The Dodgers, at 4-2, were in second place by one game behind the Houston Astros, and observers continued to note that something felt different with this team. It was particularly noticeable whenever a Dodger player hit a home run, as Rick Monday did in the rubber match—his first as a Dodger—in a 4–3 win over the Braves on April 13. Whenever this happened Lasorda made a point of greeting his players at the top step of the dugout and hugging them like a proud uncle. This ritual bolstered the image of the Dodgers as one big happy family enjoying themselves in the California sunshine. And perhaps because of the manager's enthusiasm, players continued to give the manager credit for changes that had come to the team. "You can sense the difference in the dugout," said Lasorda's third baseman, Ron Cey. "We are more aggressive because Tommy is an aggressive manager. He shows his emotions and it reflects on the club."[14]

Despite the positive results of the first week of the season, the team knew it had yet to be truly tested. But they didn't have to wait long. On April 15 they traveled to hostile San Francisco to begin a long twelve-game road trip against their Western Division rivals, the Giants, Reds, Braves, and Padres. Fans need not have worried. In San Francisco the Dodgers swept the Giants in a three-game series, outscoring their rival 19–7. Reggie Smith had two home runs in the first game, had another in the second game, and then nearly got into a brawl with Montefusco in the third game. After striking out Smith in the first inning, Montefusco had issued a verbal insult to the slugger, and Smith had to be restrained from charging the pitcher. Once relative calm was restored the Dodgers won a crazy back-and-forth game, 7–6. When the dust had settled Smith stood near the top among league leaders in offense, with three home runs, thirteen RBIs, and a batting average of .395.

Though it was still early in the season, players were almost giddy over the team's prospects. "I tell you," said left-handed starting pitcher Doug Rau, "this is a real treat for me to pitch with all those runs." Reggie Smith agreed with the pitcher. "This is more than a one-dimensional club," he said. "This is a team that can hurt you in many ways. We have more than one guy who can hit it out."[15] Lasorda, for his part, couldn't stop talking about how everyone on the team was playing a part. "The way things are going," he said, "managing is easy."[16]

The team's success continued. The Dodgers traveled to Cincinnati and quickly took two straight in a short series. After the second game, a 3–1 win that was the Dodgers' seventh in a row, the Reds' manager dared again to shrug off the Dodgers' success. "They're not much different than any other team," Anderson said. "Somewhere along the line they're going to lose four or five in a row and they'll have days just like we had today. They didn't beat us today, we beat ourselves. . . . When you only get five hits," as the Dodgers did that day, "you're not going to beat many people." Lasorda countered the remark by saying, "Tell Sparky that when we hold the other team to one run, we're not going to lose many, either."[17] Much of Anderson's bluster must have come from an early premonition of what might come. At the end of the season's second week his 4-8 Reds were in last place in the Western Division, while the 9-2 Dodgers were in first. And just when it seemed things couldn't get any better for his bitter rival,[18] a new Dodger slugging star would emerge for the team during the next series against the Atlanta Braves. In early spring training Tom Lasorda had slotted his third baseman, Ron Cey, into the crucial cleanup-hitter position. Alston, in 1976, had tended to put Steve Garvey in the slot, though Cey had occasionally appeared there as well. On Lasorda's team Cey had flown under the radar as cleanup hitter for much of the first three weeks of the season, but in Atlanta something finally clicked. Against Atlanta in the first game

Cey hit a double and a single. In the second game, on April 23, Cey homered and singled with four RBIs, and in the third game he doubled, homered, and knocked in five runs. The Dodgers took two of three from the Braves, raising their record to 11-3. In San Diego Cey continued his tear, going seven for thirteen with three home runs and five RBIs over four games as the Dodgers swept the Padres. On April 28 the Dodgers stood in first with a 15-3 record, and Cey's batting line on the season was otherworldly. In eighteen games he had collected eight home runs, a .448 batting average, .990 slugging percentage, and twenty-six RBIs.

There are so many working parts to any baseball team, and so many opportunities for things to go haywire during the long season, that Dodger fans had to remind themselves to take in stride the Dodgers' fast start in 1977. Still, all could agree on one thing: despite having to manage so many diverse working parts, the team's new manager had acquitted himself admirably. Lasorda's veteran players were all playing at, or above, their career marks, and, with a 15-3 record as of April 28, his Dodgers were within spitting distance of the franchise's best start—the 22-2 record that the Dodgers had recorded in Brooklyn in April 1955. With all this under his belt, and more, one would think the new manager would be ecstatic, resting a little easier and focusing on keeping the team on track over the long season. Yet several niggling things kept Lasorda occupied during the season's first month.

For instance, Lasorda remained concerned about the Dodgers' overall lack of power. Beyond Cey and Garvey, who had eight and six home runs, respectively, on April 28, there was not much to speak of. Smith had slumped after his early displays of power, and both Baker and Monday, each with just three home runs thus far, had been less than spectacular. With that issue in mind, and with Al Campanis coming to a quick dead end in his talks to acquire slugging Mets first baseman–outfielder Dave Kingman, the team signed an aging free-agent slugger—Boog Powell—to hold down a bench spot. Powell, who was thirty-five and stood at six foot five and 250 pounds and had been hampered in 1976 by torn tendons in his ankle, had come to Vero Beach to ask for a tryout after being released by the Cleveland Indians on March 30. Powell cleared waivers on April 5 and was signed by the Dodgers to serve as a pinch hitter and backup first baseman.

Worse than the question of power, however, was another niggling issue that continued to worry Lasorda. Back on April 7 disgruntled Dodger pitcher Don Sutton—who, by his own admission, was never going to join the Tom Lasorda Fan Club—threw a fat grapefruit in his first pitch to the first batter of the season, Gary Thomasson. When Thomasson, a journeyman outfielder who was never going to be confused with Willie Mays, put the pitch into the grandstands, Lasorda was shocked. While Sutton returned to his workmanlike self after the initial blast and gave up only three more hits the rest of the way, winning the game 5–1, something about that first pitch stayed with Lasorda. After the game Lasorda was magnanimous about his first win as manager, saying the Big Dodger in the Sky "could not have planned it any better," but privately, Lasorda couldn't shake the feeling that the home run was another of the veteran pitcher's ways of sticking it to his manager. After all, Sutton had been clear after Lasorda's hiring that the veteran pitcher didn't appreciate Lasorda's showbiz way of working the press, and the pitcher had also told the press, when asked, that he would have preferred his friend and former teammate Jeff Torborg as manager. Characteristically, Lasorda, while not pleased with Sutton's antics, made a joke of the situation. "I know they intended to send the first ball used on opening day to the Hall of Fame," Lasorda told the press, referring to the new Rawlings ball. "But they planned to mail it to Cooperstown—not have it fly itself direct."[19]

Sutton, for his part, continued to fashion himself as the team's black sheep, though in many ways this made him a walking contradiction. After all, as Lasorda would be the first to acknowledge, no one on the Dodgers hated to lose as much as Sutton. "Don has about as complex a personality as anyone I've ever met," said his Dodger pitching teammate, and fellow southerner, Burt Hooton. "He's a very generous individual who'll talk to anyone while the rest of us just say 'Hi' and keep going. At the same time, he's an extremely competitive person." Dodger coach Monty Basgall, who had first discovered Sutton in the early 1960s when he worked as a scout for the team, concurred. "He's an odd guy in a way. He's very independent. He knows what he wants, and he goes after it." Born in the rural Gulf Coast region to a poor but hardworking family of sharecroppers, Sutton referred to himself as a "nothing semipolished hick," even though his dedication to his professional practice was anything but unpolished. Sutton not only had become, by 1977, one of the winningest Dodger pitchers in history, but had also become enough of a fixture in the large Los Angeles to marry a smart local urban girl—his wife, Patti—and form his own corporation, SuttCor International, which managed a local restaurant and a deli. In person, Sutton lived a clean life—no smoking, no drinking—in keeping with his Christian upbringing, but he also spoke his mind often enough to get himself in trouble with his teammates and occasionally the fans. "He's not the kind of guy you want to get into a verbal battle with," his pitching coach, Red Adams, would later say. "He's quick with the whip."[20]

All the contradictions—the southern affability and wit, the sharp focus on his personal goals, his dislike of the PR aspects of the sport, and his abiding will to win—made Sutton a challenging teammate to get along with. And because of his particular vantage point as a veteran Dodger who had stuck with an underachieving team for more than ten seasons, Sutton seemed to feel it was his right to question the approach of the team's new manager. Throughout spring training and well into the season, Sutton took every opportunity to defy Lasorda. And though the two would eventually reach a state of shaky détente, Lasorda would harbor doubts about his ace long after they had both gone elsewhere. "If I had to pitch one guy in a Game 7, it would be Don Sutton," Lasorda said years later. "I loved him. But sometimes I was one of the only ones."[21]

It's perhaps a testament to the sheer power of Lasorda's personality that, despite his failure to win over Sutton, he was still able to bring a lot of strong personalities into his orbit. Ron Cey, for instance, could easily have been as prickly about Lasorda as Sutton. After all, Cey was often overlooked for his contributions to the team and overshadowed by the team's other stars, particularly the highly popular Steve Garvey. This was despite the fact that Cey was an All-Star who had brought much-needed stability to the Dodgers' hot-corner spot. Furthermore, Cey, like Sutton, had lingering frustrations over contracts that he felt didn't acknowledge his true value to the Dodgers. At the same time, however, Ron Cey was his own unique personality on the team. Though he once said he felt like a "bit actor waiting to get my big chance," he would be the first to acknowledge that he was not as Hollywood glamorous as some of his teammates.[22] He wasn't as daunting at the plate as Jimmy Wynn or Reggie Smith and was not the all-around athlete that Dusty Baker was. He was not the All-American hero that Rick Monday was, and he was not the public darling that Steve Garvey was. Born in Tacoma, Washington, in 1948 to a middle-class family with working-class roots, Cey epitomized a certain Dodger spirit.[23] After the age of eight, all he ever wanted to do was play Major League Baseball, though he'd made the decision without fully realizing the challenges he'd face. "If I'd known the circumstances I'd have to overcome, I probably wouldn't have felt so strongly about it," Cey told *Sports Illustrated* in early May. "I was fortunate to make it, even though a lot of people said I never would."[24]

Watching Cey stand at the plate in 1977 was like watching a blacksmith approach a hot furnace. His arms were short and steely, and his hands were as meaty as welding gloves. His bat was an iron hammer, and he swung it with a quick and controlled fury, which, when his timing was on (like it was in April 1977), gave it a great deal of pop. Perhaps the best word to describe Ron Cey as a ballplayer was *solid*. Cey was solid in the way that a stone monolith was solid. This was also his biggest liability. His sturdy, muscular 185-pound, five-foot-ten body was unique in baseball—with thighs as large as an offensive lineman's and calves that were particularly short. His lower body's structure in fact gave Cey a distinctive gait that led directly to his nickname: the Penguin. Still, Cey took full advantage of what assets he did have—although he lacked pure speed, his quick hands and a quick first step made him a solid fielder at a tough position, and his leg strength added to his power at the bat. Also, because of the challenge he had faced in convincing baseball people he could play the game with his particular physical frame, Cey had developed the mental toughness and workmanlike habits required to play the hot corner at a high level. By 1977 the Dodgers' third baseman had played on three straight National League All-Star teams.

Despite his struggle to overcome his own limitations, in early 1977 Cey credited his success thus far to Lasorda. The manager, he said, had given Cey freer reins even as he expressed greater expectations for his third baseman. Indeed, thus far most of the Dodgers were much the same as Cey—responding well to Lasorda. After the sweep of the Padres in San Diego, the Dodgers were batting .305 as a team and averaging three more runs per game than in 1976. To end April the Dodgers played two games at home against the Montreal Expos and won both of them. Amid much fanfare and attention from local and national media, Ron Cey knocked in two runs in the first game, and then, after going hitless in the first six innings of the final game, he slugged a solo home run in the seventh to help cement the win. The blast gave Cey his twenty-ninth RBI, a feat that broke a Major League record for the first month of the season. Ron Cey was named National League Player of the Week for April 18–24, and he was also the obvious choice for National League Player of the Month for April.

On May 1 the Dodgers, at 17-3, stood atop the Western Division by a crushing seven and a half games over their nearest rival, the Cincinnati Reds, which was said to be the largest lead ever for a team after the first month of the season. And the Dodgers continued putting on a show well into May, as people around the nation started to take notice. On May 16, in an article titled "In L.A., It's Up, Up and Away with Cey," *Sports Illustrated* lavished high praise on the Penguin and the Dodgers. "A major league baseball season is not supposed to be a 100-year dash," wrote author Larry Keith.

> It is a marathon, an endurance test demanding strong will, a steady pace and reserve strength for a finishing kick. . . . But from the very start of the season the Los Angeles Dodgers have been going flat out, crushing the opposition and setting new standards for early excellence. They have won with force, and they have won with finesse. They have been awesome at home and on the road, in the warmth of the afternoon and in the chill of the night, against hard-throwing righthanders and against curve-balling lefthanders. They won their opener, have kept on winning and give every indication they plan to win some more.[25]

On May 6, after a convincing 9–3 win over the Philadelphia Phillies, the Dodgers' record stood at 22-4, a stunning ten and a half games ahead the Reds. On May 17, powered by Don Sutton's sixth win against no losses, the Dodgers beat the Phillies again to move twelve games ahead, and, on May 26, after beating the Astros 4–3, the Dodgers led the Western Division by twelve and a half games. Sportswriter Don Merry pointed out that this was the team's largest league lead over a second-place opponent since the move to Los Angeles. Even during the Koufax and Drysdale era, no Dodger team had so dominated its opponents.

The team continued rolling for much of the next month. At the end of May the Dodgers' record stood at 33-15; its team batting average was, at .290, about .40 points higher than opponents were batting against them. Five of the team's starters were hitting over .300, and even the usually weak-hitting catcher, Steve Yeager, was batting a surprising .290. Ron Cey and Reggie Smith were near the top of league leaders in home runs and RBIs, and Steve Garvey was right behind. And the starting pitching had been, for the most part, outstanding—the team's overall ERA was just 3.35, best in the league. In other words, the team was showing it was as good as Lasorda had believed. This Dodger team, with its furious approach to the game and its voracious appetite for winning, seemed far removed from nearby Tinseltown. As if in response, then, in early May a new team nickname began to appear in local media. And by May 7 the name had already gained currency among some of the team's followers, as evidenced in a letter to the *Los Angeles Times* that day from a fan named Mario P. Basich. "Well, we finally came up with a name for the local boys," Basich wrote, "'The Big Blue Wrecking Crew.'"[26]

Much of the inspiration for the name must have come from the way the team had been demolishing its opponents, though it's probably more likely that someone wanted a name as catchy and powerful as that of its chief divisional rival. Or as Basich concluded in his letter, ""I hope they live up to it [the nickname] when they meet the 'Big Red Machine.'"[27]

TEN

A John Wayne Kind of Adventure

Kids today don't have any fantasy life the way we had—they don't have Westerns, they don't have pirate movies . . . the real Errol Flynn, John Wayne kind of adventures.

—George Lucas

May turned to June in 1977, and all across the Southern Californian basin attention turned to summer pursuits. For many people around Southern California—particularly school-age boys—this meant focusing on the Los Angeles Dodgers baseball club, whose cast of heroic young players loomed as large as comic-book heroes. All over the city, boys in backyards, in their driveways, and at suburban parks imitated the batting strokes, fielding stances, and pitching deliveries of their favorite Dodgers, passed Topps cards back and forth, and bugged their families to take them to Dodger Stadium. All of which explains why the buzz around the Los Angeles ball club was growing as the season wore on. By June 1, after just twenty home games, Dodger Stadium had drawn 767,306 fans. This total, best in the league, projected out to a full-season attendance of more than 3.1 million—a total that would shatter the Major Leagues' single-season single-team attendance record. To many across L.A. in 1977, the Dodgers had simply become the hot summer ticket.

On May 26 the Dodgers took a ten-inning game from the Houston Astros, expanding their lead in the West by a comfortable twelve and a half games over the Reds, who had lost in San Francisco. Despite the Dodgers' runaway lead, the Reds themselves seemed unalarmed, perhaps even cocky, as they prepared themselves to fly into Los Angeles to take on the Dodgers for three head-to-head games starting on May 27. Before the series Sparky Anderson, perhaps seeking to employ every possible weapon in the looming battle, acknowledged that this Dodger team was a good one before quickly qualifying his assessment. "Well, it's not going to be enough," said the Reds' manager. "I want to see how Lasorda reacts when it turns. We've won with soundness, not somebody losing their coconut. We're solid people. We acted like pros, looked like pros, and did our job. The Dodgers are going to look back some day and realize in the long run this is a better way."[1] The fun is in the chase," Reds second baseman Joe Morgan added. "And I have never had more fun than catching the Dodgers the past two years." Reds catcher Johnny Bench concurred: "We'll get it together and when we do we'll win it again."[2]

The Dodgers responded to the Reds' cavalier dismissals on the field. In the opener, in front of a sold-out crowd of 53,055 at Dodger Stadium, the lineup socked seventeen hits in a 10–3 victory. After the game the Reds were chagrined. "It was embarrassing . . . humiliating," Joe Morgan said bitterly. "I felt right then and there we had reached rock bottom. We couldn't be pushed down any further. We only had one way to go." Sparky Anderson seemed bemused and alarmed. "We can't expect help from any other team," he said. "We've got 16 games left with the Dodgers. We've go to win at least 12 of them or." Anderson completed his thought by blowing a kiss, as if saying good-bye to a chance at a third straight world championship. Even Cincinnati's rank-and-file players seemed torn in two by what had happened. "We're not really worried," said pitcher Pat Zachry, who was only in his second year with the Reds. "I mean, we're worried. But not really. . . . Oh I guess we're worried."[3]

Lasorda, though he knew better, could not help but swagger a bit after the game. The Dodgers' thirteen-and-a-half-game lead in the Western Division was the largest first-place lead the team had had since its move from Brooklyn. "If I were in their position," said Lasorda, "I'd be worried. If you're in trouble, isn't it natural to be worried?"[4] The swagger was understandable. Like any gunfighter in the midst of a long showdown, it took a good amount of ego for Lasorda to do his job. And while there's no record that Lasorda knew John Wayne, a local boy from the suburbs east of Los Angeles who was a noted Dodger fan—having once praised Sandy Koufax on his 1973 spoken-word album, *America, Why I Love Her*—it's certain that Lasorda knew of John Wayne (what American didn't?). So it made sense that the Dodgers' manager was beginning to resemble one of Wayne's interchangeably iconic movie characters, such as Rooster Cogburn, John Chisum, or Hondo Lane. (Years later, in fact, a future Dodger named Billy Bean would compare Lasorda to the gunslinging movie star when describing his first meeting with his new manager in 1989. "Tommy Lasorda is the baseball equivalent of John Wayne," said Bean. "He wasn't just a manager; he was a legend.")[5]

Unfortunately for the gunslinging Dodgers, the final two games of the series against the Reds dealt the local team a sharp setback. On May 28, the day that one sportswriter noted was the twentieth anniversary of the day the National League approved the move of the Dodgers to Los Angeles,[6] the Reds beat the Dodgers, 6–3, on twelve hits, including two home runs by George Foster and one by Ken Griffey. Sutton took the disappointing loss, giving up all of the Reds' home runs (and all six runs) before being sent to the showers after just three innings. Afterward Lasorda refused to make a big issue of the game, or of Sutton's ineffectiveness: "I'm not concerned," he said. "Even Cy Young got knocked out twice in a row the year he won 36 games. So now three guys have been knocked out twice in a row . . . Cy Young, Sutton and, yeah, Lasorda." The next day, on May 29, the Reds erupted for eight runs off four home runs, including a Johnny Bench grand slam and the fourth homer by George Foster in the three games at Dodger Stadium. While Dodger pitcher Rick Rhoden, who was looking to become the Majors' first eight-game winner, lasted longer than Sutton the day before, going into the sixth inning before getting knocked out, the result was the same. It was a loss. After the game the Dodgers still held an eleven-and-a-half-game lead over the Reds, but this was the first series loss by the Dodgers all season, so Lasorda was understandably disappointed. "This was a tougher loss," he said before changing the subject.[7]

There was no time to staunch the bleeding, however, as the Dodgers boarded a plane to Houston immediately after the loss for a Monday-night game at the Astrodome. Against the young, hard-throwing right-hander Joaquin Andujar, the Dodgers promptly lost their third straight game, 5–3. It was the second straight time the Dodgers had lost to the second-year pitcher. On the next night, May 31, the Dodgers lost to the Astros again, 5–2, getting shut down by the team's ace J. R. Richard and outhit by a couple of former Dodgers—catcher Joe Ferguson, who hit his ninth home run, and outfielder Willie Crawford, who had two hits and an RBI and scored a run. It was the Dodgers' fourth straight loss—the first such losing streak of the season—and that, coupled with a Reds winning streak, cut the team's lead in the West to just nine and a half games.

Dodger reaction to these losses varied. Don Sutton blamed them on a change in the team's emotional makeup, although he didn't seem much concerned about it. "We just seem to be less enthusiastic recently," he said. "The season is a series of peaks and valleys. The idea is to take advantage of your peaks and keep your valleys as shallow as possible. There is no team in history that ever had all peaks and I didn't expect we would be the first." Second baseman Dave Lopes, meanwhile, thought the losses were the ironic result of having played so well for the first part of the year. "Give those other teams credit," he said. "They've been playing good ball against us. In fact, from here on out every team is going to be up for the Dodgers, ready to beat the (bleep) out of us. We've been getting a lot of publicity all season long and I don't think some of the other teams like it."[8]

John Wayne would have well understood Lopes's assessment, having many times played the role of a hero fighting against the odds, surrounded by enemies on all sides, outgunned and overmatched and in dire straits. Born Marion Morrison, Wayne was raised in modest circumstances in Glendale, California, by a pharmacist and his wife. After losing a football scholarship at the University of Southern California because of an injury, Morrison went to work for a local film studio, and, in time, he began to appear in bit parts. Now called John Wayne, he landed his first starring role in 1930 at age twenty-three, in the flop *The Big Trail*. He went on to star in nearly 150 films over the next forty-five years, often reflecting a kind of wry, self-aware swagger that was completely in tune with America's self-image at the time.

In 1976, in his last role in *The Shootist*, Wayne played a dying gunslinger hoping to live his last days in peace even though he has become a mark for old enemies seeking vengeance. The film is set in 1901 in Carson City and plays up the fact that, at the time, the trappings of the Old West were dying out. In 1976 Wayne was in fact struggling—both with the state of Hollywood, which seemed to be fading into something far less appealing, and with his own mortality. In 1973 Wayne had observed a new generation of young Hollywood stars and filmmakers create the iconoclastic western *High Plains Drifter*, in which inhabitants of a dusty Old West mining town are depicted as craven and murderous.[9] By 1976, at the time he made *The Shootist*, Wayne was old and tired, a survivor of a late-1960s battle with lung cancer, and it showed in the film. The script even somewhat reflected Wayne's disillusion. "You told me I was strong as an ox," his character, John Bernard Books, says after being told he has a terminal disease. "Well, even an ox dies," replies the doctor.[10]

Whatever the source of his concern, Wayne certainly had a point—the culture was changing, eschewing age-old traditions as the nation's largest generational cohort came of age and inevitably forced their values on the established culture. And Hollywood was not immune to the change. "Los Angeles was full of tumult," writes entertainment writer and film critic Patrick Goldstein of the time. "There was a raw, infectious energy in the air, inspired by a sense that the cultural world was shifting under our feet." Driving the changes in Hollywood, as *Los Angeles Times* film critic Charles Champlin pointed out in 1969, was a major shift of power in the Hollywood studios—from an "Old Hollywood" approach that was suddenly failing to attract an audience to a daring new approach seeking to connect with the interests and ideals of younger (that is, baby boomer) moviegoers. Film critic Paul Schrader suggested that, in the years between 1969 and 1971, "the industry imploded, the door was wide open and you could just waltz in and have these meetings and propose whatever. There was nothing that was too outrageous."[11] In 1967 two movies—*Bonnie and Clyde* and *The Graduate*—one violent and sensational, the other sexually provocative and emotionally raw, rocked the industry by attracting surprisingly large audiences. Other similarly innovative and edgy film projects followed over the next few years. And before anyone realized it, there was a new movement in filmmaking—dubbed "New Hollywood" in the press—led by a new generation of directors, producers, auteurs, screenwriters, and young stars whose values developed out of the counterculture of the second half of the 1960s.

The New Hollywood approach to moviemaking yielded some of the most artistically brilliant and original Hollywood movies ever—*The Fox* (1967), *Point Blank* (1967), *Easy Rider* (1969), *Paper Moon* (1973), *Chinatown* (1974), *Dog Day Afternoon* (1975), *Taxi Driver* (1976), and the like. But even considering the social commentary and artistic accomplishment of these films, by the second half of the decade audiences were, like John Wayne, just a little fed up with all this heavy, heady, disheartening stuff. As early as 1971 moviemakers were wondering how to deal with the divisions of the times. During the production of George Lucas's first film, the bleak, dystopian *THX 1138* (1971), his filmmaking mentor and friend Francis Ford Coppola challenged him to write a script that would appeal to mainstream audiences. The result, *American Graffiti* (1973), was a surprise hit for Lucas, noted for its crowd-pleasing nostalgia. The results inspired Lucas. "When I got done with *Graffiti*," he said, "I saw that kids today don't have any fantasy life the way we had—they don't have westerns, they don't have pirate movies, they don't have that stupid serial fantasy life that we used to believe in. . . . What would happen if there had never been John Wayne movies and Errol Flynn movies and all that stuff that we got to see all the time. I mean, you could go into a theater, sit down and watch an incredible adventure."[12]

For his next film, then, Lucas decided he wanted to continue entertaining the audiences in the way that Hollywood used to do. "I thought: we all know what a terrible mess we have made of the world," Lucas said. "We also know, as every movie made in the last ten years points out, how terrible we are, how we have ruined the world and what schmucks we are and how rotten everything is. And I said, what we really need is something more positive." When asked what his next project would be, Lucas was blunt. "I'm working on a western movie set in outer space," he replied, referring to the idea that would eventually become a film called *Star Wars*. When the interviewer looked uneasy, Lucas laughed. "Don't worry," he said. "Ten year old boys will love it."[13]

Although Lucas was certain in 1973 that he had an idea that would work for Hollywood, the execution of his idea took time to develop. He was never a particularly facile writer, and in this case his sources of inspiration—Joseph Campbell's books on mythology, the great westerns of the heyday of Hollywood, the presidency of Richard Nixon,[14] the American involvement in Vietnam—did not easily translate to a script, especially for a populist, entertaining adventure story. Lucas worked on the treatment and script for *Star Wars* for three years, struggling to get the tone and plot just right.[15] He rewrote his *Star Wars* script three times in succession, submitting each draft to his contacts at the studios and getting rejected each time. Through it all Lucas's health suffered. He grew isolated from friends and family. Finally, in early 1976 the fourth draft of Lucas's nascent space swashbuckler finally seemed to have the right story elements in place. Even then Lucas worked with two script doctors, Gloria Katz and Willard Huyck, to turn the fourth *Star Wars* script into a final preproduction script. Then, despite his hard work, most of Hollywood's studios at the time—Warner Brothers, MGM, United Artists, and Universal—took a pass on *Star Wars*. The project was saved at the last minute only when a studio on the verge of bankruptcy, Twentieth Century Fox, decided to take a gamble on it.[16]

After many trials *Star Wars*, George Lucas's old-fashioned tale of romance, adventure, swashbuckling swordplay, princesses in distress, and cloaked villains—all set *in space*—finally made it to movie houses in late May. Meanwhile, out in the bright daylight, the Dodgers were suddenly becoming reacquainted with the feel of the earth beneath their feet. Their easy streak of domination over the rest of the National League came to an abrupt end, and, just as Sparky Anderson had predicted, the reality of the long season settled over the team.

As if responding to a silent cue, over the next few weeks a growing number of fans wrote in to complain: about Lasorda's use of his bullpen, his deployment of outmanned young bench player Ed Goodson—a rare left-handed batter on the Dodgers—in key game pinch-hitting situations, and his directing of Steve Garvey to swing more for the fences (which they claimed was threatening his usual dependability at the plate). "I hate to throw cold water on the fine start of the Blew Wrecking Crew," wrote one fan to the sports page in early June, "but the holiday weekend had all the earmarks of those late May days of the last couple of years when Ye Olde June Swoone has cursed our local heroes. . . . It might be a repeat of 1975 and 1976."[17]

If the season had been a John Wayne movie, or even a newfangled outer-space throwback to the western adventures of the past, it was at this point in the story that, from out over the horizon, a cocky hired gun would appear to deal with the town's enemies. A chief candidate for this role was a player that the Dodgers thought, when they obtained him before the season began, would bring plenty of firepower to their lineup: Rick Monday. And indeed, the outwardly genial, six-foot-three, two-hundred-pound outfielder, who had become immediately popular on the team, was a deeply competitive gunslinger. "My one goal," said Monday before the season had begun, "is to have Sparky (Cincinnati manager Anderson) watch the World Series on television and to see Dodger blue on his set."[18] Yet in the early part of the season Monday had barely factored in the Dodgers' attack. In the first regular-season game, on April 7, Monday went hitless. By the end of the month he was batting only .253 and had just 3 HRS and 10 RBIS, at best a middle-of-the-road sort of performance—especially compared to teammates like Cey (9 HRS, 29 RBIS, .403 average), Garvey (6 HRS, 22 RBIS), and Smith (16 RBIS, .344 average).

The pressure on Monday to produce mounted as the season continued. On the first day of May, in the fifth inning of a game at home against the Expos, Monday overswung at a pitch by the Expos' Steve Rogers and topped a dribbler down the first base line. As he took off Monday's spikes caught in a divot, and he went down hard to one knee as Rogers forced him at first. As he kneeled just off the plate, gingerly testing his knee, the Expos' caustic manager, Dick Williams, began chattering at the veteran. "Fuck your leg and get the fucking hell out of there" is what Lasorda reported Williams said (though diplomatic Expos catcher Gary Carter said that Williams was yelling that he should forget Monday and keep the pitcher warm), and the embattled Monday was in no mood to hear it. He moved toward the Expos' bench, gesturing and barking back at the team's manager before being restrained by Lasorda and home plate umpire Dutch

Rennert. Williams, incensed, led his team out onto the field for a confrontation, and the Dodgers rushed out as well. Although no punches were thrown and the conflict calmed, Monday was still steamed about the incident after the game. "I respect Williams as a manager," Monday said. "He knows baseball . . . but personally I dislike the man. He and I will settle this later. At some point in time I will be there and he won't have 25 guys in front of him."[19]

Despite the swagger, however, the biggest setback to Monday in 1977 was still to come.

With the team struggling to stave off its hungry rivals, before a game on June 1 against the Astros Tom Lasorda stepped in front of his players behind closed clubhouse doors at the Death Star–like Astrodome. It was an unusual moment for the emotional Dodger manager. Although Tom Lasorda was widely known for his motivational skills, he was not known for his subtlety. But the manager was struggling with mixed emotions. A day earlier, on May 31, during a tight game against the Astros, Lasorda had watched as one of his key players went down. While racing for a sinking line drive off the bat of Julio Gonzalez in the seventh inning, the score tied at 2–2 and two runners on (with one out), Monday's foot got caught in a seam of the Astrodome's artificial turf, and he took a tumble. He stayed in the game, a 5–2 loss, but afterward his back stiffened. The next day, scratched from the lineup, Monday watched from the trainer's room in the visitors' clubhouse of the Astrodome as Lasorda tried to inspire his players with just a few choice words. What Lasorda exactly said at the closed-door meeting was not recorded, but he did later explain he was trying to light a little fire under the team. "I reminded them of their capabilities," Lasorda said, "and reminded them how they got to where they are today, on top of the mountain. I told them they didn't get there by accident."[20] Whatever was said, it worked. After Lasorda's speech, the Dodgers ended their longest losing streak of the season so far by beating the Astros, 6–2.

Two days later the Dodgers lost a tough battle at home—1–0 in extras—against the Padres. Don Sutton pitched superbly for nine innings, scattering five hits and giving up no runs, but the Dodger hitters eked out only two hits in eleven innings. On June 4 the Dodgers beat the Padres by exploding for nine runs thanks mostly to Ron Cey (who hit his league-leading fourteenth home run in the first inning), Reggie Smith (thirteenth home run), Steve Yeager (fifth home run), and new call-up Glenn Burke (three hits and two RBIs). And the Dodgers completed a sweep of the Padres on June 5, with Doug Rau recording the win, his sixth of the season against just one loss.

But the team would lose its next series, against a suddenly bitter rival—the Chicago Cubs. Described before the series as a collection of "rejects, cast-offs, throw-ins and unwanteds from other teams," the Cubs found themselves a surprising 32-19 in early June—good enough for first place in the National League East Division by two and a half games over the Pirates. Before the Dodger series the Cubs' tough old-school manager, Herman Franks, downplayed any talk of his team's underdog status. "I don't remember sayin' this spring that we don't have a chance," Franks told *Times* reporter Don Merry. "I don't recall sayin' nothin' like that. All I remember sayin' is that if our pitchin' holds up and the guys play hard, we'll be competitive."[21] His rough talk would turn even more combative as the series against the Dodgers played out, revealing that Franks harbored some bitter jealousy from his former life as a longtime coach with the Dodgers' bitter rivals, the Giants.

The trouble started in the first game, which the Cubs took 3–1, thanks to some clutch hitting by a couple of Dodger "castoffs"—Ivan DeJesus and, poignantly enough, Bill Buckner. When asked after the game about his two hits and key RBI, Buckner, who was making his first appearance in Dodger Stadium since being traded during the off-season, admitted that he was "very much psyched up for the Dodgers." He also quickly added that he "wasn't trying to prove anything to them," but according to observers he was pleased with what he had done. Other people associated with the Cubs were not as conciliatory about Buckner or the Dodgers. "He had yet to cut the umbilical cord," said a Cubs beat writer. Several players suggested Buckner still bled "Dodger Blue." Franks went on to cast further disdain at the Dodgers general manager, Al Campanis, for unloading "damaged merchandise" when they dealt Buckner to the Cubs,[22] and while Buckner went hitless in game 2, the riled-up Cubs scored ten runs before the fourth inning en route to an easy 10–4 victory over the Dodgers.

The final game was a consolation victory, but the Dodgers took no real solace. Starting pitcher Don Sutton, hassled by the Cubs' bench all afternoon, was accused in the eighth inning by Buckner and Frank of doctoring the ball. And while the umpire found no evidence when he searched Sutton, the irascible veteran pitcher was removed from the game and fined one hundred dollars for using profanity. The Dodgers were clearly losing the psychological war against the Cubs—the team that, if the season had ended after this game, would be the Dodgers' opponent in the playoff for the National League Championship. And that wasn't the worst of it. Also in the third game, for the second game in a row, Dodger outfielder Reggie Smith was rattled by the taunting of Cubs fans. The first incident had occurred after the Dodgers' 10–4 loss and before the bus trip back to the team's hotel, when Smith was signing autographs outside Wrigley Field. Someone in the crowd shouted racial slurs at Smith, upsetting the Dodger outfielder until his teammates could calm him and get him on the team's bus. This second time, in the final game of the series, it was a fan sitting in the stands behind home plate while Smith was at bat in the third game. Smith started after the fan before he was grabbed by teammates Dusty Baker and Steve Yeager. "I've been hearing this crap for 15 years," Smith said after the game. "You try to ignore racial remarks, but sometimes you can't . . . sometimes they are too personal. I'm so heated up I've got to walk it off."[23]

And so June would go—up and down, back and forth, a long war of attrition among the great powers of the National League. After the demoralizing losses to the Cubs, the Dodgers faced another tough team in the St. Louis Cardinals. Adding to the confusion, Tom Lasorda had to take leave of the team in the middle of the series to visit his ailing mother back home in Pennsylvania. It was bad enough for Lasorda that the Dodgers lost the game, 8–7, but the manager also had to cancel an appearance on *The Tonight Show*, an appearance that the Dodgers' PR Department had worked to get for much of the past two months. (Lasorda would not get another chance until nearly a year later, in April 1978, when his friend Don Rickles was filling in as guest host.) On June 12, with Lasorda back with the team, the Dodgers lost the final game against the Cardinals, 5–2, while the Reds swept a doubleheader against the Montreal Expos. As a result the Dodgers' lead in the division had fallen to just seven and a half games. Tom Lasorda was a grim figure in the clubhouse. "Sure I'm concerned," he testily responded when asked if he was aware that the Dodgers' divisional lead had dropped by six games in only two and a half weeks. "Anytime you lose 10 of 15 you have to be concerned. But I've believed in these guys all year and I still do. It's not that they're not trying because they're all hustling . . . all giving 100 per cent. I still feel fortunate we are where we are."[24]

Lasorda's concern would not be assuaged—at least not in the short run. That is, just when it seemed the news couldn't get worse for the Dodgers, when it seemed that the evil Red Machine of Cincinnati couldn't get any more menacing, suddenly it did. On the morning of June 16 the headline of the sports page told the story: "Reds Obtain Seaver; Mets Acquire Zachry, Flynn and Two Minor Leaguers for Cy Young Winner." Tom Seaver, a four-time twenty-game winner, the veritable ace of the Mets who had been the linchpin in one World Series victory in 1969 and another World Series run in 1973, was headed to the Reds. With a solid 3.00 ERA and 7-3 record for the last-place Mets in 1977, Seaver would bring to Cincinnati what it had lacked, even during its recent dominance of the National League since 1970—a legitimate top-of-the-rotation starter. "They got a helluva player" was all Tom Lasorda would say after hearing of the trade.[25] And Sparky Anderson's laughter could be heard all the way from Cincinnati, where the Reds had just beaten the Phillies 8–7 in ten innings to move to seven games behind the Dodgers.

As the Dodgers' season slowly, inexorably unraveled, George Lucas's *Star Wars* was launching itself into the stratosphere. The all-engrossing, swashbuckling outer-space fantasy, with its clever gadgetry, colorful characters, and stunning visual effects, had instantly found its audience. According to Peter Biskind, Lucas's particular genius was to take the avant-garde sensibilities that he learned in film school—the Marxist ideology of a master editor like Eisenstein, the critical irony of an avant-garde filmmaker like Bruce Conner, and so forth—and fuse these techniques to American pulp. *Star Wars* pioneered, according to Biskind, the "cinema of moments, of images, of sensory stimuli increasingly divorced from story."[26]

Lucas was surprised, he later reported, at how big a hit his film was, but he shouldn't have been.[27] The simple good-triumphing-over-evil morality tale that Lucas had crafted offered an uplifting message that was perfect for the country's sullen historical moment, giving them at last something to cheer about. In the first weekend *Star Wars* earned $1.5 million, an impressive take in the film's initial limited release. In week two the film expanded from thirty-two to forty-three theaters (in thirty-one cities) and took in $3 million. At each theater, according to studio executives, "it set house records" for ticket sales. The furor continued even when the movie went to widespread distribution after week three. On June 4 a veteran movie theater manager at the Avco Center Cinema in Westwood, Albert Szabo, told Lee Grant, a *Times* reporter, that he'd never seen anything like the reaction to this film. "They are filling the theater for every single performance. This isn't a snowball, it's an avalanche." Grant described crowds that lined up every day at eight in the morning. "They bring food from home in brown paper bags," Grant wrote. "Some, returning for the second, third and even more times. . . . They go in there and have a ball, cheering and applauding. It's a phenomenon."[28]

Even professional film reviewers were effusive. Associated Press called *Star Wars* a "dazzling galactic swashbuckler . . . a comic strip come to life . . . eye-popping special effects." *Variety*: "Wow . . . boffo . . . meteoric . . . super-socko." *Time*: "A grand and glorious film . . . a combination of *Flash Gordon*, *The Wizard of Oz*, the Errol Flynn swashbucklers of the 30s and 40s . . . a remarkable confection . . . a riveting tale." And on and on. By the end of the third week of the film's release, *Star Wars* was bringing in so much money that Fox's stock price had doubled. At the end of its first theatrical run Lucas's fantasy had become the most successful Hollywood movie up to that time, earning a domestic gross of more than $307 million and hundreds of millions more from the European market. And it made a fortune for Lucas, Alec Guinness (who had negotiated for 2.5 percent of the film's profits), and almost anyone associated with the film.

Still, despite the frenzy of accolades and ticket sales, the film's otherworldly success also had stark ramifications for the American film industry. Prior to *Star Wars* the special effects in Hollywood movies had not changed in any significant way since the 1950s. To create his vision for *Star Wars*—of dazzling views of strange imaginary planets, menacingly realistic spacecraft, strange alien monsters and robots, laser blasts, light flashes, laser sword fights, and endless explosions—George Lucas had, through a side company called Industrial Light & Magic, done something wholly new. "Like *The Birth of a Nation* and *Citizen Kane*," wrote noted film critic Roger Ebert some years later, "*Star Wars* was a technical watershed that influenced many of the movies that came after. . . . It linked space opera and soap opera, fairy tales and legend, and packaged them as a wild visual ride." *Star Wars,* according to Ebert, "focused the industry on big-budget special effects blockbusters, blasting off a trend we are still living through. . . . In one way or another, all the big studios have been trying to make another *Star Wars* ever since."[29]

Star Wars was also revolutionary because it created a franchise mentality in Hollywood in the form of spin-off toys, figurines, games, and other merchandise.[30] The "action" figures and associated toys earned millions and millions of dollars and changed not only movie merchandising but the American toy industry. They also put Hollywood on a distinct path for the foreseeable future. Or as Paul Schrader, who wrote the screenplays for such heavy 1970s dramas as *Taxi Driver* and *Raging Bull*, explained in more dire terms, "*Star Wars* was the film that ate the heart and the soul of Hollywood," Schrader said. "It created the big-budget comic book mentality."[31]

Through the rest of June, with the newly adolescent-minded country's head aswim with images of distant planets, intergalactic space airliners, and funky alien creatures, baseball's annual pennant race seemed to take a back seat just as it was beginning to heat up. In the American League, on June 14, five teams—the California Angels, Minnesota Twins, Texas Rangers, Chicago White Sox, and Kansas City Royals—were within spitting distance of first place in the Western Division. In the Eastern Division, meanwhile, three teams—the Boston Red Sox, Baltimore Orioles, and New York Yankees—were separated by just two games. And in the National League East, three teams—the Philadelphia Phillies, St. Louis Cardinals, and Pittsburgh Pirates—were neck and neck as they chased the Cubs, whose early surge had put them four and a half games ahead of the second-place Pirates.

After another loss to the Cubs on June 17 and a Reds win against the Expos, the Dodgers' division lead fell to just six and a half games. It was the team's smallest lead since April 28. Since their seasonal high-water mark after their win over the Reds on May 27, when the team's winning percentage was .750, the Dodgers had won eight games and lost eleven. Again, team observers wondered if the Dodgers were destined to run out of gas. It wasn't until June 18, at home again against Chicago, that the team finally showed signs of returning to life. Veteran left-hander Tommy John and shortstop Bill Russell combined to give the Dodgers a come-from-behind 2–1 win over the Cubs. John went the distance in the game, and Russell had three hits, scored a run, and helped turn four double plays to keep Cubs base runners at bay. John improved his record on the season to 7-4, and Russell, who had been another of the few Dodgers who had not performed up to expectations thus far at the plate, raised his seasonal average, thanks to a recent eight-game tear in which he was batting .457, to a respectable .272.

In the games that followed the team slowly and surely returned to its earlier winning ways, increasing its distance from the Reds and the rest of the division and rewarding Lasorda for his confidence in them. On June 19, during a 3–1 win over the Cubs, a brawl broke out on the field after Cubs starter Rick Reuschel hit Reggie Smith with a pitch, and Smith charged the portly pitcher, punching him in the side of the head. Once the dust had settled Smith and the Cubs' Reuschel, catcher George Mitterwald, and manager Herman Franks had been ejected by home plate umpire Ed Sudol. In the Dodgers' next series against the Cardinals at home, they took two of three. Then, after splitting a series in Cincinnati against the Reds, the Dodgers won three of four in Atlanta against the Braves and four straight in San Francisco against the Giants. After the final win in San Francisco—a three-hit, 4–0 shutout tossed by Don Sutton that was the team's fifth straight win, twelfth win in a row at Candlestick Park, and sixteenth win in the previous twenty-one games—the Dodgers found themselves back in front in their division by ten and a half games.

Lasorda was effusive over the team's return to its winning ways. "Every day, it's something new," he said after the sweep of the Giants. "One day it's Cey, the next day it's Smith and then it's Garvey. It's like Don Sutton so eloquently said a few months ago—playing the Dodgers is like fighting an octopus. You may keep seven of his tentacles occupied but the eighth one will get you."[32]

ELEVEN

Heroes and Villains

I always try to act as though there is a little boy
or a little girl around, and I try never to do
anything that would give them a bad example.

—Steve Garvey, to television reporters during the 1974 World Series

As an athlete, I am no one to be idolized. I will not
perpetuate that hoax. They say I don't like kids. I think that
by refusing to sign autographs, I am giving the strongest
demonstration that I really do like them. I am looking
beyond mere expediency to what is truly valuable in life.

—Mike Marshall, to *Sport Illustrated*'s Ron Fimrite, August 22, 1974

Numerous observers have pointed out through the years that baseball mimics the feel of daily life. For one thing the baseball season is long. Spanning from the preseason in late February to the postseason in later October, the season has strong tidal ebbs and flows, high peaks and low valleys, fast-moving stretches and painful slowed-down passages. To some the length of the baseball season is criminal. "The season starts too early and finishes too late," said Indians, Browns, and White Sox owner Bill Veeck, "and there are too many games in between."[1] To others, though, the duration is part of the sport's particular appeal. "Baseball is a game of the long season," wrote John Updike, "of relentless and gradual averaging-out. . . . Of all the team sports, baseball, with its graceful intermittences of action, its immense and tranquil field sparsely settled with poised men in white, its dispassionate mathematics, seems to me best suited to accommodate, and be ornamented by, a loner. It is essentially a lonely game."[2] Baseball players themselves have reacted to the season's length with similarly mixed emotions. Giants third baseman Al Gallagher, in 1971, sweepingly described the effect of baseball in his life. "There are three things in my life which I really love," he said. "God, my family, and baseball. The only problem—once baseball season starts, I change the order around a bit."[3] Pitcher Jim Bouton, who became widely known for his 1970 tell-all baseball book, *Ball Four*, put it even more poignantly: "You see, you spend a good piece of your life gripping a baseball, and in the end it turns out that it was the other way around all the time."[4]

Having been, by 1977, a baseball man for more than thirty years, Tommy Lasorda well understood how long the baseball season was and how this fact tended to level things out over the long haul. This must have been on his mind, in fact, when a sportswriter asked him whether he thought the team's tailspin at the end of May was just the law of averages catching up with the team. "I don't know about that," he quipped. "I never studied that branch of the law."[5] Despite the team's recent woes, as the midway point of the 1977 season approached Lasorda knew he had plenty to crow about. His boys had played well, and, despite the highs and lows, they held, at the end of June, the best record in the Major Leagues. The team's pitching had been predictably solid, its fielding adequate, and a number of everyday position players were having career seasons. Each day, it seemed, someone new was stepping up, making a crucial play in the field, or getting a timely hit that helped the team win.

Despite his blustery ways Lasorda was not dumb. He was well aware of his job duties. Among the most important, of course, was his responsibility for putting the best Dodger lineup possible out on the field each day. And as June turned to the midseason month of July, and thoughts around the league increasingly turned to the looming stretch run toward the playoffs, Lasorda had some deep concerns about his lineup, particularly when it came to the crucial position of center field. After the incident at the Astrodome on May 31, the resulting day-to-day status for the regular center fielder, Rick Monday, forced Lasorda to weigh his options, and he realized he had no choice but to recall Minor League prospect Glenn Burke to the team.[6] On June 3 Burke had made his first start of the season for the Dodgers, grounding out twice before walking once in the game. Monday felt well enough to appear as a pinch hitter in the tenth inning of the eleven-inning loss, but not well enough to avoid striking out against Rollie Fingers. On June 4 Monday started the game, but his back stiffened up again, and he had to give way to Burke in the first inning. Burke promptly proceeded to go three for four and knock in two runs in a 9–4 win over the Padres. Over the next two weeks, between June 4 and June 19, Monday played sporadically, batted just .214, and had just two RBIs. Burke fared little better at the plate over this period, hitting just .194, though he did cover far more territory than Monday in the field. Monday briefly broke from his funk on June 20, smashing three hits, including two home runs, but the worst news was yet to come. On June 22 team doctor Frank Jobe announced that Monday's sporadic back spasms were due to an unnatural spinal curvature. Although Monday had always had the curvature and had not been bothered by it, Jobe placed Monday on a special exercise and weight-reduction program to help deal with the issue. "We're hoping it will be only another couple of days," said Dr. Jobe, but Monday would remain ineffective through much of the summer.[7] He sat out completely between July 13 and August 5 and appeared only in spots afterward. By the end of August, with just over a month left in the season, Monday's average had fallen to .246, and he had collected only twelve HRs and forty-one RBIs (compared to twenty-four and ninety-eight for Cey and twenty-eight and ninety-four for Garvey, the team's two most productive hitters). The performance was a far cry from what the team had expected from its All-American hero of a center fielder.

Although Monday's disappointing production was an obvious concern for Lasorda, this was not his only worry. As was usual for baseball teams over a long season, various players spent time on the bench in 1977 to nurse injuries and ailments. Dave Lopes missed ten days with a bruised hand. Bill Russell sat out with a severely twisted ankle. Lee Lacy missed nearly a month with a wrist problem, a result of the June fight against the Cubs. Reggie Smith sat out with a sore knee, Steve Yeager with a twisted ankle, and so on.

Fortunately for Lasorda, however, the team's pitchers were healthy and, in most cases, far exceeding the manager's expectations. Tommy John has fallen into the workmanlike professional routine he was known for, showing no open signs of dissent as he compiled a 9-4 record. Don Sutton, too, had been excellent. On July 13 Sutton was picked as one of the eight pitchers named to represent the National League in the All-Star Game. His 10-3 win-loss record, eighty strikeouts against just forty-two walks, and 2.47 ERA were enough for rival manager Sparky Anderson to extend the invitation, the fourth of Sutton's career.[8] Three other Dodgers would join Sutton at the All-Star Game. Ron Cey was chosen by fans as the starting third baseman, and Steve Garvey was chosen at first base. Garvey, of course, was well known. And Cey, who had been on fire early, had raised his own stock in the minds of many fans. Additionally, Reggie Smith was chosen by Sparky Anderson as a backup outfielder. Reggie Smith had displayed plenty of firepower for the Dodgers thus far, with a .440 on-base percentage, a slugging percentage of .595 (as of July 14), and seventeen home runs. He had also done much to once and for all cement his reputation around the league.

The book on Reggie Smith had long been that he was a trouble-making player with a hair-trigger temper and a saucer-size chip on his shoulder. Incidents this season against the Chicago Cubs and St. Louis Cardinals—in which Smith had charged pitchers after getting hit by them—had been chalked up to that reputation. Yet, at the same time, on Lasorda's Dodgers he had shown a different side. "I don't know where he got that reputation," said Lasorda of his right fielder. "The only thing I know is when I became manager I told him I needed him and he put his arm around me and told me he would never let me down. Believe me, there have been times when his leg was bothering him and he went out and played anyway. When he said he wouldn't let me down, he meant it. I don't care what anybody else says about Reggie Smith. I think he's one of the nicest guys I ever met." Even Sparky Anderson pointed to Smith as a key to the team's success. "Lopes and Smith are the whole difference," he said. As for his past reputation as a player on the Boston Red Sox and St. Louis Cardinals, Smith shrugged. "I had a temper and at times it would get out of control. [But] maybe subconsciously I was rebelling.

I was determined to be myself," and not the ballplayer that everyone said he should be.[9]

If Lasorda was pleased to see Smith become comfortable in his skin, he likely was ecstatic to see that Sutton had remained professionally sharp and focused as the season wore on. On July 18 Sutton was named, for the first time in his career, the National League All-Star team's starting pitcher. As a result a local sports columnist noted that the ordinarily irascible and outspoken pitcher seemed happier than ever. "All my childhood I dreamed of the day when I could pitch in Yankee Stadium," Sutton said after hearing the news. "I played many an imaginary game in Yankee Stadium. . . . To finally pitch in Yankee Stadium will be an incredible experience for me. I don't know how I'll handle it." Still, despite the warm feelings, the old Sutton had not completely faded. Asked if Walter Alston's replacement, Tom Lasorda, was responsible for the Dodgers' success so far in 1977, Sutton's answer was blunt: "I don't think so. Tommy's got the kind of club where all he has to do is make out the lineup."[10] The comment wounded Lasorda, and while Sutton smoothed things over by apologizing to Lasorda and saying that he had just been kidding and was embarrassed how the quote came across, the resurgence of Sutton's defiance was worrisome. After all, Dodger fans wondered, could a lack of team cohesion be the cause of another second-half collapse?

Adding to Lasorda's anxiety over the Dodgers' situation was an additional concern about the team's pitching that surfaced of late. While the Dodgers' starting rotation—Tommy John (9-4, 3.48 ERA thus far on the season), Doug Rau (10-1, 3.86), Bert Hooton (8-3, 2.66), and Rick Rhoden (10-5, 3.97)—was one of the best in the league and a key to the Dodgers' stability in keeping atop the NL West,[11] the state of the team's reliever corps was a different story. On July 16, after a rough week for the Dodgers' closer, Charlie Hough, letters had poured into the sports pages of the local papers. The key issue, it seemed, was the growing perception that Hough had a tendency to give up hits and walks in key situations. For instance, on July 10 the Dodgers played a doubleheader against the Padres. In the first game in the afternoon, with the team leading 5–4 after six innings, Hough entered the game in the top of the seventh. After giving up a walk and a double before escaping his first inning, Hough gave up the tying run in the top of the eighth and two more runs in top of the ninth to earn a 7–5 loss.[12] The loss was Hough's eighth of the season (against four wins), and things were no better when Hough entered the nightcap with one out in the ninth and the game tied 4–4. The first batter who faced Hough, George Hendrick, singled to right, knocking in the go-ahead run from second base. Although Hough would not get credit for the loss, as the runner belonged to starter Rick Rhoden, the failure of Hough to hold this game after his loss in the earlier game incensed many team followers. "Shame on the Dodgers for not providing Lasorda with relief pitchers!" wrote one fan later in the week. "No one except Garman has done any winning." Another fan called Hough a "cracked rhinestone," wondering how long Lasorda would continue to allow him to let games get away. Yet another fan suggested that, with Hough, the Dodgers' chance of winning the pennant was becoming "slim and impossible."[13]

Despite the furor Lasorda remained committed to his knuckleballer. Although Hough was not one of the newly emerging breed of power-throwing, lights-out closers, he had still amassed nineteen saves for the Dodgers by the time of the Padres doubleheader, and his ERA was a respectable 2.74. Still, with Hough's recent ineffectiveness as the All-Star break approached, the Dodger manager was worried about the bullpen. When reliever Mike Garman came down with a strained groin during the same week of Hough's undoing, the team was suddenly desperate. On June 19 the Dodgers announced they were calling up young left-hander Lance Rautzhan from their AAA team in Albuquerque. A sign of how desperate the team was could be seen in the fact that Rautzhan's record in the Minors was a mediocre 4-4 with a 4.96 ERA in twenty-eight appearances. Attempts to justify the call-up by pointing out Rautzhan's 3-1 record and four saves in his most recent appearances only further highlighted the team's nervousness.

The fan furor over the Dodgers' mediocre relief pitching, even in the midst of a highly successful season, was baffling to Lasorda. "Charlie . . . has done a tremendous job for us," he said, "and that's one of the reasons we're where we are. He's a fine young man. . . . I just can't figure it out. I guess if the fans pay their money, they're entitled to boo."[14] On the other hand, Lasorda might have added, sports fans love to cheer a winner—a fact that helped explain the abiding popularity, across Los Angeles, of Steve Garvey. Out of all the Dodgers who contributed to the team's success in 1977—players like Don Sutton and Ron Cey and Tommy John and Reggie Smith—Steve Garvey exhibited, in the minds of local fans, the characteristics of a clear and honest winner.

As if to quantify the matter, on July 12 it was revealed that, at the close of the fan balloting for the All-Star Game, Garvey not only was the top vote getter in both leagues, but was also the first player at any position ever to receive more than four million votes.[15] So what was it that fans liked about Steve Garvey? Well, for one, there was the way he handled the bat. Garvey was a hitter's hitter, always well prepared, often able to come through when it most mattered. "Garvey is the best hitter I have ever seen," Reggie Jackson said after his Oakland A's had faced the Dodgers in the 1974 World Series. "Steve Garvey is a right-handed Lou Gehrig," said veteran Yankees scout Clyde Kluttz in 1975. "Garvey with a bat in his hand is a candidate for the Hall of Fame," said another scout.[16] And in fact, despite Cey's monster month of April, by the All-Star break Garvey had uncomplainingly and steadily passed Cey, at least when it came to two measurable statistics—Garvey had twenty-two home runs to Cey's eighteen, and he had eighty RBIs to Cey's seventy-six. The fact was that Garvey was such a good, pure hitter that his success was almost taken for granted. His consistent production, in fact, was such a given that for years his nickname, in certain circles, was "Mr. Consistency."

Interestingly, Garvey's emergence as a star very nearly never happened. Although Garvey had always shown promise at the plate, he had never proved he could play in the field. Brought up originally as a third baseman, Garvey could not overcome a bum arm, the result of an injury from his years playing college football at Michigan State University. (The same scout who suggested his bat might take him to the Hall of Fame also said, "Garvey with a ball in his hands is a candidate for the post office.")[17] While trying to break in as a Dodger regular at third base in 1971 and 1972, for example, Garvey made forty-two errors in 133 starts at the position. By 1973 rumors circulated widely that the Dodgers were ready to trade him.

Confused and frustrated, Garvey walked into the office of Dodger general manager Al Campanis and insisted on knowing what the Dodgers planned for him. Campanis told Garvey that he was still considered an integral part of the team, and there would be no trade. Then, according to Garvey, everything changed. On June 23, 1973, the team played a doubleheader against the Cincinnati Reds. Bill Buckner, the Dodgers' regular first baseman, had been struggling of late, his batting average having dropped forty points from the year before, so Dodger manager Walt Alston made a snap decision, penciling in Steve Garvey's name on the lineup card at first base. Garvey, who had played but once or twice at the position, said nothing; he was not going to give up a chance to play because of a niggling detail like experience. And here, at last, he began to thrive, batting .304 during a half season of first base duty. The next season, in 1974, Garvey played so well that he was a surprise choice, as a write-in candidate (because his name was not on the ballot), to start the All-Star Game. He then went on to astonish nearly everyone by being named the All-Star Game's MVP, leading the Dodgers to the World Series, and then winning the National League MVP Award and the first of four Gold Glove Awards.

In 1974, 1975, and 1976 Garvey batted .312 or better and accumulated two hundred hits. In this Garvey credited his ability to go with pitch locations and send solid line drives all over the ballpark. He was, as he put it, a contact hitter, and his swing essentially lacked a major weakness. Adding to his appeal among fans was Garvey's distinctive batting and playing style. Garvey's forearms were large and burly,[18] and his upper body and legs were in solid condition, the result of a disciplined and focused exercise regiment. As he stepped into the box Garvey was a focused matador, his movements smooth and deliberate, an act of complete concentration. Garvey's practice swings were just short and smooth chops, a little like a matador waving his cape at a bull. But the most distinctive aspect of his swing was how the first baseman held his head throughout his at bats. His eyes were always pointed slightly downward at the plate, his head still and focused and oriented to the strike zone like a compass needle pointing to the Dog Star. Garvey credited the stillness of his stance with much of his ability to be a good contact hitter. And he would keep this poise even after he had uncorked his most violent, slashing swing. This was not the violent, upward-angled swing of a Babe Ruth or Reggie Jackson. Garvey's approach was compact and whiplike. He used his hips, torso, and arms like a hydraulic engine. And while Garvey did not have tons of natural home run power, his bat was never lacking in pop.

Adding to Garvey's appeal was his personal story—a good, old-fashioned, all-American rags-to-riches Dodger Blue sort of tale. Raised in Tampa, Florida, where his father was a bus driver who often drove charter buses during spring training for the Brooklyn Dodgers, Garvey grew up dreaming he'd one day play for the team he knew as a kid. He even was an occasional Dodgers batboy in spring training, a fact that no screenwriter could have written with a straight face. "I was an only child," said Garvey in 1975, "which wasn't too bad. I always had balls available for me because we had 11 grapefruit trees in the yard. In the spring I'd take the little hard grapefruits that had fallen off and I'd hit them with a broomstick. I'd be the whole Dodger lineup: Charlie Neal, Gilliam, Campanella, Snider, Hodges."[19]

While at Michigan State University, where he played football and baseball, Garvey was selected by the Dodgers in the first round of the 1968 draft. He then dropped out of school, signed a contract to play in Ogden for the Dodgers' rookie team, and never looked back. Ten years later, all across Los Angeles, kids worshipped Garvey. And parents approved of their kids' worship of Garvey because he, by all accounts, was a Good Guy. While the 1970s was an age of the anti-hero, replete with imperfect figures—like Randle Patrick McMurphy, Travis Bickle, and Alex de Large (not to mention Pete Rose, Dave Kingman, Dave "the Cobra" Parker, among others)—who marched to their own drummer, fought against authority, and refused to live up to anyone's expectations but their own, Steve Garvey was a rare public exception to this rule. In public Garvey appeared clean-cut to a fault—his hair, in an era known for wild styles and poor hygiene, was always carefully coiffed, his face neatly shaved. Garvey was accessible, seemingly honest and earnest. He never swore, spat, or rubbed his crotch in public. He never drank, smoke, chewed, spat, or swore, and he always had a kind word for a kid or a gentle old lady. To Dodger fans Garvey was a somewhat brawnier version of Luke Skywalker.[20]

He was a younger, shorter, more modern version of John Wayne. He was a more athletic and burly Richard Cunningham.

For people like Tom Fallon, conventional law-and-order guys who simply wanted their towns and streets to be, above all else, safe places to raise their families, Garvey was a breath of fresh air. Even more remarkably, to hardworking small business owners like Tom Fallon, Garvey was a delight because he seemed to somehow "get" that he owed something to the team, and to his fans, for his endless good fortune in being able to play this sport. He was widely involved in the community and in good charitable works. And, perhaps most important in 1977, he never got himself into contract disputes. He seemed grateful, even, for the money he earned to play on a team he seemed to love. "They come along so rarely," wrote *Chicago Sun-Times* columnist Tom Fitzpatrick in 1975. "First, there was Frank Merriwell. Then along came Jack Armstrong. Now Steve Garvey."

With Garvey's shining star eclipsing his various teammates', it was almost inevitable that resentment would build. With his looks and clean-cut persona Garvey was even courted by Hollywood. "If you want to quit playing ball today," they reportedly told him, "we'll get a series for you." Still, according to a later account written by wife Cyndy, Garvey's popularity was no accident. An agent had first approached Garvey during his appearance in the 1974 All-Star Game. "Your husband," the agent told both of them at dinner a few weeks later, "is the quintessential all-American boy. He's everybody's sweetheart. And I can show you how to capitalize on that. . . . You're very hot right now. And your contract year is coming up. I'll negotiate for you with Campanis. I'll work out some tax shelters. Handle your investments. Line up endorsements." The agent went on, explaining how to get Steve more and better press coverage, set him up for lucrative commercials and television work, and arrange speaking engagements and high-profile charity work. "That's the image we want."[21]

The homespun, squeaky-clean Garvey image was further encouraged by the public relations office of the Dodgers, a team whose front office well knew the value of creating positive images in the minds of the public. Even the venal Lasorda, who, by 1977, had coached and managed Garvey for five years on the Dodgers and two years in the Minors, readily played along. "If he ever came to date my daughter," Lasorda told reporters, "I'd lock the door and not let him out."[22] Long before 1977 Lasorda had adopted the former batboy as a kind of favored son. Garvey usually rode in the coaches' bus, sitting with the manager and the other coaches and soaking up baseball banter. He always seemed destined for bigger and better things. In time his nickname on the Dodgers became "the Senator," for the postplayer career goals he supposedly harbored.

But if Steve Garvey of the Los Angeles Dodgers sometimes seemed too good to be true, the truth about Garvey was that, while he was not completely opposite what he appeared, he certainly was more complicated. For one, Garvey, despite all his outward charms, was not widely popular on his own team. This problem went back to his time in the Minor Leagues. Unlike many of his peers Garvey didn't drink or smoke and often seemed judgmental about players who did. This stance caused plenty of friction. "You don't have to get drunk," Cyndy Garvey told him in those years. "But couldn't you just drink a beer or two? They'll like you better."[23] Garvey would hear nothing of it, refusing to waver from his personal goals. This was something that had been part of his character since childhood. Garvey, according to his father, never grew his hair long, never rebelled in any way, even in the rebellious 1960s. When his fellow college kids in the heady late 1960s were wearing tie-dye and cutoffs, Garvey wore slacks and monogrammed sweaters. Garvey said he even hated to dance, because to do so in the 1960s meant losing control.

Over time Garvey gained real enemies on the team. When the Dodgers were winning, the resentment and antipathy remained mostly in check. In interviews teammates sometimes talked distastefully about the "Madison Avenue" image of an unnamed teammate. One time, after getting thrown out while attempting to bunt himself on base, Garvey was nonplussed when he caught two teammates high-fiving each other. But what was he going to do? Garvey simply wasn't a drinker, and he wasn't good at leering at women and cutting up with the boys. In some ways it was inevitable that, as Garvey's star rose and he became more removed from his teammates, the gentle facade of tolerance would eventually implode. After his breakout season in 1974, players like Cey, Sutton, and Mike Marshall—all of whom had made significant contributions to the team's success—

couldn't understand why Garvey received so much more recognition than they did. Then when the Dodgers collapsed in 1975, clubhouse ill will toward Garvey bubbled up to the surface. "You want to know something," one Dodger starter anonymously told *San Bernardino Sun* reporter Betty Cuniberti in June of that year. "Steve Garvey doesn't have a friend on this team."[24]

It was a simple statement, and one that rang fairly true, but almost immediately the Dodger brass moved to save face. A closed-door team meeting was called to clear the air and settle any outstanding issues. What exactly was said at the meeting remains a mystery, but afterward a number of Dodgers emerged to give Garvey some due. "Maybe we're less mature," said Dave Lopes, "but the other eight starters look at baseball as a game. Garvey thinks of it more as a business. That's fine with me. It's just not my bag." Said Lee Lacy, "All I'll say is Steve is a friend." Jimmy Wynn, who also said he counted Garvey among his friends, sympathized because the same sort of jealousy had dogged him when he played in Houston. And Ron Cey suggested he was willing to offer a halfhearted détente: "I don't mind what Steve does. If he wants to go out of his way to be the clean-cut kid, that's fine—so long as he doesn't interfere with my style. Sometimes he has interfered." Garvey's reaction, meanwhile, was revealing in what it did not reveal. "I'd rather not discuss it" was all he would say.[25]

By the middle of 1977, Garvey and the rest of the team seemed to have put their personality conflicts mostly behind them. Likely helping ease the tension was the appointment of Garvey's old endorser Tom Lasorda to the manager position. Garvey had also given his stature a small boost by agreeing, at Lasorda's request, to change his approach at the plate and help provide the team with more power. And for a good spell through the first half of the season, Garvey, like the rest of the Dodgers, was quite successful. Although he had hit more than twenty homers just once in his career thus far (twenty-one HRS in 1974), by early August he was leading the team in home runs, with twenty-six. None of his teammates could argue that Garvey was not contributing to the team's success, and team observers in the press and stands also took giddy note of Garvey's surge. "Perhaps Garvey would get 200 RBIS," said one commenter.[26]

By the end of July 1977 Garvey, in his quiet, methodical way, had proved naysayers wrong. And as the season turned to August, with the Dodgers over their rough stretch and again leading the Western Division by a comfortable fourteen games, no one suspected that the high ground Garvey occupied was about to fall out from under him, plunging him into the deepest, darkest valley of his career.

TWELVE

Dog Days in Dogtown

They're like sleeping in a soft bed.
Easy to get into and hard to get out of.

—Johnny Bench, on slumps

Two hundred years of American technology has unwittingly
created a massive cement playground of unlimited potential.
But it was the minds of 11 year olds that could see that potential.

—C. R. Stecyk III, on the California-based
skateboarding phenomenon of the late 1970s

Southern California has always been at the mercy of the elements. With its warm sun and relatively dry vegetation, broken only by periods of monsoon-like rain, the Los Angeles basin suffers from drought, reservoir depletion, and brush fires, alternated with raging flash floods and hillside mud slides. In 1977 the usual bounty of the region—in which the sunny landscape was inviting and locals were thriving—by August had turned to a long dry stretch. Going back to 1976 the entire state had experienced the most severe drought conditions of the past hundred years, a span of dryness that caused severe damage to the state's agricultural system, depleted runoff water to an all-time low, and forced forty-seven of the state's fifty-eight counties to declare a state of emergency. "If the drought continues for merely another 30 days," wrote *Time* in March, quoting officials at the National Oceanographic and Atmospheric Administration, "we've got a good chance of another Dust Bowl."[1] Because of the conditions, cities across Southern California banned lawn watering, families emptied out their swimming pools, and officials rushed to build an emergency desalination plant and an emergency water pipeline.

In addition to the heat and the dry weather conditions, lingering economic woes and other uncertainties weighed on the local population. Jobs were hard to come by, and young men in the suburbs and along the coastal communities of Los Angeles lingered on street corners and at watering holes and video arcades, looking for something to fill their hot and empty summer days. Meanwhile, while the local baseball team had provided some distraction—thus far avoiding the "traditional June Swoone" that had upended fans' hopes in recent seasons—in the August heat and dryness Angelenos began to hear, in hints and whispers, a single word in reference to their team. It was a somewhat leaden, unpoetic word, but with the unusual quality that it sounded pretty much exactly like what it meant: *slump*. In August 1977 the Dodgers were stuck in a slump so severe that it seemed, even after the team had built an insurmountable lead in the National League West, their season was still at risk.

After a victory over Montreal on July 31 the Dodgers stood in first place by fourteen games over the Reds, but between August 1 and August 7 their divisional lead had fallen to eleven and a half games after they lost six of seven road games against the Expos, Mets, and Phillies. After splitting four games at home against the Reds between August 8 and August 11, for the next two weeks afterward, in games against the Braves, Giants, Cubs, Cardinals, and Pirates, the team played .500 ball and let their division lead slip to eight and a half games on August 26. And while a divisional lead was certainly welcome for the Dodgers at this point in the season, considering that a good stretch of games still remained in the season—and many of those games were against the team's divisional rivals—there was legitimate cause for concern.

The causes for the Dodgers August slump were several—cold bats, a struggling bullpen, a falloff in the effectiveness of Dodger starters Don Sutton and Doug Rau—but no reason was more jolting to Dodger followers than what had happened to Steve Garvey. In August "Mr. Consistency" found himself, for the first time in his career, mired in a major slump.

It came about like this: On August 2, after losing the previous game in twelve innings to the last-place New York Mets, the Dodgers' two leading hitters, Ron Cey and Steve Garvey, both unleashed home runs in a 7–2 victory. It was a high-water mark on the season for both players. Garvey, who had twenty-six home runs against Ron Cey's twenty-two home runs, was leading in the power race on the Dodgers, though Cey was ahead in runs batted in, ninety to eighty-seven. After the game Cey hardly seemed pleased with his and his teammate's accomplishments thus far this year. Instead, he seemed to feel slighted, particularly in comparison to his teammate. "I don't think," Cey said, "that anyone would think of me in MVP terms no matter what I did. I don't want to belabor the point. It's just the way I feel. I'm using what's happened in the past as a frame of reference. What's the highest I've finished before [in MVP balloting] . . . 15th?" Garvey, meanwhile, was bemused when reporters asked him to answer the same question, as if he were unaware that a rivalry existed between the Dodgers' two hottest hitters. "I feel that to this point I'm having a better year than in '74," he said plainly, and brushed off any talk of postseason honors. "But it's really too early to think about the MVP. You never know what will happen over the last two months."[2] A simple response; however, the talk about hit totals, slugging stats, MVP Awards, and other peripheral things must have gotten into Garvey's head. Two days later, after going three for four and raising his average to .301 in a loss to Philadelphia on August 5, Garvey went hitless in four at bats, striking out once. On August 7 it was the same story: another hitless game, another loss. August 8, in a 4–0 victory over the Reds, Garvey again was blanked in four at bats. And on August 9, in a 4–0 loss to the Reds, Garvey was oh for three. Between August 6 and August 12 Garvey would be completely hitlesss—it was the first such seven-game stretch of his career.

And the slump continued. Between August 6 and August 23 his average fell steeply—from .301 to just .275. The newspapers, fascinated by this unprecedented tailspin by the former MVP, spun the numbers. "He now has only seven hits in his last 65 at bats, an average of .113," a sportswriter mused on August 24. "He is only 36 for 176 since July 4, an average of .205. He has only 12 RBI and four home runs in those 45 games, of which the Dodgers have lost 25, and he has gone 17 straight games without driving in a run."[3]

Leading up to August, predictably, Dodger watchers had talked about how Lasorda's preseason directive to Garvey "to hit for more power" had led the first baseman to make some risky adjustments in his swing. But Garvey had dismissed the concerns. "I haven't changed very much at all," Garvey told a local columnist in mid-August, before describing exactly how he had changed his swing. "Just at certain times, I might be a little more conscious of going for the fence. . . . And then I'm dipping my right shoulder just a little lower to get more leverage on my swing." By late August, however, Garvey, was at a loss to explain what was wrong. "I feel I hit a few balls well enough in that period to have some hits," Garvey said on August 24, "but . . . I've tried to be philosophical. I tell myself that maybe it's just the last three years catching up with me, that better hitters than I am have gone through worse slumps. It's some consolation . . . but not much."[4]

As Garvey's, and the team's, slump dragged on through August, Lasorda pondered his options. In every scenario, however, Lasorda realized that if his first baseman didn't come around, there was no hope. Who was he going to play, *Ed Goodson*? (On August 23, at the height of Garvey's slump, Goodson was batting .190 and slugging .286; he was not an option.) But then Lasorda knew the ways of baseball players, how their spirit and drive rose and fell from one week to next. And he knew how fundamentally sound Garvey was as a ballplayer. There were no weaknesses in Garvey's swing, he told himself. It wasn't like pitchers were fooling him left and right—the hits just weren't falling, which sometimes happened even with the best players. Lasorda wasn't going to panic; he was going to stick with his first baseman until he started hitting again. When asked about Garvey Lasorda said:

> At one point or another, everyone gets into a slump. Steve never had one and I suspect that he felt he never would. Now what you have is one of the proudest and most intense competitors in baseball fighting himself. There's really nothing mechanically wrong. It's all mental. The problem is in trying to stop a snowball. We've given him rest.

We've had him take extra batting practice. The only thing I can try to tell him is the same thing that I have tried to tell Cey . . . "Relax, hold your head up, you're still the same hitter who helped put us 9½ games ahead of the Reds."[5]

Lasorda's decision not to worry about Garvey was a practical one. After all, in late August Lasorda had plenty of other concerns to worry about. As of August 25 the Dodgers collectively had batted only .229 over their previous forty-seven games. Over the same period the team's record had been just 21-26, making August the Dodgers' first losing month of the season. If September continued in much the same way, Lasorda knew, and if the Reds got hot as was their habit late in previous seasons, then . . . Lasorda didn't want to even ponder what would happen.

No, Lasorda knew in his heart, the team would hit again. Garvey would hit again. This was a team of destiny, he told himself. The Dodgers would not keep losing. The Great Dodger in the Sky, such as he was, wouldn't play such a nasty trick on him. Not when he had brought the team so close to the ultimate goal. Not when the World Series was within the team's grasp.

Slumps have a long history and special kind of lore in baseball. The very idea of a "slump" in baseball goes back at least to 1893, when a newspaper writer in Philadelphia scratched his head in print over the terrible recent performance of several East Coast teams by writing, "Their temporary 'slump' is hard to understand."[6] By the latter part of the twentieth century, slumps were not only a "soft bed," as Johnny Bench suggested, but accepted as part of the toll of playing the game. They were also a natural preoccupation for men trying to survive at the highest levels of physical performance and athletic achievement. Over time a great amount of folklore and pseudoscience about the potential causes, and likely cures, for slumps had developed. As Billy Williams, the Cubs star of the 1960s and '70s put it, "A slump starts in your head and winds up in your stomach. You know that eventually it will happen, and you begin to worry about it. Then you know you're in one. And it makes you sick."[7] As was suggested with Garvey, many players blamed slumps on efforts to overreach, the tendency to force things with a bat that should just occur naturally. "Homers are the root of all evil," said Curt Blefary, an Orioles outfielder in the 1960s who won the Rookie of the Year Award before seeing his career cut short by inconsistent production. "You hit a couple and every time up you're looking to hit the ball out. First thing you know, you're in a slump." A home run hitter no less than Reggie Jackson had, earlier in his career, spoken trenchantly about the desperation of a player in the midst of a slump. "So many ideas come to you," he told *The Sporting News* in 1970, "and you want to try them all, but you can't. You're like a mosquito in a nudist camp. You don't know where to start."[8]

As for remedies there was quite an array—from the common belief that a slumping player should sleep with the ugliest female stranger he could find to Rogers Hornsby's suggestion that one should try to hit the ball straight back at the pitcher (as that was supposedly the largest unprotected area of the field of play). The great Babe Ruth, after a prolonged slump in 1933, attributed his comeback in 1934 to eating scallions. Meanwhile, Roy Campanella, the great Dodger catcher whose bat helped him win three National League MVP Awards, had a simpler, somewhat Yogi Berra–like theory, as quoted in *Life* in 1953: "When you're hitting, you hit, and when you're not hitting well, you just don't hit."[9]

Despite all the lore surrounding baseball slumps, it is one of the strange ironies of the sport that when one happens, it is almost always an unexpected surprise. This helps explain why so many fans and reporters in 1977 seemed caught off-guard by the idea of Steve Garvey's, and the rest of the Dodgers', extended late-summer slump. The Dodgers had played so far above their rivals for so long by this point, it simply didn't compute. And so Dodger fans suffered through Garvey's first slump as it stretched on and on and on through the dog days of 1977. At the same time, after the forced merriment of the nation's bicentennial celebration had at last worn off, much of the country seemed seriously off-track. From the moribund stock markets and continued psychic fallout from Vietnam and Watergate to continued worry about the country's heating-oil supply and the anger over gas shortages, America was simply in the dumps. So uncertain were the economic times in August 1977 that *Time* said the country was on a "roller-coaster to nowhere," its problems seemingly entrenched and all but unsolvable. Although inflation had slowed slightly in 1977, and corporate profits had increased for the first time in several years, the stock market told a story of disappointment, as analysts noted that the bread-and-butter small-time stock investors were staying away from Wall Street. "The 25-to-40-year-olds are not in the market anymore," suggested *Time*. "They probably have lost money and had a bad experience. I think we are going to have difficulty attracting those people back."[10]

For Tom Fallon, 1977 was a tale of two realities. Despite the constantly dire economic predictions, Fallon's hardware store was slowly, incrementally growing and providing a reasonable living for his family. Tom Fallon had come to California with an ability to work hard. And he had passed on the same work ethic to his children. All through 1977, as Tom's sons Jim and Ken settled into the business, the three men were a whirling force of activity. If they weren't busy building shelving and counters, moving truckloads of stock from one spot to another, shifting and selling and moving and transferring and expanding it all in the endless search for profitability, they were plotting bigger and better things. When the store became pressed for space, Tom checked around and discovered the owner of the business behind his store was looking to sell the larger space and the land it was situated on. He convinced his sons of the value of the buy and over the summer supervised the store's move. Once there the three began the process of reconstructing and reshifting and rearranging the space all over again. This meant long, strenuous hours for everyone and stress on both of the young families of Tom's sons. James in particular never seemed to rest. Even when he was home on rare occasions, he was a flurry of activity—building an extra patio on the back of a new house and transforming the raw, hard-packed dirt and rocks of Cucamonga into a yard with planters, a new lawn, rock gardens, and, after a swimming pool was added, a new redwood deck.

As a result Tom Fallon was establishing himself as a pillar of this small suburban town, Cucamonga. And he was taking great joy in the fact that so many of his children and grandchildren had come to settle nearby. His two sons Kenneth and James had moved their families, including six grandchildren (two girls and four boys), to the region after buying partnership shares in the store, and a younger son, Patrick, had recently started working on an hourly basis at the store, hoping to save up enough money to buy his own partnership share. It all was something of a dream come true for Tom Fallon going back to his youth when, separated from his other four siblings—two sisters and two brothers—and enduring the abuse of the brutal nuns who ran his orphanage in Philadelphia, he swore someday he would always keep his family close by. If you don't have family, Tom realized then and now, what do you have?

Still, content as Tom Fallon was in the summer of 1977, he recognized that people across the Los Angeles area were in a funk. This was especially true, it seemed, of young people. Everywhere Tom went in L.A. that summer, the streets were overrun by unkempt boys and young men. With not much to do in the heat and with the bad economy, they lingered on sidewalks, at parks, in parking lots. Tom, who by nature had a kind and optimistic heart, was still annoyed at these boys. Often, on weekday afternoons, he would have to chase kids away from the parking lot behind his store, where they practiced moves on their skateboards and made an annoying ruckus for his customers. Even as he chased the kids away, however, Tom Fallon worried. He knew, after all, from long experience that things could always get worse. In fact, the signs were widespread. Several times in recent weeks, for instance, he had been awoken in the middle of the night by his store's alarm service. And it was not just petty larceny that afflicted sleepy Cucamonga. One day that August, on a hot and dusty summer afternoon, one of Tom's grandsons, who lived with his parents in a rental house just a few blocks from Tom's own home, had been terrorized by two neighbor kids with a switchblade knife. "Let's crucify him," one of the kids had said to the other, before the two ran away laughing. It may have been an older kid's idea of a joke, but it wasn't at all funny to Tom.

Mayor Tom Bradley well understood that the national—and localized—economic slump was affecting ordinary families and small businessmen like Tom Fallon. He also understood that this slump was very like any baseball slump, much of it caused by ingrained thinking, by gut-wrench defeatism. Bradley had become something of an expert in slumps since being swept to office in 1973, since he had gotten an earful of nearly constant complaint about the times. And while at first there was some merit to all the complaints, especially after the energy crisis of 1973 had led to the greatest economic downturn since the 1930s, by 1977 Bradley could see that much of the dejection in his city was self-created.

For four years, then, between 1973 and 1977, Bradley worked hard to stabilize the leadership of his growing city. He was methodical in his approach. He opened up city hall in a way that had not been seen before, making city commissions and positions available to women, minorities, and the disabled. He met constantly with important interest groups and city scions, made appearances all over town, and methodically helped transform what had been a conservative white urban center into one of the most diverse and diversified cities in the United States. Over the next stretch of years, with Tom Bradley providing the impetus, Los Angeles would develop a brand-new skyline and revitalize its financial and business districts. Bradley spearheaded an effort to clean up, reconstruct, and modernize Los Angeles Harbor, turning it into a vibrant locus of international trade. Whatever his methods, in time Bradley, quietly and without touting his own role in the effort, helped turn Los Angeles into one of the world's great metropolitan centers.

Leaders around the rest of the nation in 1977 could have learned much from how Bradley had risen above the troubles of the times. Politicians everywhere across the nation in those years were widely loathed, paying the price for people's frustrations in the post-Watergate era. By 1977 President Jimmy Carter was fast becoming the most visible focal point for this national upset. Though elected on a wave of hopeful sentiment by an electorate looking for change, the luster of Carter's presidency did not last long. In the August 1977 article on the nation's dragging investor confidence, *Time* had much to say about this. "The Carter Administration," the magazine suggested, "seems unable to inspire any confidence in investors." This, of course, was unfair. Jimmy Carter had assumed the office of the presidency just six months earlier, and the nation was struggling with a cold winter and shortages in heating fuel, as well as the continued fallout from the Watergate conspiracy, the Vietnam crisis, and continued economic malaise. Was it any wonder that Carter seemed stuck at the gate?

On February 2, 1977, just two weeks after his inauguration, President Carter give a televised address dressed in a sweater. In the speech Carter announced that the development of a national energy policy was urgent, suggesting the United States was the only major industrial country without one. He pledged to work on creating a clear policy and establishing a new energy department to consolidate efforts to deal with the nation's energy needs, and he asked the nation for help in this effort. After the speech, the president was widely ridiculed, including on the superhip NBC TV program *Saturday Night Live*, indicating that Carter would have to get to work without the traditional honeymoon phase usually given to new presidents. A few months later, on April 18, 1977, Carter gave another more formal and far more dramatic televised address from the Oval Office to announce his national energy policy. "Tonight I want to have an [slight pause] unpleasant talk with you," he said bluntly, "about a problem that's unprecedented in our history. With the exception of preventing war, this is the greatest challenge our country will face during our lifetimes. . . . It is a problem we will not solve in the next few years, and it is likely to get progressively worse through the rest of this century. . . . We simply must balance our demand for energy with our rapidly shrinking resources. By acting now, we can control our future instead of letting the future control us."[11]

By some measures this speech was more of a success than his previous one. It laid the groundwork for the establishment of the strategic petroleum reserve, the modern solar power industry, and the national conservation movement, and it encouraged millions of Americans to insulate their homes. But by other measures the speech failed miserably. It was a speech that people simply did not want to hear. They wanted solutions to the nation's problems, not complicated acknowledgments of the extent of them. On May 5, 1977, in the aftermath of his speech, Carter pointedly visited the poster child for energy overconsumption in America: the vast freeway-blanketed Southern Californian basin. A background chorus to his fact-finding tour of the region was an increasingly agitated U.S. Congress. And in California, meanwhile, at least one prominent local politician saw the flaw in Carter's approach.

On June 2, 1977, just a few weeks after Carter's visit, former actor and governor of California Ronald Reagan addressed the energy crisis from his own vantage point. Speaking on his radio show to Californians who were stuck "sitting in long gas lines," Reagan said he understood why people were "angry." But it wasn't the oil companies that were causing these problems; it was the Department of Energy, whose bureaucratic regulations were slowing the efficient production of gas for the nation's consumers. In other words government was the problem. Get rid of the government, let the market regulate itself, and there would be plenty of oil for all.

Whether Carter heard Reagan's energy message is not on record. Having met with Tom Bradley, the popular Los Angeles mayor who was then cruising to victory in a bid for a second term, it is likely Carter wondered what the mayor's secret was. Bradley was facing down many of the same problems as Carter—a seemingly intractable energy problem, which L.A. was feeling as acutely as anyplace in the country; nasty political opponents on all sides, including mayoral opponents who were levying racially charged accusations against him; an uncertain and disparate voting coalition as the base of his support; and strong ambivalence, if not antipathy, from the business community—yet he had somehow maintained a markedly high level of popularity. Carter marveled at his old ally from the previous election season and then headed back to the snake pit in DC, still no closer to an easy solution to his growing problems.

Despite the seeming return of the energy crisis, Californians, especially young ones, still found ways to have fun and enjoy themselves in the hot summer of 1977. This was nothing new, of course. Though Tom Fallon was too old to have experienced the surf craze, his sons had been mad about the new surfing craze that engulfed California in the 1960s, and Fallon watched as the two boys' lives quickly began to revolve around the surfer lifestyle. Of course, by 1977 the two Fallon brothers had given up the surfing habit, as had many young Californians. In fact, in the tough 1970s kids in depressed and gas-strapped families for the most part had to forego the beach and make due with more of a more landlocked fad: skateboards.

Although skateboarding had first been popular way back in the

1950s, interest in the pastime fell off. Part of the problem was the fact that early skateboards were nothing more than cheap pieces of wood on which clay or metal skate wheels had been affixed. These boards were crude, poor at gripping the asphalt, and often lost their ball bearings in midride, which sent riders tumbling off the board. In 1970, however, a surfer named Frank Nasworthy saw the problem and decided to do something. Using the new, more technologically advanced urethane wheels being made for roller skates, he put them onto flexible wooden boards, in the process improving the ride, increasing comfort, and setting the stage for a resurgence of interest in skateboarding.

A key development in local skateboard interest came in the early 1970s with the founding, in Southern California, of a competitive surf team composed of boys (and one girl) between the ages of twelve and sixteen. The Zephyr Competition Team, or Z-Boys, took its name from the Zephyr surfboard shop that was located in a rough, graffiti-strewn neighborhood of North Santa Monica called Dogtown. In its early days the Z-Boys team practiced surfing in and among the ruined Pacific Ocean Park pier. The emblematic failure of the former amusement park was the perfect locus for this group of scrappy, daring kids, whose hardscrabble lives were punctuated by street violence, broken homes, drug peddling, and failed dreams. Because the large tilted wood pilings and steel beams of the ruined pier jutted from the water, the local surf style relied on sharp cutbacks, daring bursts of speed, and an unreal sense of agility and bodily awareness to survive and thrive. And in time the Z-Boys became admired for their skill and agility.

Inevitably, the Z-Boys discovered the new skateboards. Because the wind shifted on the California coast around ten every morning, surfing would end early in the day. Out of sheer boredom some Z-Boys decided to try skateboarding, and they were impressed with how the polyurethane wheels allowed them to mimic their surfing style on local playgrounds, many of which had sloped retaining walls. By 1975 skateboarding had grown popular enough that promoters of the sport organized the first competitions since the heyday of the 1960s. And the so-called Del Mar Nationals, a skateboarding meet held at the Del Mar Fairgrounds in the seaside town of Del Mar, saw the national debut of the new Z-Boy style.

While skateboarding eventually would become all but synonymous with teen rebellion, in 1975 the bulk of the competitors at the competition were relatively clean-cut, well-behaved types—mimics of the "young sportsmen" ideal of the classic 1960s surfers. Dressed in their team uniforms of blue Vans sports shoes, Levi's jeans, and blue Zephyr T-shirts, however, the Z-Boys turned heads at the event even before competition began. In the "freestyle" competition in particular, which took place on a flat stretch of pavement somewhat like the ice rink of figure skating, Zephyr team member Jay Adams stunned the public with an idiosyncratically expressive display of twisting, spinning dance-like moves on his board. Afterward, just like that, skateboarding was reborn.

By the late summer of 1977 the Z-Boy style had filtered out to Tom Fallon's distant suburb of Cucamonga, causing him mild bemusement despite his familiarity with the surf life through his sons. Kids all across Southern California, even as far away as Cucamonga, adopted the Z-Boy attitude and style: Vans sneakers, Hang Ten shirts, long feathered hair, peach-fuzz facial hair, and so on. Local skaters would even, a few months later at the end of 1977, be able to hobnob with their heroes in Upland, just one town over from Cucamonga. The Upland Pipeline, one of the first great skateboard parks in California, became home to a generation of suburban skaters and host to occasional appearances by actual Zephyr team members.

Had he been paying attention, Tom Wolfe may have appreciated the Z-Boys' uniquely syncretic character, if not their particular aesthetic. In a long essay called "The Kandy-Kolored Tangerine-Flake Streamline Baby," which Wolfe had written for *Esquire* back in 1963, he had chronicled the particularly Californian penchant for cross-pollinating influences—the local sunshine, beach culture, street chic, Latin gangs, and so on—in the service of spicing up one of the region's dominant cultural preoccupations: working on and driving cars. Among the established cultural influences on the Z-Boys were the wild colors and flash of the hot-rodders, low-riders, van fetishists, and vehicle customizers who proliferated around Southern California at the time. The team also added elements from their own cultural preoccupations: the long and tousled hair of rock heroes like

Led Zeppelin and Black Sabbath, the casualness of California beach design, the tattoos and street looks adapted from gang graffiti, and so on. All of this is a long way of relaying the fact that the effect of the Z-Boys was greater than its parts. In sum, the group created a new model of how to be a kid in Southern California in the 1970s.

As the Z-Boys' influence grew, so did their confidence, and their skill and daring in maneuvering on banked surfaces advanced. In the summer of 1977 the Z-Boys suddenly got an extra nudge in their ongoing development from the weather. A long drought in Southern California that summer had desiccated the landscape and made water scarce, which in turn led to an intriguing discovery.[12] Because of tight local restrictions on water use, many local residents had been forced to empty out their private swimming pools. To the Z-Boys these emptied structures would make a natural locus for their experiments. All that summer, whenever anyone heard rumor of a pool, the Z-Boys sneaked in, drained any excess water if necessary, and, until someone chased them away (or it grew too dark), skated the pool's banks.

Eventually, skateboarding enthusiasts and observers would look back at the summer of 1977 and view the guerrilla pool skating of the Z-Boys as the birth of what came to be known as "vertical skating." The exact tale of the birth of the phenomenon went something like this: As summer turned subtly to fall across the region, one day during a skating session at a pool in Santa Monica (which was so popular it was nicknamed "the Dogbowl"), a Z-Boy named Tony Alva invented a stunning new maneuver. While skating the banked edge of a pool, Alva cleared the lip at the top of the side of the pool with his board and, spinning back around in a full 180-degree circle, landed back on the wall of the pool and continued skating. This was the sport's very first aerial trick and the launching point, literally and figuratively, for everything that would come—in skateboarding, in snowboarding, in wakeboarding, skiing, rollerblading, and so on. Not only had the Z-Boys, in the space of just three years, completely revived and revolutionized skateboarding, but in the drought of 1977 they laid the foundation for a whole range of daring "extreme" sports that would proliferate in the years ahead around the world.

THIRTEEN

The Right Stuff

If you want to grow old as a pilot, you've got
to know when to push it, and when to back off.

—Chuck Yeager

I was just hoping somebody got the license number.

—Steve Yeager, Chuck Yeager's cousin, after being flattened in a play at the plate by Pittsburgh's Dave Parker in August 1977

Despite the Dodgers' recent struggles, in August it became clear that, barring some unexpected catastrophe, the Dodgers would at least limp into the playoffs as winners of the Western Division in the National League. On August 16, with just forty-three games remaining in the season, the Dodgers stood atop the Western Division by eleven games over the second-place Reds, who were themselves struggling. Now, Lasorda realized, he needed to balance the urge to push his Dodgers to win games against his desire to be sure that his players were rested and ready for October. That is, as the playoffs loomed, Tom Lasorda's main concern was Mission Readiness.

Chief among the Dodger manager's concerns was, of course, Steve Garvey's slump. No matter how long he pondered the options, he saw precious few ways to salvage the situation if Garvey didn't come around. But then Lasorda knew Garvey. The slump would fade, and Mr. Consistency, Lasorda knew, would eventually start hitting again.

Beyond Garvey Lasorda was plenty worried. Something was generally off with the Dodgers. Perhaps Sparky Anderson had been right. The hungry, fired-up clubhouse he had helped create in December had faded to something much more tepid. Instead of playing like the explosive unit they were in April, May, and June, his boys had lost their pop.

As if his team's decaying energy wasn't enough, at the end of August Lasorda had another concern. *What in holy hell,* he wondered, *was he going to do with Steve Yeager?* The starting catcher was a compelling character on the Dodgers and a generally unappreciated factor in the team's success ever since he had become their regular catcher in 1974. In 1977 Yeager was considered by many to be as good behind the plate as perennial All-Star (and future Hall of Famer) Johnny Bench. Quick, strong-armed, and sure, Yeager was, according to Lou Brock, the premier base stealer of the era, the "best-throwing catcher in the game."[1] Famously, one of Yeager's throws to second base was clocked arriving at ninety-four miles per hour. Twice during his career Yeager would lead the league in the percentage of base runners he caught stealing, and overall he would throw out a respectable 38 percent of base stealers. Yeager was also, in many ways, the quintessential 1970s-era Dodger. Born in Huntington, West Virginia, Yeager had been drafted out of high school in 1967 as a top athlete who had lettered in three sports. Yeager developed through the team's farm system alongside the vaunted draft class of 1968. When he arrived in Los Angeles for his first call-up in 1972, he still had the vaguely square look of a small-town boy—dated sideburns, too short haircut, unfashionably oversize glasses, a vague deer-in-headlights stare. By 1977, however, in his fourth season as the Dodgers' regular catcher, Yeager was a far cry from his rookie self. Part of this might have been genetic predisposition. Steve Yeager is the cousin of the highly decorated American test pilot Chuck Yeager, the first man to break the sound barrier in 1947 and a noted tough customer. (Not only did Chuck Yeager break the sound barrier, but he do so with two painful broken ribs from a recent horse-riding accident.) Chuck Yeager was also a natural leader, serving as the founding commandant of the U.S. Air Force's Aerospace Research Pilot School, which produced astronauts for the National Aeronautics and Space Administration (NASA) and the U.S. Air Force.[2]

Steve Yeager's own astronaut-like bravado manifested in several ways. By 1977 he had ditched the geeky glasses, grown out a full head of wavy hair, let the California sun tan his face to an appealingly weathered look, and taken on the lifestyle of an L.A. playboy. As of 1976 Yeager had emerged as a major social figure on the team, well known for late-night carousing at the bars and music clubs of his adopted city.[3] So notorious had his exploits become that a divorce from Brenda, his wife of eight years, was followed by a marquee wedding to local rock musician Gloria Giaone. The wedding would be a noted social event in the city—occurring on the steps of city hall with Tom Bradley in attendance.[4]

In the mid-1970s Steve Yeager became particularly valuable to the Dodgers because of his on-field leadership. He was a master at managing the game from his position and at handling both inexperienced pitchers and world-weary veterans. For instance, Yeager had solved a particular problem on the Dodgers in 1977 when Lasorda decided to use knuckleballer Charlie Hough as his closing reliever. When Hough pitched Yeager made use of an oversize catcher's mitt, and, putting practicality over comfort, he turned his hand around to catch the ball with his palm facing upward instead of in the more customary upright position. In this way Yeager minimized the number of wild pitches that you'd expect from a knuckle-ball reliever.

Even beyond his innovative and dynamic backstop play, it was what Yeager did in 1976, after a freakish accident nearly took his life, that perhaps gives the best sense of the catcher's character. On September 6, 1976, as the Dodgers played out the last month of another disappointing season, Yeager stood in the on-deck circle in a game against the San Diego Padres. With the Dodgers leading 3–0, Bill Russell was at bat against junk-ball pitcher Randy "Junkman" Jones. When the shortstop got a piece of one of Jones's pitches, his bat shattered, sending debris flying in the direction of the on-deck circle. Yeager fell, stricken, and when Dodger trainer Bill Buhler reached the catcher he found a piece of bat the size of a small dagger jutting from his neck. Buhler dared not dig around the area where the catcher's jugular vein, windpipe, esophagus, Adam's apple, and crucial nerves were located. Instead, Yeager was rushed to the hospital, where he underwent ninety-eight minutes of surgery and had nine pieces of wood removed from the region. The surgeon afterward, in examining the recovering catcher, touched a spot on Yeager's neck and said if the wood had struck here, he would have had thirty seconds to live. Yeager would not play for the Dodgers again in 1976, and, even after he seemed fully recovered, there was concern, because of lingering damage and sensitivity to his neck area, about his suiting up again. After all, catchers' necks are vulnerable to foul tips and other blows, and he couldn't risk any further damage to the area. But Yeager was not one to be kept back—he came up with an idea and brought it to the team's equipment manager, Bill Mueller.[5] Together they invented a catcher's throat protector, sometimes dubbed the "King Tut," which would give Yeager some measure of security. At least Yeager's career seemed secure until the daredevil catcher had Tom Lasorda tearing his hair out all over again.

People have, through the years, compared baseball to any number of other activities. Philip Roth compared it to writing, all but attributing his success as a writer to his love for baseball. Jackie Robinson said baseball is like a poker game: "Nobody wants to quit when he's losing, and nobody wants you to quit when you're ahead."[6] Wes Westrum, a Giants catcher in their years prior to leaving New York, said baseball is like church. "Many attend," he explained, "but few understand." Ty Cobb said baseball was "not unlike war." Joe Garagiola, in his book *Baseball Is a Funny Game*, called the sport a "drama with an endless run and an ever-changing cast." And Walter O'Malley, the Dodgers' owner up until 1977, said, "Baseball isn't a business, it's more like a disease."[7]

In the figure of Steve Yeager we can perhaps see that baseball has another more distant analogue: astronautics. Look at it this way: The long baseball season is a procession of dull, empty stretches broken by sudden bursts of activity. The trick to playing, or managing, or even rooting for a baseball team through the season is knowing, as astronauts do, when to pour it on, how to scan the horizon or the deep empty reaches of space and know when to turn on the rocket boosters. Baseball players and astronauts face similar work conditions. Each of them, when they are at the top reaches of their profession, maintain themselves in the peak condition needed to maintain a poised readiness. They are able to wait and to watch and to keep their mental faculties and physical bodies sharp enough to perform, over and over, difficult, risky, and complex tasks. Perhaps because of this dichotomy in activity—the need for quiet readiness, punctuated by quick, risky, often violent motion and activity—the participants of these two pastimes have another thing in common. In each field participants operate under an unspoken honor code of bravery, silence, and machismo. Alan Shepard's famous prayer, said to have been created on the spot just before his first mission into space, gives a good sense of the attitude of anyone daring and brave enough to do what astronauts and ballplayers are paid to do: "Please, dear God, don't let me fuck up."

Having in common some genetics, Steve Yeager must have had something of his cousin Chuck's attitude about the dangerous risks of each of their chosen professions. The way Tom Wolfe had explained the character of test pilots and astronauts, in his *Rolling Stone* articles of 1973, is revealing. "The main thing to know," Wolfe wrote, using the voice of an imaginary collective astronaut—a kind of space-traveling Greek chorus, if you will—"is that the capsule right now is filled up with three colossal egos. Ti*tan*ic egos, one might say, but of a type you've probably never known in your life . . . because it is extremely doubtful that you have ever been involved in a particular competition known at *The Right Stuff*." The Right Stuff, or a kind of fearless, surpassingly reckless, adventurous spirit imbued with almost endless doses of strong ego, was what space travel was all about, according to Wolfe. "It's a vast competition," he continued in the collective astronaut voice,

> [and] the main thing to know about an astronaut, if you want to understand his psychology, is not that he's going into space but that he is a flyer and has been in that game for fifteen or twenty years. It's like a huge and very complex pyramid, miles high, and the idea is to prove at every foot of the way up that pyramid that you are one of the elected and anointed ones who have *the right stuff* and can move ever higher and even—ultimately, God willing, one day—that you might be able to join that very special few at the very top, that elite who truly have the capacity to bring tears to men's eyes, the very Brotherhood of the Right Stuff itself.[8]

To Wolfe, Chuck Yeager, who had been the first pilot to break the sound barrier, was the epitome of the Right Stuff. It was this very American characteristic that made it possible for President John F. Kennedy to look to the skies and tell a crowd gathered at Rice University, with a certain kind of swagger, "We choose to go to the moon." That America swagger, after all, was very recognizable to a 1960s public used to seeing countless westerns—like *Rawhide*, *Maverick*, *Gunsmoke*, *Rio Bravo*, *The Alamo*, *How the West Was Won*—on television and on the silver screen. "Up to the time of Kennedy's death in 1963," Wolfe continued, "the space program was a cowboy operation. We were riding hell for leather to try to catch up with the Russians. To find out if there were Indians over the next hill, what you did was ride at full gallop over the next hill. That way you were *sure* to find out; there was no time to be fooling around with scouting reports." America's blind bravado, ironically, was very nearly the downfall of the space program before it even got off the ground. While Kennedy still lived, in fact, NASA was called before the President's Science Advisory Committee to present its plans for going ahead with the first manned American space flight. The USSR had put Yuri Gagarin into orbit in April 1961, and the United States hoped to put Alan Shepard into space immediately afterward, but the program was undeveloped at best, with little significant test data and a lot of unanswered questions. The gathered scientists were shocked, telling Kennedy it would be suicide to go forward with the current plan. "But Kennedy, God bless him," wrote Tom Wolfe in the collective voice of the astronauts, "told us to go ahead if we felt we could do it. Our reaction was: Well, *there's one way to find out!* It was cowboy stuff . . . and it was a beautiful time. . . . Everybody who came close to the program in those days—we can't think of any exceptions—got caught up in the mystique of the Right Stuff."[9]

As a rule ballplayers, being young men in prime condition and in the peak of life, are prone to playing with the reckless abandon of cowboy astronauts. What did such men have to fear, after all? They had their whole lives, all their playing careers, ahead of them. Yeager, of course, had already learned—in 1976—how quickly a player's career could come to a fluke end. But then the catcher, with his macho bravura, had promptly forgotten this lesson. On a bus during spring training before the start of the 1977 season, Yeager talked with a reporter about his love for another even more physical sport. "Love football," Yeager said. "Love that contact. Sometimes I regret not taking one of all those scholarship offers and playing football in college. I was a quarterback. I could throw the ball 70 yards. . . . There's nothing like the sound of two bodies cracking together."[10] Yeager then spoke of the "contact men" that he most respected around the league: Pete Rose, Bob Watson of the Houston Astros, and, as fate would have it, the massive outfielder Dave Parker of the Pittsburgh Pirates.

On August 24, 1977, ironically thanks to Dave Parker, Steve Yeager would again learn a lesson about his own human fragility. He would also make a play that, arguably, staunched the team's recent bleeding and set them up to make a final push for the pennant.

In the eighth inning of a tight game against a tough Pirates team, on a Wednesday-night game in Pittsburgh on the day after the Dodgers had just lost two straight to the Cardinals in St. Louis, the Pirates' star outfielder Dave Parker stood on second base with the score tied at 1–1. On the mound Tommy John got set to face Al Oliver, a dangerous hitter. In the stands at Three Rivers Stadium, twenty thousand fans roared for their team. John threw his pitch, and the Pirates' outfielder laced a line drive to right field for a base hit. Parker, who had good speed despite his size, did not hesitate, rounding third base and heading for home. After fielding Oliver's hit Dodger right fielder Reggie Smith's throw was right on line, if a bit short, bouncing twice before it reached home plate. To make the tag Yeager had to take a step forward to catch the ball and then turn to face the onrushing Parker. That step made all the difference. Unable to set himself, Yeager was sent flying backward, head over tail, by Parker's headfirst lunge at the plate. Parker rolled over the top of the catcher like a train gone off the tracks, but in the aftermath it was Yeager who untangled himself and got up first. He held up the baseball to show the umpire Parker was out, and then he collapsed back down onto the plate as manager Lasorda and the Dodgers' team trainer came to his aid.

After the game Lasorda was of two minds. On the one hand, old

Tom loved to see this kind of grit from one of his boys. He couldn't help but have a special fondness for ballplayers who put it all on the line for the good of the team, for players who exhibited his own idea of the "Right Stuff": Garvey, for example, who had not missed a game in more than three seasons; Reggie Smith, who played through all kinds of injuries; and of course Yeager, who thought nothing of taking a bullet for his teammates.

Because of Yeager's play at the plate, the Dodgers remained tied with the Pirates and went on to win, in ten innings, 2–1. "To hold onto that ball," Lasorda gushed afterward, even as the rattled Yeager was being examined on the training table, "called for some kind of determination, for some kind of outstanding play."[11] At the same time, Lasorda thought, the Dodgers were likely headed to the playoffs and, possibly, after that the World Series. He well knew he could ill-afford to lose such a valuable cog as Yeager.

When Yeager woke up the next day stiff, sore, and unable to play, Lasorda faced an immediate dilemma. If he put his catcher on the disabled list, then Yeager would not be allowed on the Dodgers' playoff roster because he would not be considered "active" on the prescribed cutoff day of August 31. At the same time, leaving Yeager on the roster while he could not play—for however long he could not play—left the team shorthanded. After a few days of deliberation, Lasorda gambled. He kept Yeager on the active roster and inserted into the lineup the team's only remaining option at the position, thirty-one-year-old career backup catcher Johnny Oates. It was a major risk. If Oates got injured, Lasorda had only two emergency backups with any catching experience of any kind: thirty-nine-year-old Manny Mota, who had played a few games at the position for the Pirates nearly fifteen season years earlier, and the thirty-five-year-old current Dodger bench warmer Boog Powell, who had spent time behind the plate in high school.

The uncertainties and dilemmas continued. As with any baseball team at the tail end of summer, minor aches and pains of all sorts riddled the clubhouse. The day after Yeager's flattening by Dave Parker, a sudden crisis afflicted the Dodgers' middle infield. Backup utility man Teddy Martinez, playing for Dave Lopes, who was sitting out his fifth straight game with a stiff neck, was knocked down by a Pirate sliding into second base. Martinez left the game, the trainer fearing it was a season-ending ligament tear. And it was; Martinez would not play again in 1977. Rick Monday's back problems continued to limit his playing time and to damage his effectiveness when he did play. This as Reggie Smith struggled with a sore knee, Dusty Baker showed worrisome signs of trouble with his legs, Charlie Hough struggled to pitch with any consistent effectiveness, and so on down the lineup.

Then there was the sporadic thorn in Lasorda's side, Don Sutton. As the 1977 season wore on, Lasorda realized that he and Sutton simply were destined never to get along. "I always figure twelve players on the team are going to love the manager," he said several years later, perhaps remembering his experiences with Sutton, "twelve players are going to hate the manager, and the twenty-fifth player is going to have a gun loaded with three bullets and three blanks."[12] On the 1977 Dodgers Sutton was Lasorda's half-loaded gun. And at the end of August, much to Lasorda's chagrin, the gun suddenly seemed fully unloaded. Whereas the veteran pitcher had been, around the time of the All-Star Game, in the midst of one of the best seasons of his career, with ten wins against just three losses and an ERA of just 2.47, in the weeks that followed he suddenly couldn't buy a win.

After Sutton's victory on July 4 someone had pointed out to him that he had recorded 186 lifetime victories as a Los Angeles Dodger, just one shy of the number of wins Don Drysdale had recorded as a Dodger in L.A. Sutton's next win would thus tie him as the all-time wins leader of the Los Angeles Dodgers. On July 9, in a close game against the San Diego Padres in front of a crowd of nearly forty thousand at Dodger Stadium, Sutton pitched magnificently for nine innings, scattering five Padre hits while matching his career high for strikeouts with twelve and holding his opponents to just one run, only to see the team lose 2–1 when Charlie Hough gave up a run in the tenth inning. In the fifth inning of the game, an incident took place that may, or may not, have rankled Sutton. While people around the league had long suspected that Sutton occasionally employed an altered ball—either by marking it with some sort of tool, which was the source of his nickname, "Black & Decker," or by using a petroleum product to create a sort of "spitball"—by 1977 the idea had become a kind of ongoing psychological battle. That is,

Sutton often used the appearance of cheating to get in the head of opposing hitters, while opposing teams accused Sutton of cheating as a way of getting him off his rhythm. Al Dark, the Padres' manager, did just that, hoping to disrupt the pitcher in the midst of a tight game. Whether Sutton was rankled this time, or perhaps had pushed himself too hard to win this game, the eventual loss was the first of a long, tough string for the pitcher.

Over the next month Sutton grew increasingly ineffective. On July 14 Sutton lost a close game, 4–3, against the Astros. In his first start after the All-Star Game, on July 23 against the Expos, he lost 6–4. After a no-decision against the Phillies on July 27, Sutton had the worst outing of the season on August 1, giving up nine hits and six runs in five and two-thirds innings against the lowly New York Mets. And on August 12 Sutton blew a sure win by giving up four runs in the top of the ninth and losing to the Braves at home, 5–2. By mid-August Sutton's amazing season had all but collapsed, his record falling to 10-7 and his ERA gaining an entire run in just six weeks.

Not that there weren't bright spots for the Dodgers in August, hidden behind the scrim of slump and injury that had defined the past month. Plenty of his Dodger players, Lasorda had to acknowledge, were playing their hearts out. Tommy John, for instance, has quietly won sixteen games, against just five losses, while lowering his ERA to 2.57. The starting pitching in general, in fact, was solid—effectively keeping the team in the playoff hunt despite the rest of the team's struggles. Rick Rhoden won his sixteenth game on August 31. Doug Rau had thus far won thirteen games (against just five losses). And Burt Hooton, though he'd hit some rough spots,[13] had recorded a strong ERA of 2.71.

Taken on the whole the team's lineup had had a solid season at the plate despite the recent struggles. Cey had cooled some after his fast start, but he had twenty-four home runs and was fast closing in on one hundred RBIs. Reggie Smith was batting a solid .313 and had twenty-five home runs. Dusty Baker had managed twenty home runs. And both Russell and Lopes had been solid, contributing batting averages over .280 and solid play in the middle infield. And because it was the Dodger Way to think down the road to the future, Lasorda could take solace in the fact that the wider organization was thriving. Three of the team's five Minor League affiliates were in first place in their leagues. On the team's AAA franchise, the Albuquerque Dukes, several obvious prospects—Pedro Guerrero, Rafael Landestoy, Ron Washington, Rick Sutcliffe, and Dave Stewart—were waiting in the wings. Hank Webb, while not spectacular, had pitched well enough that the Dodgers were considering calling him up to Los Angeles in September. And Claude Westmoreland, who had not made the team in spring training, attracted some attention in Albuquerque by setting a new Minor League record by homering in seven straight games. With the team shorthanded after losing Teddy Martinez, the Dodgers' front office might have briefly pondered bringing Westmoreland up, but since he would have been a major liability in the field, it never happened.

Despite the continuing concerns the future was still bright for the Dodgers, as was its present. Lasorda had no way of knowing it, but as August wound down the seeds of a final team turnaround were being sown by an unusual managerial move. On August 27 the Dodgers announced the signing of a wiry forty-one-year-old former Major League outfielder who had been playing in the Mexican League for the past three years. Originally from Venezuela, Vic Davalillo was a left-handed contact hitter with decent speed, who had rarely struck out in thirteen seasons spent with the Indians, Angels, Cardinals, Pirates, and A's. The signing gave the Dodgers an intriguing one-two punch off their bench, the ageless Davalillo batting from the left side of the plate and Manny Mota, who in August 1977 was batting nearly .400 (and had an on-base percentage over .500), batting from the right side. Over the last month of the season, Davalillo would bat a solid .313 (fifteen for forty-eight) while pinch-hitting and filling in ably at the team's trouble spot, center field.

And there was more encouraging news to come. On August 28 Steve Garvey finally let loose at the plate. It was a stunning turnaround. In a convincing 11–0 win over the Cardinals, Garvey went five for five, collected fourteen total bases, scored five of the team's eleven runs, and knocked in five runs. "It's great to be back," Garvey told reporters after the game. "A day like today has a tendency to make you forget any hard time the last couple of months."[14] Incidentally, thanks to Garvey, on August 28 Don Sutton finally got his 12th win on the season and his 188th as a Dodger. He had at last moved past Drysdale into first place on the all-time Los Angeles Dodgers wins list.

The next day, as if confirming Garvey's, and the team's, reemergence, while the Dodgers first baseman batted in the first inning of a game against the Cubs, the notorious Kissing Bandit, Morganna, rushed home plate. Garvey at first hid behind the umpire, but then allowed her to kiss him on the check before she was ushered away by stadium police. The Dodgers got the win in the game, their fourth straight, and just like that the Dodgers were back in business. Suddenly, they seemed as loosey-goosey, and deadly effective, as they had been in April. On August 30 during the team's regular "Kangaroo Court" session—a regular team gathering designed to allow players to blow off some steam by pointing out each other's foibles and mistakes—word came that Don Sutton had been fined five hundred dollars for leaving the team recently for two days to do color commentary at the Little League World Series in Williamsport, Pennsylvania. When Lasorda asked Sutton to step to the center of the clubhouse, the pitcher presented his manager with a meringue pie in the face—all to the merriment of his teammates. "Lasorda was my defense counsel," Sutton explained later, "and I wanted to show him what I thought of the job he had done."[15] Lasorda reportedly took the pie incident well, indicating that perhaps the event had been prearranged beforehand as a way of releasing some of the team's recent tension.

The good vibes continued growing. Before the game on August 31 the team rejoiced when Tommy John announced to his teammates the birth of his second child, a son named Thomas Edward Jr. Also that day news would come down that Mayor Bradley, in a move meant to honor the now retired former owner-president of the Dodgers, had proposed to the city council to rename Stadium Way O'Malley Way.[16] Then, perhaps most important, on August 31 Steve Yeager started the Dodgers game against the Cubs after sitting out for a week. That he would go two for four and score a run in the 5–0 win over Chicago was a bonus, indicating that Lasorda had survived his gamble. Steve Garvey, meanwhile, had one hit and an

RBI, continuing his recovery from his slump. Vic Davalillo, filling in for the still struggling Rick Monday, had three hits and scored two runs, and Manny Mota got a crucial pinch hit in the eighth inning of the game. The multiarmed octopus of Sutton's imagination had returned.

After the game the Dodgers took their final step toward the playoffs by ending their Boog Powell experiment. The beefy Powell, who had not contributed the power that the Dodgers hoped for in 1977, would end his season, and his Major League career, in Los Angeles without collecting a single extra-base hit. On September 1, while the expanded roster opened the door to a host of hopeful young players—including Webb, Landestoy, Ron Washington, Jeffrey Leonard, Bobby Castillo, and Lance Rautzhan—to join the team, Powell was released. On September 9, after Tommy John got his fourth win against the Reds on the season, and his eighteenth overall, the Dodgers stood thirteen and a half games atop the Western Division. Their magic number was now just eight with twenty-one games left to play. Even Johnny Bench could read the writing on the wall. "To be realistic," said the Reds' star catcher, "we don't have much of a chance. We're due for a comeback, but it's probably too late."[17] On September 20 the team clinched the pennant on another stellar pitching performance by Tommy John—this time his nineteenth win on the season—and a rare home run by Rick Monday, his fourteenth of the season. After the game, in a jubilant clubhouse, Tom Lasorda hugged and thanked everyone for their effort, lavishing particular praise on his thirty-four-year-old left-hander, whom he had decided to name as his opening starting in the playoffs. At a lull in the celebration Lasorda moved to the center of the clubhouse and said, "I want to congratulate all of you. It's been an honor to be your manager."[18]

A few days later, on September 22, Lasorda turned fifty. At the team party that night, the second in three days, the Dodger manager stood up and spoke, saying that the pennant had been a great birthday present, but the lavish party funded by the team's Kangaroo Court money was not so bad either.

FOURTEEN

Gonna Fly Now

> Ah come on, Adrian, it's true. I was nobody. But that don't matter either, you know? 'Cause I was thinkin', it really don't matter if I lose this fight. It really don't matter if this guy opens my head, either. 'Cause all I wanna do is go the distance.
>
> —Rocky Balboa

The divisional playoff system in Major League Baseball was, in 1977, still a relatively recent invention and a somewhat odd event. On the one hand, these playoffs—established in 1969 and officially called the League Championships Series (LCS)—felt somewhat trivial, an unwanted annoyance. After all, they weren't the World Series, which had a history stretching back, in some form or another, more than one hundred years.[1] By the 1970s the World Series was a spectacle and a life-changing event—for those who played in it, of course, but also for even casual fans of the game who often demarcated the moments of their lives based on when their home team last won a Series. But the League Championship Series was much more difficult to grasp and get behind.

The World Series was where heroes were created and where images of athletic prowess became part of the national imagination. The LCS, on the other hand, seemed like a formality, something you had to swallow in order to get to the main course. "If there really was such a thing as Tom Lasorda's big Dodger in the sky, he would never have created a playoff," wrote one L.A. sports columnist who fretted about the team's chances in the LCS in 1977. The writer thought it was a "little sad for Los Angeles" since its dream of a season was likely about to end at the hands of the powerful Philadelphia Phillies, who had clinched the Eastern Division title on September 27. "The Dodgers didn't quite do their 3 million at the gate, but they did just about everything else—first out of the gate, first all the way in the National West, first to clinch, first in attendance, first in pitching, first in double plays, first in Chinese dinners to go, first in victory parties, first in center fielders hanging upside down and first in blue this, blue that and big blue adjectives from the immortal Bill Russell to the incomparable Davey Lopes. . . . But so short, so bitterly sweet, and whatta way to go."[2]

Despite the seeming pro forma quality of the League Championship Series, however, players did not approach the games as an afterthought. "There's more pressure on you in the playoffs than in the World Series," said pitcher Tommy John some years after his playing career. Toward the end of September, when Tom Lasorda announced that John would receive the honor of starting the Dodgers' first playoff game in 1977 in Philadelphia, the veteran left-hander took a deep breath and tried to prepare himself. "If you lose in the playoffs, that's all they remember about your season, no matter how good it was. The World Series is the gravy you enjoy after getting by the playoffs. There's more press, more attention, and every pitch gets magnified. No matter how much you try to prepare yourself for it, you can't fully appreciate what it's like pitching for the first time in your first playoffs."[3]

By 1977 the unique quality of the League Championship Series meant that the psychological battle to gain an edge, inspire your own players, fluster your opponents, and get public sentiment behind you often began weeks in advance. On September 24, just four days after the Dodgers clinched a spot in the playoffs as sure winners of the National League's Western Division, the Dodgers' Don Sutton assessed the team's chances against the Phillies. While conceding that Steve Carlton, Philadelphia's ace, was the best pitcher on either team, he all but dismissed the rest. "Overall their [pitching staff] doesn't match up to ours," he said. "And you can also legitimately say that on the basis of this year alone [Tommy] John has been Carlton's equal."[4] Sutton went on: "[Our] team has more pitching depth, better defense, more guys capable of delivering offensively and a more consistent offense. I don't mean to take anything away from the Philadelphia offense, but as for big guns you're really only talking about Greg Luzinski and Mike Schmidt. They'll have to hit a lot of solo home runs to beat us. By contrast, we have a handful of guys who can break it open with one swing. I think we have an advantage in offense as well as in pitching. It's just awfully tough to stop us completely."[5]

The Phillies were listening to Sutton, intently as it happened. While Lasorda's hungry young players thought of themselves as a team of destiny, the Phillies, who hailed from a struggling, older, and more overburdened eastern city desperate for a winner—Philadelphia—were just hungry. Like Rocky Balboa, the fictional boxer from the gritty streets of Philadelphia who won the hearts of movie audiences in the summer of 1976, this Phillies squad had the aura of a people's team. Loaded with the unhittable ace Steve Carlton, a nearly unhittable bullpen, dangerous sluggers like Greg Luzinski and Mike Schmidt, and speedy base stealers like Greg Maddux, Larry Bowa, and Bake McBride, the Phillies had won 101 games (compared to the Dodgers' 98) in the tough National League East. After Sutton's comments had been fully digested by the team, the Phillies began deploying their own artillery to fight the battle of words.

On October 2 Los Angeles papers led with the news that the Phillies were telling one and all how happy they were to be facing the Dodgers in the playoffs, as opposed to the Cincinnati Reds. The Reds, after all, had dispatched the Phillies from the playoffs the previous season in three straight games. Adding to the shock of this pronouncement was a biblical tinge of betrayal. Phillies manager Danny Ozark, who for thirty-one years before his move to Philadelphia had been a player and coach in the Dodger system, gave his former team only token respect.[6] "They have their strengths and we have ours," he said. "They're not the toughest, because Cincinnati knocked the beans out of us. We haven't won a game in Cincinnati in, I think, nine games. We played .500 against the Dodgers this year. So if you ask me which I'd rather play again, I'll take the .500 club."[7]

The psychological war was under way. The comments by Ozark, which were echoed by several of the team's players, were deemed unacceptably dismissive by Lasorda and quickly found their way to the Dodgers' clubhouse bulletin board. With a week still left in the regular season, various Dodgers, tired of hearing nothing but Reds, Reds, Reds despite all that they had accomplished this season, had murder on their breath. They were ready for the battle of their lives.

Frank Sinatra, who sang the national anthem at the Dodgers' home opener back in April, threw out the first pitch of the first game of the National League Championship at Dodger Stadium on October 4. It was nearly the prettiest pitch thrown from the home side all night. Thirty-four-year-old starter Tommy John, who was making the first postseason appearance of his long career, struggled with nerves from the start, giving up four runs off four hits and three walks before getting pulled in favor of Mike Garman in the fifth inning. That inning was particularly painful, as the normally composed John began by hitting the opposing pitcher, Steve Carlton, with a pitch before surrendering two Phillies runs that gave the team a 4–0 lead. Adding to John's woes was a lack of support in the field—thanks to two errors by Bill Russell, all four of the runs he gave up were unearned. And while the Dodger battery would rally, tying the game 5–5 in the seventh on a Ron Cey grand slam, the team ultimately let the victory slip away when reliever Elias Sosa gave up two runs in the top of the ninth.

So much for murder on their breath. "That wasn't us out there tonight," said an angry Steve Yeager after the game. "I don't know who the hell it was, but it wasn't us." Other players agreed that the occasion had done them in. "I think you are a little more nervous about a game like this," said Steve Garvey, "because it's something you're not in all the time. We hadn't been in it since '74."[8] The Phillies, however, were brimming over with confidence after the game. "The Dodgers have to beat us tomorrow," said Greg Luzinski, Philadelphia's burly outfielder who looked more like a meatpacker than a Major Leaguer, "or as far as I'm concerned, it's all over. They'll have to win three in our ballpark, where we've played .750 ball. . . .[9] We have a different attitude [than last year]. . . . [W]e're hungrier." Phillies third baseman Mike Schmidt, meanwhile, agreed: "Last year we had a bunch of young guys trying to achieve a goal. We just didn't have enough drive left at the end to beat the Reds. Now we feel we're going to win the championship . . . that someone is going to have to take it away from us."[10]

For a day hearts across Los Angeles raced. At a glance the Dodgers already looked beaten. They seemed to have little of the Phillies' hunger and bite. After their sloppy play in Game One, the Dodgers looked like Little Leaguers playing against a team of full-grown men. Only Tommy Lasorda, the eternal scrapper, optimist, and native of a Philadelphia suburb, seemed unaffected by recent events. "You still got to win three games to win the playoffs," Lasorda said after the loss, "and they won only one. Like the guy said, one flatulation does not make a windstorm. And one game doesn't win the playoffs."[11] Bold words, to be sure, but Lasorda meant what he said. More important, he had a plan to start the windstorm.

Considering how he had acted throughout the 1977 season, it was inevitable that Lasorda would take a can't-fail attitude going into Game Two of the League Championship Series. Though he had been in the league and around the Dodgers for the better part of three decades, and had experienced all the highs and lows of the baseball life, he was still in essence a rookie manager. He was just happy to be here, after all, and certain that he would find a way to steer his beloved team to its final goal. He saw no reason he should contemplate losing or allow any doubts to creep into his thoughts. He was also was willing to try anything to get results. In his office after Game One's tough loss, therefore, Lasorda weighed his options.

Ten hours after Game One, the inner areas of Dodger Stadium were all but empty—except for a lingering Lasorda, a couple of sportswriters, a cleaning crew, and, surprisingly, Bill Russell. The shortstop, who was widely considered the goat of the game because of his two critical errors, stopped by Lasorda's office before leaving and spoke to the gathered writers and his manager. "I'll take you all out to dinner," Russell glumly joked. "My money from Vegas should be here any minute. The gamblers have got to pay me a bundle for this one." Lasorda looked at his young shortstop. He knew he could have taken a stern approach, as Alston might have. He could have yelled and ranted and told Russell his teammates expected more of him, but something, some slight inkling, told him that might be exactly the wrong approach to take this time. Lasorda knew his boys. He knew they could play better than they did. He knew this not only from his own experience, but because of a letter he had just received from a prominent fan from back east. "Dear Mr. Lasorta [*sic*]," the letter began, "I feel that I know you personally as I have been an ardent Dodger fan for 30 years." That would have been 1947, the year that Jackie Robinson first broke into the league. "Please win the playoffs and go into the World Series. . . . I am 79 years old and this may be the last opportunity to see my Dodgers in a Series. Please give the team my love and devotion. I shall be listening and watching you on TV every game. Sincerely, Lillian Carter."[12]

Now, in the emptiness of Dodger Stadium, he wondered what it would take to get them out of their own heads, force them to lighten up, and just go out and do what they were capable of doing. Then it came to him. Lasorda gave Russell a slight nod and a smirk, and, in front of the reporters, he yelled at Russell, just a bit too loudly for the small confines of his office. "Cut that out. You can't feel bad. You got us here. Just a couple of tough breaks. So what? You'll be the hero again tomorrow. We'll all be feasting again tomorrow on the fruits of victory."[13] Russell departed with the slightest trace of a smile playing at the corner of his mouth. And Lasorda picked up the phone. He had a plan.

In the tense Dodger clubhouse before Game Two, Tom Lasorda entered and announced he had someone with him who wanted to say a few words. A short, slightly plump, balding middle-aged man stepped out from behind the manager and walked into the middle of the room. "Hello fellas," barked Don Rickles. "And thanks, Tommy Lasorda. Look at him." He pointed at the manager standing in the doorway and at his most prominent feature. "Look at that stomach. You think he's worried about you guys? No way. If you guys lose, he's gonna tie a cord around his neck and get work as a balloon." The clubhouse exploded in laughter, and Rickles began working the room like a pro, poking fun at Sutton, Garvey, Russell, Cey, and others each in turn. He told the team that if they lost tonight, they'd "all be waiting tables at the Sahara Hotel in Las Vegas tomorrow night." When he got to veteran Tommy John, he stopped and opened his eyes wide. "And look at T. J. He makes a million dollars a year, and he wears trick-or-treat underwear." When Dusty Baker, chuckling, stuck out his hand to shake Rickles's, the comic deadpanned: "Don't do anything. I'll give you my TV. Whatever you want." And on and on he went, until the clubhouse was as loose and noisy as any high school locker room.[14]

It was an odd moment, but the ploy worked. The Dodgers took Game Two, 7–1, on the strength of a complete-game performance by Sutton and a grand slam by Dusty Baker in the fourth inning. The team was solid in the field, showing none of the jitters of the day before, and the team's shortstop did redeem himself just as Lasorda said he would. "I just felt a lot more relaxed," said Bill Russell, who had collected two hits, scored two runs, and ended the game by turning an unassisted double play. "It wasn't like opening night in the playoffs. . . . I was booed a little (before the game) but I expected that. I deserved it the way I played last night. It was funny. I just laughed."[15]

In Game Three Los Angeles continued the fight. In front of a full rough and raucous Philadelphia crowd of nearly sixty-four thousand, the Dodgers kept pace through seven innings, fighting their way to a 3–3 tie. Notably, in the second inning, the Dodgers' first run came on a scrappy effort by Garvey, who scurried from first base on a long double by Dusty Baker—although Phillies faithful claimed then, and afterward, that the Dodger first baseman never touched home plate. In the bottom of the eighth, however, the Phillies seemed to get the upper hand at last, scoring two runs when the Dodgers, in shades of Game One, committed two errors. And with Gene Garber on the mound for the ninth, who had thus far shut down the Dodgers in two innings of relief, things were looking good for the home team. When Garber retired Dusty Baker on a grounder to third and Rick Monday on a grounder to second, the seventh and eighth straight batters he had retired on ground outs in the playoffs, the home crowd stood in anticipation of a victory. It was at this moment that Lasorda decided to gamble.

With two out in the top of the ninth and his team down 5–3, Lasorda called back his catcher, Steve Yeager, and sent up forty-year-old veteran Vic Davalillo to pinch-hit. It was perhaps the biggest call of the veteran ballplayer's life, but you wouldn't know it to look at the pinch hitter. Stepping up to the plate, Davalillo was calm. Years later he would reveal that he went to bat with a plan. Though Davalillo must have looked ancient to the young Phillies, he knew he still had good foot speed. As he approached the plate, he noted that the right side of the infield was playing well back to protect against any extra-base hits. Recognizing that "he was being given a gift," Davalillo "decided to take what was being given him . . . and dragged a perfect bunt past the mound."[16] He just beat out the throw from second baseman Ted Sizemore.

Next, Lasorda sent Manny Mota up next to pinch-hit for the pitcher, Lance Rautzhan. Mota hit a fly ball to left field that appeared to be the game ender, but the slow and clumsy left fielder, Greg Luzinski, booted the ball badly. Postgame commenters and armchair managers around the country would wonder, loudly and often, why Ozark had left Luzinski in the game, when it was a perfect moment for a defensive replacement. Ozark explained that yes, while he had done such a thing in certain key games throughout the years, in this game the situation was unique; Luzinski was due up third in the bottom half of the inning, and Ozark wanted to keep his slugger in the game just in case the Dodgers rallied to tie. Whatever the case, when the dust had settled, Mota stood at third and Davalillo had scored, bringing the score to 5–4. The crowd was suddenly silent, while the Dodger bench hooted and roared. Lopes came up next and smashed a hard grounder toward third that hit a seam in the Veterans Stadium artificial turf and bounced off Mike Schmidt's knee. Phillies shortstop Larry Bowa picked up the ball and fired it to first, but Lopes beat out the throw while Mota scored the tying run. Again, commenters at the game, and afterward, would suggest that the umpire at first blew the call—that Lopes was obviously out. Whatever the case a few moments later Lopes took second on an errant pickoff attempt by pitcher Gene Garber, and then Bill Russell singled up the middle, sending Lopes around to score the go-ahead run. In the bottom of the ninth, reliever Mike Garman held on to get the win, and the Dodgers were ahead in the series 2–1.

One night later, on a wet Saturday night at Veterans Stadium, the Dodgers clinched by outlasting the Phillies through several rain delays. The final score didn't matter much (it was 4–1; Baker hit another key home run and was unanimous choice for the series MVP), as this game was anticlimactic after the drama of Saturday. Afterward, as his players celebrated with laughter and showers of champagne, Lasorda was feisty. "All anyone has talked about during the playoffs," he shouted over the noise, "is that the Dodgers couldn't win here at the Vet. . . . Everyone in the country thought this Philadelphia club was better than ours. But we showed them on the field who's the greatest ballclub in the league."[17]

After the game the Dodgers celebrated their National League victory in true Philadelphian style, feasting on Italian food at the Lasorda family restaurant just outside the city into the wee hours of the morning. Meanwhile, over in the American League, the Yankees and Royals had tied up their series. Someone asked Lasorda again which of the two teams he would rather face in the Series. This time, perhaps mindful of the bulletin boards that doubtless were prominent in both clubhouses, he did not bite. "I asked God for all the help he could give me in this series," he said. "I'm not going to ask him for anything in that one."[18]

A day later the Big Dodger in the Sky gave Lasorda his answer, even if he hadn't asked for one. In Game Five of the American League Championships Series, the New York Yankees beat the Kansas City Royals in dramatic fashion. Having been shut down for the most part by the Royals' left-handed starter, Paul Splittorff, in the ninth they faced the Royals' ace pitcher Dennis Leonard, who had led the American League that season in wins (with twenty) but had seldom pitched relief during his career. Adding to the drama was a controversial move that had been taken by the Yankees' controversial manager, Billy Martin (of 10 Cent Beer Night fame). Before the game Martin had informed his erstwhile slugging star, outfielder Reggie Jackson, that he would not be starting the game. Part of this was (likely) the manager's lack of respect for Jackson, whom he thought was a malingerer and a liability in the field. But Martin also loved to play the odds, and he had decided that keeping the free-swinging Jackson from the Royals' starter, Paul Splittorff, who was well known for his ability to shut down the Yankees' stacked lineup of left-handed batters, would make the proud Jackson hungry to prove his manager wrong if called upon to pinch-hit late in the game.[19] Whatever the reason the ploy worked out splendidly for Martin, as Jackson got a key RBI single as a pinch hitter in the eighth against reliever Doug Bird. In the ninth inning, bolstered by the extra run they had scored in the eighth, the Yankees quickly knocked Leonard out of the game on their way to scoring three runs and securing a 5–3 victory.

So the Dodgers would face the Yankees in the 1977 World Series. The contentious, sniping, self-sabotaging New York Yankees. The Bronx Zoo, as they would be called in due time. The Yankees. The Dodgers' ancient archnemesis. The team that, between 1941 and 1963, had met the Dodgers eight times in baseball's championship and had emerged victorious in seven of those meetings. The New York Yankees. *Right from the frying pan*, as an Italian family like Tom Lasorda's would say, *and into the coals.*

There couldn't have been two more different teams in any World Series year than the Dodgers of Los Angeles and the Yankees of New York in 1977. The Dodgers, the team of Hollywood stars and young floppy-haired playboys, were America's team. Popular, prosperous, and sexy, the Los Angeles Dodgers represented the youthful side of America and all the country's potential for the future. They were situated in California, after all, under the sun and among the starlets of Hollywood. And they had even won over former Old Worlders like Frank Sinatra (born across the river from New York City in Hoboken, New Jersey) and Don Rickles (born in Queens). New York, on the other hand, was another world—a city of corrupt politics, brownouts, serial murderers, and a crumbling, uneven infrastructure. The Yankees represented the past, the old ways, while the Dodgers were the future. The Yankees were the increasingly money-focused, corporate face of baseball, while the Dodgers were the postmodern team who still honored the baseball traditions of the past. Whichever side of the country you came from, this World Series looked to be, if anything, an epic battle of values and likely a major economic boon for ABC TV, which would be broadcasting the Series, and for Major League Baseball.

Tom Fallon had mixed feelings about the Dodgers' World Series opponents. On the one hand, Fallon recalled how the Yankees had long dominated the Bums, his team from back when he was a young man trying to establish a family in Menands. To Fallon the Yankees represented, even back then (and much more so now, in the 1970s), the old America that he had tried to leave behind. The rusting, crumbling America of the Bronx, the Brooklyn shipyards, the New Jersey Turnpike, and seedy Times Square. Still, since Fallon had moved west to Southern California more than twenty years ago, the Los Angeles team had all but shrugged the Yankee monkey off its back. After all, the Koufax teams had won three World Series for Los Angeles, and one of them—in 1963—had been a remarkable four-game sweep of New York. And while Fallon would have loved to see such a thing again in his lifetime—imagine another sweep of the Yankees!—deep down, in the pit of his Dodger-loving stomach, he was worried. Those damn Yankees had beaten us so many times before. God, how he hated those Yankees.

Fallon was not alone. In 1977, or in most other years, the great majority of baseball fans had good reason to dislike the Yankees. "Rooting for the Yankees is like rooting for a yacht," said newspaper columnist Jimmy Cannon. "Hating the Yankees is as American as pizza pie, unwed mothers, and cheating on your income tax," suggested Chicago columnist Mike Royko. "Most all good Americans hate the Yankees," wrote one wag during a lull in the Yankees' dynasty. "It is a value we cherish and pass along to our children, like decency and democracy and the importance of a good breakfast. Along with the Pledge of Allegiance, hatred of the Yankees should be part of the naturalization test for new U.S. Citizen. If it were, everybody would pass."[20]

It wasn't just that the Yankees won so many championships, though they had won a lot of them—twenty by 1977, more than twice the number of their closest rivals. What really rankled so many baseball fans around the country, rather, is the way the Yankees won them. Starting at least as far back as the 1950s, the New York Yankees won by stacking the deck in their favor. Part of it was money. With a large ballpark, and with the support of a large and rich city, the Yankees always had money—more than most teams. But another part of it was a very un-American bit of odds rigging. According to author Michael Shapiro, starting in the late 1940s the Yankees treated another big-league team, the Kansas City A's, essentially as a high-level farm team. Because Yankees owner Del Webb was pals with the owner of the Kansas City A's, Arnold Johnson, the Yankees were able to pilfer the A's top players in order to keep their own lineup sharp. "Under Johnson," Shapiro wrote, "Kansas City became the place where the Yankees sent the inexperienced, the untested, and the unwanted."[21]

Obviously, every team seeks any competitive advantage to help it win ball games. All teams, on occasion, pull off trades that are underhanded or deceitful—recall the Cubs' accusations regarding the Dodgers' unloading of Bill Buckner, after all. When it came to how the Yankees treated the A's for more than a decade, however, competitive advantage was raised to a fine-art form. Between 1955 and 1959 alone, fourteen trades took place between the two teams, sending stars and solid role players like Roger Maris, Hector Lopez, Ralph Terry, and Johnny Blanchard to New York in exchange for no-names like Jerry Lumpe, Tom Sturdivant, Marv Throneberry, and Johnny Kucks. As a result in these five seasons in particular the A's finished in eighth place (out of eight teams) once and seventh place three times; the best finish they could muster, in 1955, was sixth place with a record of 63-91. Over the same period, the Yankees finished first four times and won two World Series titles. In 1957 the shenanigans were so obvious that a congressional subcommittee investigated whether the two teams had colluded in their transactions.[22] The results of the investigation were inconclusive,[23] though the results on the baseball field were not. Over a fifteen-year period between 1949 and 1963, the Yankees appeared in all but two World Series, emerging as world champions in ten of those years. Among fans and players of other teams that had none of the Yankees' advantages, many wondered what use it was to play the long season when it was all but preordained that, year after year, the Yankees would win. Paul Richards, the manager of the Baltimore Orioles in the later 1950s, saw in the systemic futility of the American League a sign of baseball's eventual demise. "If the American League history of the next decade approximates that of the last," Richards suggested in a *Look* article late in the Eisenhower decade, "and every sign today indicates that it will, then the League will die. . . . The cause of the debacle will be the strangulation of competition and interest by the overlong dominance of the New York Yankees."[24] Richards cited, as evidence, that overall baseball attendance had fallen off through the years of Yankee dominance. And this was true *even* in the city of New York, where the Yankees brought home their championships.

Beyond the basic unfairness of the Yankee's consistent dominance, people also tended to dislike the pinstriped players themselves—viewing them as haughty, distant, reactionary, ruthless, superior, and unapproachable. Joe DiMaggio, Babe Ruth, Hal Chase, Carl Mays, Whitey Ford, Billy Martin, Bobby "Dark Cloud" Murcer, Thurman Munson—these were not nice men, as a rule, not guys you'd want on your side when the chips were down (though the chips were rarely ever down for the Yankees, of course). As the old joke put it: "When the Yankees go out for dinner, they reserve twenty-five tables for one." An old-school sportswriter, Jack Mann, who covered the team during the 1950s for *Sports Illustrated*, said the Yankee clubhouse "held all the carefree charm of a dentist's office." Bill Lee, who pitched for the Yankees' rival the Boston Red Sox during the 1960s and '70s, had perhaps the best assessment of the typical Yankee character: "The more self-centered and egotistical a guy is, the better ballplayer he's going to be. You take a team with twenty-five assholes and I'll show you a pennant. I'll show you the New York Yankees."[25] One very telling indication of just how bad was the team's culture was the fact that the Yankees were one of the last teams to field an African American player. The team's management long expressed open distaste for the idea of a black player in pinstripes, and even when catcher Elston Howard broke the team's color barrier in 1955—eight years after Jackie Robinson first played for the crosstown rival Brooklyn Dodgers—his manager saddled Howard with the dismissive nickname "Eightball."

Not that the Yankees would disagree about their own loathsomeness. Babe Ruth, the Yankee star of the 1920s and '30s, readily acknowledged how much and how widely he was hated. "I don't mind being called a prick or a cocksucker or things like that. I expect that."[26] Indeed, Ruth was a horrific teammate; he quarreled with his manager, got into fistfights with teammates, and feuded with rivals like Leo Durocher and Lou Gehrig, with whom he seldom spoke. Meanwhile, George Weiss, the Yankees' general manager through the glory years of the 1950s, found his own players so repugnant that he hired private detectives to follow them around at night. Casey Stengel, the team's manager for seven of its championship titles during those years, was well aware that his players caroused, drank whiskey, and got into fights off the field. "But I have found," he explained, justifying his tolerance for bad behavior, "that the ones who drink milkshakes don't win many ball games."[27]

It perhaps should come as no surprise, considering the character of the team, that the Yankees of the 1950s and '60s had relatively few diehard fans. As a rule baseball fans in the Big Apple had been fonder of the city's National League franchises—first the New York Giants, then the lovable Brooklyn Dodgers, and finally, after both of these teams left for the West Coast, the New York Mets. Even during the Mets' first season, a disastrous embarrassment in which the team lost a record 120 games, New Yorkers openly revolted against the boringly perennial champion Yankees. Though the Yankees would win the World Series in 1962, it was the Mets that won New Yorkers' hearts. "You see, the Mets are losers, just like nearly everybody else in life," wrote New York newspaperman Jimmy Breslin in 1963. "This is the team for the cab driver who gets held up and the guy who loses out on a promotion because he didn't maneuver himself to lunch with the boss enough. It is the team for every guy who has to get out of bed in the morning and go to work for short money on a job he does not like. The Yankees? Who does well enough to root for them, Laurence Rockefeller?"[28]

By the early 1970s the national hatred of the Yankees had cooled somewhat, as the team was wallowing through a string of mediocre seasons. The Yankee deceit of the past was forgotten, and the city of New York too, once proud and full of bluster, had become something of a shadow of itself. In recent years New York had suffered through the bad management of a corrupt city government, through garbage and other union strikes, power shortages, a highly publicized string of serial murders by a killer known as the Son of Sam, and even bankruptcy.[29] Still, in 1977 the seeds of a new generation of Yankee hatred had been sewn by two important events. The first, which occurred in 1971, was the publication of Jim Bouton's seminal tell-all baseball memoir, *Ball Four.* In the book, which covered Bouton's efforts to pitch during the 1969 season with the Seattle Pilots and Houston Astros, the author also looked back, with brutal honesty, at the venal qualities of various Yankees—especially Mickey Mantle, whom Bouton portrayed as a heavy drinker and a womanizer—at the tail end of the team's glory period in the early 1960s. The second event was the arrival, in 1973, of one man: a new Yankees owner named George Michael Steinbrenner III.

Steinbrenner and the Yankees were a match made in heaven. By all accounts a self-serving, self-righteous, complex, and manipulative human, Steinbrenner, who had made his fortune in the shipbuilding industry, was head of a purchasing group that bought the team from the Columbia Broadcasting Service for the paltry sum of $8.8 million. Promising fans above all else that he would return the team to its winning ways, Steinbrenner was immediately controversial and polarizing. He got into legal trouble in his first year as owner by trying to hire manager Dick Williams away from the A's before his contract was up. In 1974 he was convicted of making illegal contributions to Richard Nixon's campaign for reelection (and for obstruction of justice during the investigation), and he was suspended from baseball for two years. When he was allowed near his team he quickly alienated himself from his players by enforcing, among other things, a strict grooming code.[30]

Still, despite his obvious flaws Steinbrenner was successful at his primary goal: he turned the team into winners again. After finishing in fourth place for three straight seasons, in 1974 the Yankees surged to second in the AL East, just two games behind the Baltimore Orioles. Two years later, in 1976, the Yankees were back in the World Series, after being shut out from the Fall Classic for the previous twelve seasons. New York dropped four straight games in the 1976 World Series to the Cincinnati Reds, but they entered the 1977 season with high hopes. After the loss Steinbrenner had all but guaranteed Yankee fans a World Series win, and, as if to put some muscle behind his proclamation, he went out during the off-season and signed several high-profile free agents—Don Gullett and, notably, Reggie Jackson (as well as Catfish Hunter, signed a year earlier)—purchased the contract of Jim Wynn, and traded for left-handed pitcher Mike Torrez and catcher Cliff Johnson. While the team's returning core—namely, catcher and team captain Thurman Munson, slugging third baseman Graig Nettles, speedy center fielder Mickey Rivers, and Cy Young–winning reliever Sparky Lyle—was likely more important to its success, many baseball fans around the country saw the free-agent signings (especially of Jackson) as a return to the unfair competitive advantage of the Yankee teams of the 1950s. Steinbrenner further incited the animosity of fans of opposing teams by appointing, as the team's new manager, the feisty former Yankee player Billy Martin.

Across the country, to ordinary people standing in gas lines, shaking their heads at all the rising prices and wondering how to make ends meet, the privilege of the Yankees and Steinbrenner was just too much to take. The Yankees had always been privileged, always had unfair advantages. And now, in an era when it seemed the big guy—the corporate giants and stuffed shirts and overentitled—were increasingly gaining all the advantages, the Yankees of 1977 seemed to symbolize the basic unfairness of America. In Cleveland, for instance, on September 5, 1977, local radio station WWWE staged the very first "Hate the Yankees Hanky Night." The Indians, who were on their way to a ninety-loss season and a fifth-place finish (out of seven teams) in the American League East, had at that point lost thirteen straight games to the Yankees going back to the middle of the previous season. The promotion was a success, as 28,000-plus fans (compared to the team's seasonal average of 11,115 fans per game) watched the Indians sweep a doubleheader that day against New York. (The Indians promptly turned back around, though, and lost their next three games against the Yankees over the next three days.)

Despite the national ill will, during the first half of the 1977 season the Yankees were mostly mediocre. As late as June 21 the team's record was a disappointing 36-31, and the team was stuck in a tie for second place, four and a half games behind the Orioles. A key problem for the team was the clubhouse atmosphere, filled as it was with strong personalities and egos, as well as a manager who clashed repeatedly with his owner and his most high-profile player, Reggie Jackson. At one point or another during the season, most of the team's mainstays—including Munson, Reggie Jackson, Graig Nettles, and Mickey Rivers—spoke of their deep desire to leave New York. But the team turned things around in the second half of the season. Jackson's bat heated up. Billy Martin toned down his antics. The Yankees, realizing they had talent, started working together. And in the end the team fought its way into a second straight World Series appearance.

FIFTEEN

Klieg Lights, Smoke Bombs, and Three Massive Bombshells

The Dodgers hated going into New York
because of the fans, who were obnoxious.

—Tommy John

Pardon me for asking, sir, but what good
are snub fighters going to be against that?

—Gold Leader, *Star Wars, Episode IV: A New Hope* (1977)

The difference between Los Angeles and New York in 1977, and between the characters of their two baseball teams—one a national darling of sorts, the other a national nemesis—helps explain the incoming narrative of the World Series. Earlier in the summer, when the Yankees first began to surge, a sports reporter in Los Angeles made a connection that would later become commonplace, comparing the Yankees to the "evil Empire" of that summer's breakout movie, *Star Wars*. Then, on the day before the series, the great local doyen of old-school sportswriters in Los Angeles, Jim Murray, was even more explicit. "For the Dodgers," wrote Murray, "the problem is beating a team that was put together like Standard Oil or U.S. Steel. This Yankee team should be listed on the Wall Street Big Board. It wasn't put together like most teams, it was bought on the commodity market. These are just a bunch of hired guns, athletic Hessians. . . . It's baseball's version of the Krupp Works."[1]

So this World Series of 1977 would be, in the view of many observers, a showdown between the peaceful, idyllic planet of Alderaan (a.k.a. Elysian Park) versus the Death Star in the Bronx. It was left up to the Dodgers to stand up for all the underprivileged, overtaxed, endlessly struggling underdogs of the universe against the juggernaut Yankees. It was a last gambit by old Obi Wan O'Malley finally to defeat the villainous Darth Steinbrenner.

This was all, of course, an overstatement, a result of the fact that the World Series of 1977 was revisiting a classic rivalry—the Dodgers versus the Yankees—at the exact moment that a worried country was desperate for something to distract it from its troubles. Just six days before the first game of the World Series, President Jimmy Carter had paid a much-ballyhooed visit to the blighted projects, burned-out buildings, rubble-strewn lots, and garbage-choked streets of the South Bronx. The president's grimly understated assessment of the dire state of the neighborhood—"A very sobering trip," he said—appeared in *Time* and on the front page of the *New York Times*. The fact that Carter had come to announce plans for a national initiative to redevelop and turn around such blight seemed beside the point; for at least a brief time the neighborhood just south of Yankee Stadium was a symbol of America's growing sense of disgrace and shame.

Once the lights came on at Yankee Stadium and the roar of the crowd could be heard ringing out across the Bronx, people, at least for a time, forgot the depressing reality of the times and fixated on the narrative of these games. Starting on October 11, 1977, the true-blue Dodgers and "evil" Yankees played six drama-filled games. At times it seemed either team could have taken the Series. Both were explosive, had capable pitching and wily and competitive managers, and knew how to win. In the end, though, of course, only one team would win.

Back on September 29, when the Yankees had clinched their division, a magnanimous Tom Lasorda, whose team had been the first in the league to clinch a playoff spot, called Yankee manager Billy Martin to congratulate him. Lasorda and Martin were friends, unlikely though that may have seemed. It helped that both had come from similar molds. Both were sons of tough Italian immigrants and marginally talented athletes who had succeeded through their own guile and will. Both had risen to the top in one of the most difficult of all human pastimes, the upper echelon of the professional sport of baseball. Both were charismatic leaders, each in his own way, and both possessed very capacious egos that often served them in their pursuit of winning. Still, in the first meeting between Lasorda and Martin, the two had been anything but friends. Mickey Mantle, the great Yankee star of the 1950s and '60s, told the story to an L.A. sportswriter. One day in 1956 the first-place Yankees were playing against the last-place Kansas City A's, to whom Lasorda had been traded by the Dodgers. According to Mantle, several A's batters had been brushed back by the Yankees' pitcher. As Mantle told it the A's manager then yelled, "That's what's wrong with this lousy club! Everyone is afraid of the Yankees." At that Lasorda went to his manager and insisted he be put in the game. Lasorda then knocked down the first two Yankee hitters and threw behind the heads of Hank Bauer and Billy Martin. "Well, you can guess what happened next," said Mantle. "Martin yelled something, Lasorda yelled back—and pow. The two of them went after each other like pit bulldogs. In the middle of the action, Bauer tried to get at Lasorda, who shouted at him between punches, 'Stay out of this, Bauer. This is an Italian fight.' . . . When the blood dried, Billy and Tommy shook hands and they became great pals."[2]

Whatever the reason for their friendship, despite the differences in the franchises they worked for and loved, Lasorda admired Billy Martin and sincerely supported the embattled manager's efforts to lead the rival Yankees to the Series. "I look at Billy and I see myself," Lasorda told reporters after the two met at a Manhattan restaurant the day before the first game of the World Series. "It's never come easy for him. He's had to scrape and hustle. . . . I sympathize with what he's gone through this year. He has to be Manager of the Year. He's put up with so much and yet here he is." Reportedly, many in the baseball world were startled by the meeting of two World Series–rival managers, but both Lasorda and Martin were unapologetic about their social meeting. "It's strictly a personal thing. Billy and I are friends," said Lasorda. "To be managing a team in the Series and to have that team playing a Yankee team managed by Martin is the ultimate for me. . . . We're like brothers." Martin, for his part, pointed out to reporters that the meeting did happen on Columbus Day, "and us Italians have to stick together."[3]

What the rival managers talked about has not been recorded.

Perhaps the two men shared memories of old times, of fights they'd both fought, of people they once knew. Possibly they bonded over the frustrations and vicissitudes of their positions. It is certain, however, that they dared not speak about their teams and the battle they would be fighting in a few days. "Bill and I are friends, was all Lasorda said of their dinner when asked, before he tellingly added: "But when we're on the field, it's a war."[4]

War, indeed. The first skirmish of the 1977 World Series occurred even before the first game started. On Monday, October 10—Columbus Day in New York—the Dodgers had arrived in New York, chartered a bus, and headed out to Yankee Stadium to get in some light practice before the opening game on Tuesday evening. "When the bus arrived at the House that Ruth Built," wrote a writer who was embedded with the team for the Series, "a howling mob of 100 or so youths descended happily on it, some slamming fists on windows, all of them jeering as the Dodgers ran a gauntlet of abuse."[5] That the incident disturbed many of the Dodgers is evident in later comments made by some of the more vocal Dodgers. For now, however, Lasorda's squad rushed inside and bunkered down until the real fight began.

Game One of the 1977 World Series was played on Tuesday, October 11, in front of the Yankees' unruly home crowd. In the top half of the first inning, in the midst of an early Dodger rally, a second critical skirmish took place. With two Dodger runs already in, and Reggie Smith at first base with one out, Steve Garvey came to the plate. On a 3–1 count Smith took off toward second base as Yankee pitcher Don Gullett delivered a sharp fastball on the inside corner. It was not a particularly good jump; Smith was not trying to steal. Instead, with contact hitter Garvey at the plate the calculating Lasorda had called for a hit-and-run. "If I can't run a guy on a 3–1 count with Garvey hitting I better get out of the game," Lasorda would say afterward. "I'd do that a thousand times in a row. One thousand times. There was never a doubt in my mind about that play."[6] Unfortunately, and portentously, contact hitter Garvey miscalculated and overswung at the pitch, missing badly, and Smith was flat-footedly thrown out by Yankee catcher Thurman Munson. Was this a potential Series-altering event? Probably not. But had Garvey gotten wood on the ball, perhaps poking a hit through the gap on the left side of the infield where Yankees second baseman Willie Randolph had moved to cover second, it's likely Smith would have scored. And this would have given the Dodgers a first-inning lead of three runs that may have knocked the starter Gullett out of the game. Instead, the Dodgers settled for just two runs, and Gullett remained in the game, eventually pitching into the ninth inning.

While these two small early battles would play a role in the ultimate outcome of the World Series, they were of less consequence than what took place later, in the top of the sixth inning and the score 2–1. With one out Garvey bunt-singled his way on base. One out later Glenn Burke poked a soft single through the right side of the infield that seemed to take forever to reach the outfielders. Garvey tore around second, and, as he rushed to third, Dodgers third base coach Preston Gomez noticed that right fielder Reggie Jackson had backed off to let the weak-armed Yankee center fielder, Mickey Rivers, field the ball. Gomez signaled, just a bit late, for Garvey to go home, and the first baseman, who had slowed momentarily, now scrambled to reach the plate. Rivers's throw was a bit short and slightly offline. Thurman Munson, the Yankees catcher, caught it a bit up the first base line, and then swung around and dove to tag Garvey as he slid. And here is where fate intervened, putting its stamp on the outcome of the game and the entire Series.

It was a close play. In replays it appears that Garvey beat the tag, sliding just around the diving reach of Munson. Garvey certainly insisted as much after the game. "I was safe," he said. "I came through the outside of the plate and he had to dive back toward me. I thought I had my right toe in there."[7] Unfortunately for Garvey and the Dodgers, however, the home plate umpire, old Nestor Chylak, who had been the plate umpire for the 10 Cent Beer Night debacle (and so had a history with Billy Martin), had set himself a good ways down the first base line. In the TV announcer's booth, after Chylak had called Garvey out, Tom Seaver was the first to point out the obvious. "The umpire is out of position!" Seaver yelled. "The umpire is down the line! He's not even in the picture! Where is he?!" With Munson's body shielding the play at the plate, Chylak essentially had to guess what happened, and he gave Munson the benefit of the doubt. Garvey immediately leaped to his feet, arguing that Chylak had not seen the play. But no amount of arguing would overturn Chylak's judgment call, even if his judgment was just a guess. Garvey was out. The game remained tight, and, even though the Dodgers still led, it was beginning to feel like this was not going to be their night.

The final moment that determined the results of Game One, the event that everyone would be talking about afterward, came in the bottom of the twelfth inning of what had become a deadlocked game. With runners at first and second and no outs, Dodger reliever Rick Rhoden, who was normally a starter for the Dodgers and seemed somewhat out of sync here, faced Yankee veteran backup outfielder Paul Blair. This was the same Blair who had factored prominently in the Dodgers' 1966 World Series loss against Blair's team of the time, the Baltimore Orioles. In that Series Blair, a twenty-two-year-old platoon outfielder who was paid the league minimum in 1966 (eight thousand dollars), crushed a monster home run off Dodger pitcher Claude Osteen in the fifth inning of the third game to secure a 1–0 victory for his team. The Orioles would eventually sweep the Dodgers in four games.[8]

In the 1977 Series Blair, now a defensive specialist for the Yankees at age thirty-three, had replaced Jackson in the field in the ninth inning. Batting against Rhoden in the twelfth inning, Blair dug in. Twice he attempted to move the runners over with a sacrifice bunt, and twice he bunted foul. On a two-and-two pitch, however, Blair smacked a grounder just out of Bill Russell's reach, sending Willie Randolph home with the winning run. Yankee fans, who had been restive since about the eighth inning—when they started throwing streamers and toilet paper rolls out on the field—mobbed the field.

Game Two's results on Wednesday also had the quality of predestination, the game's outcome never in doubt after the Dodgers took a quick 2–0 lead on a Ron Cey home run against Catfish Hunter in the top of the first inning. They extended the lead to 3–0 in the second on a home run by Steve Yeager and then to 5–0 on a two-run homer by Reggie Smith in the third. While the Yankees scored a run in the fourth, for the most part they were quiet, as Burt Hooton, the Dodgers' starting pitcher, pitched masterfully for nine innings. The

Yankees managed just five hits against Hooton's "knuckle curve." ("It's one hellacious pitch," said Dodger catcher Steve Yeager after the game.) The final score was 6–1.

The only drama in Game Two, in fact, came from the Yankees' fans, who were again unruly and disruptive throughout the game. In the ninth inning play was halted after fans threw firecrackers and a smoke bomb onto the field, and then, after Reggie Jackson tossed the device back over the right-field fence, play was disrupted all over again when several successive fans got loose on the field before being tackled by stadium security officers. The moment was so ugly that ABC TV commentator, and noted New York apologist, Howard Cosell fumed. "I want to make something clear to the viewers," Cosell said, interrupting his cocommentator, Tom Seaver, "We are not showing the antics of America's young heroes, because we don't want to encourage this kind of activity. It is tasteless, it is wrong, and we don't want any part of it." And this was just the tip of the iceberg. As would come out after the game, fans had been dangerously abusive to the Dodgers from the start of Game Two. First, it was a nameless obscene chant that rose up in the left-center-field bleachers. "That we can tolerate," said a Dodger bullpen pitcher who was located just below the bleachers. What the team couldn't tolerate, he explained, was the other stuff that came from the stands. "Whiskey bottles, beer bottles, little rubber balls. They were throwing anything they could get their hands on. The bad part was the security officers out there were doing nothing. . . . This is something a ballplayer shouldn't have to put up with. You get hit in the head by a beer bottle and it's all over." Another target of the fans, right fielder Reggie Smith, was unfortunately unable to avoid the Bronx missiles of Yankee Stadium. "Somebody hit me with a hard rubber ball," he said. "Right on top of the head. It jammed my neck down. It was like somebody hit me with a hammer."[9]

After Game Two the crowd's antics throughout the first two games would be the talk of the Dodger clubhouse, at least until the news of a major kerfuffle in the Yankees clubhouse made the fans' antics seem anticlimactic. The Yankees' troubles started, as with many of their problems in 1977, with something Reggie Jackson said. When asked by a reporter about Billy Martin's decision to pitch Hunter, who hadn't started a game since September 10 because of various injuries,

Jackson had answered bluntly. "In a World Series," Jackson asked, "how do you make a decision like that on a guy like Hunter? Cat did his best but he hasn't pitched in so long. . . . [A]h, the hell with it." A day later, on reading Jackson's comments, the fiery Martin went ballistic. "If I'm going to back that ass," Martin reportedly said, "why doesn't he back me? I didn't knock him when he messed up that play the other night" (when Jackson forced weak-armed Mickey Rivers to field a ball to the outfield with Garvey trying to score), "so what business does he have knocking me?" Martin paused to catch his breath, before he continued frothing. "This isn't a one-way street. He has a lot of growing up to do. He's having enough trouble in the outfield without second-guessing the manager. We have a chance to win the world-championship and we're not going to do it with our mouth."[10]

Jackson, for his part, was apologetic afterward, suggesting he had been misrepresented. "It seems that more times than not everything Reggie Jackson says becomes controversial," said Jackson. "Either I don't say it properly or it's taken the wrong way, out of context. Maybe I said it the wrong way last night. I was emotional. I was talking about a friend. If the timing was wrong I'll take the blame." Jackson was then asked again, for the umpteenth time, about his relationship with Martin and whether he intended to second-guess him. "I haven't really said anything about the manager all year," Jackson continued, absurdly enough. "What's between Billy and I is between Billy and I. I have nothing to say about how he manages the team. I don't know how to handle a pitching staff. I don't know how to handle myself." After Jackson's clarification, reporters then went back to Martin and asked if he felt the latest act in this "persistent soap opera" would affect his team's chances in the Series. "No," Martin said. "Reggie's teammates don't pay any attention to him and why should I?" Yankee captain Thurman Munson took Martin's comments one step further. "I couldn't give a bleep about Billy Martin's or Reggie Jackson's comments," said the pugnacious catcher. "I do think it's unfortunate that at a time when we have a chance to win the championship, there's a guy out there trying to second-guess the manager. . . . I used to know what was going on around here but I stopped mixing drinks a long time ago. I've got only five more games at the most to worry about all this crap."[11]

With the Yankee clubhouse burbling, and the controversy over the Yankee Stadium hoodlums still roiling ("What a World Series!" wrote one Dodger fan to the *L.A. Times*. "The New York Muggers vs. the L.A. Huggers"), it was difficult to discern what tilted the next two World Series games. Now back in Los Angeles, in front of the generally laid-back home crowd, the Dodgers barely had time to pause before the next two games were over.

Tommy John, pitching in the first World Series game of his career (in his fourteenth season), started off Game Three with a rough first inning, giving up three runs on a slew of Yankee hits. And while the Dodgers tied the game in the bottom of the third inning on a three-run home run by Dusty Baker, the team never really seemed to be in the game. The Yankees went back ahead, scratching a run out in the top of the fourth, following that with another run on a string of singles in the top of the fifth. And that was pretty much it. Mike Torrez, the Yankees' hulking (six-foot-five) right-handed starter, stymied the Dodgers' right-handed hitters, completing the game for a 5–3 win.

The loss was disappointing and frustrating—to fans, players, and the Dodgers' management, who wanted to rid the bad taste of Yankee Stadium from their palates—but after the game various Dodgers worked hard to sell an alternative narrative. "Tommy John pitched a hell of a ballgame," said manager Tom Lasorda, explaining that none of the Yankees' nine hits was hit particularly hard. "Not to alibi, but their fourth and fifth runs were on balls hit off infielders' gloves. I thought the guy pitched a hell of a game." Steve Yeager added only that Munson's sharp double down the left-field line had been solidly struck. "Rivers was jammed and got a soft liner that turned into a double. Jackson was fooled on a breaking pitch and chinked a single to left. Piniella hit one that had eyes to get it through the infield."[12] John, somewhat dejected and alone in the clubhouse after the game, even tried to put a good spin on the loss. "Heck," John said, "Sandy Koufax, Whitey Ford, and Don Drysdale have all lost World Series games." And his teammate Dusty Baker was more bluntly optimistic after the loss. "We ain't losing," he said. "We're just behind."[13]

But Game Four was a similar story to the previous game. The Dodgers' starting pitcher, left-hander Doug Rau, gave up three quick runs in the top of the second inning, and the Dodgers' only runs came on a two-run home run in the bottom of the third by Lopes. The Dodgers had several scoring threats against Yankees starter Ron Guidry—most notably a leadoff single by Cey in the seventh inning and a one-out double by Cey in the ninth—but both rallies fell short. In the end it was another loss—this time 4–2—and the Dodgers' sense of desperation and disappointment, even in the face of Lasorda's eternal optimism, was growing.

In fact, as a notorious incident in the top of the second inning would reveal, Lasorda himself may have been more frustrated with his team than he let on. Before the game ABC TV had asked Lasorda to wear a microphone so they could use his comments as continuity to provide insight during key moments. Apparently, however, Lasorda almost immediately forgot he was wearing the device. When the Yankees had strung together four straight sharp hits against Rau to start the inning, Lasorda went to the mound intent on removing his pitcher. "You give me a sign, Red," Lasorda said to his pitching coach, Red Adams, as he left the dugout. "When I get out there, I'll mess around for some time. Okay?" At the mound, however, Rau immediately set Lasorda off by asking to be left in the game.

"Fuck no!" Lasorda yelled at his pitcher. "You can't get the fucking left-handers out for Christ al-fucking-mighty." When Rau protested by saying he felt good, Lasorda continued laying into his pitcher. "I don't give a shit, you feel good—there's four motherfucking hits up there. . . . I may be wrong, but that's my motherfucking job. I'll make the fucking decisions here." And so on it went, for nearly three minutes as Elias Sosa warmed up in the bullpen. The tirade got so intense at one point that Dave Lopes tried to intervene. "Just back off the mound," Lopes said. "You wanna talk about it, talk about it inside. . . . This is not the place to be talking about it Okay? That's all I'm trying to say. Fucking jump on me, shit. I'm just trying to avoid a scene out here Okay?"

"That's right," Lasorda agreed, before turning back and laying into Rau. "It's fucking great for you to be standing out here talking to me like that. . . . I'm the fucking manager of the fucking team. I gotta make the fucking decisions, and I'll make 'em to the fucking best of my ability. . . . I can't fuck around, we're down two games to one. If it was yesterday it would be a different story. . . . We can't give 'em two more this fucking early."

After the game it was impossible for the Dodgers' manager to disguise his disappointment. "Now we've got our backs to the wall," said Lasorda. "It's going to take a hungry club to come back from 3–1." Still, he couldn't help but try to rally his team. "They did it against the Phillies in the playoffs," he said, suggesting they could do it again.[14] He even held a closed-door clubhouse meeting with the team before Game Five, delivering an impassioned pep talk to his boys. "I told them I was extremely proud of them, of what they'd accomplished," Lasorda said. "I told them, 'You beat a hell of a Cincinnati club and then everybody thought Philadelphia was going to wipe you off the face of the earth in the playoffs, but you didn't believe it. You've had a few tough breaks in the Series, but I wouldn't trade this club for any in baseball.'"[15]

Still, the optimism was a hard sell for this Dodgers team, who no doubt saw the lights of Yankee Stadium shimmering on the road ahead. As third baseman Ron Cey put it, in response to Lasorda's pep talk: "It's tough to play a game from behind. It takes three now for us to win. What in hell else is there to do?"[16]

In Game Five veteran Don Sutton gave the team a victory at home by keeping the Yankees' bats quiet through six innings, long enough for the Dodgers' sluggers to get untracked for once. The final score, 10–4, disguises the fact somewhat that the Yankees were never in this one. (They squibbed pairs of runs in the seventh and eighth innings after the Dodgers had rolled to a 10–0 lead.) For the Dodgers Dusty Baker led the team with three hits, while Garvey, Lopes, Russell, and Lacy each had two. Steve Yeager and Reggie Smith had each smacked home runs. Still, it was a hollow win. While it helped further Sutton's legend as the team's "meal ticket" pitcher—as he still had yet to lose a postseason game over his career (against five wins)—the players had one thing on their minds. "Going to New York doesn't bother me," Dusty Baker said, tellingly revealing what was foremost on his mind after Game Five. "I wouldn't care if I was in Vietnam if I was playing in the World Series."[17]

After the win in their last game in Los Angeles, Don Sutton said he still believed in his team. "I don't profess to be a prophet like Jeanne Dixon," Sutton said. "But I believe there will be seventh game on Wednesday and that we are a good enough team to win it all." Steve Garvey, meanwhile, explained that he too had a good feeling about the Dodgers' chances. "I said before the game that we'd win the Series. . . . I just got this feeling. I have a lot of confidence in our next two pitchers, Burt Hooton and Tommy John, and I knew pride would take over today."[18] Yet, despite the optimism, the Yankees were winning the 1977 Series. They had, thus far, simply played better baseball. They had gotten more clutch pitching, had better and more timely hitting, and had fielded better and hit better in the clutch than the Dodgers. Some people may have said the Dodgers should be winning the World Series, yet they were not.

Behind the numbers, in fact, Howard Cosell had inadvertently stumbled upon an essential difference between the Dodgers and the Yankees during Game Three. Filling time during the lull of several slow innings, Cosell brought up a graphic that showed where each of the starters on each team had come from. In the bottom of the fourth inning, he showed that five of the Dodgers' eight position players (Cey, Russell, Garvey, and Yeager) had come up through the Dodgers' system after having been scouted and drafted by the team. "Basically the Dodgers build their team through the farm system," Cosell said. "Basically . . . [t]he Dodger building processes have not changed ever since Branch Rickey first installed them, and then Mr. Walter O'Malley took over from him in the early fifties." Then, in the top of the seventh inning, Cosell showed a similar graphic for the Yankees' lineup. Of the eight position players on the team, only one, Thurman Munson, had come up through the Yankees' system. The vast majority of the team had come to New York through trades and free agency. "And so you can see that this team was structured differently," Cosell explained. "They didn't come with farm origination and the long developmental process that the Dodgers deploy."

The more organic development process had made of the Dodgers a kind of family. Many of these players, despite their relative young ages, had played together for nearly ten years—having come up together through all levels of the farm system, growing together as they each became full-grown men. As an organic, less manufactured product, the Dodgers were as flawed and human as any family—especially compared to the Yankees. In particular, the Dodgers' lineup suffered from a heavy right-handed bias. That is, with their strong battery of right-handed hitters—Lopes, Russell, Cey, Garvey, Yeager, and Baker all hit from the right side—the team left itself somewhat vulnerable when opponents threw right-handed pitchers against them. And while Lasorda and Campanis had attempted to address this weakness somewhat by trading for left-hander Rick Monday, that had not turned out well after Monday's back injury. It was no accident that right-handed starter Mike Torrez, picked up for just a half season by the Yankees to fill a need, was able to win two key games against the Dodgers in the Series, going all the way in both. The Yankees, meanwhile, were a more "manufactured" (and well-paid) team with a much more balanced battery and pitching staff.

It was also no accident that the Dodgers, who were somewhat short on left-handed pitching, had no answer to the most high-priced, ill-fitting, and controversial cog in the Yankee machine: a left-handed power hitter who had already earned the nickname Mr. October by the time he stepped up to the plate in Game Six of the 1977 World Series.

For Dodger fans recounting what happened after the fourth inning of Game Six in 1977 World Series is akin to a southerner's recounting of the burning of Atlanta or a Japanese citizen's recounting of the last days of World War II. And recounting the events are further complicated by the fact that, in the minds of the deepest of Dodger fans—those diehards who lived and breathed all things Dodgers in 1977, who watched every possible minute of the World Series, and who, at age eleven, say, had lived a life mostly sheltered from soul-crushing disappointment—the events that began with no outs in the bottom half of the fourth inning were when one was forced to reckon with a hard truth about the world. That is, three particular moments in Game Six, which seemed to come as quick as lightning strikes, or sucker punches from a playground bully, were the stuff of waking nightmares and countless adult therapy sessions for millions of poor Angelenos who had to witness the events. The devastation was just so massive, the Dodgers' destruction and desolation just so complete. And it was made all the worse by having to watch the rusted-out, crumbling, belligerent, and uncouth Old World city of New York rejoice at crushing the hopes and dreams of the people of Los Angeles.

After the Series ended, as if to pile on additional injury, it was revealed that local Yankee fans had, before Game Six, found the hotel rooms of two Dodger players—Dave Lopes and Steve Garvey—and left stark messages for the players. "The guy said," reported Lopes, "'We're gonna show you how crazy New York fans are.' He said he was going to shoot me."[19] In the end it was all so demoralizing and devastating that it's still difficult for some Dodger fans from that time to put the actual events into words. Still, to keep the historical record clear, one must try.

Game Six started innocuously enough. The Dodgers, as they had in three of the first five games, scored first in the first inning, when Garvey tripled home two runs. They held the lead until the fourth inning, when, with the score at 3–2, the meat of New York's lineup—Munson, Jackson, and Chris Chambliss—was due up to face Happy Hooton. At this point there was some reason for Dodger fans, and for the team, to be hopeful. In Game Two Hooton had all but shut down the team's heavy hitters. Munson had only gotten one hit, a single, while Jackson had gone hitless in four at bats, striking out twice and grounding into a double play, and Chambliss had gone oh for four with one strikeout. However, Munson ripped a sharp single to left field, after which one of the TV announcers commented that, thus far, Hooton seemed to be having some trouble locating his knuckle curve. "He's gotta get that pitch established and get it over if he's going to be effective," said Tom Seaver. Lasorda, aware of the problem, watched Hooton carefully, his face a mask of worry. Yet with his shaky bullpen Lasorda had no choice but to hope that Hooton could get through a few more innings.

After the single by Munson Hooton took the ball from Lopes, who had received it from Baker, and he scraped his right foot across the front of the pitching rubber as Reggie Jackson came to the plate. Jackson looked placid, as though his mind was elsewhere. He could have been a Tibetan monk, getting ready to recite morning prayers. Hooton, his face the usual mask of misery—upper lip curled, eyebrows furrowed—stared down at Jackson from his perch on the mound at Yankee Stadium.

And here is where time slows down for the Dodger fan. Here's where one wonders what Hooton must've been thinking at this particular instant, what he thought would be just the right pitch to throw to the dangerous left-handed slugger—who was in his element, in front of the boisterous New York fans, looking out at the easy pot-shot that was the fence in right field. Here's where one might wonder why Hooton didn't throw a different pitch to this dangerous bruiser.

Up until now, unlike in the League Championship Series, Jackson had had a good World Series. Not a historically great one, but a good one. He had hit just over .350 with two home runs, and while he'd batted in just three runs from his position as cleanup hitter, he had scored seven runs in the first five games, a number that was just two shy of the World Series record. As Hooton leaned back and lifted his left leg to start his stretch delivery, Jackson stood absolutely still, almost unconcerned, peering at Hooton in a sleepy sort of way. As Hooton finished his kick and started his throwing motion, Jackson still had not moved, except to dip his knees slightly. Hooton delivered his pitch, a fastball that Yeager wanted down and in but that crept up right into Jackson's wheelhouse. In an instant Jackson uncorked, rotating his sizable linebacker's upper body and powerful arms in a roundhouse swing that, once his bat connected with the pitch, put the ball well back in the lower deck of the right-field grandstand. The boisterous New York crowd leaped to their feet, erupting in glee, as Jackson ran the bases in his unique bouncing trot.

The game and the Series were, for all intents and purposes, over. Hooton, who clearly had nothing in the tank to shut down the Yankees, was removed after throwing a few pitches to Chambliss. His relief, Sosa, gave up a bloop hit, and another run, and the Yankees now led 5–3 in the bottom of the fourth.

In the fifth inning disaster would repeat almost exactly as in the fourth. With two out Jackson again came to the plate with a runner at first. Again, he looked calm and self-possessed—though just a tad less so—and again he turned on a first-pitch fastball from a Dodger right-hander (Sosa, this time) and parked it in the stands out in right.

The Yankees now led 7–3 and would not give up the lead. The Dodgers' battery, their spirits no doubt crushed by the stunning turn of events, fell completely silent through the sixth, seventh, and eight innings. By the time Reggie Jackson returned to the plate in the bottom of the eighth, the score still 7–3, there was not much hope for the Dodgers. To win now would have been something just short of a miracle. And the Dodgers showed no signs of being able to create another miracle.

Jackson led off the eighth inning. This time right-handed knuckleballer Charlie Hough was pitching. The crowd stood up and offered an ovation, and now, perhaps aware of what he had already accomplished, Jackson looked anything but placid. He stood more upright than he had in earlier innings. He fidgeted at the plate and seemed completely unprepared as Hough began his high leg kick. The ball came fluttering in—a good-looking looping knuckler that came in low. In the last instant this time Jackson unleashed a powerful uppercut swing. What should have been a high pop-up to center somehow kept carrying, and carrying, and carrying, and everyone in the ballpark—the fans, the announcers, the Yankees, and most especially the Dodgers—could hardly believe it. The ball seemed to have afterburners on it, landing some 470 feet away, in the darkened part of the stands way out in no-man's-land beyond center field. In his autobiography some years later Jackson would reveal that everything he did in this at bat—the agitated demeanor, the oddly upright stance, the seeming lack of readiness—was premeditated. "The key to hitting a knuckleball is timing," Jackson wrote. "I got this from Sal Bando, who was a great knuckleball hitter with the A's. He taught me about how to hit it: 'Just stand there, Reggie. Don't even get into your stance. Just face forward, and take a nice full cut.'"[20]

Whatever the case it was Jackson's third straight home run, and Hough's was the third straight pitch to Jackson to leave the park. It was a historic feat of athletic prowess, and it had killed the Dodgers in the 1977 World Series.

Interlude

Postorbital Remorse; or, There's Always Next Year

I will express now what I had in my mind at the beginning, that this could well have been the series of the almighty dollar against the Big Dodger in the Sky.

—Keith Jackson, in the ninth inning of the sixth game of the 1977 World Series

I think there are going to be a lot of Reggies born in this town.

—Bill Lee, after witnessing the last game of the '77 World Series

You have to be fearless. You have to defy that Big Loss in the Sky.

—Steve Garvey

Some years after the 1977 World Series, long after the ball field at Yankee Stadium had been freed of ecstatic and unruly New York fans, after the confetti and vomit and broken glass had been swept from the grandstands, and after all the furor had died down, Jonathan Mahler reported in his book *Ladies and Gentlemen, the Bronx Is Burning* on the widespread notion that the Yankees' dramatic World Series victory, and Jackson's Ruthian display of home run power,[1] had all but pulled a bankrupt, crime-riddled, and corrupt city out of the depths of despair. "The tabloids wove Reggie's three mighty blows into their narrative of the city's struggle for survival," Mahler wrote, citing, among other sources, a *New York Post* editorial titled "Who Dares to Call New York a Lost Cause?" Coming fifteen years after the last Yankee world championship over San Francisco in 1962, the win in 1977 certainly did thrill a city hungry for some good news, even if the tabloids' claims were somewhat dubious. "What Reggie Jackson did here Tuesday night," wrote Mike Gonring, a staff reporter for the *Milwaukee Journal*, "in the sixth and deciding game of the World Series would have been unbelievable, had not so many people witnessed it." Gonring noted that, for the series, Jackson had slugged five home runs in all and ten RBIs, which were both records. "It was totally preposterous. Absolutely incredible," the scribe wrote, echoing the near-universal sentiments of baseball fans around the country.[2]

In the weeks immediately following the Series, Reggie Jackson lapped up the accolades and attention, in one moment affecting an *aw-shucks* kind of humility and in the other boasting in the manner of Muhammad Ali or Broadway Joe Namath. "Love me or hate me," Jackson crowed to one interviewer in the aftermath of Game Six, "but you can't ignore me."[3] In interviews Jackson attributed his success not to his own playing prowess but to the Lord ("God allowed me to do that") and to some sort of humanitarian impulse ("I'll tell you what I was thinking . . . *I did this for all of us. Take it. Enjoy it. And let's do it again*").[4] And to anyone who had doubted him, Jackson spoke bluntly. "At last I feel I'm a Yankee," he said.

Later, before the start of the 1978 season, a more circumspect Jackson admitted that, for much of 1977, he had hardly felt secure about his role on the team. "To me, the Yankees were always Mantle and Ford, Joe DiMaggio, and Ruth and Gehrig. . . . But now I think I belong."[5] In his autobiographical account of the 1977 and 1978 seasons, published long after his playing days, Jackson would go much deeper. "I know all the stories about how I said they'd name a candy bar after me if I played in New York," Jackson said. "How I was longing to come and play on the big stage and become Mr. October. Most of it is just that—stories. I was already a star before I came to New York, and I was going to take my star with me anywhere I went. In fact, New York was about the last place I thought I would end up." As to what was Jackson's first choice of team to play for before the 1977 season, he gave a surprising answer. "My real first choice was the Dodgers," Jackson wrote.

> To me, the Dodgers made perfect sense. They were a good team. I played in the World Series there in 1974 [while he was on the Oakland A's], and the ballpark felt small to me. . . . I always hit the ball

> very well there. I always loved the environment there. . . . They had a manager who was full of energy in Tommy Lasorda. They had a great farm system, great ownership in the O'Malleys. I always admired the family: They were minority conscious, and they had always been community conscious. There were the team that signed the first black player, Jackie Robinson—they had a great history. Their values were something you wanted to be around.[6]

Jackson pointed out that his left-handed bat would have been a great complement for a team overloaded with right-handers. Furthermore, he continued, Jackson was, unlike with New York, very fond of the city. "Los Angeles was a good spot for me in many ways, on and off the field. . . . And I know the Dodgers wanted me. Al Campanis, their general manager, was always trying to get me in a trade. A small ballpark, in a fast league. It was the place dude!"[7]

Success, of course, provides the means to whitewash over all manner of misbehavior and contention. Not only were the drama, backbiting, and sniping in the Yankees' clubhouse in 1977 erased by Reggie Jackson's epic three swings, but his feat on that one October night in the Bronx changed the very way he was perceived as a ballplayer. The truth was this: Yes, Jackson was at times a dangerous, often very intelligent, if flawed hitter (his tendency to overswing, and his prodigious ego about his ability, meant that he went down swinging an inordinate amount of the time). However, he was rarely admired by his teammates, his managers, even by the fans. In fact, Jackson was often derided as one-dimensional, or a showboat or hot dog, and even as a loafer who cared little for the welfare of his team. Throughout the 1977 season Billy Martin in particular had been open about his disdain for Jackson.[8] And while Jackson suggested that Martin's feelings about him were racially motivated, the truth was that many on the Yankees' coaching staff (and its player roster, truth be told) had problems with Jackson's high self-regard.[9]

Even Reggie Jackson's hallmark nickname, "Mr. October," did not originally mean what it came to mean. The nickname had been coined as a sarcastic jab at Jackson by Thurman Munson, who had found the outfielder as repugnant as anyone, at the *beginning* of the World Series, not at the end. How sarcastic is up for debate. Many believe that Munson was pointing out how terribly Jackson had played during the AL Championship Series against the Kansas City Royals. (Jackson had gone two for sixteen in the crucial series, collecting just one RBI and no extra-base hits.) However, Jackson would contend that Munson was still somewhat jokingly supporting Jackson when coining the nickname. "It was after the second game of the Series," Jackson said, "and he (Munson) was sticking up for Martin against me. He told the media, 'Billy probably just doesn't realize Reggie is Mr. October.'"[10] Whatever the case Jackson embraced the nickname, and after his mighty heroics in the World Series the nickname just seemed to fit.

A well-developed ego is, of course, a crucial trait for many successful ballplayers. Even among Tom Lasorda's seemingly congenial and clean-cut Dodgers, there was more than enough ego to go around. What else would explain the bitterness that filled the Dodgers' visiting clubhouse that night after the World Series ended? As the world celebrated the Yankees' victory and Jackson's unprecedented personal triumph, the Dodgers were in a dark mood. In one corner Charlie Hough, the pitcher who served up the third of Jackson's home runs, sat on a trunk, looking, according to one reporter, like "a broken prize fighter." "He hit a good pitch," Hough said, "down and away. Of course, he hits them down and away. Whatever it was, he exploded." Next to Hough, meanwhile, utility infielder Lee Lacy shook his head in slow wonder, bitterly repeating the slugger's name within earshot of reporters: "Reggie Jackson . . . Reggie Jackson . . . Reggie Jackson . . ." In another corner Ron Cey stood in front of a mirror, staring at himself vacantly, while Dave Lopes and Rick Monday sat in front of their lockers, heads down and avoiding eye contact with anyone. Catcher Steve Yeager, for his part, was unwilling to be so conciliatory. "I hope you're not coming over here expecting me to say something," he told reporters. "Because I got nothing to say. We got beat. We just got beat."[11] The team's flight home to Los Angeles was similarly torturous. The coaches and a few players sat, slouched and silent, in the front of the plane in a darkened cabin. A few other players, meanwhile, blew off steam and frustration in the back of the plane. When the team reached Los Angeles, only a small subdued crowd greeted them. Without ceremony the Dodgers each went their separate ways for the winter.

Under Lasorda, however, the Dodgers were careful to strike a certain positive, laid-back, California-esque pose at most times, so once the shock of losing the World Series wore off, the team quickly reverted to form. Don Sutton and Steve Garvey were quick to publicly congratulate the Yankees in general, and Reggie Jackson in particular, for the win. "I think it was a night when he released a lot of emotional tension," said Garvey of Jackson's season-redeeming Game Six. "It sure was some performance. I have never seen one like it in my life in a championship game situation." "Nobody on the Dodgers should feel ashamed," Cey said, once he was able to speak. "Give credit where credit is due. The Yankees made all the right plays. Their pitchers made the good pitches and their hitters got the big hits."[12]

If the Dodgers' response to the loss was confusing, there was probably a good explanation. This was, after all, Lasorda's team, and the conflicting emotions were a reflection of his style. Outwardly, Lasorda kept a positive outlook, talking about how his players had come together, rising to the challenge in a tough transitional year. "There were things on the line," said Lasorda, "for me and for the team. People said that you can't be a big league manager and remain close to your players. They said that with today's attitudes and salaries you can't indoctrinate a feeling of loyalty and pride in an organization. I think I proved those people wrong on both counts. My players are proud to be a Dodger in the same way that players used to say that it's great to be a Yankee. . . . I think we strengthened the attachment between our fans and Dodger blue." Still, despite the optimistic words, Lasorda's deeper feelings about the World Series loss were more conflicted than he let on. Lasorda's ego had been bruised by the dramatic loss, and if you looked closely you could see signs. For one thing, Lasorda had, from all the stress and hard work of his first season as manager, put on thirty-five pounds of extra weight. And after the Series Lasorda was slightly defensive when asked about the team's prospects for 1978. "I already have a motto," Lasorda said. "'We did it before and we can do it again.'" In fact, on October 20, two days after Lasorda and the Dodgers had returned home to L.A., the manager's positive outlook was all but gone. "We had a tremendous season in many ways," he told Dodger beat reporter Ross Newhan, "a gratifying season for the organization, the manager, the players and the fans . . . [But] we had a long flight home, and we're disappointed that we couldn't bring Los Angeles a world championship. . . . I don't want to take anything away from the Yankees. We're too professional to do that. They beat us and there can be no alibis about it. Yet, there is no way that I can consider New York the better team. I wouldn't trade clubs, period. Man for man I have to take the Dodgers over the Yankees."[13]

As Lasorda had been certain it was his destiny to lead the Dodgers to a world championship in his first season at the helm, the wound left by not accomplishing this feat would in time become very clear. And as Reggie Jackson's fame grew in the aftermath of his Series performance, Lasorda and many of his Dodger players (and Dodger fans) would grow increasingly bitter about the loss. Accordingly, at the start of the winter break one wag wrote to the local paper, expressing a simple sentiment no doubt felt by millions: "To whom it may concern: Damn Yankees!" All winter at home in Fullerton, even as he kept himself busy in preparations for the coming season, Lasorda quietly, internally seethed. The wound remained so raw that in spring training, after a game against the Yankees with little at stake and even less meaning, Lasorda would gloat over the Dodgers' 7–3 win, telling a reporter that he had waited five months to get these guys. In fact, the seething wound to Lasorda's ego would apparently never heal. Even in 2010, more than thirty years after the fact, Lasorda used the occasion of a broadcast-booth visit with Reggie Jackson, Tim McCarver, and Joe Buck during a Fox Game-of-the-Week broadcast to attack his old nemesis. When Joe Buck inevitably brought up Jackson's remarkable feat in the 1977 World Series, Lasorda quickly blurted out: "A blind pig will always find an acorn." While Jackson attempted to insert some self-deprecating humor into the moment, Lasorda remained unrelenting. If he had had an opportunity to pitch to Jackson, Lasorda said, he would have "put him on his back."[14]

The unsettling fragility of the strong ego was much on the mind of Tom Wolfe in the fall of 1977. In his *Rolling Stone* "Post-orbital

Remorse" articles from several years earlier, he had identified the characteristics that drove the men of America's space program—their hypercharged egotism, their otherworldly competitiveness, their self-absorbed drive to achieve. Every one of the astronauts, and many involved in the space program, thought the spirit of the time—the driving force of the Right Stuff[15]—so crucial to the program and to America's need to achieve that none of them seemed to worry about the negative side effects: the damage to their personal lives, the addictions and mental health issues, their destroyed relationships, and so on. "We were cowboys, and the space program was a cowboy operation. It might have made the whole goddamned thing more open, more honest, more real, more lovable, if you will, and the better for all of us in the long run. But there was nobody who was going to tell that there was a whole side of us that was spelled MANIAC."[16]

Many of the wives of Dodger players may have well understood what the astronauts' spouses had to contend with: the fallout from an ego that had been lifted to the heights of human achievement, whether it be the rarefied air of outer space or the unlikely playing ground of the World Series. Baseball players are understandably protective of their personal lives, preferring to escape to relative obscurity after a season of intense competition, endless road travel, all-consuming focus on the game. Still, decompression into personal life for ballplayers was likely as difficult as it was for astronauts. In baseball postseason fallout takes many different forms. Fans and players and team management—all suddenly thrust into the emptiness that follows a disappointing end to the season—have little relief but the well-worn clichés: "There's always next year," or "We just got a bad break," or "The team will definitely bounce back from this." For many Dodgers life might have been just as it was for Steve Garvey, who, after the World Series in 1977, was faced with a return to his home life after many intense months away. "It's an empty feeling," said Steve Garvey of the impending off-season. "It's like writing a book without a climax."[17]

For Cyndy Garvey life after the 1977 World Series seemed somehow irrevocably changed. "The plane ride home to Los Angeles was torture," she wrote in a tell-all account of her life as a Dodger wife. "Steve and I sat up front, with the coaches. In the back, I could hear the players loosening up, having a few drinks and celebrating how far they'd gotten. They were singing and laughing. Even though they'd lost, even though they'd been unlucky, they knew they were young and healthy and damned good ballplayers." In the cabin where the Garveys sat, light was dim. The team's coaches slumped miserably in their seats. Lasorda, who seemed particularly distraught, supposedly sneaked drinks out of a briefcase.[18] Garvey did not speak much to his wife on the five-hour flight, breaking his silence only when a reporter stopped by to get a quote. "When we got back to Los Angeles," Cyndy Garvey wrote, "a small crowd of fans was there to greet us. All the passengers on the plane pulled themselves together and got off. . . . Nobody talked to us. I held on to Steve's arm and we went home alone."[19] From this moment forward, according to her account, Garvey would grow increasingly distant from his wife, preoccupied with things other than his family. And while Garvey, as a prominent star player on a team that had won the National League Championship, was in high demand—appearing almost around the clock at charity events, banquets, baseball clinics, publicity events—there was also, as Cyndy would discover some years later, no small amount of deceit driving Garvey's distance from his family.

Wolfe would describe the range of problems that astronauts had after completing their space missions, even to the point of giving this particular phenomenon a name: postorbital remorse. It wasn't a clinical diagnosis, as the psychiatrists had departed from the space program early on in its history, but something based on later reports by the astronauts about their struggles. In particular, the early astronauts suffered, once they realized they would never again travel to space, a kind of "holy hell." Scott Carpenter was the first astronaut to describe postorbital remorse. "The point is it dawned on him," wrote Wolfe, "that he wasn't going up again. The adventure was finished. There was no suitable encore to your final space flight. He had spent fifteen years ascending the mighty pyramid of flying and three years staring into the Jaws, training for this one flight, and he made it, and accomplished what he had set out to do—and suddenly he had no future."[20]

In these articles about brave and extraordinary men who faced life after accomplishing something truly remarkable, Wolfe hinted that he identified, however distantly, with their emotions. His collective-astronaut voice, at one point in the story, tried to convey the post-orbital struggle by speculating what it might be like if a writer, who had just written a great book, was told by the publishing world that "each writer gets a chance to publish just one book" and after that book the writer had to "step aside forever and let other writers have their shot at it."[21]

This was a telling thought. By late 1977 Wolfe himself had been grounded, as a writer, for several years. After the four-part "Post-orbital Remorse" series hit the newsstands and caused a broad sensation, Wolfe planned to write a grand, comprehensive biographical history of America's space program. In fact, Wolfe imagined this book well could be his breakthrough work, the one that would attract a vast, new, more mainstream audience that would cement his reputation for the ages. Spurred by this vision Wolfe lined up a publisher and editor and signed a contract. He organized his past notes and categorized them, then drew up plans. But then he hit a snag. Perhaps it was the daunting scope of the subject—fifteen years of very involved history, dozens and dozens of complex interviews, important national cultural ramifications—but for the first time in his career, Wolfe found himself at a loss to write the story.

Now it was three years later. Wolfe, seeing his city all aflutter from an epic World Series win by the hated New York Yankees and the repulsive Reggie Jackson, and full knowing his epic book on America's space program was languishing, had a choice to make: either redouble his efforts to finish his master work for the ages or give up the whole idea altogether and start over. Wolfe made his choice. By November he was back in the hunt for the Right Stuff.

For two other Toms the long winter that followed the Dodgers' loss in the 1977 World Series also presented crucial moments of decision. By the fall of 1977 Tom Bradley had all but put the racially divisive election of 1977 behind him and begun to focus on issues that would move his city toward the future: his efforts to grow the local economy and prop up local businesses; his burning drive to help the city cope with a growing host of social problems such as entrenched poverty, rising crime, gang violence, and so on; his desire to move Los Angeles into the forefront of a more international, global era; and, related to all of these, his wish for Los Angeles to host the Summer Olympics in 1984. The full reasoning behind Bradley's desire to bring the Olympics back to Los Angeles was complex. On the one hand, he was convinced that the Games would bring significant benefits, both tangible and symbolic, to his beloved city. But on the other hand, Bradley had other, more personal, reasons to want the Games. Bradley had witnessed the results of the previous Los Angeles Olympics in 1932 when he was an impressionable fourteen-year-old. With his home just within walking distance of the Olympic Village in Baldwin Hills, where the athletes stayed during the Games, Bradley found himself drawn toward the world's great athletes of the era—especially African American sprinter Eddie Tolan, who earned the nickname "world's fastest human" for his feats at the 1932 Games. And while he could not afford the eleven-dollar ticket to watch an event at the Coliseum, Bradley caught glimpses of the Games through slats in a fence at the stadium, and he read about the great athletes' exploits in the daily paper. Later, he climbed the fence of the stadium to watch a favorite track event. "The one-hundred-meter dash turned out to be the most exciting event of the entire Olympics," Bradley recalled. The memory never left him and may have been a chief inspiration for him to bring the Games back. "It may have been Bradley's concern for the youth of Los Angeles," wrote Bradley biographers Gregory Payne and Scott Ratzan, "and his memories of what the Olympics of 1932 had meant to his own impoverished boyhood that made him so determined to bring the Olympic Games to Los Angeles for 1984, despite the possible political consequences to himself."[22]

By November 1977, meanwhile, Tom Fallon had realized something about his struggle to build his business. Sure, things were fine overall. Customers seemed to enjoy coming in to the hardware store, if only to buy a few bolts and share a word with the owners. But with the region around them booming, and new tracts of land being cleared and graded every day for new housing, business could have been even better. What he needed, he thought, was something more, some master plan that could make his enterprise as successful as others around town were becoming. Fallon needed to do something.

After moving to Alta Loma just prior to becoming a partner with Nelson Hawley, Tom Fallon had gone on a fact-finding tour. He had talked with people, listened to what made them tick, and tried to understand what were their hopes and dreams were. Ultimately, Fallon came to several sharp conclusions. The first was this: the boomtown mentality and the expansive economic drive that ruled Southern California had arrived in the Cucamonga area and were not likely to go away anytime soon. And the second conclusion was this: the key to local boom-time success was one thing, land. That is, he knew that in order to realize for his family a semblance of California-style economic success, he needed to purchase as much land in and around Cucamonga as he could. Despite this realization, however, he wondered in the months after the 1977 World Series exactly how he could pull such a thing off. And this was when everything suddenly changed.

On November 30, 1977, Cucamonga voted on a referendum along with two adjoining unincorporated Southern Californian communities—Alta Loma, where Tom Fallon owned a home, and Etiwanda, where his grandchildren went to school and played in Little League—on whether to merge as one incorporated city called Rancho Cucamonga. All three bedroom communities, located as they were in the foothills of the Sierra Madre range along the path of old Route 66, had long been separately known for little other than producing wine, being the punch line of a running Mel Blanc–Jack Benny gag, and for some fairly quirky history. For instance, in 1960, before plans were scuttled, a developer sought to build a Bible-land theme park in Cucamonga. Add in a sensational unsolved murder or two from back before the war, and you get the gist of the spirit of the place. By merging into a larger city, Rancho Cucamonga hoped to leave behind its colorful dusty-outpost past and become a place more worthy of serious development.

For Tom Fallon, the incorporation confirmed that his theory was correct—that there were money and success to be had in owning local land. Fallon also, in the aftermath of the vote, began to hear the rumors: that the city governments of all three communities were increasingly intent on attracting corporate developments to fatten the local tax base and that housing and other developments would be increasingly upscale. Fallon knew, then, that his window of opportunity was shrinking. He had to take action soon. Which was how, in the days and weeks that followed the disappointment over the Dodgers' loss to the Yankees, Tom Fallon changed the destiny of his business, and of his family.

PART 2
1978

SIXTEEN

Rediscovering Baseball

The ironic and most remarkable aspect of Reggie Jackson's feat is that for a moment there, on that littered, brilliant field, he—he, of all people—made us forget.

—Roger Angell

It breaks your heart. It is designed to break your heart. The game begins in spring, when everything else begins again, and it blossoms in the summer, filling the afternoons and evenings, and then as soon as the chill rains come, it stops and leaves you to face the fall alone.

—A. Bartlett Giamatti, "The Green Fields of the Mind," *Yale Alumni*, November 1977

The ripples that spread out across the country in late 1977 as a result of Reggie Jackson's World Series heroics swept up many of the hardened purists of the time. That is, the disillusioned masses of baseball fans who had loudly bemoaned the changes to their sport just a year prior suddenly realized, in the winter of 1978, that the ground beneath them had shifted. "The ironic and most remarkable aspect of Reggie Jackson's feat," wrote *New Yorker* writer Roger Angell, "is that for a moment there, on that littered, brilliant field, he—he, of all people—made us forget."[1] Beyond New York, in far-off places like Youngstown, Ohio, and Milwaukee, Wisconsin, people were ecstatic about baseball again. Fans young and old forgot their recent complaints about the state of the game. Suddenly, the entire nation was abuzz about the American pastime. ABC TV estimated that a healthy number of fans—between 110 and 120 million of them—had tuned into the World Series in October. In 1977, led by the Dodgers' record-setting attendance mark of more than 2,955,000 fans,[2] the overall attendance for the league reached 38 million, a record for the sport and a rise of 14 percent from the season before. The Dodgerland fans had flocked to Dodger Stadium, but so had baseball fans all across the country come out for their team. A Harris survey conducted after the 1977 season showed that, for the first time in nine years, more adult sports fans in 1977 had followed baseball than football, though this was by only a scant margin (61–60 percent).[3] Further, during the off-season advance ticket sales were booming. Twenty-five of the league's twenty-six teams reported increased preseason sales, and nine clubs, including the Dodgers and Yankees, reported record preseason sales.[4]

After the 1977 season, it became obvious that, while baseball's modern free-agent system still rankled, most fans had all but accepted the changing game as a fait accompli. And why not forget one's misgivings about free agency? After all, the free agency that so many had feared would bring about the demise of baseball had done the opposite. The game was exciting, its popularity booming. And free agency had played a role in this—making it possible, among other things, for Reggie Jackson's remarkable, generation-defining achievement to happen. Even the victims of Jackson's handiwork—the Dodgers and their fans—had to concede that some much-needed excitement had returned to baseball. "Only a few years ago," wrote a columnist in the *Los Angeles Times*, "baseball was being subjected to mournful scrutiny by commentators who, having wrung their hands dry, pronounced the game moribund. They mispronounced it rather badly. Baseball has in fact never been more robust."[5]

A good sign of the thaw in the attitudes of disgruntled and disappointed baseball fans was the return of a time-honored baseball tradition: Yankee hatred. That is, it was clear in the aftermath of the Yankees' stunning and shattering victory over the Dodgers that the country was split once again along traditional lines. At the end of 1977 you either were ecstatic to see the Yankees on top again or were disgusted by that fact. "Some authors," wrote Gordon Verrell in *The Sporting News*, "went so far as to suggest that the World Series between the Dodgers and the Yankees was really an exercise matching the 'good guys' against the 'bad guys,' the result of which obviously says something for black hats and other unsavory types."[6] Across the country people derided the Yankees, self-important owner George Steinbrenner, the even more self-important star Reggie Jackson, and feisty manager Billy Martin. Commenters dismissively ridiculed the Yankees as "the best team that money can buy" and suggested that, for the good of baseball, the team should be dismantled. That the cries were soundly ignored, and the Yankees dug right back into free agency in the off-season to purchase the contracts of free-agent pitchers Andy Messersmith, Rich Gossage, and Rawly Eastwick, did not really matter. The fact was, all the Yankee-centered tumult and disagreement meant one important fact for baseball: the sport mattered again. People cared about baseball.

So at last, after a long lull, baseball at the dawn of 1978 was finally starting to evolve with the times, growing in its marketing savvy and learning to leverage its inherent charms against its competition. As baseball commissioner Bowie Kuhn suggested, people in the late 1970s, stressed as they were and overcome by the struggles of the time, were realizing the charms of a more leisurely, fun, and family-friendly game. "I have pretty consistently maintained that this kind of feeling was going to work to baseball's benefit," Kuhn said. "I've been saying that for probably five years. We as people live in a fairly frenetic society and we are looking for something that takes us away from some of the more extreme pressures. Baseball has a charm that seems to fit that need. . . . More people hunger for a more leisurely pace and baseball matches this mood perhaps better than more explosive sports." And it wasn't just karma. Kuhn also cited, in addition to the perceived rediscovery of the "game's gentle charms," that the league was simply working better. There was more balanced competition in baseball, an appealing increase in offensive firepower among the game's stars, as well as more aggressive and coordinated marketing strategies, direct-mailing efforts, and reasonably priced tickets at "pretty, clean, nice ballparks"—all contributing to the sense that baseball was a fun family game. "Clubs are doing a much better job of marketing than ever before," Kuhn said.[7]

In light of baseball's improving prospects after the close of the 1977 season, and in view of the looming 1978 campaign, Tom Lasorda reasserted his enthusiasm for the game. "He told the team," said one of Lasorda's players, "that the best possible thing that could have happened to us this season was winning the World Series. The second best possible thing was to lose the World Series."[8] The rest of the Dodgers, and all the team's fans and supporters, seemed to follow Lasorda's lead. In time the winter that came after Jackson's three death blows was not a time for bitterness and disgruntlement. Instead, it was a time for self-reflection and preparation. Meaning, the team, its fans, and owners looked back to consider exactly what the team had accomplished in 1977 and forward to ask if it was possible for them to do even more in 1978.

For Dodger third baseman Ron Cey, the answer was an unequivocal yes. "We—the Dodgers—have a winning attitude," Cey told an interviewer in January, just before the team was to begin winter workouts at Dodger Stadium. "Every year we start out with the same primary goal—the world championship. When you have that kind of attitude, a winning one, everyone tries that much harder." Tom Lasorda had often gone so far as to say the key to the Dodgers' success in 1977 was "love," but people were learning to take much of what Lasorda said with a grain of salt. Cey, for his part, acknowledged his manager's tendency for hyperbole, but he didn't completely dismiss Lasorda's assessment. "True," he said, "the whole thing has been exaggerated, but it does run true quite a bit, and it hasn't been altogether overdone. You can sense it. You can see it. You can feel it. Anyone who'd been around the clubhouse could feel it, too."[9]

The key to the Dodgers' winning attitude, in other words, according to Cey, was a sense of unity—a unity that observers half marveled at, half belittled. The Dodgers were certainly not for everyone. While Gordon Verrell had pointed out that the Dodgers so-called "'one-for-all, all-for-one' reputation was widely heralded in poetry and song through the 1977 season, hitting a peak in the World Series,"[10] Howard Cosell had taken umbrage at the team's particular character in the second game of the World Series. "I'd like the viewers to note before you close out, Keith," Cosell had said to his cohost, Keith Jackson, "these Dodgers are not full of jubilation, jumping over one another. They're a kind of passionless team. They don't have the outward fire of the Yankees." Tom Lasorda, of course, would likely have taken sharp exception to Cosell's words. "The most exciting thing to me," said the manager in January 1978,

> is how the fans have identified with the team. What we saw in our attendance I've seen again in the reception when I'm out speaking. We got more than a thousand letters between the time the World Series ended and every one, in some form or another, was an expression of support for our philosophy and approach. Frank Sinatra told me he had never seen a team capture the heart of a city in the short time that the Dodger blue did. I even got letters from writers all over the country saying how much they respected the way we handled ourselves.[11]

Tom Lasorda had in fact taken to barn-storming for his beloved Dodgers during the off-season, spreading his Blue Gospel constantly, even after suffering dysentery while on a scouting trip in the Dominican Republic.[12] And why not? The Dodger manager was in great demand. In short order Lasorda appeared on the TV game shows *Tattle Tales* and *Hollywood Connection*; hosted a thirty-minute Super Bowl preview; traveled to Spain, Florida, Pennsylvania, Canada, Mexico, and Arizona (in addition to the Dominican Republic); and attended events, often in his honor, hosted by the Variety Club, Cystic Fibrosis Foundation, Lions Club, Elks, Moose, and baseball writers' organizations in Philadelphia, Houston, St. Louis, and New York.[13] While Lasorda's breakneck pace raised a lot of eyebrows, and the pointed concern of Dodger president Peter O'Malley, Lasorda shrugged. "Look," he said, "how can you get tired doing what I'm doing? I'm blessed. I have my health, a marvelous family, and the only job I've ever wanted. I work for the best organization in baseball, in a city with the best fans. My players took me to the World Series in my first year as their manager. In the last year I've been on the *Tonight, Tomorrow* and *Today* shows. I was on the cover of *Sports Illustrated* even before I managed my first major league game. Only in America could this happen to the son of an Italian immigrant. I'm only trying to put something back in. . . . That's what life is all about, isn't it?"[14]

Make no mistake, however; through the whirlwind schedule of fetes, charitable events, and chances to crow about his Dodgers, Lasorda never took his eye off the bigger prize: getting his team back to the World Series in 1978. As he did prior to his first season as manager, in his scant spare time Lasorda plotted and schemed about his lineup, his players, and how best to employ them in the coming year. He planned, he said, to hold individual meetings with his players, just as he did the previous year. "For one thing," Lasorda told a reporter, "I want to convince Garvey, Smith, and Ron Cey that they can be even more effective with more rest." And as he did prior to the previous Christmas, Lasorda wrote letters to each of his players, as well as his coaches, to relay how much he valued each of them. "[I] told them that I wanted to share any honors I had won because they were the people who had made it possible. I told them they were not only outstanding talents but outstanding human beings, that I would need their resources again in 1978 and I wanted them to go to spring training with the same enthusiasm and desire" as they had before the 1977 season.[15]

"This is a young team that has the ability to be better than it was last year," Lasorda said firmly, "that can be more productive in each of the next several years. . . . The players know they can win. They know what it takes to reach the World Series and they want to do it again." When someone asked again if he didn't want to rest a bit before starting the difficult road to a world championship, Lasorda balked. "Rest? Hell," he exclaimed, "I'm ready for spring training. I'm ready to go get 'em again."[16]

As you might expect of any team that has lost the World Series, especially in as dramatic a way as L.A. did in 1977, the Dodgers did not spend the winter in static hibernation. Lasorda, ever in search of a competitive edge, knew he had several pressing concerns left unaddressed from the 1977 season. Foremost, Lasorda knew the bullpen had to be shored up, especially considering the several key injuries and the inconsistent performance of the team's closer, Charlie Hough, who had recorded just three saves in the final two months of the season. The signing of free-agent reliever Terry Forster gave Lasorda an additional bullpen tool, but there were still some other very burning questions lingering as spring training approached. Would Rick Monday return from his injury and be effective in the crucial center-fielder position? Could the team sharpen its already proficient starting pitching even while assuaging the unrest of several veteran starters? And what could give the Dodgers an edge over the ever-hungry Cincinnati Reds, who had improved their own pitching staff through the acquisition of former Oakland A's star Vida Blue? As a result of these concerns, the Dodgers' camp, led by general manager Al Campanis, was one of the more active during baseball's winter meetings in Honolulu, and Dodger pitchers Don Sutton and Rick Rhoden were mentioned often in trade rumors. Sutton was reportedly offered to the Texas Rangers in exchange for their star pitcher Bert Blyleven, who had long made it known he wanted to play ball in his home state of California. And Rhoden, meanwhile, was one of four players being offered to the San Diego Padres in exchange for outfielder Dave Winfield.[17] None of these deals came through, however, so Lasorda had to settle for former Dodger outfielder Willie Crawford, who had played with the team during its run to the 1974 World Series.[18] While Crawford's star was clearly descending in 1978, Lasorda hoped he could provide, off the bench, another solid left-handed bat.

Inevitably, as spring approached and the Dodgers sought left-handed hitters and better options in the outfield, observers increasingly speculated on the future of embattled veteran Rick Monday. Considered a major disappointment for the Dodgers in 1977—perhaps the only real disappointment in a season of great highs—Monday was philosophical about his tumble on the AstroTurf in Houston on May 31. "It led to my most frustrating season," said Monday to an *L.A. Times* reporter before the 1978 season. "The pain and back spasms and the other problems lasted 3½ months." Compounding the problem, and adding to Monday's and his team's frustration, was the fact that the source of the outfielder's pain and inability to play was not truly understood. "It was like playing ball in chains," said Monday with a shudder. "When you don't really understand an injury, it really upsets you. I've had broken bones and things like that, but this was my first serious problem. With a fracture, you can see the cast. You understand what's wrong. A back injury is like dealing with the unknown."[19] When Monday was finally well enough to play regularly in September, he took pains to explain, it was so late in the season, and he had missed so much time, that his timing at the bat was off-kilter. He went through the playoffs and World Series, he said, feeling "out of synch." And while he had a decent playoff series against the Phillies, getting two hits, including a double, in seven at bats, Monday was completely ineffective against the Yankees. He batted .167 with three strikeouts in twelve at bats and was replaced in two games by the weak-hitting Glenn Burke. In 1977 Monday had collected the worst numbers of his Major League career: a meager .230 batting average, a weak .383 slugging percentage, and just 15 home runs and 109 strikeouts in 456 plate appearances.

To his credit, the ever-competitive Monday, who was of course fully aware of what was at stake for the World Series runner-up, had two messages to send to Lasorda and anyone else in the Dodger front office who might be reading. First, he wanted to let it be known how committed he was to this team—to the point of suggesting his own struggles didn't matter. "If I could go back to May 31," he said, "I'd still dive for that ball. If they hit one at me tomorrow and I can catch it by diving for it, I'll do the same thing again. You can't baby yourself and play this game." When pressed further if he had strong feelings about playing for the Dodgers, Monday, who grew up in nearby Santa Monica, didn't hesitate in his answer:

> Do you remember the thrill you had the first time you were actually on the road to Disneyland? Going to the Dodgers was like going to Disneyland for me. I had never been at a training camp with more than one field. Everyone in the world wants to play for the Dodgers. . . . There's an awareness here that we're all in the same boat together: The secretaries, the O'Malleys, the batboys, the PR people, the players. Everything is "we." This is a unique organization. If something's bothering you, you know you can bring it up. The Dodgers don't let things smolder within like they do on some clubs. And corrections are made in constructive ways. In short, I like the Dodgers.

Further, Monday wanted it to be known that the Dodgers didn't need Winfield or anyone else—they already had their center fielder. Monday was ready to play and contribute to the team's cause. "This winter," he said, "I've come all the way back. My timing is OK again and I'm ready for the season. Make that: I'm looking forward to the season. . . . I expect to pick up my career where I left off last May."[20]

As for any specific personal goals, Monday demurred. "In 11 years in the major leagues," said Monday, "the only goal I've had is to get into the World Series. Now, having played in one, my goal this year is to win it."[21] The World Series would have to wait, of course, as there was, in fact, a long road for the team to travel before it could win a championship. Indeed, if the winter was any indication, that road might hold any number of bumps and disappointments. In mid-February the Dodgers returned from a team trip to Hawaii, where they had competed in the *Superteams* competition for ABC TV. While the Dodgers had done well in the competition in the past, emerging as victors in 1974, this year they were outclassed by the Dallas Cowboys and Kansas City Royals, who eventually won it all. A big factor in the Dodgers' loss in the competition was their performance in the eight-man canoe race. Not only did the Dodgers lose the race, but their rudder man actually fell out of the boat. The name of that waterlogged crew member? The ever-disappointing Rick Monday.

Of course the *Superteams* defeat was mostly symbolic, and not to be fretted over too seriously, but more disturbing news reached the team on February 24. One day earlier the team's retired owner, Walter O'Malley, had fallen ill while flying in his private plane to Florida. So severe was the illness that the plane was immediately rerouted to Rochester, Minnesota, where the seventy-four-year-old O'Malley was checked into the Mayo Clinic for tests and observation.

If fans of the team were looking beyond Walter O'Malley's hospitalization for some positive news, it came to them at the very end of February. In the San Joaquin Valley, about 170 miles north of Dodger Stadium in a small town called Lindsay, a local junior high school held a ceremony. But it was no ordinary ceremony. In attendance, in addition to the expected coterie of teachers and students and their parents, was a new principal named Bob Edwards. Also, more surprisingly, there were four TV crews and perhaps a dozen reporters from nearby city papers. And there were two guests—Steve Garvey and his wife, Cyndy—on hand to celebrate the rededication of a school that had been so unruly and troubled just a year earlier that it was almost closed down.

It was a cool and overcast day. All that month of February 1978, an unusual amount of rain had fallen on Southern California. Whereas the average rainfall in Los Angeles in February was about 3.8 inches, over an eleven-day period 8.2 inches of rain fell. (March would see an additional 4.2 inches.) This might not sound like much precipitation compared to many parts of the country, but in Southern California this amounted to a major monsoon,[22] and the dry, hard-packed ground in Los Angeles could not absorb the water. As a result across the Los Angeles basin residents had to cope with flash floods, mud slides, sinkholes, and the like. Out in Cucamonga, where the flooding and accumulation were particularly bad, empty lots filled with water and entire sections of certain roads completely disappeared overnight. The problem was so bad that, when parents found it increasingly treacherous to get children to schools, local school districts closed for the better part of a week in mid-February. And as water levels rose, Cucamonga Hardware saw a run on sandbag kits.

In Lindsay in late February the ceremony at the school was marked by a sense of relief and joy, as not only had the rains slowed, but there were various tangible signs of change around the school. Walls had been repainted from a dull yellow to Dodger blue. Graffiti had been cleaned and covered up by a mural of Peanuts characters playing baseball. And a new large picture of Steve Garvey was hung over the trophy case. Principal Edwards noted that the school had upgraded its curriculum and that fighting and gang activity had decreased, and then he spoke of the entire reason for the ceremony and the most dramatic sign that this was a wholly renewed place: the school's new name. "It's not just the name change which has turned the school so completely around," Edwards told the gathered students, parents, teachers, and journalists. "It's just that Steve Garvey gave us reason to do all this. Now people in the area are going to say, 'Oh, yeah. Steve Garvey Junior High School, that action place where things are really popping.'" After Edwards finished Garvey stepped up to the mic and spoke seriously, telling the kids that he would keep working hard and they should too. The crowd of 370 kids burst into applause, stomped their feet, and cheered loudly. The first baseman who had starred in All-Star Games and in the World Series seemed genuinely affected by the adulation. "This," said Garvey as students rushed to surround him, "is all a little scary."[23]

Spring training for the Dodgers in 1978 began on March 1 with a markedly different atmosphere from a year earlier. Much of this was due to Tom Lasorda. Whereas he had been overly blustery and vocal in his uncertain first spring training as the Dodger manager, now, in his second, he was more circumspect. "I don't know if we can get off to a 22-4 start again," Lasorda told a reporter. "That's asking a lot. We'll get ready the same way we did last year and hope we can start just as fast . . . Our people are talented enough and young enough to be more productive than they were in '77. They now know they belong, that they can win. They have character and respect. They know what the rewards are and they want it even more than before. They know everyone will be gunning for them, that they can't live on their laurels."[24]

A few days later, of course, Lasorda had reverted to his usual overconfident self. "The only questions mark I can see are that we don't know how many games we'll win it by and who we'll play in the fall classic." Then, much as he had on the first day of camp a year before, Lasorda made a major announcement. Having obtained the endorsement of the team president, Peter O'Malley, and several of the team's veteran players, Lasorda had decided to appoint Dodgers second baseman Dave Lopes as the team's captain. Lopes would be the fifth player to hold the position on the Dodgers since the team's first captain, Pee Wee Reese, held the position from 1949 to 1958. He would also be the team's first captain since Willie Davis held the position in 1973. Lasorda, in choosing Lopes, was well aware of the particular spirit of his team, filled as it was with a number of strong and independent spirits. "We have a number of guys of equal qualification," Lasorda said afterward. "But you can only have one leader, one captain, and I've always felt Davey is a natural. I look for him to play a prominent role in the same way a coach does. I look for him to serve as a liaison between the players and myself."[25]

Lopes, for his part, was in tune with his manager in recognizing the need to focus on player relations in the Dodger clubhouse.

"There are always situations where a player is reluctant to go to the manager," said Lopes. "There are liable to be incidences of animosity and turmoil. By understanding my teammates' personalities and maintaining rapport with the manager and coaches, I can possibly head off these situations." Tellingly, after the appointment was announced and players responded with applause, several players told pointed jokes. "Captain?" said Tommy John, looking over at a teammate whom he later admitted he had never found likable. "Everyone knows that Ron Cey is our leader." ("Maybe," Lopes reportedly responded with a laugh, "but Ron isn't stopping at captain. He's going right on to commissioner.") After the joking subsided players seemed to agree that the move would likely serve to alleviate much of the behind-the-scenes stresses on the clubhouse. "It's difficult to put into words," said Ron Cey, "but there is no doubt in my mind that this was a good step, that Davey will be more than an honorary captain. He tried to do a lot of things last year but was restricted by not having the official title. This will give him the weight he needs, will give an impact to his suggestions."[26]

Of course, Lasorda couldn't help but take some credit for Lopes's ascendance to the position, as well as his infield partner Bill Russell's blossoming. "Davey Lopes and Bill Russell were exactly alike," said Lasorda of his middle infielders' early days. "Davey wouldn't say two words all night. And you didn't know Russell was around until the game started. I took them everywhere. I was always trying to draw them out. They now represent the two most dramatic personality changes I've ever contributed to." And while this could have been another instance of Lasorda's bluster, in fact Lopes was the first to agree with his manager. "Lasorda pushed me toward being even more aggressive, more extroverted," said Lopes. "He instilled a lot of his own personality in me, both in my approach to baseball and in my personal life." Lasorda's transformation of Lopes was so complete by spring training in 1978 that some around the baseball world had actually dubbed the formerly timid and retiring second baseman something approaching the opposite—a showboat, or a "popoff." To that Lopes took umbrage. "I wouldn't call myself a popoff at all," he said. "I don't say things just to satisfy my ego or spirit. . . . Yet if you ask me a question, I'll give you the honest answer."[27]

His agreement with Lopes struck, Lasorda kept a close watch in the early days of spring training and made no bones about his increased expectations for his players. Lopes, he said, would be completely recovered from several injuries that slowed him down in 1977, and so he expected more steals from his speedy second baseman. Cey, who, after a record-setting month of April in 1977, was stricken by a groin problem and fell into a slump, would be more relaxed and consistent. Dusty Baker would continue his recovery from leg injuries. Lasorda even had hope for his light-hitting catcher. Steve Yeager came to spring training having replaced his regular aviator-style eyeglasses—after he had broken six different pairs of them in 1977—with new soft contact lenses, which he swore gave him much sharper vision. "I can now see Chub Feeney's autograph on the ball when it's being pitched," said Yeager, laughing. "Before, I had trouble reading road signs at night. . . . Seeing this well is a brand new feeling. I'm excited. I've got to believe that if you can see a lot better, you should be able to perform a lot better."[28] Lasorda would expect more from his rugged backstop's bat.

And so on down the lineup. Terry Forster would bolster the bullpen. Rick Monday would make a comeback similar to Dusty Baker's in 1977. Stalwarts like Don Sutton, Steve Garvey, Reggie Smith, and Tommy John would continue to star. Even the bench would contribute, with a range of quality talent in Lee Lacy, Teddy Martinez (if he could recover completely from his injury), Willie Crawford (if he could return to form), and tough backup catchers Jerry Grote and Johnny Oates. And then, of course, there were the ageless pinch-hit specialists, Vic Davalillo and Manny Mota.

"Look at that," Lasorda bellowed across the Dodger practice field during morning calisthenics. "Look at Mota and Davalillo. They must have a hundred years between them." The actual number of years that the two ballplayers shared in 1978, if official records can be believed, is eighty-one. "People say I'm a connoisseur of antiques, that it's the only reason I'm keeping Mota and Davalillo around." All joking aside, the presence of both players—each in their forties and each from modest baseball-centric families who grew up in Latin countries (Mota from the Dominican Republic, Davalillo from Venezuela)—was a remarkable thing, and all parties seemed aware of the fact. "I am very happy," Davalillo said, when asked how he felt to be there. Very early in the spring Davalillo compared life in the Mexican League with life in the Major Leagues. "In Mexico," he said, "you get 100 pesos meal money. That's four American dollars a day. In the big leagues, you have to tip that much a day." "I feel very good about being back in the majors," he told a reporter a bit later that spring. "I didn't think it would happen, . . . not at my age."[29]

Manny Mota, the man whom Walt Alston once said would "roll out of bed in December and go 4-for-4," echoed his teammate's sentiments. As a child Mota said, "we used oranges and lemons for baseballs, and we made mitts by sticking our hand into a paper bag. . . . I dreamed about having spikes and gloves and a real baseball to play with. I still think a lot about those memories. They are good ones for me."[30] Now, many years later, after sixteen seasons in the big leagues, Mota was facing a major milestone. Long considered to be one of the game's great pinch-hitting experts, Mota would start 1978 just twenty-two pinch hits behind the all-time leading pinch hitter, his former Pirates teammate Smokey Burgess. Of the record Mota was unequivocal. "I want to stay until I catch Smokey," he said. "I would like to catch him this year but I will be proud to catch him anytime." Within hearing range of his teammates and manager, however, Mota was more humble. "It is nice to be back. It is nice to be back with determination. I know that as I get older I have to work harder."[31]

That both Davalillo and Mota would make the cut out of spring training gave hope to aging fans of the team. Not every one of the Dodgers' projected role players had the favor of their manager. Lasorda had in fact lost patience with two young Dodgers—namely, Glenn Burke and Ed Goodson—who had stalled in their development. "Glenn can run, field and throw," said Tom Lasorda very early in spring training. "He hasn't proved to us he can hit." Lasorda had a point. Though Burke had outstanding speed, was an excellent fielder, and had performed extremely well at every level of the Minors, in two years of part-time play in the Majors he had yet to generate anything at the plate. (His slugging percentage in 226 plate appearances in 1976 and 1977 was a woeful .312.) "I'm convinced Monday is sound," Lasorda continued, "which means I'm left to balance the bench. I've got right-handers like Manny Mota and Lee Lacy who have showed me they can hit better than Burke and I have people like Crawford and Davalillo who I have to keep because there will definitely be times when I'll need the left handers." Translation: he had little need for weak right-handed hitters like Burke and Goodson. Perhaps anticipating fan reaction regarding Lasorda's statements, Dodger general manager Al Campanis had his own things to say on Burke and Goodson. "In Burke's case," said Campanis, "he is out of options. He can't be sent to the minors without his permission. He must be traded and I expect there will be interest in him. . . . In Goodson's case, . . . he can be released, traded or consider playing in Japan."[32]

The ongoing decision about whether to shelve these two players would, at least in one case, prove to have some lasting ramifications. Interestingly, Campanis himself had perhaps sealed the fate of at least one of these players when he had announced, several weeks earlier, that because of payroll concerns, the Dodgers were going to hold the traveling roster this year to twenty-four regular players, as opposed to the usual twenty-five. Goodson, after a lackluster spring, was released outright by the Dodgers on March 17; he would never, after eight seasons in the big leagues, appear in another Major League game. As for Burke, the jury was still out, but just barely. Burke survived spring cuts when Willie Crawford, who struggled through a far worse spring that Burke's, was cut outright by the team at the very end of the spring exhibition season on March 30. Teddy Martinez, meanwhile, would survive spring cuts and start the season as the Dodgers' utility man. On the pitching staff, amid even more brutal competition, Lance Rautzhan, who had been on the Dodgers' roster in the 1977 World Series and pitched well in spring training, would be sent back to Albuquerque in favor of another reliever, the locally born screwball-tossing Mexican American right-hander Bobby Castillo. Hank Webb, who had made an appearance with the team as a September call-up in 1977, but was now pushing twenty-eight, could not turn his presence on the forty-man roster into a spot on the Major League team. He would return to Albuquerque in April and never appear in another Major League game.

SEVENTEEN

Paradise Defiled

There was never a region so unlikely to become
a vast metropolitan area as Southern California.
It is . . . a gigantic improvisation.

—Carey McWilliams, *Southern California: An Island on the Land*

At the dawn of 1978 Los Angeles was an uncertain city. L.A.'s former self-confidence and swagger had been gradually shaken by the events and conditions of the 1970s, and now, in the new year, many Southern Californians seemed to be suddenly waking from a long daydream. "Of course," *Time* had written in a July 1977 reappraisal of its 1969 article mostly lauding the Golden State, "the California dream was doomed from its inception; a society based on the illogic of instability is no society at all." Back in 1972, in his book *California: The Vanishing Dream*, author Michael Davie noted that despite the wealth, sunshine, talent, and knowledge in California, "worldly happiness" was, for some reason, fleeting. "The economic and technological machine was grinding on," Davie wrote, "but fewer and fewer people thought that its whirrings were a prelude to a better future."[1] In 1971, two years before the roiling economic crises of 1973 that would hit California hard, a poll had already revealed that half the state's recent arrivals, and a full third of its permanent residents, would leave the state, given the chance. The next year migration to California crashed—to around thirty thousand, or one-tenth the annual rate of three hundred thousand who arrived during the 1960s.

It wasn't that the state was significantly more troubled than anywhere else in the country in the 1970s. Rather, as *Time* pointed out, it was that the utopian image of Los Angeles from its heyday in the 1950s and 1960s so harshly clashed with daily life in the 1970s, which was defined by traffic congestion and air pollution, job losses and economic instability, racial conflicts and other results of the postwar patterns of development and consumerism. Living in 1970s Los Angeles was a tedious proposition, and the fantasy of the California paradise was seeming more and more just that—a fantasy. Now, after promoting itself as the golden land of opportunity for a half century, the resulting unfettered growth had led to very real systemic and infrastructural problems. For the typical Angeleno in 1978 days were thick and hot as soup, and life was organized around freeway commutes and long delays, sore lungs and red eyes, slow trips to auto body shops and busy shopping centers, the hassle of long workweeks and the struggle to earn a hard dollar. Living in Los Angeles meant you had to be ready for ceaseless work, because not doing so meant you would fall behind the vast roving mechanical herd of the other freeway-bound residents of the region. In short, real life in California was anything but a pleasant stroll along the seashore. As a result, the magazine explained, the problems there seemed somehow more jarring than in the rest of the country: "The loss seems greater in California because there the expectations were so much greater than elsewhere. . . . California has clearly lost the magic it once had."[2]

The death of the California Dream was something few people truly wanted to acknowledge. However, as the troubled decade of the 1970s wore on, more and more Californians could no longer ignore the hard truths about their lives and the falseness of the dream. If a singular moment epitomized this dawning realization, it was one that occurred during the hippie-bohemian summer of 1969. In the Los Angeles hills located just north of the fantasy factory of Hollywood, in a house on Cielo Drive, lived the diminutive Polish-native filmmaker Roman Polanski with his wife, Sharon Tate. Polanski was, most famously at the time, the director of the unusual horror film *Rosemary's Baby*, which includes a scene in which a young woman (played by Mia Farrow) is raped and impregnated by Satan. Polanski's life up until 1969 had seen its share of deep trauma and tragedy. Born a Polish Jew before World War II, as an eight-year-old boy he somehow survived the final purging of the Kraków Ghetto, when his father, who had been lined up to board a train to the Mauthausen-Gusen concentration camp in Austria, pushed him away and denied knowing him. Somehow Polanski survived the war, mostly by hiding in barns or forests and eating whatever he could steal or find. After the war he was reunited with his father, who had somehow survived.[3] In time Polanski attended the famed Polish film school in Lódz, and eventually he made a number of highly regarded films—including *Knife in the Water*, which was nominated for a Best Foreign Film Oscar in 1962. *Rosemary's Baby* was his first big Hollywood break, and it was a smash success. Afterward, Polanski was one of the leading lights in Hollywood.

What thrust Polanski into the middle of California's looming identity crisis was a traumatic event that occurred on August 9, 1969. Polanski had married the beautiful young actress Sharon Tate, star of his 1967 horror spoof, *The Fearless Vampire Killers*, in 1968. In February 1969 the Polanskis, flush from the success of his first Hollywood film, rented a house at 10500 Cielo Drive in the Benedict Canyon neighborhood that was owned by Rudi Altobelli, a manager of stars such as Henry Fonda and Katharine Hepburn. Previous to the Polanskis, the house had been, as fate would have it, rented by music producer Terry Melcher and his girlfriend Candice Bergen. By 1969, however, Melcher and Bergen had split up, and Melcher had moved to a house in Malibu. But it was while he still lived on Cielo Drive that Melcher had set in motion the wheels that would lead to tragedy.

In retrospect, it is easy to discern how the California sense of openness and *do whatever feels right* played a role in what happened next. Though the arriviste Polanskis had no way of knowing, the canyons north of the downtown—Laurel, Benedict, Topanga—had been ground zero for much of the region's hedonistic impulses that reached their peak in the late 1960s. The region became known for wild parties, drug use, open and rampant sex, and the presence of clinging fringe elements—ranging from the nubile young "groupies" at the houses of rock stars to the looming presence of some dark and mysterious local cults. Terry Melcher, a noted profligate with a nasty drug habit, was said, tellingly enough, to have grown tired of the chaos and impositions of the canyon life before he finally left for the relative calm of Malibu.

A story that emerged later may help explain Melcher's frustration. Sometime in 1968 he had attended a party at the Pacific Palisades house of Beach Boy Dennis Wilson. There, Wilson introduced Melcher to a young singer named Charles Manson. At the time Manson and a group of mostly female followers, who called themselves the "Manson Family," had befriended Wilson and his songwriting partner, Gregg Jakobson. Wilson and Jakobson talked Melcher into coming to hear Manson play. Nothing came of it—Melcher wasn't interested enough to book a recording session—and afterward Manson felt betrayed. He told Manson Family members that Melcher had broken his promises and that he was intent on keeping Manson's music from the world. On August 8, therefore, the increasingly agitated Manson directed family member Charles "Tex" Watson to go to the house where Melcher used to live. "I want you," Manson said, "to totally destroy everyone in that house, as gruesome as you can."[4] According to another family member's later confession, Manson picked the house simply to send a message to Melcher.

Much has been written and said about the Manson Family's spree of murders, so there's no need to give another recounting here. On the evening of August 8, 1969, the world changed not only for Roman Polanski and his family and friends, but for all of Los Angeles. At the Polanski residence that night were his wife, Sharon Tate, who was more than eight months pregnant; a friend of Tate's named Jay Sebring; a Polish screenwriter and friend of Polanski's named Wojciech Frykowski; and Frykowski's girlfriend, Abigail Folger, heir to the coffee fortune and an employee in the Welfare Department of the city. Polanski, who was away in London at the time working on a screenplay with his partner, Andrew Braunsberg, for a film called *Day of the Dolphin*, had asked his friends Frykowski and Folger to take care of his pregnant wife until he could return on August 12. Early the next morning in London, on August 9, Polanski received the news in a call from his manager. According to Braunsberg, Polanski was profoundly devastated. Not only had he lost his beloved wife and their unborn son, but he had lost the promise of family stability and contentment—something he had not experienced since the years before World War II. At the press conference a few days later, Polanski, visibly stricken and distraught, berated the press for spreading wild and unfounded rumors about the couple and what had exactly happened at the house.

In time, once the details of the crime got out, the sense of devastation that Polanski experienced spread far and wide across Los Angeles, shattering the illusion of California as a modern-day paradise. "After Sharon was murdered," said Andrew Braunsberg, "everybody was totally freaked out. It was a very weird time. The highest paranoia. The transition of this hippie kind of existence in L.A. to this brutal awakening of an understanding that these kinds of absolutely horrible events can happen. . . . It changed everything overnight in L.A." Gene Gutowski, meanwhile, a film-producer colleague of Polanski, put it more succinctly. "It was the end of a fairy tale," Gutowski said, "for Roman, for everybody."[5] In retrospect, as *Time* suggested in 1977, it was obvious that the wild and wholly open ways of Hollywood would eventually prove problematic and that the illusion of a Southern Californian paradise, where profligate and reckless behavior was its own reward, would eventually unravel.

Whatever one thought of the killings on Cielo Drive, almost no one in the Los Angeles area was left unaffected. "On August 9, 1969," wrote Joan Didion at the end of the 1970s, "I was sitting in the shallow end of my sister-in-law's swimming pool in Beverly Hills when she received a telephone call from a friend who had just heard about the murders at Sharon Tate Polanski's house on Cielo Drive. The phone rang many times during the next hour. These early reports were garbled and contradictory. One caller would say hoods, the next would say chains. There were twenty dead, no, twelve, ten, eighteen. Black masses were imagined, and bad trips blamed. I remembered all of the day's misinformation very clearly, and I also remember this, and wish I did not: *I remember that no one was surprised*."[6] Tom Bradley was one of those most deeply affected by that day, as he had a personal connection to the murders. Earlier in the spring of that year, during his first attempt to unseat corrupt incumbent mayor Sam Yorty, then council member Bradley had gotten to know Abigail Folger when the young heiress began volunteering for, and contributing to, Bradley's mayoral campaign. At the time Folger, who was described by colleagues as outgoing and capable, if a bit eccentric, had come to realize how little effect she was having on the city's massive social problems. The suffering she was seeing daily in her job in the Welfare Department was getting under her skin, and so she pinned her hopes for change on Bradley. When Bradley became the victim of a smear campaign and lost the election to Yorty, Folger grew even more disillusioned and withdrew somewhat from public life. Ironically, this was how she and the struggling screenwriter Frykowski agreed to house-sit for Polanski, and take care of his pregnant wife's needs, in the lead-up to the August murders.

As a city council member at the time, and twenty-one-year veteran of the Los Angeles Police Department, Bradley, of course, had a long-standing concern about the rapidly rising violent crime rates in his city throughout the 1960s.[7] Still, while he was intensely concerned about the problem, he had a more nuanced understanding of its full nature. "There were many voices [in the city] calling for stiffer penalties and tougher sentences," write Bradley biographers J. Gregory Payne and Scott Ratzan. "As a former police officer, Bradley agreed that steps had to be taken in that direction."[8] But, Bradley knew, the shallow, quick-fix solutions proposed by politicians completely misunderstood the root causes of the problem.

Seeing the complex city from his vantage point as its chief administrator, Bradley viewed L.A.'s crime problem as multifaceted and immune to simplistic policy fixes. Confined to a life of squalor and broken homes in the poorest parts of town, young Angelenos of color in general lacked resources, family support, even the access to education that could pull them out of their dire situation. With few available ways to obtain clothes and food, many young people turned to petty crime. After that it was only a matter of time before the crimes grew more serious. "Bradley was well aware of the syndrome," suggest Payne and Ratzan. "Many of those he had played with as a kid had gone down the same road, ending up with nothing but a jail record."[9] The fact that Bradley witnessed the struggles against criminality up close with his daughter—whose problems with drugs, petty crime, and incarceration continued—also gave him an intimate understanding of both the personal tragedy and the abiding seriousness of the problem of crime in Los Angeles.

With the systemic cards stacked against a wide array of the region's young people, Bradley knew that any long-term solution to the problem of crime would necessarily require a more dynamic and multitier effort. In 1977, Bradley noted, roughly one out of every two black and Hispanic youths in Los Angeles was unemployed. Therefore, shortly after his reelection to the mayor's office in that year's election, Bradley spearheaded a program called Operation HEAVY, which employed the resources of city hall, the police department, and the Los Angeles Unified School District to provide juveniles offenders with counseling, recreational opportunities, job training, and job placement as an alternative to a life in the criminal justice system. Although Bradley had no illusions that his program alone would solve one of his city's most entrenched problems, he did consider it a good first step. Bradley also helped develop a summer youth program, SPEEDY, that provided jobs to tens of thousands of disadvantaged students during the summer of 1977. These two initial efforts were widely praised across the city, even by factions that were politically opposed to the mayor. For instance, longtime Republican political operative Francis Dale, who had recently served on the Committee to Re-Elect Richard Nixon, praised Bradley's programs, saying they "contributed to the city's most valuable resource—its youth—[and] are exactly what every city across American should be doing more of."[10]

Although his programs to address the root causes of youth crime in L.A. gained accolades, Mayor Bradley knew there was much more that needed to be done. Despite that he worked so hard—nearly sixteen hours a day, seven days a week, so that he barely slept and almost never spent a moment of private time with his family[11]—and despite that he maintained a calm and upright public image while in office, Bradley was privately distraught about the social ills that plagued his city. As a result he increased his resolve regarding bringing the Olympics back to Los Angeles. In 1974, with Bradley's direction, Los Angeles had submitted a fairly strong bid to host the Summer Olympic Games in 1980. It was only one year into Bradley's first term in office, and already he was convinced that the spectacle of the Games would help inspire the city and its young even as it made Los Angeles a leading city of international trade and travel—an American gateway to the so-called Pacific Rim. Although L.A. lost the bid for the 1980 Olympic Games (to Moscow), Bradley was not surprised. After the decision was made, however, the atmosphere was reportedly quite cordial on all sides, and representatives of Los Angeles's Olympics bid returned home with the sense that the International Olympic Committee (IOC) would welcome a future bid by the city. According to John Argue, the president of the Southern California Committee for the Olympic Games, representatives of the IOC "liked Bradley. . . . He was sincere, and has a real spirit that reflects the Olympics. He just hit it off with them from the very beginning."[12] As a result Bradley immediately began working behind the scenes to build support for his planned bid for the 1984 Games.

In 1977, however, with the public increasingly focused on the city's growing internal problems, an Olympics bid began to seem like anything but a wise public policy decision. To many Angelenos, in fact, the Olympic Games likely would mean a host of additional problems for the city. For one, there were the costs to host the Games, which had been skyrocketing in recent years—especially in the Summer Games that had occurred in 1976. No one wanted to saddle Los Angeles with crushing debt simply for the privilege of hosting two weeks of sporting events. Additionally, with local crime rates rising, many worried about the potential for crime or violence to mar the Games. "There were rumors," write Payne and Ratzan, "that the Olympics would result in an influx of terrorists coming to Los Angeles, and fears of a repeat of the 1972 Munich tragedy. . . . There were even those who warned of national security threats—waves of Communists infiltrating Southern California and fanning out throughout the United States." Despite the mayor's strong belief in the eventual benefits of bringing the Olympics back to L.A., a growing chorus of critics and policy makers became increasingly wary of the real benefit of the Games. "Even on the Mayor's own staff," said Anton Calleia, who was Bradley's budget director at the time, "there were those who strongly opposed Bradley pursuing the Games, [who] thought it was politically a very damaging issue."[13] Bradley, however, resisted the counsel of his advisers and pressed on to realize his vision.

The people of Los Angeles weren't the only ones wary of holding the Olympic Games. On November 1, 1977, the day after the application deadline for bids for the 1984 Olympic Games had passed, the International Olympic Committee announced it had received a bid from just *one* candidate for the Games—Los Angeles. (The city of Teheran, in Iran, was said to be pursuing submitting a bid, but in the end did not actually complete one.) To the media IOC executive director Monique Berlioux noted that this marked the first time since the start of the modern Olympics movement that only one city had applied to hold the Games. She also noted, much to the relief of Mayor Bradley, that all that remained was for the representatives of L.A.'s Olympics committee to submit answers to an IOC questionnaire. Assuming the city's responses were adequate, a vote by the IOC to approve the bid was likely.

As fate would have it, however, the road to a second Los Angeles Olympic Games, something that only two previous cities—London and Paris—could boast of, would see many more roadblocks.

That the first of these roadblocks involved another wide-ranging and far-reaching crime scare only reinforces the growing sensitivity of Angelenos toward their culture of violent crime. On October 18, 1977, just a few weeks before Los Angeles submitted the only bid for the 1984 Summer Olympics, a nineteen-year-old woman named Yolanda Washington, who worked as a waitress but also moonlighted as a prostitute in Hollywood, was found dead near the Forest Lawn Cemetery in the Hollywood Hills. The victim's body had visible strangulation marks around the neck and rope burns on her wrists and ankles. Police initially chalked the murder up to a rape gone wrong, but on November 1 police discovered another body in La Crescenta, just north of downtown. Eventually identified as fifteen-year-old Judith Lynn Miller, a runaway who had turned to prostitution, her killing was markedly similar to that of Yolanda Washington. Miller had been abducted in Hollywood, raped, strangled, bound, then dumped, most likely from a car, in a quiet hillside residential area of the city.

Over the next four weeks six similar murder scenes were discovered, each following the same pattern: victims were captured somehow, raped or tortured in some way, strangled, and dumped on a hillside. On November 23 the decomposed body of twenty-eight-year-old aspiring actress Jane King was found near Griffith Park. By now law enforcement officials had established a task force to catch the ostensible serial murderer—or murderers, as officials were convinced this was the work of at least two killers—whom they dubbed the "Hillside Strangler." By early December, then, with officials in Los Angeles offering one hundred thousand dollars for information leading to an arrest, the word was out. Fear and paranoia settled over the city.

It's somewhat difficult today to imagine exactly how Angelenos felt in late 1977 and early 1978—or how New Yorkers felt a year earlier about the Son of Sam killings, or Bostonians felt in the early 1960s about the Boston Strangler. After all, Americans in the twenty-first century have become inured to such stories, living as we do with a hyperawareness of the potential for violence, inundated as we are with a constant flood of death and murder in movies, on TV, on the Internet, and in all forms of American popular entertainment. In the 1970s movies like *Star Wars*, *Jaws*, and other gaudy blockbusters were breaking new ground in depicting cartoonlike, highly desensitizing images of violence. In the decades that followed, after several decades of gory "slasher" films, high body-count action movies, zombie gore fests, and news coverage of serial murderers like John Wayne Gacy, Jeffrey Dahmer, and Ted Bundy, violence seems commonplace. But in late 1977 and early 1978, it wasn't. Suddenly, everyone in California was acutely aware that a vicious serial killer was loose in the city, claiming victims in nearly every corner of the region—in La Crescenta, Glendale, Hollywood, Angeles Crest, even the hills near Dodger Stadium. No place in the area seemed safe.

The Hillside Strangler's activities tailed off early in 1978. The last documented murder in L.A., the tenth over the course of four months dating back to October 17, was discovered in Angeles Crest on February 16. Though it may have been the last official "Hillside" strangling, the mounting concern and near hysteria forced Mayor Bradley to make a public statement on crime. And this in turn would lead to a fateful decision. On March 28, 1978, Bradley appointed a new chief of its police department, Darryl Gates, a veteran police investigator who had led the search for the Manson Family, formed the city's first special weapons and tactics (SWAT) unit, and innovated tough countermeasures against the city's growing street gangs. Bradley chose Gates to help bolster the mayor's reputation as tough on crime. Little did either man know what actually lay in store for him and the city in the years to come.

EIGHTEEN

The Redemption of Rick Monday

Do you remember the thrill you had the first time you were actually on the road to Disneyland? Going to the Dodgers was like going to Disneyland for me.

—Rick Monday

The Dodgers' opening spring-training game in 1978, ironically enough, was against the New York Yankees in Fort Lauderdale. On March 10 the Dodgers took the cold and windy night game, 7–3. The team's pitchers held Yankee slugger Reggie Jackson to a single in his two at bats and the rest of the New York lineup to just four other hits. The Dodgers, meanwhile, were sparked by Ron Cey's home run and three RBIs and Rick Monday's two hits, including a solo moon shot to right-center field.

Despite this slight vindication of the disappointment of the team's most recent game—back on October 18 in the World Series—the atmosphere in the Dodger camp was different this year. In 1977 Lasorda had instructed the team's veterans to play, eat, work out, and take breaks together for much of spring training. In 1978 he held many Dodger regulars in reserve. It may have been Lasorda's intention to ease the veterans slowly back into the game, and to reduce injuries this season, but it may also have been an indication of a new sense of confidence in the Dodger camp this year. The team had less to prove this year after their World Series appearance. They could focus on other, more pressing, concerns.

After their opening exhibition-season win, the Dodgers dropped four straight games—14–3 and 5–2 against the Atlanta Braves on

March 11 and 12, 7–5 against the Twins on March 13, and 7–2 against the Montreal Expos on March 14. The Minnesota game, ironically, was marred by complaints that the Dodgers had failed to field a serious lineup. "Why the hell do we schedule all these exhibition games if the players don't need them?" said a Twins team official, peeved that few Dodger regulars appeared in the game. "We spent a lot of money advertising the appearance of the National League champions and this is what we get for it. I'm disgusted." Lasorda shrugged off the complaints. "You hear the same complaints every spring. It's inevitable. My decision last spring to keep our eight players together proved to be a success for various reasons. I play them every other day and I leave them the option of asking to play on the days when they normally wouldn't. . . . You can't accommodate everybody. What's wrong with Rhoden, Hooton, Davalillo, and Burke? Those guys all played in the World Series last year." (In addition, an anonymous Dodger official was harshly dismissive: "I don't think anyone would know the difference even if Minnesota didn't bring its regulars.")[1]

On March 15 the team's record stood at 1-4, which was a far cry from the full-bore attack of the season before—though of course both records meant virtually nothing. Beyond the team's record, though, Lasorda had his worries. Reggie Smith had sat out a couple of games nursing a sore back. Without Smith the Dodger outfield was in rough shape. Willie Crawford had reported to camp at a heavy 240 pounds, quickly earning the nickname "Whale" from Lasorda. And although the veteran reduced his weight to 221 pounds in just a few short weeks, at the plate he was showing few signs of his former effectiveness. "He's worked very hard," said Lasorda of Crawford. "He's been in uniform from seven in the morning to five at night. In fact, he's worked too hard. He's made himself weak. He's not swinging the bat the way he should be. I told him to take it easy, that he doesn't have to do it overnight, that I want him ready in April, not mid-March."[2] Others, such as Ron Cey, Dusty Baker, and Steve Yeager, had thus far been surprisingly inept at the plate. And the Dodgers' defensive play was uncharacteristically sloppy as well, with the team recording seventeen errors in its first nine games.

One clear bright spot in the midst of the up-and-down play, however, was none other than last season's biggest disappointment—Rick

Monday. Monday entered the preseason with a lot to prove. In the first game of the exhibition season against the Yankees, Monday had hit a long home run close to the deepest part of the ballpark in Fort Lauderdale. "The home run off Figueroa relieved a lot more of the frustration from a season in which I had not been able to perform anywhere close to what I had hoped to," said Monday, who had come to camp fit and lean at 206 pounds. "Figueroa had pitched winter ball and I had kind of expected to be blown away, especially considering that the first game of spring was being played at night under bad lights . . . The injury is behind me. I have not had any problem, discomfort or stiffness. I've been running around like a kid."[3]

Despite Monday's resurgence, the team's exhibition-season struggles continued. It may not have helped that the health of the team's aging owner—Walter O'Malley—continued to be a question mark. The various medical complications after his abdominal surgery back in February carried on into the spring, causing ripples of uncertainty down through the team's administration, into the clubhouse, and perhaps out on the field. After a couple of wins—against Baltimore, 8–4, on March 16 and against the Twins, 12–1, on March 17—the Dodgers lost two more against Houston and Montreal. After nine games the Dodgers' record stood at a disappointing 3-6, and Lasorda must have taken some alarm at the fact that all six of the team's preseason losses had come at the hands of rival National League teams. Certainly, this fact, and the Dodgers' sloppy play, had been noticed by others around the league—including none other than their nemesis Sparky Anderson, who still seemed unimpressed at the Dodgers' accomplishments of the previous season. "In my opinion," said Anderson, "the Dodgers still have to play catch-up with us. They may be wearing rings that the organization gave them as a token for making the playoffs, but the big stone still isn't there, it still isn't a World Series ring. What happened last year wasn't a true test, and didn't really prove anything because of the way we had to completely rebuild our pitching during the season. This year will be the test and the Dodgers are going to have to beat us two years running, which no one has done in my eight years here." Other members of the Reds concurred with the team's manager. "Maybe I'm wrong," said Pete Rose, "but on an overall basis I think we have more players who have performed more consistently that the Dodgers. If you put the teams next to each other and had every player perform up to his capability, to his career statistics, we would win."[4] In other words the Reds were not going to let the pennant get away again without a fight.

Lasorda, pointedly, offered no comments about the Reds in his postgame press reports. "I'll leave that to Sparky," said Lasorda. "At this point, I'm only interested in our own preparation and at this point I'm pleased with our progress. I remain confident that we will be a better team than we were last year. These guys tasted the fruits of victory. They know what it takes. They want to do it again, and they have worked very hard. I'm positive they will be ready physically, mentally, and fundamentally."[5] The Dodgers responded to Lasorda's optimism by recording two straight wins—a 14–1 blowout of the Rangers in which Rick Monday went four for four with a home run and a 6–1 win over the Braves. On March 22 the Dodgers followed up with a close loss in an eleven-inning game against the Orioles, 9–8. In the game, a classic spring-training tilt characterized by poor play and missed opportunities, both teams had six errors *apiece*. The Dodgers lost in the bottom of the eleventh inning, in fact, when Dodger utility man Lee Lacy committed two errors on one play, first kicking a grounder and then throwing wildly past first base to allow the tying and winning runs to score. With their record now 6-7 on March 23, the Dodgers followed with three straight convincing wins—12–1 over the Mets, 5–0 over the Yankees, then 6–2 over the Mets again on March 25. In the most recent game Rick Monday shined yet again, going two for two against the Mets with a triple and three RBIs.

With these signs of life from the team at last, Walter O'Malley must have finally felt inspired enough to make an appearance in Vero Beach. Fresh from his stay at the Mayo Clinic, O'Malley appeared at the head of the Dodgertown conference table on March 25 and pointedly lit a cigar before holding court. "I feel so damn good right now," O'Malley told a reporter. "A combination of Irish whisky and Florida citrus seems to be all I ever need to recover from my physical problems." When asked about the team, and if he had had any contact with harried manager Lasorda, O'Malley laughed and cracked a joke—"I told Tommy that when he goes to the mound to take a pitcher out, his belly is now getting there a minute before the rest of his body does"—before growing serious. "Actually, I've learned not to get too emotional about what happens in the spring. Everything has a way of finding its level."[6]

The next day another convincing win, 12–1, over the Houston Astros raised the team's exhibition record to two games above .500, and the Dodgers' general manager weighed in with thoughts about the Dodgers' prospects in 1978. Saying that the team compared favorably to the Snider-Robinson-Campanella era of the 1940s and '50s, Al Campanis said, "We will have the best rounded team in the 21 years that we have been in Los Angeles." His assessment, he continued, was based on five factors. The first four were related to the clubhouse personnel he had brought together: the core of players who had brought home a National League pennant the previous year, particularly its consistent top-end starting pitching; the addition of left-handed reliever Terry Forster, who was having a very good spring thus far; the resurgence of Rick Monday, whose injuries seemed to be behind him; and the improved reserves on the Dodgers' bench. The final factor was a surprise, and an indication of the ability of the Reds to continue pushing the organization's buttons: Campanis suggested the team was strong because of Tom Lasorda's burning and angry drive to win. "I think Tommy genuinely hates the Cincinnati s.o.b.," said Campanis. "When Walter Alston retired and Sparky said, 'now the Dodgers are going to find out just how good a manager Alston was,' Tommy felt he was being belittled. He was quick to pick up on it and hasn't forgotten it." Campanis then ended his statements with a mild jab at Anderson. "I'd hate to have a man of Tommy's temperament and motivational ability genuinely mad at me."[7]

After finishing the grapefruit season with two straight losses that dropped the Dodgers back to .500, at 9-9, the team flew back to Los Angeles for the opening of the Freeway Series against the Angels on the last day of March. The results couldn't have been more disappointing—not only was the game in Anaheim a rare rainout, called in the fourth inning with the Angels leading 5–0, but Reggie Smith slipped on some wet turf during the game and injured himself. Afterward, Smith was angry. "I told myself," said Smith after the game, "'take your time.' I was going real slow and I still couldn't hold my feet. My left leg went out and I felt something go in here."[8] Smith pointed to his right groin area.

Adding to the sense of disappointment for the defending National League champions was the news that came to the clubhouse sometime during the game. Former Dodger third baseman Billy Cox, who had been one of the so-called Boys of Summer and played on three National League pennant-winning teams in Brooklyn in the late 1940s and early 1950s, had died of cancer the night before the game in Anaheim. Add the fact that Iron Man Steve Garvey, who started the season having played every game during the previous two seasons, twisted his ankle in the rainy conditions at Anaheim Stadium, and suddenly the Dodgers seemed more vulnerable than a league champion should be. Lasorda, for his part, seemed eager to get on with the season. "I didn't want to see any more people getting hurt," Lasorda said plaintively. "At least we got some of our work in . . . We're coming up to the season now and we've got to play; we've got to get our work in."[9] On April 1 the Dodgers lost a close one to the Angels, when the American Leaguers scored two runs in the bottom of the ninth inning on a two-out single by outfielder Rick Miller. A day later the Dodgers lost again to the Angels, unofficially giving the American League squad a sweep over Lasorda's boys, their first since 1964. The Dodgers' preseason record dropped to either 9-11 or 9-12, depending on whether you counted the 5–0 game that had been halted in the fourth inning.

Despite the clouds over the team, there was some good news for at least for one player. Although team management had declared that Glenn Burke was likely to be on the chopping block at the end of spring training—a fact made even more likely by the surging Rick Monday—it was announced on April 2 that Burke would actually be on the team's twenty-four-man roster when the season opened on April 7. It helped that the Dodgers' experiment with Willie Crawford had failed, leaving open an outfield spot. In addition to this news, the Dodgers announced that although the team's stellar young right-handed pitching prospect Bob Welch would not be on the team's opening-day roster, since there were already five starters slated for the start of the season, he was being awarded the Dearie Mulvey

Award as the team's most outstanding spring-training rookie in 1978. Welch had posted a 2.08 ERA and struck out twelve batters in thirteen innings pitched during the exhibition season.

The Dodgers finished spring training with a loss in Arizona—6–5 against the A's—and then promptly hopped on a plane for Atlanta for the season opener against the Braves. On the plane players were chastened. Although a number of the Dodger starters—Reggie Smith, Ron Cey, Bill Russell—had been hampered by niggling injuries, several players and coaches were worried about the team's mind-set leading into the opening week of the season, in which the team would play six road games against division rivals Atlanta and Houston. "If you were to ask me if I sense a complacency here," said Bill Russell, "my answer would be that I can. If being complacent is to think, 'Hey, we're the league champions, we don't have anything to prove again, we just have to go out there and everything will take care of itself,' then yes, I think there's complacency here." Russell lowered his voice before continuing. "We played like rookies instead of major leaguers this spring. We shouldn't play like we did no matter who's in the lineup. I'd like to have the attitude of last spring. I'd like to have the winning pattern of last spring." Russell's manager somewhat agreed with the shortstop's assessment, though he couldn't help but be optimistic as well. "It's true," said Lasorda. "We've given some games away. I don't like that at any time. I would be more concerned, however, if it had happened with our regular lineup. The injuries have been a setback, no doubt about it. I was quite pleased with our conditioning, our progress and the playing time the regulars had been receiving when we left Florida. Since then we've pretty much come to a standstill in all areas. Yet our regulars will be out there Friday [on opening day] and that's when it counts. A week from now no one will remember our spring record."[10]

Other Dodger players, meanwhile, were much more circumspect regarding the team's recent play, its 10-14 final spring exhibition record, and the various fits and starts among its presumed starting lineup. "Last spring was different," said Dave Lopes. "There had been a complete change of command. Everyone was more emotional, more motivated about spring training. I'm not saying that the attitude isn't as good now . . . it's just that the emphasis is different. . . . The concern is to come out of spring healthy." Ron Cey, who was nursing a hamstring injury, concurred with the sentiment of his captain. "The major consideration," said Cey, "is that we may not be as aggressive as we will be later on. We many have to play it cautious for a few games so that we don't aggravate the injuries and risk being out longer than we already have. The situation forces us to be at our best mentally."[11]

Opening day for the defending National League champion Dodgers on April 7, 1978, had a familiar air about it. On the mound for the Dodgers in Atlanta was the veteran right-handed "ace" of the team, Don Sutton. It would be the seventh such start for Sutton, a feat that tied him with Don Drysdale for the most opening-day pitching starts. It was, of course, an indication of Lasorda's adherence to baseball orthodoxy that he remained committed to offering Sutton the honor. In Sutton's own words, he didn't belong on the mound on this day. "On the basis of last year," Sutton said before the game, "Tommy John deserves this start. On the basis of this spring, Bob Welch deserves it. I don't really deserve it on any basis other than longevity. It's like giving a special trial to the senior partner in a law firm." He also quickly added that he wasn't going to turn the honor down: "When something exciting is going on," Sutton said, "I would rather be in it than on the sidelines. I'm a lousy spectator. I honestly think if there had been more of a race last year, I'd have been more effective down the stretch. I'm not attempting to rationalize for an unsatisfying record (14-8). I'm simply a person who responds when something is on the line."[12]

If he was worried about his complacency in the face of the Dodgers' excellence in 1977, after opening day in Atlanta Sutton may have only had more concerns. Before a sellout crowd of nearly forty-three thousand at Atlanta Stadium that also saw the very first managerial appearance of the Braves new skipper, Bobby Cox, the limping, gimpy Dodgers stuck it to the Braves with a fourteen-hit, thirteen-run barrage of offense in which every starter had at least one hit. Sutton certainly started the game shakily enough, giving up runs in each of the first four innings, before settling down and letting the Wrecking Crew do its damage. "I allowed myself to get caught up in the excitement," said Sutton afterward. "I was trying to throw harder than I'm capable of throwing. It used to be that when I'd give up three runs early I'd go looking for the guys in the white jackets and padded cells. With this team, however, my only philosophy is to keep us close. I know that unless we're absolutely killed early we'll general rally."[13] When the dust had settled, Sutton had pitched seven innings for a 13–4 win, improving his all-time record against the Braves to 26-11, and the Dodgers had evidence that their punchless spring training was likely an anomaly.

Beyond the win the bigger story of the game was the performance of Rick Monday. Having ended the exhibition season with a .302 batting average, Monday came to opening day confident that he was ready to play in 1978. Monday went four for five in the game, scored three runs, and knocked in four RBIs. Additionally, he played hard in the field from the start, attempting a leaping, twisting grab in the first inning off the Atlanta Stadium wall on a long fly ball off the bat of Braves center fielder Rowland Office. After the game Don Sutton sought out Monday to thank him for the attempt to rob Office of his early home run. Monday, watching the veteran pitcher walk away afterward, was amused. "There's a lot of Missourian in all of us," said Monday, chuckling. "We all have to be shown. Even Sutton didn't believe my back was better. He let Office test it in the very first inning."[14]

All through April Monday would continue his tear, doing his best to prove doubters wrong. And the Dodgers, following Monday's lead, got off to a solid start. After sweeping the Braves in Atlanta, they traveled to Houston for a series-opening 5–2 win. Though they lost the next two games against the Astros, by the close scores of 1–0 (against Houston ace J. R. Richard) and 11–10, there seemed to be some fight in the squad. The last game, a wild shoot-out in which neither Sutton nor Houston starter Joe Niekro nor any other pitcher in the game could seem to get anyone out, was lost when Dodger rookie pitcher Bobby Castillo gave up the tie-breaking run on a fielder's choice in the bottom of the ninth. "They end up beating us with a couple chinkers," the feisty Lasorda said after the game. "The kid (Castillo) makes a hell of a pitch to Howe [who led off the ninth with a double] and he doesn't hit the ball hard enough to be caught. Alou hits a little roller and if it's two feet the other way we're still playing. The Astros got a little lucky."[15]

On April 14 the Dodgers hosted the team's first home stand of the season against Atlanta, Cincinnati, and Houston. After sweeping the Braves in the first two games of the stand, the Dodgers lost two of three against the surging Reds—whose cockiness had returned somewhat, thanks to a 9-4 record and possession of first place in the NL West. The Dodgers, however, at 7-4, were not far behind. And Rick Monday continued to fuel the team's hopes. In the final game against the Reds, Monday's two home runs (he now led the league with six) were key in a 5–4 win. In the four-game series against Houston, the Dodgers won three times, with Monday contributing another home run in the final game. After beating Houston and ending the home stand, the Dodgers, at 10-5, were solidly in second place, just a half game behind the Reds. On April 25 the Dodgers then traveled to Cincinnati, beat the Reds twice, and took over first place by half a game in the Western Division.

This is where things stood at month's end. And while the results of this April in no way resembled the results of April a year earlier, the Dodgers had to be pleased with the results. What's more, they had to be more than pleased by the play of their suddenly resurgent Rick Monday. For the month of April Monday led the Dodgers with a .353 average and .754 slugging percentage. He had hit eight home runs while knocking in twenty-two RBIs, even while his strikeout total, usually swollen by his free-swinging habits, remained low. (On May 1 Monday had struck out as many times, eleven, as he had walked.) The center fielder, in fact, had almost single-handedly carried the Dodgers through the month. While sluggers like Cey, Smith, and Baker had yet to get on track, Monday had been the key scoring catalyst in six of the Dodgers' wins in the season's first month. Without Rick Monday, it is safe to say, the Dodgers' season as of May 1 would likely have been heading in a different direction altogether.

NINETEEN

Every Day We Pay the Price

Open letter to Walter Alston: I want to offer my apologies for ever having rapped you for being The Quiet Man during your years with the Dodgers. Compared to loudmouthed Tommy Lasorda, silence is indeed golden.

—Letter to the editor, *Los Angeles Times*, June 24, 1978

The rivalry between the Reds and Dodgers being what it was, and lasting as long as it had by 1978—the two teams finishing first-second in seven of the previous eight seasons—it's no surprise that their habit of sniping about each other should intensify early in the season. After the Dodgers swept the Reds in Cincinnati at the end of April, Joe Morgan unloaded on the Reds' rivals in blue and their manager. "He is a smart ass," Morgan exclaimed, referring to Lasorda's poking fun at Sparky Anderson for closing the Reds' clubhouse to reporters thirty-five minutes before each game. "What Sparky does in this clubhouse is none of his (Lasorda's) business. Sparky doesn't go around popping off about Lasorda hugging and kissing his players. They're all a bunch of hypocrites over there. Running together before every game and I know they all don't like each other. I just read in the *Sporting News* where they're all mad at Steve Garvey again." Morgan was referring to a recent *L.A. Times* article, picked up by *The Sporting News*, in which sportswriter Skip Bayless suggested that Steve Garvey was the "loneliest Dodger," primarily because his teammates refused to accept him, his personality, and his image. Though Dodger players and team officials were quick to discount the story—Lasorda said there was "no problem" on the team, and several teammates were nonplussed that the issue seemed to be lingering after having been dealt with several years before—Morgan couldn't help but try to stir things up. "I guess Joe doesn't have enough to worry about in his own clubhouse," Lopes said in response to Morgan's rant. "All along the Reds have seemed to be interested only in what we're doing."[1]

The next day Lopes tipped his cap to the Reds on field as he ran with teammates. Rick Monday cracked jokes. "Maybe Joe would feel better about it if we held hands while we ran," he said. "The way they run on an individual basis, maybe they're the ones who don't like each other. All I know is the way Morgan pops off, they should hang a sign over his locker which reads, 'consultations now in order.'" Garvey noted that the comments seemed more personal and cynical than usual, and not in the spirit of the rivalry between the teams. And Lasorda simply shook his head. "I don't care what he says," Lasorda said. "Probably just couldn't think of anything else. Last year, he kept saying that it was fun chasing us because he knew the Reds would catch us in August. We made it so much fun for him that he must have laughed all the way through the playoffs."[2]

The truth was, though Morgan had no way of knowing it, and as the Dodgers were still unaware, his comments were far more prescient than the usual tossed-off locker-room insult. In a quick few months the Dodger clubhouse would be virtually coming apart at the seams. For now, however, the Dodgers seemed intent on focusing on winning games and continuing their push for a second straight World Series appearance.

After ending April with two quiet losses against the Cardinals—in which the Dodgers failed to score a run despite the fact that Steve Garvey extended a hitting streak to twenty games—May got under way, after a day off on May 1, with a third straight Dodgers loss. This time it was a close one, 5–4 in ten innings, against the Cubs in chilly and windy Wrigley Field. In the game Garvey had another hit, an RBI double, but the Cubs were sparked by a two-hit, two-RBI day by a former friend—the ever-gimpy Bill Buckner, whose ankle issues had persisted for yet another season. "I guess the Big Cubbie in the sky took care of us today," Buckner joked after the game, adding that while he still gets psyched up for a game against his old team, he also wished them the best. "I've also fallen in love with this city," Buckner said of Chicago, "the fans, the park, and I know that the trade was the best thing that could have happened. The way my ankle is all I could have done with the Dodgers was pinch hit. I can only play first base and, I don't think they'd have moved Garvey out."[3]

Despite the recent struggles the Dodgers remained still a half game atop the Reds in the Western Division, and they stayed that way on May 3 by beating the Cubs 9–5. Steve Garvey lost his hitting streak in the game, going oh for four, though he still knocked in two runs on a sacrifice fly and a force-out. "I was very aware, very conscious of it," Garvey said of the end of the streak. "I kept wanting to get up one more time today. I hit the ball well a couple of times but I couldn't get it to fall. Still, it's a nice feeling to open the season with a 21-game hitting streak, to go all of April without getting shut out. And I'd much rather have it end on a day that we win than on a day we lose." Despite the focus on Garvey, Reggie Smith and Rick Monday were the catalysts for the win, collecting seven hits, four runs, and five RBIs between them. Smith also had a double and a triple, while Monday had a double and a home run and made a dramatic, run-saving diving catch in the seventh inning on a ball that commenters afterward suggested was located in a spot similar to the one he had injured himself on in Houston the previous season. "People have been asking me if I'd ever attempt another diving catch and this was their answer," Monday said after the game. "Thank God it wasn't AstroTurf."[4]

In the backdrop behind the Dodgers' first win of May was an event that happened in the clubhouse before the game. After the three straight sloppy losses, Lasorda decided to call his first team meeting of the season before the game—a ten-minute expletive-fueled monologue in which the manager called into question just how dedicated members of the team were to the common cause, to the Dodger cause. The exact words that Lasorda used were, of course, never recorded, though afterward an amused Don Sutton reported that the Dodger manager used one particularly foul word in his oration 117 times (or 144 times, or 120, depending on the telling).[5] While Lasorda was mum about what he discussed with the team, when asked about Sutton's comment Lasorda replied that the four-letter word was "love. L-o-v-e. Four letters." Rick Monday, who still led the league in home runs with nine and the team in hitting with a .378 batting average, was philosophical about the meeting. "We had not played well for three days," Monday said, "and Tommy was irritated about it, just as we were. He felt some things needed to be said, to be straightened out, and it probably did some good."[6]

Despite Monday's levelheaded comment something about the blowup seemed off. Perhaps Lasorda was feeling the pressure being exerted by the Reds, and by the seemingly endless battle of words between him and rival manager Sparky Anderson, and between his players and the Reds. Another win on May 4 against the Cubs, however—this one fueled by a dinged-up and heavily bandaged Reggie Smith, who had two hits, including a homer, and three RBIs—stemmed further talk about Dodger unrest and disorder, at least for the time being. And a day later, on a day in which the baseball world watched Reds veteran star Pete Rose log his three thousandth hit—in front of a home crowd that rewarded him with a five-minute ovation—the Dodgers scored a quiet win, 7–2, in Pittsburgh against Bert Blyleven.[7] The win lifted the Dodgers' record on this extended road trip to 6-3, and, even more important, it gave them a two-game lead over the Reds in the Western Division. The mood was so elevated in the clubhouse after the game that Lasorda called his friend, and Dodger honorary mascot, Don Rickles, who was performing in a casino in New Jersey. Lasorda handed the phone over to several players, whom Rickles needled mercilessly.

The high spirits didn't last long, however. On May 6 the Dodgers lost a squeaker against the Pirates, 3–2, and in the process they lost star outfielder Reggie Smith to a possible groin pull. What's more, the Reds, having won at home against Montreal, moved to just one game behind the Dodgers in the standings. On May 7 the Dodgers let another game get away against Pittsburgh, 6–4, by allowing the speedy Pirates to steal eight bases against the vaunted arm of catcher Steve Yeager. "They stung us pretty good," said Tom Lasorda afterward. "It's the way they play and we shouldn't have allowed it to happen. On a couple of the steals, Tommy [John, the starting pitcher] let them get good leads. On a couple more, I thought a good throw would have gotten them. We were just too lax." Despite the manager's frustration, and despite the fact that the Reds were again knocking on the Dodgers' door, Lasorda expressed some relief that the road trip was over. "It seemed like we'd been on the road for a month," Lasorda said as the team prepared to return home for a much-needed long home stand—twelve games at Dodger Stadium over the next fourteen days. "We beat Cincinnati twice on the trip and we went through a lot of weather. All things considered, I think it was a very good trip." Lasorda later added that his players were still "embarrassed" by their performance earlier in the month. "I won't have to remind them about it," said Lasorda. "It's what makes this team unique. They know they played badly and they'll correct it on their own. I don't think the one game should detract from what was a very long, very successful trip. We have been a good road team in my two years (47-34 last year and 10-7 this year) and there's no reason for that except that we're a damned good team, period."[8]

Among the Dodger players who sat through Lasorda's tirade, no one was more embarrassed by his performance on the road trip than Steve Garvey. After his season-opening hitting streak ended in Chicago on May 3, Garvey had gone one for twenty-one between May 3 and May 9, and his batting average had dropped from .326 to .275. Garvey, like most of his team, was eager to get back to the friendly confines of their home stadium. "I think we've all been quite conscious," said Garvey, "of how much time we've been away. It's a real drain having to play so much on the road so soon after having spent five or six weeks in Florida. It really takes it out of you, especially when you experience the variety of weather we did on the last trip."[9]

At home, however, the Dodgers continued their recent lackluster play. After taking the first game of the home stand against the Cardinals, the Dodgers lost four of the next five games against St. Louis and Chicago. Not only did the team fall behind the Reds in the division race, but after a loss against the Cubs on May 13 they were leapfrogged by the suddenly resurgent San Francisco Giants (by a half game). The thick clouds over the Dodger clubhouse darkened, and an ominous mood settled over the manager's office. It was this mood, likely, that would soon lead to an event so notorious and raw that it changed the way the baseball public forever perceived Tom Lasorda.

To put Lasorda's looming explosion into perspective, one must consider some events going on at the same time in the wider world beyond the confines of Dodger Stadium. Back in April, a few days before the Joe Morgan kerfuffle, a monumental but not widely noted event took place down in Kingston, Jamaica. The event would not have much of anything to do with the Dodgers, or baseball per se, except to provide a sense of some attitudes and issues buzzing in the air of the time. On April 22, 1978, famed Jamaican reggae singer Bob Marley performed at the One Love Peace Concert in the troubled city of his birth, Kingston. At the time Marley was in exile from his home country and living in England, recovering from injuries after being attacked in his home by mysterious gunmen—most likely in the employ of one of the main political factions—and coping with his recent diagnosis of a type of malignant melanoma under the nail of one of his toes. Marley's, and the concert's, purpose was clear—to solve the ongoing political strife that was tearing the country apart.

The plan, simply put, was to use reggae music, which was wildly popular in Jamaica, to force the leaders of Jamaica's two main political parties, Michael Manley of the People's National Party and Edward Seaga of the Jamaican Labour Party,[10] to negotiate a peace. The One Love Peace Concert was actually the brainchild of two rival political gangsters, Claudie Massop from the JLP and Bucky Marshall of the PNP, who had been locked up together in the same jail cell after a fight. Upon talking, the two realized that they each were desperate to stop the violence that was tearing their country apart. Reggae, they decided, was the key, as was convincing exiled superstar Marley to return home and perform. After being released from jail Massop flew to London to sell Marley on his vision, and, miraculously, Marley accepted the invitation.

The concert attracted a crowd of thirty-two thousand, with sixteen of the biggest acts in reggae performing. Some of the musicians directly addressed the issue of political violence in Jamaica and the role of Manley and Seaga in fomenting it. One performer in particular, Peter Tosh, was particularly provocative, lighting up a joint onstage and directly berating the two political leaders, who were seated in the front row of the concert hall. Some months after the One Love Peace Concert, the police took revenge on Tosh by arresting him as he left a dance hall and beating him nearly to death while in custody. Bob Marley, meanwhile, took a different approach during his set of songs, repeatedly asking for peace and unity in his country, and he sang and danced with remote intensity—as if he were in a holy trance. In the midst of performing his popular song "Jamming,"[11] Marley suddenly stopped singing, started talking in a kind of stream-of-consciousness spew, and offered up a message that might have taught Tom Lasorda something about inspiring the masses. "Just let me tell you something," Marley said as the music kept playing and tens of thousands of audience members screamed and cheered, "to make everything come true, we gotta be together. . . . To show the people that you love them right, to show the people that you gonna unite, show the people that you're over bright, show the people that everything is all right. . . . What I'm trying to say, could we have, could we have, up here onstage here the presence of Mr. Michael Manley and Mr. Edward Seaga. I just want to shake hands and show the people that we're gonna make it right, we're gonna unite, we're gonna make it right." Though the two seemed reluctant, under the power of the music and Marley's exhortations, they both joined him center stage, where the singer took both of their hands, joined them to each other, and raised them over his head in symbolic unity.

Back home in L.A. at the time of the One Love Peace Concert, Tom Bradley was facing political and social turmoil and dissension that, while less orchestrated and far less violent, was still disconcerting to a leader who prided himself on his calm and steady leadership. As the search for the Hillside Strangler continued, in April Bradley's efforts to bring the Olympics back to L.A. suddenly began encountering some serious setbacks. Back on January 14 the Los Angeles Olympic Organizing Committee had submitted its responses to a questionnaire required by the International Olympic Committee as a condition of its awarding the Games to its favorite (and in this case only) bidder. In the questionnaire the LAOOC had been blunt—per Bradley's directive—regarding the facilities the city would use for the Games, detailing an austere approach to the pre-Olympiad buildup. Bradley and his team explained their basic belief that the only way to hold a successful Olympics was for the host-city organizing committee, and not the IOC, to be the final arbiter of the construction of venues and staging of events. They also wanted to have final control over the revenue.[12] While the tough stance by Bradley and local Olympic organizers was widely praised by local officials and commentators, it was immediately deemed unsatisfactory by IOC officials—and particularly by its president, Michael Morris, Lord Killanin. For shrewd political reasons, however, Killanin and the IOC remained mum on the issue for several months, submitting no formal response to the city. Then, in early April, just a few days before the target date for a planned April 11–12 summit meeting between both sides in Mexico City to hash out the details of the Games, the IOC finally countered the questionnaire's stipulations. While Bradley was traveling in New Zealand, he was caught off-guard by a reporter who asked for his opinion on the recent demands Lord Killanin had just made public. Bradley, of course, had no knowledge of the letter, which insisted bluntly that the IOC would make "all final decisions regarding the staging of the Games, even though the city would foot the bill." Uncharacteristically, Bradley snapped at the reporter, saying that he did not intend to negotiate the Olympic contract "in the public media." A few days later Bradley told a reporter simply, "We are sending staff to Mexico City to further discuss the matter. I think only at that time are we going to have any further clues as to what demands are truly bottom line for the I.O.C. and where, if at all, the city can make any adjustment in its response."[13]

Negotiations in Mexico City quickly got messy. The chasm between Bradley and his city and the IOC and its president, Lord Killanin (a.k.a. Michael Morris), was vast. The largest sticking point was the notion of the IOC granting local "control" over the Games. Instead of conducting a planning summit in Mexico, then, the two days of meetings turned into an exercise in mutual confusion—the IOC firmly stating that Los Angeles drop its demands for control and representatives of Bradley's team insisting that the city needed some mechanism to keep the Games in check. The IOC came away from the meeting loudly crowing that Los Angeles had acquiesced in its demands, while representatives from L.A.'s Olympics Committee contradicted that assessment. "We have not given away anything," said the mayor's representative Anton Calleia. "We still have the financial control which we insisted upon and at the same time, I think we have made some concessions to the IOC which are very significant to them."[14]

"The city recognizes the supremacy of IOC rules in the organization and conduct of the Olympic Games," wrote Bradley on April 12, "but the city and/or the Los Angeles organizing committee retains veto power over any and all decisions which may increase the cost of the games." When asked to clarify what exactly had happened between the two parties at the summit, Bradley explained, with diplomatic (and somewhat syntactically tortured) grace, "The essence of what took place was there were a number of clarifications which were largely semantic and some of which were more substantial which were worked out during face-to-face meetings."[15] Despite Bradley's show of hopefulness, it was noted that a final decision on the Los Angeles bid for the 1984 Games had been pushed back—at least until another summit meeting scheduled to take place in Athens in mid-May.

As Bradley's Olympics bid highlighted, sometimes good intentions are not enough to bring positive change to the world. The same could be said, ultimately, of the One Love Peace Concert. The event did little to staunch the violence on the island nation over the next few years. Within a few weeks of the concert, Prime Minister Manley, reveling in the sense of connection he had established with the Rastafarians, called for new elections and won by a significant margin. And because of this, however, a new round of fighting broke out between supporters of the two parties. In the end even the two organizers, Massop and Marshall, were both killed within two years of the concert.

At Dodger Stadium in early May, as the weather heated up and the tension of the season began to build, Tom Lasorda had trouble communicating his good intentions for the team. The Dodgers' manager, in light of the team's inconsistent performance, struggled with the feeling that he was somehow responsible, that he wasn't doing enough, and that perhaps he had somehow lost the pulse of his boys. On May 12, after the Dodgers had lost the opening game of a three-game series against the Cubs—the team's third straight home loss—and had fallen into third place, the Dodger manager held yet another closed-door clubhouse meeting. Afterward, again Lasorda would not talk about what he had said in the meeting, beyond the fact that he had asked the team to show "more aggressiveness." Other sources, however, reported that the manager may well have surpassed his previous record for vulgarity—that is, the 117 "four-letter words" that Sutton had "counted" during the previous clubhouse meeting. Whatever the content, to many it was becoming increasingly clear that, despite his reputation for being a "player's manager," Lasorda also possessed a pretty sizable dark and angry side.

The Dodgers beat the Cubs in the second game on May 13, 5–2, behind strong pitching by Tommy John and reliever Terry Forster. In the final game of the Cubs series, however, all hell broke loose. On a rare Monday day game, the Cubs overcame the Dodgers 10–7 in fifteen innings on the strength of three home runs by the team's lanky left fielder, Dave "King Kong" Kingman. Though he had come into the game struggling—batting only .221 with just four home runs on the season—Kingman smashed a two-run shot in the sixth, which cut the Dodgers' lead at the time to 3–2. He then followed with a two-run blast in the top of the ninth, which tied the game 7–7, and another three-run shot in the top of the fifteenth inning to provide the victory. The Dodger hitters, who had sixteen hits in the game, stranded fifteen runners on base. It was their sixth loss in the last eight games. "This was as tough a loss as I've ever been involved in," said Lasorda afterward, before focusing on the three–home run exhibition. "It was an unbelievable exhibition. The guy [Kingman] always seems to wait until he gets out there before he does it."[16]

In Newhan's article Lasorda sounded levelheaded, if tired and disappointed—the kind of manager that Dodger fans widely believed he was and that the press let everyone believe he was. It was, however, a somewhat less than complete view of a manager. That is, beyond Lasorda's image as a jovial, backslapping master of hugs and silly nicknames, there were a growing number of clues about a different Lasorda. None of these clues was more revealing than a later, less guarded, response by Lasorda to the loss his team had just suffered at the hands of Dave Kingman.

Sometime after the game Tom Lasorda was interviewed by Paul Olden, a reporter for local radio station KLAC-AM. According to transcripts of the interview, it began innocuously enough, with Olden asking, "Can you give us just a few basic comments about your feelings on the game?" Lasorda's response, too, was relatively mild, delivered in an *aw-shucks* sort of twang. "Well," he began, "naturally I feel bad about losing a ball game like that. There's no way you should lose that ball game. And it, uh, just doesn't make sense."

"What's your opinion of Kingman's performance?" Olden then asked. The explosive response was instantaneous.

"What's my opinion of Kingman's performance?" Lasorda responded, his voice suddenly rising.

> What the *bleep* do you think is my opinion of it? I think it was BLEEPING BLEEP. Put that in, I don't BLEEP. Opinion of his performance? BLEEP, he beat us with three BLEEPING home runs! What the BLEEP do you mean, "What is my opinion of his performance?" How could you ask me a question like that, "What is my opinion of his performance?" BLEEP, he hit three home runs! BLEEP. I'm BLEEPING pissed off to lose that BLEEPING game. And you ask me my opinion of his performance! BLEEP. That's a tough question to ask me, isn't it? "What is my opinion of his performance?"

"Yes, it is," responded Olden in a somewhat shell-shocked voice, "and you gave me an answer."

"Well, I didn't give you a good answer," Lasorda said, "because I'm mad."

From there the interview wound down quickly. Olden quickly allowed that it "wasn't a good question," and Lasorda continued his rant. "That's a touchy question to ask me right now," he said. "'What is my opinion of his performance?' I mean, you want me to tell you what my opinion of his performance is."

"You just did," Olden said.

"That's right," Lasorda said, sounding very satisfied with himself. "BLEEP. Guy hits three home runs against us. BLEEP."

TWENTY

The Ballad of Glenn and Spunky

> Managing is like holding a dove in your hand. Squeeze too hard and you kill it, not hard enough and it flies away.
>
> —Tom Lasorda

> I hear that when you get too loud in the Dodgers' clubhouse, they call you aside and say, "We don't do that."
>
> —Pirate infielder Phil Garner

Tom Lasorda's rant about Dave Kingman would become, over time, a thing of legend—a glimpse at the unguarded mind of a Major League skipper dealing with the everyday pressures of managing a baseball team. In the immediate aftermath of Lasorda's explosion, team followers and fans were astounded to discover that the carefully nurtured image of the manager as a cheerleading, jovial, backslapping friend of Don Rickles and Frank Sinatra and best buddy to his players was somewhat less than truthful. And by mid-May people all around baseball were taking note of the changed atmosphere around the Dodgers. While the team had formerly been known for its workmanlike efficiency and ability to avoid the scandals, flair-ups, and other unrest common among high-performing teams such as the Yankees and Reds, now the Dodgers seemed to have their share of internal tension. The quiet confidence that drove the previous year's squad to dominate the National League was gone, and tension ruled the day.

While the public and press were just beginning to understand the full character of the Dodgers' sophomore manager, a number of players throughout the year had already learned their lesson the hard way. Sure, there was a lot you could get away with in Tom Lasorda's loose clubhouse. "You can laugh at Lasorda," wrote Bill Plaschke some years later. "You can play jokes on Lasorda. You can treat him like a nutty uncle or a wacky grandfather. You can do things to him that players on other teams would never dream of doing to their managers. But there is one thing you cannot do to Lasorda. The manager with no rules has one sin, and it is a mortal sin." That sin? Betrayal. Betrayal to him, betrayal to the Dodgers organization, betrayal to the Dodger Way. None of these was tolerated by Lasorda. There was another good reason, after all, that Lasorda had his young players bend down on one knee to pledge their belief in the Dodgers—a reason beyond motivating them to do their best for the organization. Lasorda also wanted to let them know, in a subtle way, that disobedience came at the player's own peril. "You must not be disloyal," Plaschke continued. "You must never turn your back on him or the franchise. You must never do anything that would show a lack of respect for all he has done for you."[1] From the moment Lasorda became the Dodgers' manager in 1977, any player who betrayed him or his team simply disappeared.

Don Sutton, of course, was one player who put all of Lasorda's rules to the test. The veteran pitcher had no qualms about directly clashing with his manager. Early on in Lasorda's reign, Sutton went against one of Lasorda's few pregame rules—that pitchers had to shag fly balls during batting practice. Sutton's custom was to use this time to run, so that's what he continued doing. One day in San Francisco during batting practice, Lasorda observed that Sutton and Doug Rau were running together. "Why do you do this to me?" Lasorda asked Rau, a player who had played under him throughout the Minor Leagues. "You've been like a son to me." Rau's response: "Sutton made me do it." Lasorda then summoned Sutton. Sutton bluntly told his manager he would continue to run during batting practice. And Lasorda locked the office door. "Fine, you want to change the rule, we'll change it right here," he said to Sutton. "Let's fight right here, you and me. If I beat you, the rule stays. If you beat me, I'll change it."[2] Sutton backed down, and the manager had made his point.

To be fair, Lasorda balanced his insistence on loyalty from his players with his own unconditional loyalty to them, at least within limits. "It's simple, really," Lasorda said. "I show you the loyalty of a father, you show me the loyalty of a son. . . . That's how I am, that's what I've preached forever, that's what made our teams work so well. You show me loyalty, I will watch your back forever."[3]

With the team not playing up to its potential in May, Lasorda was not the only Dodger who was frustrated. On May 16, two days after the Dodgers' Sunday-night loss against the Cubs, Dodger beat writer Ross Newhan revealed that Reggie Smith had come back to the Dodger clubhouse and smashed a shelf. Though his public persona was not terribly colorful—particularly compared to the "other" Reggie who dominated the New York and national media—the veteran Smith was known as a strong and explosive personality. Described as a "high-spirited, volatile, bruising competitor on and off the field" in a newspaper feature profile in the summer of 1978, Smith was a key cog in the Dodgers' success. (He had been voted by teammates the Dodgers' most valuable player in 1977.) A Los Angeles native who had grown up in a strict, deeply religious household with seven siblings, Smith was taught at a young age to work hard and follow the rules. "The rules in our house were no smoking, no drinking, no coming in late, no backtalk," Smith said. "I was encouraged to do my schoolwork, play plenty of baseball and football, but I was also expected to help with egg deliveries" in his father's wholesale-egg business.[4] From this background, Smith developed an intense drive to succeed in whatever he attempted. At Centennial High School in Compton, he mastered several sports: the one-hundred-yard dash, Golden Gloves boxing, football (he was recruited by a half-dozen colleges), and, most of all, baseball.[5] Smith approached baseball with an intensity that was daunting. "Reggie's a foxhole dude," said his teammate Dusty Baker some years later. "If it was war or a baseball game, there wouldn't be another person I want next to me."[6]

In 1978 Reggie Smith was the same person he always was. Married to his high school sweetheart, Ernestine, Smith strove for accomplishment and achievement. At home he played music with his family, having learned to play seven musical instruments, and he taught his children the same values he had been taught. "We begin with the usual parental subjects," Ernestine said, "morality, honesty, responsibility, studying hard. Then we extend the guidance to other areas. We're not fanatical preachers . . . but Reggie makes a special effort to pour his heart out to kids who have fewer opportunities." Smith concurred with his wife and then tried to justify his intensity. "Someone once said," he explained, "'Knowledge is the only instrument of production that is not subject to diminishing returns.' And I believe it. . . . I'll go out of my way to read and study. Ernestine and I are two of a kind in that way." The two discussed some of their recent learning experiences—a Vladimir Horowitz concert, the King Tut exhibition, and an attendant study of ancient Egyptian history—before Smith continued. "The explanation is simple," he said. "We didn't go to college and we're trying to become more well-rounded by reading and learning."[7]

Smith's Dodger teammates, of course, were well aware of Reggie's various passions. They called him the Professor, often testing his knowledge with questions and once even hanging a sign on his locker that read THE PROFESSOR IS GIVING LECTURES ON KING TUT. "He was very intelligent," said teammate Dave Lopes years later, "and everything he did he wanted to become good at doing. He worked hard in the off-season at something new every year. . . . One year it was an airplane pilot, and he got his license. One year it was photography. . . . Every Spring Training, we'd ask ourselves, 'What's coming next?' Reggie didn't ever settle for doing things half-assed."[8] According to Lopes, Smith had also become, by 1978, perhaps the most accomplished of the team's needlers, serving the crucial role of keeping things as "loose as possible in the clubhouse" in order to clear players' minds of their worries and frustrations. "A good needler gets downright personal," Lopes said in describing Smith's approach. "He'll try to shock you by saying the worst things he can think of about your wife or you—or any part of your life. He holds nothing back. But he does it in a way that if the guy getting the needle is human, he'll laugh. That's the goal."[9]

On May 15, one day after the loss to Kingman and the Cubs, Reggie Smith was the key in a close 7–6 win against the Pittsburgh Pirates. In the game Smith smashed two singles, hit a two-run home run, had two stolen bases despite his sore legs, and then came up to bat in the ninth with bases loaded and a chance to win the game for his team. "With a Dodger Stadium crowd of 35,290 chanting 'Reggie, Reggie,'" wrote Newhan, "the right fielder drove [a] double into the right-field corner to cap a three-run, last-gasp assault that burdened Bert Blyleven with his fourth defeat in six decisions."[10]

Lasorda's team, riled up from Smith's heroics, swept the Pirates and prepared to meet the first-place Giants at home. Before the series, however, Lasorda decided to administer another necessary system shock to the team. On May 17 the Dodgers announced the trade of Glenn Burke, the once-promising outfield prospect who had come to the end of his rope with the team, to the Oakland A's for twenty-nine-year-old outfielder Bill North. The Dodgers sold the trade as a win-win for both teams and both players. For the Dodgers North was an upgrade from Burke, who had never seemed to figure out how to hit Major League pitching. North would benefit as well by returning to the limelight. (The Oakland A's had finished dead last in their division the season before, with a 63-98 record.) Critics, however, questioned the trade's wisdom. North, they suggested, was not the player he once was. Though a switch hitter who gave the Dodgers a much-needed left-handed option and a speedster who had led the American League in steals three times, North's playing time in 1977 had been limited to just fifty-six games due to various injuries. And in 1978 North was batting just .211, with almost no power.[11] Sure, Burke's numbers were even worse than North's at the time of the trade, but it still seemed to many that the ceiling for the twenty-five-year-old center fielder was much higher than North's. "Once we get him cooled down a little from wanting to play all the time," Dodger coach Jim Gilliam had said of Burke sometime before 1978, "frankly, we think he's going to be another Willie Mays." Fans, too, were upset at the trade. "If Glenn Burke's absence," wrote two fans, "causes the Dodgers to lose the division title—as it may, considering his importance last year—we all can thank Walter O'Malley's greedy, quick-profit business sense." And according to a Dodgers beat writer at the time, even several veteran players on the team were distraught. "You don't break up, disrupt a team going as well as it was going, to make change," Lopes said later. "I didn't feel it was going to make us a better ball club. . . . It was probably not the real reason why things happened."[12]

In fact, a number of things about the trade failed to add up, at least on the surface. If the management was truly concerned about the clubhouse atmosphere and attitude of the players, they likely hadn't improved matters things by going after North.[13] A member of the free-spirited and loose "Swingin' A's" of the early 1970s, North seemed initially upset about the move to the constrictive and conservative Dodgers atmosphere—not least because it meant he had to shave his beard, which he kept because shaving tended to irritate his skin. Dodger management shrugged off the issue, saying that North's agent had indicated he would be receptive to the trade. But the arrival of North was tainted with other complications, including his continued leg problems and confusing life choices (North had recently been arrested for possession of cocaine).[14] And though the Dodgers' new center fielder said the right things when interviewed by the press a few days after his arrival in L.A. ("I'd like to play every day but I'm about winning," he said. "I'm about making a contribution in any way I can"), he also had this to say about his transition from the wild and contentious A's. "I've been to the mountaintop, and nobody can take that away from me," he said. "Now it's mostly about money. I want some. I've enjoyed the fruits of the game, I've had a good career. Now I want to make some money."[15]

Also not adding up were the reasons the Dodgers gave for shipping off Burke. After the trade the team's upper management let it slip out that one of the reasons for the move was that they considered Burke a "troublemaker," and as evidence they cited his "frequently expressed desire to play regularly." But what professional baseball player *doesn't* want to play regularly? Furthermore, from all reports Burke was anything but a "troublemaker" inside the clubhouse. "He was the life of the team," said Lopes a few days after the trade.[16] "He was the guy who kept the chemistry going in the clubhouse."[17] Tellingly, Burke had been particularly popular with some of the team's most problematic stars, Reggie Smith and Steve Garvey in particular, as well as with clubhouse leaders Lopes and Baker. Known for blasting disco music from the tape deck in his locker and reaching across the divides of a very diverse clubhouse, Burke had a ready and wide smile and a distinct penchant for making "Ali-esque pronouncements regarding his baseball and basketball ability," all of which were widely appreciated by a team weary perhaps of the franchise's dry professionalism and seeking to clear their minds of the stress of the long and difficult season. Indeed, according to common lore Burke had been the catalyst for inventing, or at least helping to popularize, a gesture that would become nearly ubiquitous in years to follow: the high five.[18] "God, it's quiet in here," remarked one player in the days after Burke's departure.[19]

The real reason the Dodgers decided to let go of their long investment in the hulking and speedy athlete who had been dubbed "King Kong" by his teammates will likely never be known. Certainly, the Dodgers needed a left-handed bat, and a proven bat—both of which Burke was unable to provide. But Burke's intangibles—defense, speed, clubhouse cutup—would seem to warrant better treatment, or at the very least an opportunity to finish the full season. However, the team had had several clear concerns about Burke's behavior. In the Minors Burke fought with managers and kept personal habits that were different from other players—living at the YMCA, for example, rather than in a house with some of his teammates. Dodger upper management worried increasingly about how to "reach" the offbeat young player, and general manager Campanis took two unusual steps with Burke. First, during Burke's first year as a roster player, Campanis assigned Reggie Smith to room with the younger player and keep an eye on him while the team was on the road. Then, a while later, Campanis called Burke into his office and offered him a bonus of seventy-five thousand dollars if he would settle down and get married.[20]

So what was the exact nature of Dodger concern about Burke? A lifelong friend of Burke's, who had played sports with him on the basketball courts of Oakland and at Berkeley High School, spelled it out thusly: "They traded him not for his baseball ability but for his life choice."[21] In fact, if Burke was surly on occasion, or seemed to behave strangely after the games or in his personal life, it could well have been because of a deep secret he was trying to keep from his team. It was a secret that he had come to understand fully only in 1975, while playing in the Minors and still a year away from being called up to the big leagues. "The vast majority of the players and management never really got to know me that well," Burke said of his Minor

League experience, in which he played for six different teams over six seasons. "They never questioned why I didn't have the outwardly sexual drive of the average ballplayer." The truth was, as Burke discovered at age twenty-three in 1975, while playing in the team's AA franchise in Waterbury, Connecticut, he was gay.[22]

Throughout the beginning of his career, in various small Minor League locations, Burke carefully and tentatively explored local gay nightlife. "I knew I was going to have to make changes in my life to continue my homosexual lifestyle while staying in the closet," Burke said. "I knew even then that 'coming out' would be baseball-suicide." He had a number of close calls. "I used to go to this bar in Waterbury called the Road House Cafe," Burke said. "As I was leaving there one night, one of the owners of the Waterbury Dodgers saw me coming out. We didn't exchange words, but I gave him one of those looks that said, 'Well, I know you're not going to tell.' But he never said a word to anyone. Turns out he was just as 'guilty' as I was."[23]

The gay lifestyle meant contentment and joy on one hand for Burke, but on the other hand it meant a good deal of extra stress, especially after he attained his ultimate goal of playing in the Major Leagues. He had to deceive the twenty-four teammates and numerous coaches who saw him every day. "When we were on the road," Burke said, "I would wait until my teammates were either in their rooms for the night or out on the town before heading out to gay bars and parties. I would anxiously flag down a taxicab while practically covering my head so no one would notice me. If someone did, I never acknowledged them. I was even fearful that the cab driver would notice I was a ballplayer, so I would always tell them to pull over a block or two from where I was going. No straight dude will ever know how difficult this charade is to play." The deception wore on Burke. "I became extremely paranoid. Even though I was very careful about concealing my homosexuality, there were more than a few occasions I thought someone from the front office had someone spying on me. And there were also times I was convinced everybody was whispering about Glenn Burke, the in-hiding Dodger homosexual."[24]

"I'm sure he played in fear," said his Dodger teammate Dave Lopes years later, "the fear of the fact that it's going to get out that he's gay and once it comes out, you're going to take abuse. Face it, society isn't ready for that. If there are any gay players, even today [in the mid-1990s], and you would think that there probably are, that's why they choose not to come out, because they know their careers are going to be ruined." Reggie Smith, another Dodger teammate, agreed with Lopes: "Homosexuality was taboo. I'm not going to sit here and say it was anything different. I'm sure it would have ruined his career. He would have not only been ostracized by his teammates, but management would have looked for ways to get him off the team, and the public would not have tolerated it."[25] In recent years, in fact, Burke's teammate and friend Dusty Baker has speculated that the Dodger management knew about the young player's hidden life as a homosexual, and that was a good part of the reason for his dismissal. "I think the Dodgers knew," said Baker. "I think that was why they traded him."[26]

After his playing days Glenn Burke spoke much more bluntly about the prejudices he thought had eventually ruined his playing career. Glenn Burke said of the trade on May 16, 1978:

> Little did anyone know why I was really traded by the Los Angeles Dodgers to the Oakland A's. [What] the Dodgers would receive in exchange was Billy North, a player who had watched his batting average drop 64 points in the previous two years. . . . I, on the other hand, was only 25 years old, had started in two World Series' games for the Dodgers in '77, and had proven to the team and fans alike that I was a speed-demon on the base-paths and one of the better defensive outfielders in baseball. And if given the chance to play on a regular basis, I would have been a great hitter too.

The real reason for the trade, according to Burke, was because they *knew*. "In the Seventies," Burke said, "the Dodgers were drawing three million fans a year. They had a pristine, clean image. Management was afraid of my sexual orientation, even though I never flaunted it. To this day, the Dodgers deny trading me because I was gay. But it was painfully obvious. . . . The Dodgers just never gave me a chance."[27]

As to how the Dodgers knew his secret, Burke, despite the care he took in guarding his secret, probably made one crucial mistake. At the time Tom Lasorda was not only a company man—loyal to the conservative and tradition-minded Dodgers—but also a man of his time, deeply committed to staid, safe, Frank Sinatra–approved heterosexual and male-centered middle-American conventions. Lasorda was also, however, a father in deep denial, at least publicly, of the open homosexuality of his son, Tom Lasorda Jr., whom everyone called "Spunky." Spunky Lasorda was a thin, sprite-like, sharply handsome young man of just nineteen years in 1977. He wore his blonde hair long, in the fashion of the time; regularly dressed in women's clothing; and preferred, despite a childhood spent following his father as he worked for Minor League Baseball teams around the country, the dazzling gay nightclubs of Hollywood over the green grass of a baseball park.

Though much divided Tom Lasorda from his son, much also bound them. "They had a great deal in common," wrote Peter Richmond in a GQ story.

> Start with the voice: gravelly, like a car trying to start on a cold morning. The father, of course, spends his life barking and regaling, never stopping; he's baseball's oral poet, an anti-Homer. It's a well-worn voice. Issuing from the son, a man so attractive that men tended to assume he was a woman, it was the most jarring of notes. One of his closest friends compared it to Linda Blair's in *The Exorcist*—the scenes in which she was possessed. . . . Then, the most obvious similarity: Both men were so outrageous, so outsized and surreal in their chosen persona, that, when it came down to it, for all of one's skepticism about their sincerity, it was impossible not to like them.

As described by friends who knew him at Sunny Hills High School in Fullerton, where the Lasordas lived in a middle-class suburban home, Spunky Lasorda moved through school with uncommon "style and self-assurance." He was "invariably dressed impeccably" and often surrounded by a group of fashionably beautiful young women. "He was as beautiful as his friends," said a high school classmate, filmmaker Cat Gwynn. "He had none of his father's basset-hound features. . . . [His] bones were carved, gently, from glass. . . . [And while] it was very obvious that he was feminine . . . none of the jocks nailed him to the wall or anything. I was enamored of him because he wasn't at all uncomfortable with who he was. In this judgmental, narrow-minded high school, he strutted his stuff."[28]

That Glenn Burke would befriend the openly gay son of the manager of his baseball team was inevitable. It was also ill-fated. "I have bitter-sweet memories of Spunky," said Burke years later. "We were great friends. He had a tremendous sense of humor. He was a transvestite some of the time, but not all of the time. And extremely flamboyant. . . . Spunky and I were a lot alike in many ways and very different in others. We were alike in that we both were disappointments in Tom's homophobia and unwillingness to deal with the whole situation." Because Spunky could not be completely open and out front with a father unwilling to accept who he was, he had long felt victimized by Lasorda. And so Burke, who was beginning to realize that Lasorda treated him differently from other players and wondered if it was because of his sexuality, shared a bond with Spunky. The two also shared, according to Burke, a sense of humor. Often they talked of dealing with their frustration with Tom Lasorda by staging a *Guess Who's Coming to Dinner* sort of moment, in which Spunky would deck himself out in pigtails and "all the female trimmings" and bring Burke to dinner at the Lasorda family home. They, of course, never dared act on their subversive little fantasy. "Tommy would have shot us in the head," Burke laughed. "Then he would have had a heart attack and died."[29]

Despite outward signs that Tom Lasorda was in some denial about his son's secret life, the father was, as many noted, deeply supportive, even protective, of his son. "He talked lovingly about his father and their relationship—they had a very good relationship," said another friend of Spunky. "I was surprised. I didn't think it'd be like that. You'd think it'd be hard on a macho Italian man. This famous American idol. You'd figure it'd be [the father saying] 'Please don't let people know you're my son,' but it was the opposite. . . . There had to be acceptance from his mom and dad. Tommy had that good self-esteem—where you figure that [his] parents did something right." Though it's difficult to know for sure, it appears that Tom Lasorda's protectiveness led him to take direct action in 1977 to end Burke's relationship with his son. That is, around the time Spunky had befriended Burke, Lasorda encouraged Spunky to move to West Hollywood to pursue his dream of a fashion career. "[Spunky] couldn't see me anymore," Burke said later. "The Dodgers had paid him to stay away from me. Spunky was a real pussy to end our friendship like that. A pure pussy! . . . I guess Tommy just couldn't stand me being friendly with his son Spunky. . . . But I'm not bitter. Bitterness doesn't solve shit."[30]

Ironically, the Dodgers' success with Lasorda as their manager in 1977 may have played an additional role in Burke's trade. Because of the pennant race, the outfielder's efforts to lead a double life became, in his words, "a little tougher. . . . [I] was suddenly in the limelight because of the team's success. We were on National television everyday now and, without sounding too bold, I was a big handsome guy with a good sense of humor. Girls suddenly were coming out of the woodwork to hang out with me. . . . They just wanted to be seen with me. If I had been straight, I would've had a field day." By the end of the 1977 season, in fact, as the Dodgers were on their way to taking the Western Division title, Burke guessed that most people on the team knew his sexual orientation because of his reluctance to take up the offers. "The tell-tale signs were beginning to surface," he said. "Some players would ask with a grin, 'Is Glenn waiting for his "girlfriend?"' Or, 'Don't bend over in the shower, here comes Glenn.'"[31]

Considering all that came to pass in 1977, Burke later admitted that he should have seen the trade coming. Once the trade did come, however, Burke quickly became resigned to, even hopeful about, leaving the Dodgers. "I remember thinking that the Dodgers didn't give me a chance to be the next Willie Mays," said Burke. "But maybe the A's would."[32]

Considering the fate of both Burke and Lasorda Jr. however, Burke's later regrets are to be expected. Under the even more intolerant Billy Martin, the ex-Dodger's playing career with the A's ended quickly—a little more than a year after the trade. (Martin had taken to taunting the young player with homophobic epithets even as he gave the outfielder scant regular playing time.) At the time that he recounted this story, in the mid-1990s, Burke was to that point the only baseball player who had ever come out as gay. He was also in hospice care, his health long ruined from AIDS-related complications that came from a life of drug abuse and other misbehavior.

"The point I'm trying to make here," he said from his hospital bed, "is that the Dodgers are arguably the sharpest organization in all of sports. They knew I was gay, and were worried about how the average father would feel about taking his son to a baseball game to see some fag shagging fly balls in centerfield. . . . A great part of society still doesn't know how to deal with homosexuality. And there is no sport that accepts gays less than baseball."[33]

That's not to say that Burke forgave anyone for their insensitive and hurtful behavior. "Spunky died of AIDS-related complications a couple of years ago [in June 1991, at the age of thirty-three]," Burke said. "It's somewhat tragic, but Tommy is still in denial about Spunky's sexual orientation and how he died. He tells his friends Spunky died of pneumonia only, not AIDS complications. I feel bad for Tommy that he lost his son. It must be very painful to bury your child. But he should stop being a jerk and accept Spunky for who he really was."[34]

TWENTY-ONE

Ain't Talkin' 'bout Love

It's very romantic. It gets a hold on you. You love it and you hate it. It's a whore, but it's a fertile mother: L.A., to me, is what America is all about.

—Don Henley

Though it wasn't exactly television history, on March 15, 1977, a new situation comedy debuted on ABC TV. Set in an apartment building in Santa Monica, the show distinguished itself from the usual television fare of the time by the contemporariness of its situations, humor, and characters. In the first episode of *Three's Company*, for instance, two young female roommates, one dressed in a short dressing gown with slit leg and the other wearing a loose robe, gather in the living room of their apartment to relive the events of a wild party the night before.[1] One of them, named Janet, is hung over and embarrassed over her behavior at her former (third) roommate's nuptials the night before. "Eleanor must hate me," said Janet. "It was her wedding reception and I ruined it." To which the second roommate, Chrissy, replies: "She didn't even notice. Her labor pains started, and they rushed her off to the hospital." In the first two minutes of the program, then, we encounter two semiscantily clad young women talking casually about their single lifestyle, and we hear about a third roommate who gave birth to a child at her wedding reception. This was not your grandmother's situation comedy.

While much about the basic premise and content of *Three's Company* was typical of commercial entertainment through the ages, based as it was on farcical misunderstandings, broad physical humor, and other comedy-of-error tropes, what was new here was the show's relaxed standard for language and more mature sexual content. After the opening scene of the pilot, Chrissy goes into the bathroom to take a shower and discovers a man sleeping off the party in the bathtub. The girls take the surprise in stride—a telling bit of detail for a generation that has come to expect casual sex as part of the youthful dating life. According to one study, for example, between 1972 and 1982 the proportion of American women who endorsed premarital sex jumped by 20 percentage points to become the norm (58 percent).[2] Further, when the surprise visitor turns out to need a place to live, the two girls extend an invitation without much question. Janet even hatches a sexually charged plan to assuage their landlords, the Ropers, whose older values make them suspicious of such an arrangement. The plan is this: Jack will pretend to be gay and therefore, strangely, now acceptable to the landlords.

Three's Company, despite being dismissed by critics as "fluff," was an almost immediate success. ABC gladly renewed the show for the next season, and ratings grew. Eventually, *Three's Company* became a number one–rated show, and it reached syndication after completing a seven-year run. What struck a chord in audiences about *Three's Company* had something to do with the changing zeitgeist of the 1970s. Between 1948 and 1970 American television networks generally avoided any hint of sexual content, relying mostly on bland, more universally palatable entertainment. "They saturated the airwaves," wrote social historian Edward Berkowitz, "with variety shows, westerns, and situation comedies that featured suburban households confronting the problems of a prosperous society." It was only in the 1970s that the television networks finally realized they could appeal to a wider audience by catering to the younger generation whose values, interests, and sense of humor were markedly different from the generation before. The saucy do-it-if-it-feels-right escapism of *Three's Company* was in keeping with other hit programs of the era—most notably the "Jiggle TV" vehicle *Charlie's Angels*, which was a hit for ABC starting in late 1976. *Charlie's Angels* featured three beautiful young women who, while undertaking dangerous missions for an off-camera character named Charlie, never seemed to lack opportunity to wear skinny bikinis or other revealing clothing. While critics excoriated the show, audiences "loved it," according to critic Edward Berkowitz, "and Farrah Fawcett-Majors became a breakout star. Men worshipped her as a sex symbol . . . [and] women found her adorable and imitated her hair style."[3]

Charlie's Angels, like *Three's Company*, was also set in and around Los Angeles, and this was by design. After all, Southern California in the 1970s represented, to most Americans, something exotic and on the forward edge, especially when it came to matters of sex and love. In those days Los Angeles was "groovy." It was famed as the place where young people could get in touch with their venal sides. In the second episode of *Three's Company*, for example, Chrissy reveals that her father, a minister who lives back in the sleepy central California farm town of Fresno, refers to Los Angeles as "Sin City." For many young Americans in 1977, that "Sin City" was pretty appealing.

The culture of Southern California coming out of the late 1960s was defined by youthful hedonism. Influenced by the hormone-heavy local beach and car cultures, the drug- and sex-fueled music culture that centered around Laurel Canyon, and the warm sun and attendant sun worship, Los Angeles had become, alongside New York and San Francisco, a main locale for the nation's emerging sexual openness. In 1974 the founder of the men's magazine *Playboy* moved his headquarters from Chicago to a large Gothic-Tudor-style house located in Los Angeles near Beverly Hills. Almost immediately, the new western Playboy Mansion became famous for its elaborate, raucous, sex-charged parties. Amid the crowds of celebrities and gawkers, the avuncular Hugh Hefner would hold court while disco lights flashed, music blared, and bevies of beautiful, nearly nude young women skated, or splashed in the pool, or posed for the paparazzi.

It made sense that Hefner—the ageless elder statesman of the nation's sex industry—would thrive in Southern California once he settled there. In the middle of the Me Decade, Californians everywhere were in search of one sort of self-gratification or another. This much was clear to Tom Wolfe, at least, when he chose to focus on Los Angeles for his 1976 article on the "Me Decade" for the magazine *New York*. The article opens at L.A.'s Ambassador Hotel, in the presence of a local housewife seeking to overcome her sexual and personal "repression" by attending a session with a self-help trainer. "Take your finger off the repress button," the trainer tells a gathered crowd, leading them through an "est" training session.[4] Est training was a method of self-improvement and realization that had been invented by Werner Erhard around 1971.[5] Erhard promised that his training would teach people how to transform their lives, and between 1971 and 1984 he sold his bill of goods to more than seven hundred thousand enrollees.

"Take your finger off the repress button!" the est trainer shouted in the hotel conference room. "Let it gush up and pour out!" And the gathered, who were all now lying on the floor of the hotel conference room, did as he asked—they screamed, then screamed again, and again, each time louder and with more abandon, until at the end the room sounded like a frightened, frenzied orgy of wishful release. Wrote Wolfe:

> There are no longer 250 separate souls but one noösphere of souls united in some incorporeal way. . . . Each soul is concentrated on its one burning item—my husband! my wife! my homosexuality! my inability to communicate, my self-hatred, self-destruction, craven fears, puling weaknesses, primordial horror, premature ejaculation, impotence, frigidity, rigidity, subservience, laziness, alcoholism, major vices, minor vices, grim habits, twisted psyches, tortured souls—and yet each unique item has been raised to a cosmic level and united with every other until there is but one piercing moment of release and liberation at last!—a whole world of anguish set free.[6]

The urge to self-improve, to experience all the joy that is possible to experience in life, to live in orgiastic bliss in perpetuity—all of these impulses reached an apotheosis in Los Angeles in the 1970s. "The old alchemical dream was changing base metals into gold," wrote Wolfe. "The new alchemical dream is: changing one's personality—remaking, remodeling, elevating, and polishing one's very self . . . and observing, studying, and doing on it. (Me!)" By the later 1970s this self-absorption and concern for self-transformation became a full-time preoccupation in California. There was the nearby Esalen Institute, in Big Sur, with its Encounter sessions. There was Scientology. There was Arica, the Mel Lyman movement, Synanon, Daytop Village, and Primal Scream. The list of sects, cults, alternative communities, and alternative outlooks was nearly endless: ESP, Flying Saucer cults, the "Jesus People," the Moonies, followers of Carlos Castaneda, the People's Temple, the worshippers of the acid trip and the occult and the paranormal. "Outsiders," wrote Wolfe, "hearing of these sessions, wondered what on earth their appeal was. Yet the appeal was simple enough. It is summed up in the notion: 'Let's talk about *Me*.' No matter whether you managed to renovate your personality through encounter sessions or not, you had finally focused your attention and your energies on the most fascinating subject on earth: *Me*."[7]

In Los Angeles in the 1970s the impulse for self-gratification was so strong that it also led to the development of a multibillion-dollar sex industry. Inspired by the "free love" philosophies of nearby San Francisco and its wild late-1960s music and drug scene, Los Angeles had seen the rise of a "blossoming hippie milieu" along the stretch of music and nightclubs of the Sunset Strip and in the Strip's "bucolic annex Laurel Canyon." "Young girls are coming to the canyon," sang the Mamas & the Papas in 1967, indicating both how Laurel Canyon had entered the cultural zeitgeist and what it was that drove the phenomenon. Mickey Dolenz, a locally born boy who hit pay dirt with the Monkees, had a house in Laurel Canyon that was noted for the constant procession of Hollywood actors—such as Jack Nicholson, Dennis Hopper, Harry Dean Stanton, and so on—and fellow musicians who would come to visit and swim naked in Dolenz's pool. According to Jackson Browne, who was a younger member of the Laurel Canyon community, there was always a "gaggle of girls" who mainly lived at the house of Dolenz's "bandmate" Peter Tork and would show up at various places with "big bowls of fruit and dope and shit" and would "fuck us in the pool."[8] At the house of "Mama" Cass Elliot of the Mamas & the Papas, meanwhile, it was known that young men could go there to catch a good high—in exchange for sexual favors. Jim Morrison, who lived and cavorted in Laurel Canyon, based his song "Love Street" on his experiences.

"L.A. was all about hanging in those days," said a former music executive for MGM. "It was the constant hanging at other people's houses, which was the magic of the hills and canyons. All you had to do was drive up into Laurel Canyon and so much would happen en route." In time, the music scene of Laurel Canyon of the era added to L.A.'s growing reputation for sexual possibility and lack of abandon. As Joan Didion noted in her essay "The White Album," Laurel Canyon seemed locked in a "mystical flirtation with the idea of 'sin. . . . in 1968 and 1969.'" "Everyone was experimenting and taking it all the way," said a filmmaker from the era. "It opened up a negative force of energy that was almost demonic." Eventually, in the 1970s, the sex-charged music scene morphed. "The Sunset Strip got really ugly," said musician and writer Jan Henderson. "Let's face it, we were all doing shit we weren't supposed to, but the sharks moved in."[9]

By 1977 and 1978 much of this drug-fueled sexual decadence centered on one particular club, the Roxy Theater, which had opened in 1973 on the Sunset Strip in West Hollywood. Among the groundbreaking sexual and drug-addled escapades that occurred at the Roxy was the first American run, in 1974, of the British stage play *The Rocky Horror Show*. Also in 1974, in the small bar located above the main club, John Lennon and Harry Nilsson spent their "lost weekend" of drug abuse and other acting out. (A few years later, in 1982, John Belushi would spend the last night of his life partying in the same bar before later going home and overdosing on a fatal injection of heroin and cocaine.)[10]

At the time it seemed natural that all of L.A.'s raunchiness would be highlighted at the Roxy Theater. After all, the club's owner, Lou Adler, was a high-living, hard-partying playboy, known for fathering seven children with four different women—including the 1970s-era sexual symbol Britt Eckland, a Bond girl in 1974's *The Man with the Golden Gun* who was a regular fixture at the Playboy Mansion and in the pages of *Playboy*.[11] In the late 1970s the Roxy Theater became home to thousands of young, attractive, sexually open women who had their sights set on brushing up against fame by crawling into the bed of someone famous. Clubs all along the Sunset Strip teemed with women who were available in exchange for a few drugs and a ride up to the canyon. By the later 1970s Los Angeles's music scene was defined by a new generation of rock-fueled debauchery—in the form of oversexed, be-spandexed, and hair-teased bands like Van Halen and Mötley Crüe, whose songs became a pulsing sexual soundtrack for millions of seventeen-year-old boys and girls of the era.

Adding to the sexualized atmosphere of Los Angeles in the 1970s were the orgiastic parties and sex-fueled happenings at the Playboy Mansion in nearby Beverly Hills. "Sex," argued Hugh Hefner, the local champion of hedonistic self-fulfillment as a kind of moral imperative, was the "major civilizing influence in our society, not religion." The alternative to free love, he suggested, was "repression, perversion, obscenity, war and a crushing of the human spirit."[12]

Never mind that Hefner's vision was wholeheartedly male-centric, that his magazine and his parties turned women into one-dimensional objects of desire to be enjoyed by men, and that he himself, a man who was nearly fifty as the 1970s closed, enjoyed the sexual availability of a constant string of "apple-cheeked young women who arrived from the Midwest, eager to be Playboy centerfolds."[13]

With Hefner's slant on sex providing additional impetus, people across the nation began to view Angeleno sexual attitudes and practices with wonder, then increasing consternation, and, eventually, horror. This evolution in the views of L.A. began in the suburbs, away from the nighttime debauchery of Laurel Canyon and the Sunset Strip, where local sexual values seem to have led, at least according to one source, to a social-sexual practice called "swinging."[14] Though humans had been exploring nonmonogamous sexual activities in various ways for centuries, the practice, if the Hollywood movie *Bob & Carol & Ted & Alice* was to be believed, became common in the Los Angeles area in the 1960s. Somewhat more discomfiting to middle America, meanwhile, was the growing presence of the sex industry, both legitimate and illegal, in L.A. in the 1970s. In 1976 a nightclub owner and publisher named Larry Flynt moved the headquarters of his growing pornographic business from Ohio to Beverly Hills. Chief among the products of Larry Flynt Publications was a magazine called *Hustler*, which would become notorious for its raw sexuality, scandalous cartoons and editorials, and penchant for pushing the limits of good taste. In North Hollywood, meanwhile, a former ventriloquist named Ted Marche had established a multimillion-dollar business making dildos. Between the mid-1960s and mid-1970s, Marche Manufacturing made nearly five million of its signature sexual toy, as well as more than 350 different sexual products. "These toys," said Ted Marche's son Steven, a partner in the business, "have saved more marriages than all the preachers in the world."[15] And Angelenos were only just getting started.

By the mid-1970s the Los Angeles region also became the leading producer of X-rated films. In the early 1970s the arguable kingpins of the pornographic film industry in America were the Mitchell Brothers. Based in San Francisco, the nominal national capital of porn back then, Jim and Artie Mitchell produced pornographic films and owned a collection of X-rated cinemas and strip clubs in the San Francisco area. In Los Angeles at the time, where the proximity to Hollywood might have made the development of a porn film industry seem almost a given, it was believed that Hollywood executives spurred the local police's notorious vice squad to hassle any such production houses whenever they appeared. By the middle of the decade, however, that all began to change.

In this era, in the years before AIDS and the Moral Majority, pornography was widely accepted, even deemed "chic," by mainstream audiences. Films like *Deep Throat*, *Behind the Green Door*, and *The Devil in Miss Jones* were "hits" at movie houses. Then, with the proliferation of new home video players—the so-called video cassette recorder that played VHS-based tapes—in 1977, demand for X-rated productions only increased.[16] This was just as a growing number of young, hungry filmmakers were graduating from the relatively new film programs at the University of California at Los Angeles and the University of Southern California only to find a stagnant filmmaking industry in Hollywood. With so many out-of-work and hopeful filmmakers—such as Bob Chinn, Bob Vosse, and Steve Scott—bumming around the Los Angeles area, and the demand for porn growing, it was only natural that pornographic production houses would begin to appear.

At first the porn production houses in Los Angeles were small and based out of quiet, somewhat dull cities in the San Fernando Valley—Chatsworth, Van Nuys, Northridge, Canoga Park. But quickly, driven by the growing VHS market, porn producers and distributors began to figure things out. The adult film industry in San Fernando Valley made several high-profile smash "hits" such as *Candy Stripers*, *The Debutante*, *Johnny Wadd*, and a host of films starring a famously well-endowed porn actor named John Holmes.[17] Then, in June 1978, VCX, Inc., became the first adult video company to exhibit at the annual Summer Consumer Electronics Show in Chicago. Afterward, business exploded, as the company received orders for more than 180,000 tapes. By the early 1980s the San Fernando Valley had become the chief source for adult films, eventually growing to a multibillion-dollar industry, and VCX became the single largest manufacturer of prerecorded videotapes. In 1983 a trade magazine for the adult film industry, called *AVN*, moved to San Fernando Valley. By then, with around 90 percent of all pornographic films being produced in the area, the region had earned a new nickname: "San Pornando Valley."

It is perhaps not surprising that California's sexual freedom would begin to show signs of decadence and disease. Hollywood had, after all, seen its share of corruption scandals and other basic shadiness. In 1977 the ill-fated Hollywood director Roman Polanski was taking sexual liberties that would embroil him in a sensational criminal scandal that would in many ways exemplify the era. On March 10, according to accounts of the victim, Polanski had sex with a thirteen-year-old girl whom he had drugged with a combination of alcohol and a part of a quaalude. Though Polanski claimed that the sex was consensual, it didn't matter—under California law a person under eighteen cannot legally consent to sexual intercourse with anyone who is not a spouse. In other words, what Polanski did had to be considered rape.

The story was major news in California and around the world for much of the spring and summer of that year. Ironically enough, the criminal trial *People of the State of California v. Roman Polanski* was scheduled to begin on August 9, 1977, exactly eight years after the death of Sharon Tate Polanski. Under the various terms of an arranged plea agreement, Polanski would plead guilty to a lesser charge and receive, pending a psychiatric evaluation, only probation. Unfortunately, however, just previous to the arraignment, the judge indicated that he had changed his mind and intended to imprison Polanski. Feeling he had no other choice, on the night of February 1,

1978, Roman Polanski boarded a plane to England and left the United States forever. A day later, fearing that he could be extradited by Britain back to the United States, he flew to France, where he held citizenship. He has never returned to either England or the United States.

For moralists like Tom Wolfe, the debauchery among Laurel Canyon's musicians and groupies, the explosion of pornography in Southern California in the 1970s, and the Roman Polanski case were all manifestations of the self-absorption of the Me Decade—the idea that you could be fulfilled through the solipsistic pursuit of your own sexuality seemed in keeping with what he had observed at the Esalen Institute. Tom Bradley, meanwhile, did not make the growing presence of porn purveyors a focus for his administration, though he was certainly aware of the issue. After all, pornography had always riled up strong emotions in Los Angeles. In the late 1970s, perhaps because of the too rapid expansion of porn productions in San Fernando Valley, a number of adult shops around the area were attacked. On June 1, 1978, in particular, a bomb destroyed an adult bookstore and massage parlor on Ventura Boulevard in Sherman Oaks. This was reported to be the third such attack on pornography-related businesses in the valley in the previous two months.[18]

For Tom Lasorda's Dodgers, meanwhile, sex was an obvious, and somewhat popular, part of life in California. As Glenn Burke had hinted team members were the toast of the region and often subject to advances by available young women. Of course, American athletes have long had access to more than their share of pretty young women—just read certain passages in *Ball Four* or in the sordid 1970s-era tell-all biographies of noted baseball swingers like Joe Pepitone (*Joe, You Coulda Made Us Proud*) and Bo Belinsky (*Bo: Pitching and Wooing*), and you'll get a sense of this. Nancy Marshall, who was married to Mike Marshall when he played on the Dodgers, later wrote of those years that "most of the screwing around that occurs on the road is just recreational sex. . . . They're bored and adored, so they get laid. I think just about everyone knows about that."[19] For good reason, perhaps, players are reticent to discuss their own dalliances and those of their peers, so there's no way to quantify the extracurricular activities of any of the Dodgers of 1977 and 1978. What's clear, though, is that many on the team found love and affection among the women of Southern California. While Don Sutton married a local girl named Patti after settling in with the team in 1968, according to a *Sports Illustrated* story from 1982 there were rumors of other women in Sutton's life from almost the get-go. Patti even once told an interviewer that she had "misgivings" about marrying Don from the moment of their wedding. "Most of us are used to receiving, receiving all the time," Sutton said of his habits. "Everything is done for us. We're not used to giving at all. There's a constant sponge effect. Our priorities get way out of whack. We tend to forget that other people also need some emotional strokes. Everyone needs to feel the space they occupy is important."[20] Years later Don and Patti Sutton would divorce, and Don Sutton would marry a much younger woman.

Dusty Baker, meanwhile, who grew up in nearby Riverside, married a Grambling University student while he was with the Atlanta Braves. Her name was Harriet, and on the Dodgers Baker became known for setting up teammates with his wife's friends.[21] Flashy Steve Yeager, meanwhile, was known as the driver of much of the team's late-night carousing. In the early 1970s Yeager had already divorced Brenda, his wife of eight years, and in 1976 he had a marquee wedding to local rock musician Gloria Gaione.[22] Even Tom Lasorda, father of two and married to Jo seemingly forever, was widely rumored to have had numerous dalliances, though no confirmation was possible.

And then there was Steve Garvey. No one was more popular, and no one was more seemingly upright—the namesake of a local junior high school, a fixture in local philanthropic circles, and later a member of the board of trustees of the private Catholic University of San Diego—than Steve Garvey. But as it happened, Garvey was perhaps the most quintessentially Southern Californian when it came to matters of sex—fully embodying the dysfunction and sexual intrigue that increasingly defined local sexuality in those years.

A first glimpse of what Garvey was really about came in 1981, in a long Q&A interview in *Playboy*. After touching on the obvious topics—his thoughts on various baseball players and managers, on free agency and his salary situation, on his struggles to be understood by teammates—conversation turned, as is to be expected in a men's magazine, to sexual issues. "Why is there so much gossip about you and Cyndy," asked the interviewer, "other women, other men?" In his response Garvey bemoaned the public's inability to understand that it is "possible to have a friendship with someone of the opposite sex and to enjoy conversation or dinner without sexual involvement. . . . The gossip still amazes me." The interviewer, perhaps dissatisfied, pressed Garvey: "Have you considered having an affair?" she asked, to which Garvey responded revealingly, "It's a feeling I've had for, gosh, a couple of years now. Anything is possible. But given the relationship I have with my wife and the feelings we have for each other, the odds against it are lopsided. Of course, I've had thoughts about having an affair, but, in essence, the actuality has never happened. . . . As far as my marriage is concerned, and my love for my wife, our relationship has never reached a point which has forced me to go out and have a sexual affair with another woman."[23]

Despite Garvey's stumbling protestations, he was having extramarital sex. And a lot of it for many years—as much, in fact, as any ballplayer who wasn't claiming to be some sort of moral paragon. Later, after his playing days, Garvey's unsavory succession of dalliances—and multiple paternity suits—would of course come back to haunt him, destroying his reputation, tarnishing his case for election to the Hall of Fame, and ruining his hopes of entering politics. Though there was no ballplayer more publicly popular in his time than Garvey, and though no one seemed more upright and wholesome, he perfectly embodied all the dysfunctions and unease of L.A.'s sexual mores in those years. "Ain't talkin' 'bout love," indeed.

TWENTY-TWO

Untaxing the Golden Cow

At a time when City services and City government are under critical scrutiny; at a time when the future is viewed conservatively and our vision of what we might become are [*sic*] narrowed; at such a time it is fitting that we remember who we are; our humble beginnings; the visionaries who shaped a modern metropolis from semi-arid land; our potential.

—Tom Bradley, "197: A Time to Reflect," remarks offered at a celebration of the 197th birthday of Los Angeles

As spring came to a close in 1978, and the political rhetoric of an election season heated up along with the weather, Mayor Tom Bradley was more convinced than ever that bringing the Olympics back to Los Angeles would be a boon for every one of its residents, and he couldn't fathom exactly why anyone else would think differently. Still, Bradley had not risen to high office by ignoring the feelings and concerns of his constituents. From nearly the moment his original bid failed in 1974, he knew that there were concerns over how much the city would be obligated to pay for the privilege of hosting the Games. In fact, a wide swath of the city made it clear they didn't want to be taken to the cleaners by the IOC, as had happened in Munich, Montreal, and in fact to just about every other Olympic venue in the past half century.[1]

Because of the troubles of the previous two Olympic Games—the terrorist-marred Games in Munich in 1972 and the financially besieged Games in Montreal in 1976—Bradley had always stressed that the Angeleno vision for the Games was a "spartan" one. That is,

Bradley would not construct the type of overelaborate sports facilities and complexes that had stressed Munich in 1972 and bankrupted Montreal in 1976. "Los Angeles [needs] only a velodrome, archery range, and swimming pool," he said at the time. All other events could be accommodated in existing sports facilities around the city. But that was not all. Bradley proposed a revolutionary change when he insisted to the IOC that the city would actively seek to control costs. Among the most unusual of his cost-saving notions was to construct a swimming complex that would place two temporary aluminum pools at Dodger Stadium for the Games' seventeen or eighteen days of swimming events.[2] The focus, Bradley stressed, would be on the world-class athletes, not on "new buildings and extravagant frills."[3] He also suggested that the city would extensively seek private funding—meaning corporate sponsors—to cover costs. This was, despite the necessity, new and controversial territory.

Bradley's ideas for the 1984 Olympics were of course not only counter to long-standing Olympic tradition, but also a direct challenge to the authority of the International Olympic Committee—an organization that tended to take a dim view of such matters. "The I.O.C. sees itself like the College of Cardinals," said Anton Calleia, "or like the knights of the Round Table. They can be very difficult to deal with."[4] After the close of the Mexico City summit with the IOC on April 12, the Los Angeles team returned home hopeful that, with a few compromises, an Olympic agreement was within reach. Unfortunately, the Los Angeles City Council chose this time to express its own ideas on the matter.

Just a few days before, while the Los Angeles team was in transit to Mexico, a young and somewhat contrarian council member named Zev Yaroslavsky had published an editorial in the *Los Angeles Times*. The sharply ambitious Yaroslavsky, who had won his first election at age twenty-six in 1975 over a more established opponent,[5] saw opportunity in the Olympic-bid uncertainty. In his commentary the council member asked pointed questions. "Why do we want these games at all? What primarily motivates our bid, and what do we expect to get out of it?" After admitting that he had been naive at first, thinking the bid was "primarily motivated by confidence in our ability to stage a series of athletic events, that our citizens would seize the chance to participate in preparing for and viewing the Games, that this community—including its youth—would invest their energies in constructive recreational and athletic programs that would benefit Los Angeles for generations to come," over time Yaroslavsky realized that something far less productive and altruistic was happening. "Our bid is slowly becoming a thinly veiled disguise," wrote Yaroslavsky, "to change the way others see us. Our bid is becoming another attempt to revise our hick-freeway-surfer-laidback image." The Olympics would do little to alter that, he suggested, adding that the costs were too steep to risk the chance. "We alone will bask in the glory," he wrote. "[And] we alone will pay the psychological and financial cost."[6]

Toward the end of April the city council's growing skepticism over the Games had become a distraction in the city's ongoing negotiations with the IOC. After an April 15 speech by Anton Calleia at a Florida meeting of the U.S. Olympic Committee suggested that an agreement was imminent, three Los Angeles City Council members—Ernani Bernardi, Bob Ronka, and Yaroslavsky—loudly expressed their concern and asked that at least one Olympics "skeptic" be allowed to join the city's delegation for an upcoming meeting in Athens in May. (Bradley and his team on the city's Olympics Committee acquiesced by announcing it would allow Bob Ronka to participate.)

Another key source of "opposition" in the city government was the city controller at the time, Ira Reiner—though Reiner afterward suggested he was never truly opposed to the Olympics bid. "As Controller, I had to raise concerns about the potential cost to the city of hosting the Olympics," Reiner said. "I wasn't against the Games; I was merely against building state-of-the-art facilities at taxpayers' expense." In early May the swirling political battle continued, with all sides sending mixed signals and making contradictory statements. On May 4, perhaps feeling pressured by the comments of some city council members, the L.A. Attorney's Office sent to the IOC a "toughly worded" contract for the 1984 Olympics. The contract, which was different from the one that city officials had received from the IOC in Mexico City, included various protections for the city and legal reservations on potential Olympic costs. These protections were not likely to be favorable to the IOC, and indeed, on

May 8, the International Olympic Committee indicated that it found the contract so unacceptable that it would "not even consider it for the time being."[7]

As if matters weren't looking bleak enough, a public-opinion poll taken on the eve of the local organizers' trip to Athens revealed that a full 59 percent of Los Angeles County voters were now opposed to hosting the Games. With this as a backdrop even as the city's Olympic representatives arrived in Athens on May 15, word came to Mayor Bradley that IOC president Lord Killanin was requesting a private meeting with him. The meeting between the two was congenial, with both sides seeming to want a compromise, but then, much to Bradley's surprise, later that evening at the general meeting the International Olympic Committee announced a public ultimatum to L.A.'s Olympic representatives. In a sternly worded message the IOC insisted that Los Angeles either negotiate from the starting point of the original draft contract from April 11 or lose the Games. (To put some oomph behind the ultimatum, several days before the meeting, on May 11, IOC president Lord Killanin had been quoted in Paris saying he had lined up three potential fallback cities—Mexico City, Munich, and Montreal—in the event that negotiations with Los Angeles broke down.) In Athens, then, in the middle of May, Tom Bradley realized his Olympic dream was turning more and more into a political nightmare.

Behind the Los Angeles City Council's sudden intransigence over the Olympics was a development in the spring of 1978 that had seemed to sneak up on Bradley and the city. Though Mayor Bradley started his second term fully aware that he had won a full 59 percent of the vote against a host of opponents—including runner-up Democrat Alan Robbins, who garnered just 28 percent of the vote—Bradley would find a world of trouble from a lesser candidate in the election. This was the unimposing, jowly seventy-five-year-old retired businessman and perennial political candidate Howard Jarvis.

Howard Arnold Jarvis had been born in 1903 in a small mining town north of Salt Lake City, Utah, called Magna. Raised Mormon, as a young man Jarvis regularly worked with his father, John Ransome Jarvis, a future state supreme court judge, on campaigns for state legislature seats. After Jarvis graduated from Utah State University, he convinced a local bank to loan him the money to buy a struggling small community paper, the *Magna Times*. And by the time Jarvis was thirty, he had expanded his business to include eleven small newspapers. In 1931, as fate would have it, the ambitious young publisher attended a convention for the Republican Party in Chicago, where he shared a suite with a California district attorney named Earl Warren. According to Jarvis, Warren suggested that he move to the golden land of opportunity. In 1935 Jarvis sold off his papers and took this advice. "When I arrived there," Jarvis recalled, "I was wet behind the ears, all I had was money."[8] Despite being green to the ways of the Golden State, Jarvis set about making a greater fortune in the wide-open local economy—first purchasing an Oakland chemical firm and later, after relocating to Los Angeles, establishing a chain of home-appliance factories.

In 1962 successful businessman Jarvis ran in the Republican primary election for the right to run for the U.S. Senate seat held by the incumbent, a liberal Republican named Thomas Kuchel. "I thought Tommy Kuchel voted with the Democrats on every crucial issue," wrote Jarvis, "and I thought the Republican Party ought to have a *Republican* U.S. Senator." Though Kuchel won the primary and was eventually reelected to his Senate seat, the primary run was, for Jarvis, a "fascinating experience." During the run Jarvis honed a homespun, common-man approach that would serve him well in future political battles. "I was on the road for eighteen months," Jarvis later wrote.

> I built myself a mobile home with a toilet, a shower, radio, and television. I even had a sound system on top, and inside I had a printing press and typesetting equipment so I could go into a town and print posters and have kids hand out hundreds of them for me. I campaigned all the little towns and cities, some 400 of them. I didn't think I could do very well in the big cities, but I thought maybe I could get the country vote and beat Kuchel that way, I just had a ball traveling around the state in my van. I slept in it every night.[9]

The outsider campaign by Jarvis raised the ire of state Republican Party functionaries, and someone in the party convinced a last-minute ultraconservative, anticommunist candidate, Lloyd Wright, to enter the race as a way of splitting the conservative vote. Kuchel won the primary election handily, followed by Wright in second. Jarvis came in third.

After the election was over Jarvis, somewhat exhausted, made the fateful decision to retire from both politics and business.

> By then I had several thousand employees, and I was one of the largest industrial employers in Southern California. It was a terrific strain. I had a huge payroll and a lot of problems. . . . A lot of my friends who owned their own businesses and were about the same age I was were dropping dead, and I found myself spending a great deal of time of time going to their funerals. I felt if I didn't get out, I would probably die in the saddle at my office. It was just too much for one man. So I sold all my companies . . . to some investors from Chicago.[10]

Jarvis fully intended to take his earnings—about $750,000 (the equivalent of nearly $6,000,000 today)—and move to the Bahamas, where he would live a long life of leisure, but things didn't quite turn out as he expected. As fate would have it, in 1962 a group of Jarvis's neighbors who were struggling under the particular financial pressures of California's tax codes reached out to him for advice on how to deal with the problem. "I was invited to my first meeting on taxes," Jarvis said of the episode. "The meeting took place at a neighbor's home in Los Angeles, with about twenty ordinary people who were concerned about how fast property taxes were rising in California."[11]

The local tax problem was somewhat deep-rooted in the state's economy. Since the acceleration of emigration to California that followed World War II, land prices had been booming in California, particularly in the Southern California counties of Los Angeles, Orange, and San Diego. "The land boom had resulted in spiraling assessed valuations placed on land," wrote Jarvis, "creating monumental increases in property taxes, which the politicians were unwilling or unable to do anything about." Put another way, as the state's land boom sent the values of homes sky-high, local officials were reluctant to "lower their tax rates so as to keep the total bite relatively stable . . . [instead finding] ways to spend the extra money."[12]

The meeting of Jarvis's neighbors in 1962 was small and preliminary. While people in the group were sincere in wanting to do something about a tax system they saw as unfair and punitive, there were, according to Jarvis, "no big wheels" in the group. Many of the gathered were older, in their fifties and sixties, and growing increasingly worried about how to manage retirement on a fixed income with such unpredictable tax burdens. Confronted by the sincere concerns of his neighbors, Jarvis was intrigued, but he felt somewhat out of his element. "Up until then," he wrote later, "I had always been on the political end of things. I knew something about taxes, but I had never had a chance to specialize in them. The people at this meeting asked me to write their bylaws, which I did. Then they wanted me to be their chairman. I said I would do it just long enough to help them get on their feet. [But] the more I got my nose into taxes, the more it interested me. And the first thing you know, it was a full-time deal."[13]

Under Jarvis's guidance the group developed a set of principles to direct their efforts. The first principle was primary: that "property taxes in California should be fair and should be applied to all the property in California that should be taxed." In California, the group noted, thousands of taxable acres were off the tax rolls either because they were owned by corporations that didn't pay or because they were owned by sham charitable trusts created for the sole purpose of gaining a tax break. Second, the group "wanted taxes to be equal for everybody. . . . We felt that if two people had houses just alike, like tract houses, and the owner on the right side of the street paid $3,000 a year in taxes and the owner on the left side of the street paid $1,000 a year in taxes, they weren't being treated equally." Because of the vagaries of the property tax codes, this scenario was common in California—especially when houses sold and were reassessed based on inflated house prices, or when assessors simply picked and chose which houses they wanted to reassess. Finally, and most important, the group wanted the tax system to "be within the ability of the people who were taxed to pay for it."[14] In other words, they wanted to protect the elderly, young people, and any middle- and lower-class home owners who might not be able to afford their homes because the property tax assessment was too dear.

In time Jarvis became the state chairman of the group, which eventually was known as the United Organizations of Taxpayers (UOT). "We made up our minds," Jarvis said, "back in 1962, that government officials might continue plucking our feathers, but we were not going to allow them to do it without a lot of hissing on our part."[15] In his position Jarvis took a multifaceted approach to changing the tax code. For one, his group affiliated with hundreds of disparate smaller tax advocacy organizations and individuals from all over the state and worked hard to keep the various parts unified around a central goal: to change tax codes. In addition, to keep the wide-ranging coalition of citizens concerned about taxes connected to the organization—that is, a paying member—Jarvis intentionally aimed to be a "tax leader for the state of California," focusing particularly on the reduction of taxes. This meant he didn't try to get involved with every small local or municipal tax fight, but chose instead to be a key source of tax information for the entire state.

Jarvis traveled almost constantly, giving speeches to local community groups and writing arguments against tax-increase proposals that were placed on state ballots. Between the mid-1960s and mid-1970s, Jarvis submitted arguments to the ballots on several dozen tax increases, and, he claimed, "almost all of them . . . resulted in the defeat of some type of tax increase." Additionally, as part of his intentional effort to remain out in front of his organization, Jarvis continued filing to run for various political races around the state. He never actually won any of these races, but that was not his true intention. "A lot of stories have been written," said Jarvis, "about how I was a 'perennial losing candidate for office,' but whoever writes those stories just doesn't understand that I didn't expect to be elected mayor, or to the U.S. Senate, or to any other office. All I was doing was using my campaign as a platform for tax reduction."[16]

After 1965 Jarvis was increasingly recognized as the leader of what was now being called the "tax movement." By 1970 that Jarvis had begun to gain political muscle was evident in an article that appeared in the June 7 edition of the *Los Angeles Times.* Describing him as a "maverick Republican who once tried to start his own Conservative Party," the article gave a surprisingly level view of Jarvis and his motives. "He says he hopes before he pushes up daisies," said one associate, "he can do something for his fellow man. . . . And that's what makes him tick." As for what Jarvis's true intentions were, the article quoted him saying: "I think my philosophy goes a little bit toward the idea the less government the better, because I'm convinced that you can't put enough brains in that little town on the Potomac to run this country. I have never seen a good example of it." Detractors in the article, of course, had a different take on Jarvis. "He's got a fantastic ego," said one opponent, "and he'll do anything to feed that ego. Taxes are unpopular, so he's against taxes. He's a cornball. He's as kooky as they come." Still, no matter what you personally believed about Jarvis, the article acknowledged, he was the chief spokesperson for a large and growing number of "disgruntled California property owners" increasingly convinced they were gaining the muscle to change the tax laws. Just how much muscle Jarvis's group had, wrote *Times* reporter William Endicott, was "open to debate, but [Jarvis's] name has become well known in the past five years before legislative committees, boards of supervisors, city councils and school boards all over California."[17]

The growing awareness of Jarvis's tax movement was an offstage menace to Bradley's efforts to keep his city's Olympics bid afloat. Always supremely attuned to the political winds, Bradley was aware of the feelings of voters in Los Angeles, even before his team submitted its final bid. In a speech that declared his candidacy for a second term, therefore, Bradley made sure to highlight his budget management skills, saying that it was a "kind of enlightened stinginess" that had led him to "produce balanced budgets for three consecutive years without new taxes." In addition, Bradley pledged that, if reelected, he would "continue to streamline government" and "make it work better for all of us, for less money."[18]

Despite the mayor's hard sell, Bradley's team of organizers suffered several surprising blows in late May and early June as the public mood seemed to turn more and more cynical. With the election fast approaching on June 6, the *Los Angeles Times* announced the results of a preelection poll that focused on the key public initiative that Angelenos would be voting on: so-called Proposition 13, also known the Jarvis-Gann Property Tax Relief Initiative. The initiative had been filed through the state's relatively unique ballot-initiative process, which allowed proposed laws or constitutional amendments to be voted on in an election, provided the law's advocates collected a certain number of signatures in advance. Early on in his work with the United Organizations of Taxpayers, Howard Jarvis had realized the potential of California's ballot-initiative process.

According to the California ballot-initiative rules, advocates had to obtain the signatures of 8 percent as many voters as voted for governor in the previous election. The UOT's first attempt to launch a tax proposition yielded only about 100,000 signatures, far short of the 500,000 or so required. "We didn't even come close to qualifying," said Jarvis. But after that first attempt, in 1968 he and his group successfully supported getting an initiative on the ballot—Proposition 9, written by Phil Watson, the Los Angeles County tax assessor—that attempted to limit property taxes. Proposition 9 was attacked by the political establishment, however, and received only 32 percent of the vote in the election. In 1971 Jarvis and the UOT launched their third attempt to reduce property taxes through the ballot-initiative process and again failed. "We fell about 100,000 signatures short of the number we needed to qualify for the ballot," Jarvis later wrote. "At least that's what the politicians said . . ."[19]

According to Jarvis, the fact that the proposals kept getting defeated was ironically "encouraging" to the politicians. "They evidently felt," wrote Jarvis, "that the defeat of three straight constitutional amendments to limit property taxes gave them carte blanche to raise the cost of state government."[20] As Jarvis estimated, state spending rose from 3.1 percent of the gross state product between 1967 and 1973, to the rate of 6.5 percent a year between 1974 and 1978. By 1978, Jarvis said, nearly 15 percent of the state's workforce was composed of government employees, twice the number it had been in 1950 and well over the national average. Additionally, Jarvis claimed, with so much money in the system, the likelihood for graft and corruption was inevitable, and, indeed, between 1973 and 1976 an unusual number of legal cases against corrupt local tax assessors were filed in the state attorney general's office. With the situation growing more pressing, Jarvis and his group attempted again to raise enough signatures for a ballot initiative in 1976 and 1977, failing just short both times. In 1978, however, after establishing an alliance for the first time with a tax-relief group from Northern California run by Paul Gann, the petition for what would become Proposition 13 garnered a shocking number of signatures—1,500,000 of them. And while opponents to the initiative tried various age-old political tactics—doomsday speeches by prominent politicians, semiofficial studies predicting disaster if Proposition 13 passed, even a "fake" competing tax-relief initiative that mandated a much more insignificant tax reduction—this time Jarvis and his cohorts were prepared. They had seen it all before, and they were ready with responses even before those who opposed them took action.

All through the winter and spring of 1978, support for Proposition 13 grew among likely voters across the entire state. In March just 35 percent of voters supported the initiative, against 27 percent opposed (and 38 percent undecided). But in April that support grew to 41 percent (against 34 percent opposed and 25 percent undecided). Then, on the eve of the election in May, a clear majority of 52 percent said they supported Proposition 13, while opposition had grown only slightly, to 35 percent (and only 18 percent undecided). The numbers in Los Angeles County in the May poll were even more strongly in support of the Jarvis initiative—with 63 percent of local voters in support against just 30 percent opposed.

Though the potential passage of Proposition 13 in 1978 would have no direct bearing on funding an Olympic Games in 1984, the swirling antitax, antispend rhetoric did affect the ongoing discussions about Bradley's bid. "In the pressure-cooker atmosphere of Los Angeles," wrote *Sports Illustrated* reporter William Johnson, "with anti-spending fever rising daily in the intensifying campaign for Proposition 13, local politicians perceived that fierce attacks on the Olympics and the I.O.C. seemed to go down well with voters." When council member Bob Ronka, who opposed the Olympics bid, returned from Athens, his rhetoric was unequivocal. The IOC had "whipsawed," "double-crossed," and "backstabbed" the negotiators from L.A., according to Ronka. "Other council members joined the chorus," Johnson continued, "and City Controller Ira Reiner, known to have ambitions for higher office, announced that he and City Councilman Ernani Bernardi, long a fiscal gadfly and opponent of all manner of spending for the Olympics, were going to launch a campaign to put what amounts to an anti-Olympics referendum on the ballot next spring (the earliest it could be done)."[21]

Despite the growing political mess in his city, Bradley remained steadfast. His Olympics bid was, after all, part of a comprehensive plan to continue transforming Los Angeles and give it the sense of civic identity befitting an internationally significant city. Still, uncertainty grew. Feeling that there were few options but to show signs of surrender to the IOC, city officials announced on May 16 that they had "conditionally" agreed to the IOC's stipulations regarding the financial responsibility for the 1984 Olympics. As to what this "iffy" deal actually meant, Mayor Bradley, in a city meeting that was closed to the press, said that the city was accepting final financial responsibility for the Games, though he was quick to point out that such acceptance of responsibility was contingent on being able to obtain an insurance policy that would protect local taxpayers against any financial losses.[22] As a result of the city's "conditional" acceptance of the contract, on May 19 the IOC announced it was giving the Games to Los Angeles. But at the same time the IOC recognized the city's ploy. The award, therefore, the IOC maintained, would be only on a "provisional" basis until the city signed the actual IOC form contract and agreed to all of its rules. If the city failed to do so by July 31, the IOC maintained, the committee would withdraw the award and open a call for new bids. Though a grim-faced Mayor Bradley did his best to put a good spin on this news—saying that he maintained the city's position of not doing "anything that would place a financial liability on the city"—everyone knew that this news almost certainly had doomed the city's Olympic hopes, as everyone expected the city council not to approve the agreement.

In early June, as Mayor Bradley continued trying to find a clear middle-path compromise that would assuage critics at home while satisfying the strict conditions of the IOC, an astounding sudden turn of political tides was looming. As the June 6 election approached, it became more and more clear to observers that, for the first time in state history, voters were poised to take charge and force their government to stop spending their money. In the swirling political winds of the moment, of course, all manner of public officials took public stands on the issue. On June 1, in an obvious ploy to curry voter favor, city controller Ira Reiner published an article in the *Los Angeles Herald Examiner* that said he was joining forces with the organizers of Proposition 13 to stop the city from spending money on the Olympics. As a result, the antitax forces themselves "began to exert more and more pressure on the fortunes of the Games." The pressure would only worsen when Proposition 13 passed by an "astonishing, top-heavy vote."[23]

The passage of Proposition 13 would have a profound effect on people around the state. The resulting tax rollback, which immediately reduced property taxes in California by 57 percent, would also, experts estimated, "slash some $7 billion from the revenues of municipalities across the state."[24] Its passage also gave rise, according to historian Kevin Mattson, to a flurry of national antitax activism in 1978 and 1979. "In November 1978, sixteen states organized antitax initiatives for the ballot; twelve passed. By July 6, 1979, *National Review* celebrated Proposition 13 as a major breakthrough victory in the conservative war for America, a sign of the country's grassroots rejection of liberalism that had worked successfully as reform."[25] To many Proposition 13 signaled a post-Watergate sea change in the relationship between people and their government, the first great victory of a looming "taxpayer revolt" in the country and a turn toward an unfettered, free-market, corporate-friendly outlook among voters. To some Proposition 13 was the first cornerstone in the attempt to construct a new shrunken-government political reality.

More locally, Proposition 13 complicated Mayor Bradley and his administration's efforts to solve the city's increasing tangle of problems—including promoting affirmative action hiring in the city, developing a comprehensive rapid-transit system, integrating local public schools through forced school busing, and the ever-present problem of crime (including the still unsolved Hillside Strangler murders)—even as he dealt with floundering negotiations over the city's Olympics bid. As a result after the election the mayor was wounded and stymied, privately expressing anger and frustration. Voters in Los Angeles, he noted in 1978, were simply not showing up to voice their thoughts on matters of import to the city. "The apathy on the part of the electorate is something which has always been a problem," Bradley told an interviewer, noting that the election turnout had been scant—just 15 percent of eligible voters. "We have never had the kind of turnout at the polls that some countries have achieved. . . . I think that we cannot escape the fact that there is just a sense that a person's vote really doesn't matter, doesn't count, so why bother to go and vote."[26]

> Adding to voters' sense of futility and discouragement, Bradley reasoned, was the tangle of opinions and ideas and harmful rhetoric that had come in the wake of the Olympics negotiations and the debate over city finances and taxes. Bradley said in a public address shortly after the election: There has been so much bombastic rhetoric, all negative, about the Games, all predicting huge deficits, all voicing pessimism and gloom. Even if we could afford the most aggressive public relations program we couldn't undermine that talk. It is repeated over and over and over. It is a product of the climate of Proposition 13, of politicians grandstanding for the public. But it is also caused by terrible reporting in the media. This isn't going to cost anyone one dime in property taxes, but no one wants to listen to that. No one will listen anymore. No one will believe me. The atmosphere has been poisoned.[27]

As a result of the continuing frustration, Mayor Bradley briefly actually considered giving up the dream. But even as the sudden antitax rebellion exerted pressure to reconsider the city's financial situation, and even as the blowback from emboldened political opponents threatened his own political standing, Bradley set aside his frustration and resolved himself to see his efforts through to the bitter end. "We could say to hell with it and abandon the Games completely," Bradley said, taking pause to let his words sink in, "but I think there have been too many people involved, too much effort expended, too many months of too many lives given to this effort for me to play the demagogue for short-term political advantage and walk away from this bid. We'll stick it out."[28]

Still, with political winds blowing hot around the Olympics issue, the mayor realized he needed to come up with a different approach if there was any chance to have it accepted at last by the IOC. In early June, therefore, Mayor Bradley finally "threw up his hands" and named a "citizens' committee" to study the situation and come up with a compromise solution. "I want this committee," Bradley said when announcing his decision, "to explore all realistic possibilities for holding the Olympics in Los Angeles without fiscal risk to the city and, for now, I want it removed from all debate in the city council. We have to get the issue outside the atmosphere of city hall, where demagoguery and negativism and transparent political opportunism have made any kind of meaningful debate or decision impossible."[29] It was, to be sure, a blatantly desperate, high-minded step by the man who had led the city's Olympics bid process for much of the past five years. The only question that remained was, would it work?

TWENTY-THREE

Nothing Is Clicking Right Now

Part of the Dodger makeup is the Hollywood thing. The Dodgers have an image of being close, and they try to live up to it. But from what we hear, they're fighting among themselves.

—San Francisco pitcher Bob Knepper, May 27, 1978

After the trade of Glenn Burke to the A's on May 16, the Dodgers' season plodded onward in much the same up-and-down way as before. Between May 19 and 21 the team took two of three from the Giants to improve their long home-stand record to 7-5. On May 20 the Dodgers had announced that, just as with Glenn Burke, they were reluctantly giving up on the once-promising reliever Mike Garman by trading him to the Montreal Expos for two pitching prospects.[1] The twenty-eight-year-old Garman, who had appeared in just ten games for the Dodgers in 1978, earning no saves and no wins with one loss and a 4.41 ERA, would record thirteen saves and a 4.40 ERA for the Expos over the rest of the 1978 season before being relegated to the Minors in 1979.[2] Garman's fate was disappointing but understandable, as the big right-hander's effectiveness, which had seemed so promising early in 1977, had simply fallen off the table after he hurt his elbow in June. And the Dodgers, caught in a dogfight in their effort to earn a spot back in the World Series, simply had no time to wait and see if a middling reliever would ever return to form.

On May 22, as the team traveled to San Diego for a night game against the Padres, the Dodgers shared second place in the West with the Reds, just a half game behind the San Francisco Giants. In contrast to just a few days earlier, manager Lasorda was in a jovial mood with the press. "It's hard to predict what's going to happen through the rest of the summer," he said. "But this (the three-way race with San Francisco and Cincinnati) is great. I'm happy for baseball. This is good for our division and good for the game. . . . To see the fans' reaction this weekend to these games was great, really something."[3] The lightness in the clubhouse was short-lived, however. In San Diego the Dodgers lost two of three games. Then, after traveling to San Francisco on May 25, the team lost two of three against the Giants. Just like that, on May 28, Los Angeles had fallen back into third place, three and a half games behind San Francisco.

Part of the problem was a series of nagging injuries to Dodger regulars. Rick Monday, Reggie Smith, Bill Russell, Ron Cey, and Dave Lopes all missed time due to various strains and pulls, causing Lasorda to joke: "We've gone through so much tape I should have bought stock in Johnson and Johnson." Beyond the jokes, however, Lasorda remained frustrated with his team, again holding a closed-door clubhouse meeting before the team's May 27 game against the Giants, then exploding at an umpire after a controversial call during the fifth inning of a loss. Dodger fans too, having noticed the team's troubles thus far on the season, were quick to express their dissatisfaction. "I wonder if other true-blue fans like myself think maybe the Dodgers aren't exactly putting out 100% effort?" a fan wrote to a local paper, perhaps voicing the concerns of many team followers. "The 1978 team seems to lack determination and enthusiasm. Is it complacency or is it that they are satisfied with just reaching the World Series last year? Whatever, that winning punch is missing."[4]

With all the criticism leveled at the team, a reporter asked veteran outfielder Reggie Smith if there might not be a backlash among players over the added pressure Lasorda was creating. "No, because Tommy always speaks confidently and collectively," replied Smith, whose own seasonal frustrations were clear during the first game of the season, when he was restrained from going after a fan who had thrown a beer can at him. "It's only when you start singling out individuals that a pressure is created, that you sit there wondering, 'Who's next?' Tommy doesn't do that, and he also never fails to mention that he knows we are still going to win it."[5]

Despite all the efforts to rally the team, through much of June the

Dodgers' play was characterized by inconsistency, missed opportunities, streakiness, and plain sloppiness. The month began with a long road trip to the East Coast, during which the team's record against the Phillies, Mets, and Expos was 3-7. Afterward, the Dodgers rushed home to prepare for a two-game series against Philadelphia, a team that had swept them a week earlier. Frustration continued to mount. Now just three games above the .500 mark, the Dodgers were stuck five games behind the Giants. A spate of letters flooded into the paper, some blaming Lasorda for his angry tirades—"I'm sick and tires of reading nothing but complaints from Dodger manager Tom Lasorda," wrote one woman. ". . . There's more to this game than . . . continuously babbling"—and others blaming the team for being poor losers. "The Dodgers [are] a fast-fading group of ego trippers who are poorly led and motivated," wrote a fan from Pasadena. "What's wrong with the Dodgers? Simple: Ron Cey and Davey Lopes worry more about Steve Garvey's image than their own batting averages," wrote another fan from Irvine.[6]

The outside perspective on the team may, or may not, have been accurate. On the one hand, players took full responsibility for the team's losing ways and sought to address the problems. After an ad hoc meeting of players in Reggie Smith's hotel room on June 6, for instance, during which players discussed the need to remain confident and aggressive, some players emerged shamefaced. "Tommy can only do so much," said Smith about his decision to lead a meeting, "can only say so much before it becomes repetitive. We're the ones who have to do it and I think we all felt a need to reassure ourselves about each other's confidence, to reassure ourselves that we all still feel we have the best team, that by July and August we'll be back out front. We talked about the need to stop waiting for things to happen and going out and making them happen, about staying loose and relaxed, and regaining that old feeling, that old confidence that when we step on the field, we're going to win, period." Dodger pitcher Doug Rau, who went out and got the win later that day to snap the team's five-game losing streak, agreed with Smith, while also acknowledging his appreciation for his manager. "I give Tommy Lasorda a lot of credit. He hasn't panicked one degree during all of this (nine losses in the previous 12 games)."[7]

On the other hand, just as the Dodgers' losing streak began in June, word spread around the team and among the press corps that an old sore spot of dissension within the clubhouse had once again flared up. After a loss on June 8, noted team gadfly Don Sutton was the subject of a story by sportswriter Marty Bell. In the June issue of the magazine *Sport*, in an article called "Don Sutton Does Not Bleed Dodger Blue," the pitcher sang a familiar song. "I do not bleed Dodger blue," he said. "I don't appreciate the rah-rah style. I don't go in for all the hugging and kissing. . . . I'm also not a yelling, screaming headline grabber. . . . I don't need to be the most famous player in baseball. But it would be nice to know that I was respected and appreciated by those around me. . . . Some day, I'm going to retire with most of the Dodger pitching records and someone's going to pick up the record book and say, 'Gee, I never realized this Sutton was such a great pitcher.'"[8] Despite Sutton's statements fans responded warmly to the pitcher after a game on June 25. In a 4–3 squeaker over the Reds, Sutton pitched six somewhat shaky innings, in which he gave up nine hits and a home run to César Gerónimo. Still, it was enough to collect the win, Sutton's 7th of the season (against 6 losses), and the 197th of his career. That number, 197, moved the thirty-three-year-old veteran of twelve seasons with the Dodgers into a tie with Hall of Famer Don Drysdale for most wins by a Los Angeles Dodger pitcher. (Drysdale, who pitched two seasons in Brooklyn, had an overall career total of 209 wins as a pitcher for both cities). In the fifth inning of the game, Sutton also received a standing ovation after recording his third strikeout, and 2,283rd of his career. That total tied him for first on the L.A. Dodger strikeout list, again with Don Drysdale. "I wasn't expecting it," said Sutton, perhaps a bit too enthusiastically (considering his recent criticisms). "It was really thrilling. It was one of the greatest things to happen to me. A lot of people where important to me as I was coming up were watching on national TV. The timing couldn't have been better. I wish I could have gotten one more (strikeout) and broken the record."[9]

As if it wasn't enough that the old tensions with Sutton had rekindled, after a loss on June 9 Lasorda must've felt like throwing in the towel on the season. In the game Reggie Smith was knocked out with an injury to his shoulder, the same shoulder that, in 1976, had required season-ending surgery. Even worse, after initially consulting with doctors who said Smith might need another surgery to repair the shoulder, Smith suggested he might retire from baseball rather than have another surgery. "When it rains it pours," said Lasorda, summing up all of his current worries. Yet, dark as things seemed, it was at just this moment that several key developments finally seemed to drag the team out of its doldrums.

The day after Smith's injury the Dodgers beat Montreal in a happy fashion, manufacturing two runs in the top of the ninth off a base hit by Garvey and a walk by Cey, followed by a sacrifice bunt by Monday and a bloop double by Baker just over the head of the Expos' third baseman. "We got a break," said Lasorda, of the game-winning hit. "He (Montreal manager Dick Williams) played the infield in with one out and a one-run lead. If the infield's back, the third baseman catches Baker's chinker."[10]

Between June 10 and June 16 the Dodgers followed by rattling off seven straight wins at home, though afterward they remained in third place, still five games behind the Giants. A little more than a week later, meanwhile, the Dodgers, seeking to shore up a faltering bullpen, made an important move—calling up a twenty-one-year-old pitcher from Michigan named Bob Welch. Drafted by the Dodgers in the first round of the 1977 June amateur draft, Welch pitched the second half of the 1977 season in AA San Antonio. He did well enough in that stint to be invited to attend spring training with the Dodgers at Vero Beach in 1978, where he played well. At one point a radar gun clocked Welch's fastball at ninety-three miles per hour. "That puts him in Tom Seaver category," said an excited Al Campanis within hearing of a reporter. Sent down to the team's AAA affiliate in Albuquerque after spring straining, in eleven starts Welch recorded a 3.78 ERA and 5-1 win-loss record, which was good enough that buzz began to build around the young pitcher.

"In June," Welch said of 1978, "the general manager of the Albuquerque team started paying attention to me. One day I was sitting in the stands, keeping a chart of our pitcher, and he sat next to me and asked, 'Do you have an agent?'" Welch figured there was something going on, and, sure enough, he got the call from the Dodgers on June 18. And on June 20 Welch made his first Major League appearance—a two-inning relief stint at home against the Astros. Welch gave up one hit and no runs and recorded two strikeouts in the game. On June 24, in his third appearance, Welch pitched one and a third innings against the Reds in relief of Don Sutton (in the game in which he tied the all-time L.A. Dodger win mark), and he recorded his first save. By the end of June Welch had made enough of an impression in his three relief appearances, in which he had given up no earned runs in five and a third innings of work, that he was the focus of a feature article in the *Los Angeles Times*. "I don't know how I could be any more excited about a young pitcher," the article quoted Al Campanis as saying. "He's Major League–plus. He's akin to a power pitcher like Tom Seaver." To Lasorda, meanwhile, Welch was reminiscent of another pitcher he once knew. "I played with Don Drysdale [at Montreal in 1955]," Lasorda said, "and I see a lot of Drysdale in Welch. Similar style and characteristics. The same intensity in his eyes. Welch comes over the top and Drysdale was a sidearmer. It's about the only difference."[11]

Welch, meanwhile, seemed to have hardly taken in his good fortune. Because of an even temperament, Welch exhibited what looked like an innate self-possession. "He comes in with poise and confidence," said Lasorda. "He takes the ball and goes after the hitters." Welch, however, took pains to set the record straight. "I have butterflies," he said. "I always do. But the job is the same whether it's here or Albuquerque, whether it's Pete Rose or someone you've never heard of. I can't do the job by getting nervous about it and Lasorda seems to know that. He doesn't say anything that will make me uncomfortable. He give me the ball and says, 'It's your ball, your game.' He's really helped my confidence."[12]

Despite the boost to the Dodger bullpen from Welch's arrival, for the rest of June the team was up and down. In the ten games between June 17 and June 27, the team's record was 5-5. What ailed the team, someone pointed out, was that despite having returned virtually the same lineup that had taken the team to the Series in 1977, most of the team's regulars had fallen well short of the pace they had set the previous year. "The figures are down in every case," wrote one sportswriter, "except those of Smith," who was batting .318 and had eleven home runs as of June 9, "and Monday," who was hitting .326 on June 9 and also had eleven home runs.[13] The Dodgers' number-eight hitter, catcher Steve Yeager, was batting just .198 and had hit just one home run to date (compared to the sixteen home runs he had hit in 1977). Bill Russell, meanwhile, who batted second for the team behind speedster Dave Lopes, was hitting .256, compared to his 1977 average of .278. Dusty Baker, who had hit thirty home runs in 1977, had logged only two in the first fifty-five games of 1978. Consistent Steve Garvey, who had hit just above or around .300 over the five previous seasons, was hitting a paltry .269 as of June 9. Even the team's traditional strength, its pitching, had fallen off from the previous season, recording an ERA of 3.84 thus far in 1978, compared to the team ERA of 3.22 the season before. The Dodgers simply, continued the writer, had had "trouble regaining the former fire, feeling, and confidence" of manager Tom Lasorda's first year at the helm.

The sense of decline on the team was so palpable and frustrating that a usually somber and quiet Dodger pitcher, Burt Hooton, spoke out about the team's woes at a Sportswriters Association banquet. "Our staff had recorded only one shutout this season. Our staff ERA is around 3.80," said Hooton, before explaining that he had seen things go wrong during recent games that he had not seen in all his years of playing baseball. "Errors at inopportune times, poor base running, failure to advance a runner to scoring position, lack of hitting and then lack of pitching have all combined to hurt the team." Still, Hooton conceded, there were signs the team was coming around. "The enthusiasm is still there and it's genuine," he said. "But the division is so much stronger and that's going to make it tough to catch up if any team falls too far behind."[14]

As if in response to Happy's encouragement, the Dodgers managed to win six straight games to end the month. After beating Cincinnati on the road, 2–0, on July 1 for their third straight victory over their Western Division rivals, they remained three games behind the Giants. One bit of good news was that Reggie Smith's tender shoulder, which doctors feared would need surgery, was deemed to be merely a sprain and was improving on its own. "You have no idea what kind of load this is off my mind," Smith reportedly said after learning he would be able to play again after letting his shoulder rest.[15] While Smith's pending return did bode well for the Dodgers' chances, in late June the team received a small shock after their new relief pitcher, Terry Forster, developed chronic soreness in his elbow. Forster, who had been the team's most effective reliever thus far in 1978, would have limited availability for much of the next month.

By July 1 Smith's productive bat was back in the lineup, though his home run power was slow to return until later in the month. News that came to the team a day later provided an additional shot in the arm, when the team announced it had reacquired their former power-hitting catcher Joe Ferguson—ostensibly to provide some relief to the slumping Steve Yeager—from Houston for cash and a couple of Minor Leaguers.[16] "I'm very pleased to have Fergy back," said Tom Lasorda. "He can play two or three positions and should be able to play five or six more years. The fact that Yeager has been struggling had a lot to do with it, though Yeager is still my regular catcher, still the best defensively that I've seen." Ferguson's former, and perhaps renewed, rival for the Dodger backstop position, Steve Yeager, expressed understanding, and even some agreement, with the move. "I certainly think the trade was a good move," said Yeager. "He's a hell of a player and a valuable property since he can play two or three positions. We've always been friends. There's never been ill feelings." Still, in the strange and stilted atmosphere of the Dodger clubhouse, even this welcome news had negative repercussions, as the increasingly disgruntled Dodgers utility man Lee Lacy expressed some upset at the news. "With the acquisition of Ferguson," Lacy said on July 2, "I think my playing days with the Dodgers are over. I don't see myself doing anything more than pinch-hitting or pinch-running."[17]

It's axiomatically true that every struggling clubhouse is an unhappy clubhouse, but Dodger unhappiness was reaching a fever pitch as the team continued to underachieve over the summer. Even former players seemed concerned about the current atmosphere around the Dodgers. "The Dodgers are facing complacency," said former Dodger first baseman Wes Parker. "We faced the same problem in 1965 and 1966. In 1965, we won the pennant, then had all kinds of problems the following year. We won the pennant again, but it was a struggle. The other teams in the league were shooting for us."[18]

Meanwhile, former Dodger reliever Mike Marshall, who was now attempting to make a comeback at age thirty-five with Minnesota in the American League, offered an even nastier assessment of the team:

> If I could take the Dodger talent and give it to the Twins, we'd be 40, 50 games over .500 at the end of the year. The (Dodger) talent is immense. The attitude is (expletive). . . . Walk into the Dodger clubhouse and see how many players are sitting at their lockers reading stat sheets. Major leaguers don't read stat sheets. In this game, you have to say, "If I make an out on a grounder to second base, the runner moves over and the club has a better chance to win." Not: "I backhand the ball, I might get an error and not win the Gold Glove." That's not baseball.[19]

After beating up on the Reds in Cincinnati in early July, the Dodgers traveled back home and split four games against the Braves. Despite the split the manager was not happy with the team's play. This was particularly true of the third game, which the Dodgers lost 9–8 after taking an 8–0 lead after five innings. "It's a (bleep bleep) crime to lose a (bleep bleep) game like that," Lasorda said afterward to a reporter, who, perhaps thinking of the Dave Kingman incident earlier in the season, decided to be faithful (though still PG rated) in recording the manager's words. "A (bleep bleep) eight-run lead. A (bleep bleep) two-run lead with two (bleep bleep) strikes on the hitter. (Bleep) no. I can't ever (bleep bleep) remember losing a game like that. I can't ever remember a (bleep bleep) tougher loss."[20]

On the road against Houston the Dodgers won three of their next four games, ending the first half of the season—before the All-Star break on July 10—on a high note. The Dodgers were still in contention, perched in second place, two games behind the Giants and one game ahead of the Reds, and the sense of relief around the clubhouse was palpable. Players were well aware that, with their inconsistency thus far on the season, they could have been much worse off at the All-Star break. "To be only two back with all the injuries we have had," said Smith, "is a very good sign." Dave Lopes agreed with this teammate. "We're extremely lucky to be only two back at the break," he said.[21]

Underneath the relief, however, as one might imagine of any team managed by Tom Lasorda, the Dodgers also fully expected more success in the second half of the season. "We're . . . extremely confident," Lopes continued. "We're playing better ball than either San Francisco or Cincinnati right now and I don't think the All-Star break will hurt our momentum. We have the best depth, defense, pitching and hitting in the league. If we can avoid the injuries that hurt us in the first half, we should win it." Reggie Smith agreed with the team captain. "We know we have the better ball club," he said, "and all we have to do is go out and prove it. To be only two back with all the injuries we have had is a very good sign. We've talked all year of that feeling of being in control of a game, of feeling we were born to win, the feeling we had all last year, and now we have it again. . . . We all know we're the better team and now I feel we've plugged the gaps, spiritually and physically."[22]

The roiling relief, and sense of purpose, among the Dodger players and coaching staff was given an assist by the All-Star break. For one, the game was managed by the manager of the defending National League champion—that is, Tom Lasorda of the Los Angeles Dodgers. Plus, the National League's team involved a large contingent of six Dodgers—starters Steve Garvey and Rick Monday and reserves Ron Cey, Tommy John, Dave Lopes, and Reggie Smith. Despite some minor controversy over National League manager Lasorda's favoritism in choosing so many of his players as reserves,[23] several Dodgers were catalysts of the National League's seventh straight Midsummer Classic victory, 7–3, over the American League.

Dave Lopes, playing as a reserve, got a hit and an RBI in a big four-run eighth inning for the National Leaguers, while starter Steve Garvey recorded two hits. His first, a clutch two-out single in the third inning, knocked in two runs to tie the game. And his second, a lead-off triple in the eighth, started the winning rally for the National League. What was even more amazing about the Dodger first baseman's performance is that he did it with twenty-two stitches in his chin, from a gash he had suffered a few days before the All-Star Game. "When I went into third on the triple," Garvey said after the game, "I think I popped a stitch. But I'll take a popped stitch for a triple anytime."[24] Garvey was named the game's most valuable player, the second time he had been so honored.

With the Midsummer Classic success of Garvey and Lopes, and the news that a number of Dodger regulars who had been suffering from one ailment or another were now healthy, Lasorda and his team prepared themselves a successful stretch run. Little did anyone know, however, how wrong his assumptions would prove to be over the next month, perhaps the most troubled month for the Dodgers since before the days of Leo Durocher—so troubled that everything, the entire house of cards, nearly came crashing down on August 20.

TWENTY-FOUR

The Grapple in the Apple

I am the most loyal player money can buy.

—Don Sutton

Steve Garvey is not sure whether he wants to be a first baseman or a Pope. He's so goody, he goes out behind the barn to chew gum.

—Don Rickles on Steve Garvey

The dog days of late July and early August can be a difficult stretch for baseball teams. After more than one hundred ball games, afflictions of all sorts—aches, nagging strains, general exhaustion, and frustration—are common, even as the deepest and steamiest heat of middle-American midsummer settles over the land. What's more, as August progresses, and moods and bodies break down, players can see more and more, off in the distance just over the horizon, the promise of the looming off-season—a time when players get to join their families, take vacations, go on long hunting and fishing trips, and so on. It's no wonder that July and August are very often the make-it-or-break-it point for so many borderline teams. As of late July in 1978, while the Dodgers felt the deep malaise of summer, it was clear that the season could go any direction for Tom Lasorda's boys.

A Sunday day game on July 23, 1978, was a perfect example of the crushing weight of the dog days of baseball. Before the game the Dodgers held their annual Old-Timers Game festivities. Up in Walter O'Malley's chairman's box, former manager Walt Alston and Mayor Tom Bradley joined Dodger greats Sandy Koufax and Roy Campanella to watch star players of old—some from the Dodgers, some from rival teams—return to the field. In the game Frank Robinson crushed a Larry Sherry pitch for a home run, Maury Wills stole a base, Willie Mays made a basket catch, Duke Snider made a heads-up base-running play, and so on. The Old-Timers Game would be just about the last thing Dodger fans got to cheer about that day, as the Dodgers then lost the regularly scheduled game to the Cardinals, 2–0. The tone of the loss was set early on in the top of the first inning, when Bill Russell and Dusty Baker collided in shallow left field as both pursued a pop fly that had been hit by Cardinals shortstop Garry Templeton. Though Baker managed to hold onto the ball to record the out, both players, after tumbling to the field, were removed from the game with facial cuts and bruises. After the collision the Dodger lineup failed to provide any sort of spark against St. Louis's starter, Pete Vukovich, collecting just three hits in the loss.

In early August Dodger inconsistency continued. The team won five straight games against Chicago and Pittsburgh, briefly moving into a tie for first place with San Francisco. But then a six-game losing streak to the Pirates, Padres, and Giants between July 30 and August 4 dropped the Dodgers to a low point in the standings—four and a half games behind the first-place Giants. Mired in third place the team was actually closer in the standings to the Padres, who were just four games behind the Dodgers in fourth place. Team tension mounted and began to show itself in unexpected ways on the field, in the clubhouse, and in the comments and actions of members of the team. Tom Lasorda's explosion back on May 14, over the loss to Dave Kingman and the Cubs, was still being talked about, especially now that the Dodgers seemed to be coming apart. "I don't think it's right to make a big deal of it," Lasorda said at a sportswriters luncheon on August 9. "The guy couldn't have caught me at a worse time. I was very upset. . . . Sure, I say words around the clubhouse that I don't say anywhere else, like most people. But I've been married 28 years and my wife and children have never heard me curse around the house. I just don't think it's fair to do this." Despite his protestations "the Tape" had circulated around the country since that day in May and remained a hot topic in discussions about the Dodgers. That is, the Tape was, according to sportswriter Scott Ostler, "the first outward hint that just maybe the one, big, happy Dodger family that won the National League pennant the year before was not, after all, baseball's version of the Osmonds. More like the Cartwrights the morning after a hard night in the saloons." He went on to suggest that Lasorda was suffering a season-long "sophomore slump." "On more than one occasion," Ostler wrote, "Lasorda exploded at reporters, including one who dared suggest in print that Lasorda's relations with the press were deteriorating."[1]

To be fair Lasorda's tension in 1978 likely had an easy solution: putting an effective lineup on the field. Lasorda's regular players continued suffering nagging injuries. Almost all of his starters, with the exception of Garvey and Cey, had missed some playing time. Among the worst cases was Yeager, whose stints on the disabled list left a gaping hole in the middle of the defense. Rick Monday struggled with more back issues. Reggie Smith missed several stretches to leg and shoulder issues. So if Lasorda seemed preoccupied, impatient, and more explosive than usual, his frustration at least had a source.

Still, Lasorda's struggles to communicate extended beyond his relations with the media. On August 13, after a critical pennant-race match against the Giants, Rick Monday pulled aside several team reporters to let it be known that he was upset with a lack of communication from his manager. The issue was, on a day when right-handed pitcher Ed Halicki was scheduled to start for the Giants, Monday had assumed he would start in center field. This was despite the fact that his injuries had slowed him down and caused him to slump somewhat after the success of the first part of his season. As Lasorda watched Monday got in line and took his place during pregame batting practice with the other starters. Lasorda said nothing, but after batting practice Monday learned that Bill North was listed on the lineup card as the starting center fielder. "I just wanted to know what was going on," said the center fielder, visibly agitated. After the story was published, Lasorda called Monday into his office for a closed-door "discussion," which reportedly involved much yelling. "We had a good conversation," said manager Tom Lasorda of the event, "discussed a lot of things, and I think we're both very happy. He loves to play and there's nothing wrong with that."[2] Monday, for his part, would not say much about the discussion.

Despite the air of frustration around the Dodgers, after August 4 the team again clawed its way back into the race. Following the streak of six straight losses, the Dodgers won seven straight, mostly as a result of stellar pitching by the team's starting pitchers. By August 10, remarkably enough, Los Angeles had climbed back into a tie for first place with San Francisco. A day later, after beating the Giants at home, the Dodgers had inched ahead in the race. Though they held only a half-game lead over the Reds now, it was the team's first division lead since May 11. But things remained tense. "We look forward to playing the Dodgers more than anyone," said the chief Dodger hater on the San Francisco squad, John Montefusco. "A lot of guys here really hate the Dodgers. You hear guys here say, 'We don't care who wins the pennant, as long as it's not the Dodgers.' We're sick of the Dodgers and Hollywood. They're always on TV and you see (Dodger manager Tom) Lasorda on TV all the time. . . . I'm not saying the Dodgers don't play tough baseball. They do. But last year, every time you turned on the TV it would be the Dodgers playing somebody. It was just sickening." Other players, including some Christian-leaning players who took offense to Lasorda's "Big Dodger in the Sky" references, agreed with Montefusco. "It's just kind of the air they bring," said Giants third baseman Darrell Evans. "They always seem to be pretty cocky and expect things to happen their way."[3]

After their brief taste of first place the Dodgers lost two straight close games at home against the Giants—3–2 on August 11 and 7–6 in eleven innings on August 12—and fell back into second place. From there it was a back-and-forth footrace. On August 18 after four straight road wins, the Dodgers were back in first place by a tenuous one-game margin. After a loss on August 19, the tenth of the season for Don Sutton, the team remained in first place. Then August 20 arrived. The Dodgers were in New York for an evening game against the Mets. And in the visitors' clubhouse at Shea Stadium, something happened that changed the tone of the entire season.

For the Dodgers August 20 began just like any other day, as players prepared for an afternoon rubber match against the Mets. A day earlier, commentators had noted, during a nationally televised day game at steamy Shea Stadium, several Dodger players seemed on edge in an 8–4 loss against the Mets. Reggie Smith had flared up during an argument at second base in the first inning. Lee Lacy had argued with Mets shortstop Tim Foli during another play at second base, even to the point of charging him (he was restrained by Dodger pitcher Don Sutton, of all people). Smith later argued with Mets catcher John Stearns and home plate umpire Terry Tata over a call on a play at home. Tom Lasorda joined in with Smith. "They blow up easily," said Tim Foli of the Dodgers after the game, a sentiment with which John Stearns fully agreed. "They've been down all year and come back, they're working hard, it's hard to relax." When asked about the blowups, Smith shrugged. "I don't think we're on edge. We're just an aggressive team. We're not going to be intimidated by anybody. I'd rather be on edge and in the pennant race than in last place with nothing to look forward to but the end of the season."[4]

Despite Smith's denials, in light of what would happen on August 20, the events of August 19 revealed a team at a kind of breaking point. To understand the state of the team we should start with what was known, by fans and followers of the team who were not privy to the goings-on inside the Dodgers' clubhouse, about the two players who would figure in the events at Shea Stadium. Let's start with Don Sutton: As anyone who had followed the Dodgers over the past few seasons was aware, Sutton was not the happiest of Dodgers. On numerous occasions the veteran pitcher had expressed his feelings that he was not often accorded his due (as the longest-serving Dodger player), even as he had no appreciation for the traditions of the Dodger Way. Sutton's conflicted nature was often remarked upon. According to fellow pitcher Burt Hooton, Sutton had "about as complex a personality as anyone I've ever met. He's a very generous individual who'll talk to anyone while the rest of us just say 'Hi' and keep going. At the same time, he's an extremely competitive person." In fact, Sutton could be an acerbic teammate, quick to cut off at the knees anyone who challenged him. And his teammate for many of his years with the Dodgers Bill Russell agreed with both assessments. "Don's the kind of guy you either like or you don't," said the always easygoing Russell. "But he speaks his mind, and you've got to respect that."[5]

As a result of all of these character traits—his iconoclastic individualism, his disdain for lip service and PR, and, most of all, his often prickly personality—Sutton was, among Dodger supporters and followers and even his teammates, either actively disliked or generally avoided. Few of his fellow players got to know him. "I don't know that anybody here was ever that close to Don," said Ron Cey, "but then I could say the same thing about myself. So much of our lives is public, you keep certain parts private. One moment you feel you know and understand Don, the next you don't."[6] Still, even as Dodger fans and followers, as well as his fellow players, found it difficult to embrace the pitcher and his abrasive ways, they did appreciate Sutton's success and competitiveness over his long history with the team.

In direct opposition to Sutton, meanwhile, was the Dodgers' polite, seemingly All-American first baseman, Steve Garvey. Though a polarizing figure among many of his fellow Dodgers, Garvey was well liked by fans and team followers. To them Garvey seemed like a gentleman among the hordes. He even once served as a batboy for the team. On a team that thrived on image and tradition and hokum-filled narratives about the good old days of yore, Garvey was a nearly perfect package. Of course, it was inevitable that the clash of values represented by the two poles, Sutton and Garvey, would eventually come to a head in a real and explosive way. And on August 20, before the final game of a three-game series at Shea Stadium, it finally did.

The actual steps leading to the clubhouse explosion are fairly clear and straightforward. At the same time, however, it's difficult really to discern the reasons that Sutton did what he did and why exactly he felt it necessary to force an inevitable showdown with his teammate. While many Dodger players seemed to be baffled by Garvey, uncertain by his refusal to go out and drink with the boys after games, and convinced that his public persona as a straight-shooting paragon of virtue was too good to be true, they appreciated his contributions on the field. But not Sutton. Three days before the blowup, while the Dodgers were in Philadelphia, Sutton had been interviewed by Thomas Boswell of the *Washington Post*. Boswell, who had just seen the Dodgers dismantle the Phillies for a sweep in the defending Eastern Division champion's ballpark, was marveling about one particular aspect of the team from Los Angeles: the lack of attention paid to the Dodgers' right fielder, even when he was busy beating the pants off the home team. When Reggie Smith hit his twenty-sixth home run of the year over the right-field fence in cavernous Veterans Stadium, Boswell noted, Phillies fans "emitted only a resigned groan." As Smith crossed home plate for what would be, essentially, the winning run, "his greeting was tepid, grudging applause." Just who was this man, Boswell seemed to wonder, who was so dangerous to opposing teams yet so unknown to fans of the sport? "Who is the best-known and richest right fielding Reggie in baseball?" Boswell asked. "Reggie Jackson of New York, certainly. But who is the best Reggie? Probably Reggie Smith of the Los Angeles Dodgers—that unique star who is superb at the game's five fundamentals. Smith can run, throw, field, hit for average and hit for power."[7]

Boswell speculated at the reasons that Reggie Smith was such an unknown factor on one of the best teams in the National League. "On a team of gung-ho Angelenos, Smith is the doubting Dodger, the born skeptic who fancies solitary scuba diving, chess and gourmet cooking while watching the baseball scene with a whimsical, aloof sidelong glance." As Boswell pointed out, Smith had hit five home runs, and was batting .500, in his last five games. Reggie himself admitted to Boswell that this season had been a "difficult year . . . much harder than last year. We haven't had the power production from others, so a lot has hinged on me. Right now, I'm on a streak. It's like riding a surfboard. . . . You have to know how long to ride that wave when to pull out. In my last streak, I was too stubborn, I waited too long to go back to basics and get my swing in order from Square One. I should have backed off sooner."[8]

At this point Boswell, naturally seeking some validation for his theories on Reggie Smith, sought out the one player on the team with a similarly skeptical reputation. That is, Boswell sought out Don Sutton, and Sutton chose this precise time to unload. What happened next, in normal circumstances, would give any team pause, perhaps causing a meeting to air out grievances and relieve tensions. For the 1978 Dodgers, stuck as they were in the midst of a seemingly endless up-and-down loop, when the team daily failed to live up to the expectations it had set for itself, what followed turned the team upside down. "This nation gets infatuated with a few names," Sutton said to Boswell.

> All you hear about on our team is Steve Garvey, the All-American boy. Well, the best player on this team for the last two years—and we all know it is—is Reggie Smith. As Reggie goes, so goes us. . . . [Yet] Reggie doesn't go out and publicize himself. He doesn't smile at the right people or say the right things. He tells the truth, even if it sometimes alienates people. Reggie's not a facade or a Madison Avenue image. He's a real person. Reggie and Richie Allen are the two most totally misrepresented people I ever met. They're wonderful people with wrong reputations.[9]

The article closed on a strongly positive note—Reggie Smith expressing gratitude that he was in Los Angeles and away from the Boston Red Sox. "I've lived in the shadows of some pretty good players," said Smith. "I've had people harp at me about not living up to my potential. Well, I'm finally with a team that's perfectly suited to me. I no longer feel the pressure. . . . Now, when I step to the plate, I don't feel I have to do anything. All I have to do is my best."[10] But despite the positive words, the damage had been done.

After the article hit the DC streets a few days passed without any commotion—at least in the Dodger clubhouse. On Friday morning, August 18, a small item appeared in the "Morning Briefing" section of the *L.A. Times* with the heading "Here's One That Should Stir Some Emotions in the Dodger Clubhouse." The blurb then proceeded to repeat, out of context, the several meaty statements that Sutton had made to Boswell. Two days later, in the morning before a Sunday-afternoon game against the Mets, Steve Garvey met his manager for breakfast in a hotel in Manhattan. Holding the paper, Garvey asked Lasorda, "What would you do?" And here is where, according to Lasorda's biographer, the manager's mind went to work. On the one hand, he well knew, there was some amount of truth in what Sutton said. On the other hand, it was precisely the wrong place and wrong time—in the midst of a heated pennant race in the middle of a hot August—to say these things. But even more important than all of this, Lasorda wondered, was there a way he could turn this situation to his and his team's advantage?

"In such situations," wrote Bill Plaschke of Lasorda's actions that morning, "it is a manager's job to put out the fire. But as Lasorda knew, sometimes it was more important to start one." In watching the character of his clubhouse develop over the seasons he had been with the Major League squad, first as third base coach, then as manager, Lasorda well knew that teammates' impressions of both Sutton and Garvey had not been good for the team. Garvey had the reputation among his teammates of "being soft." Known for his reluctance to make the pivot throw from second base, for example, and for avoiding getting riled up on the field (or cutting loose with his teammates after games), Garvey was a mystery in the Dodger clubhouse. Sutton, on the other hand, was, to his teammates, just a sharp-tongued jerk. In this moment, at breakfast with a puzzled Garvey, Lasorda made a quick calculation. "I ain't going to tell you what to do," the manager said. "But if it was me, and somebody said those things in the paper about me? The first time I saw him, I would deck him."[11] Then Lasorda put down the paper, got up from the table, and left Garvey behind without looking back.

Versions of what exactly happened a few hours later vary slightly, depending on who is doing the telling. From Garvey's vantage point the incident went something like this: Infuriated by the quotes, the first baseman walked over to Sutton before the game and told him he thought the comments were inappropriate. "We are a team," Garvey supposedly said. "If there are any differences they should be kept among ourselves and not expressed in the newspapers. I've been knocked before about things I do off the field, and I don't think those things should be written about in the press. If you have to say something about me, say it to my face."[12] The two shared further words, growing increasingly heated, and when Garvey took one of the pitcher's remarks as an insult to his wife, he told Sutton he would fight him right there if necessary. In this version of the story Sutton leaped at Garvey, and the two fell to the floor, where they wrestled and clawed at each other as their shocked teammates watched. A separate story strand suggests that one teammate, perhaps Joe Ferguson, yelled, "Let 'em go. Maybe they'll kill each other." Another, more neutral, account suggests that Garvey physically picked up Sutton and then threw him into another teammate's locker. It was this loud crash that caught the attention of Dodger GM Al Campanis and manager Lasorda, who rushed in yelling "What the hell's going on?" while several Dodgers[13] managed to break up the tussle. Both ended up with bruised faces, and Garvey had suffered a noticeably bloodshot eye from where Sutton had poked him.

In Sutton's account of the incident, meanwhile, which he told to a magazine reporter several years later, the pitcher naturally laid more of the blame on Garvey. After Garvey had asked if he had said those things to Boswell, Sutton implied that a "discussion" followed to iron out "a misunderstanding between two intelligent young men."[14] Garvey, according to Sutton, had an annoying habit of emphasizing his points with finger jabs to the chest, which is what led Sutton to bring Garvey's wife into the discussion. When Garvey, again, objected to this with another finger jab, Sutton shoved Garvey, which led to the tumble to the floor. (Sutton said nothing about being physically picked up and thrown.)

And finally, Tom Lasorda offered his own interpretation of events in the clubhouse that day. As he told it, Lasorda was standing on the field before the game when a panicked stadium worker approached him to say a fight had broken out in the Dodger clubhouse, and he feared that some equipment had been damaged. "Lasorda just smiled," wrote Bill Plaschke. The manager's plan was in motion.

Whatever the true and exact version of events, after the fight, and before the flight back to L.A., Sutton sought out Lasorda and angrily told his manager he wanted to call a press conference to attack Garvey. Lasorda, reportedly, looked at Sutton and flatly suggested what a horrible idea that was. "He's too big for you," Lasorda said. "The fans love him." When Sutton called the press conference anyway four days after the fight, Lasorda and the rest of the team gathered around the TV to see what the wily pitcher would say. Surprisingly, on the whole Sutton was positive and remorseful. "For the last few days," he said, his eyes moist with tears, "I have thought of nothing else and I've tried over and over to figure out why this all had to happen. The only possible reason I can find is that my life isn't being lived according to what I know, as a human being and a Christian, to be right. If it were, then there would not have been an article in which I would offend any of my teammates."[15]

At this, supposedly, Dodger captain Dave Lopes turned to Lasorda and asked, "How did that happen?" To which Lasorda smiled and said he had no idea. "[His] ploy had worked," Plaschke wrote. "The two players who were most disliked by their teammates had beaten each other into humility. . . . Two problems had been fixed without Lasorda having to lift a finger."[16]

After the fight on August 20 the Dodgers were not the same team as before the fight. Lasorda, after interviewing both players, pointedly did not fine either of them, nor did he ask for any apologies. When he addressed the team on the matter, he was direct about what he wanted. "I don't care if you like each other or not," Lasorda said, according to an account by Tommy John. "I can't make you do that. All I'm asking is that this doesn't carry onto the field. We must play as a team. We've got twenty-five guys here. We can't have thirteen pulling from one end of the rope and twelve from the other. That won't get us anywhere. We have to pull together."[17]

Surprisingly, the team came together after the fight just as Lasorda requested. Neither Garvey nor Sutton carried their feud onto the field, and the rest of the team suddenly seemed to play with the intensity and focus that fans had been watching for all season. "The fight was cathartic in that if finally got the hostility out in the open," said Tommy John. "We played extremely well after that for the stretch run." Reggie Smith agreed with John's assessment. "That [the fight] was when we came together, realized how important we were to each other," Smith explained. "We started playing better. We're a good blend of ballplayers and that brought it all together with the feeling of, 'Let's do it together, as one.'"[18]

Indeed, the Dodgers won the game that immediately followed the fight, with Garvey providing two hits, an RBI, and a run scored. While the long-nurtured team image—of one big happy family—had been shattered, this may not have been wholly bad. No longer concerned what everyone thought of them, perhaps, the Dodger players shrugged off the notoriety of the so-called Grapple in the Apple and went about their business. For the rest of the month the team went 6-3 against the Phillies and Expos. By the beginning of September the Dodgers had settled in first place (by two games). In the first half of September the team continued winning, going 11-4 in the first two weeks of the month and rushing out to an eight-and-a-half-game lead in the West on September 15. At last, despite the fuss and notoriety, all was right in Dodger country. Finally, Tom Lasorda could stop calling team meetings. Finally, his boys were back where they should have been all season: on the way to the playoffs.

TWENTY-FIVE

Is the Force with Us?

Everything is "awesome." The Times' *You* magazine described a fountain and grunion run as "awesome" sights. Hardly a day passes in which some newspaper or magazine writer does not use "awesome" to describe some slightly above average event. . . . Aren't we overdoing it a little? Or is it a fear that most of what happens these days is actually pretty mediocre?

—Lynne Bronstein, "Underwhelmed by the World, 'Awesome,'" letter to the editor of the *Los Angeles Times*, April 30, 1977

For anyone paying attention to the news in Los Angeles in 1977 and 1978, the times were confusing, frustrating, depressing, and distressing. For eleven- and twelve-year-old boys, however, enjoying watching their favorite team in bunches, or for small businessmen trying to keep their family businesses thriving, or for a by-your-bootstraps mayor of what would soon to be the second largest city in the country, or for sophisticated East Coast writers observing the far West Coast from comfortable New York apartments—for all sorts of people, life in Los Angeles near the end of the 1970s was, if sometimes uncertain and occasionally troubling, pretty pleasant. Times were changing, certainly, but all in all life was pretty good and often, in the parlance of the times, pretty "awesome."

Awesome was a word that came into increasing use in Los Angeles in 1977 and 1978. As a neologism the word had caught on not only among postadolescents and beach-bound teenagers, but also among a wide swath of the hip-conscious mainstream. *Awesome*, in fact, had recently begun appearing in TV commercials, on television sitcoms, and all across the media. So common, and sudden, was its usage that a concerned citizen wrote into the local paper to complain. "Has anyone beside myself noticed the current rage for the term 'awesome'?" wrote Lynne Bronstein, a poet and newspaper writer who lived in Sherman Oaks.[1] For Tom Fallon's eldest grandson, who turned twelve years old just before the start of the Dodgers' 1978 season, *awesome* just seemed to fit the times. Daily life for this grandson in the late summer of 1978 was pretty *awesome*, after all. His favorite sports team, the Dodgers, who played his favorite sport, baseball, was back in first place of their division. He and his friends lived and breathed all things Dodgers in those long, awesome summers (of 1977 and 1978), trading baseball cards of their favorite players, pretending to be those players during pickup games of playground baseball, and mooning over the rare neighborhood kid who had managed to score a Dodger player autograph or other relic.

It makes sense, of course, that a twelve-year-old boy might not pay much attention to the national malaise and the raging worry about the growing mediocrity of America. Young boys who love baseball and the other trappings of boyhood are the perfect antidote, after all, to the ever-looming sense that Things Are Always Getting Worse. Old-time baseball fans might have wanted to set this twelve-year-old boy straight by informing him that the Steve Garveys and the Ron Ceys and the Davey Lopes and the Doug Raus of today couldn't hold a candle to the bright lights of baseball's past, but for what purpose? The boy would not have changed his mind and become any less of a fan of baseball, of his team, and of his favorite players. If anything, he would have shrugged. From his vantage point the times seemed just fine.

Later in life, when he wondered about it, the boy would learn that this tendency to believe that things were always getting worse was due to a particular cognitive feature of the human brain called the *negativity bias*. Psychologists have long observed that people tend to recall negative experiences more readily than positive ones, a fact that may have been evolutionarily important as a trait that keeps us out of harm's way. Of course, though, it also means—as was more than evident throughout the 1970s among baseball fans, taxpayers, and ordinary citizens afflicted with a nationalized sense of "malaise"—that humans tend to be hardwired for a doom-and-gloom outlook.

Still, it was fortunate for Tom Fallon's grandson that he was Tom Fallon's grandson, as he was one of those rare cases that proved the rule. Rather than gloom and doom, Fallon was optimistic almost to a fault—ever dreaming of a better life, ever encouraging everyone else to dream. It was this tendency, of course, that bound his grandson, and many others in the family, to Tom Fallon. It was also what led him to devise his latest get-rich plan—one that he was certain would finally get him the financial security he had long wanted for his family.

Beyond the world of Tom Fallon and his grandson, in the second half of 1978 people all over America were increasingly doubtful that things would get better in the foreseeable future. Much of the impetus for this sense of decline in the 1970s was hard economic reality. After the 1973 energy shock sent the country into sharp recession, the economy had been slow to recover. By 1977 a condition known as "stagflation," a combination of stagnant economic growth coupled with fast-rising inflation, had developed. And while President Carter had taken a number of steps to deal with it, and had given numerous speeches to assuage the concerns, nothing seemed to ease the situation.

Beyond economics another reason for the cynicism of Americans in 1978 was the inevitable social change being driven primarily by generational changeover. Simply put, the emerging adulthood of the baby boom was driving a host of social and cultural revolutions—the rise of feminism and other interest-group movements, the explosion of the suburbs, the mainstreaming of drug use, increasing divorce rates, and other trappings of the so-called culture of narcissism. With all this as a backdrop it's no wonder that *Time* would, in the summer of 1979, declare that nobody would call the 1970s "the good old days."

While Tom Fallon was hardly a qualified economist, if asked he would have said that things were not nearly as bad as everyone seemed to believe.[2] Fallon's Cucamonga Hardware, after all, had grown steadily in recent years. The store had plenty of customers, and the partners were earning a decent living. Still, Fallon wanted more. He wanted to create something truly noteworthy. And this impulse, along with his view of the times, led him to submit a wild new proposal to the partnership.

To understand Fallon's latest scheme, one would have to understand the exact spirit of Cucamonga—or Rancho Cucamonga as it was now known—at the end of the 1970s. Located on the edge of the wide, contiguous swath of development that spread east from Los Angeles, Cucamonga was still relative terra incognita. The landscape that surrounded the town was, though punctuated by the eucalyptus tree lines planted long ago as windbreak, composed mostly of dusty scrub fields. Even in 1978, after developers had discovered the area, Cucamonga was relatively open, traffic free, and mostly devoid of the polluted skies that plagued much of the rest of Southern California. In the northern part of the town, up against the foothills of the Sierra Madre, there were vast, open rock-quarry pits, yielding the gravel and stone that were being used to pave over the region. In scattered lots here and there were small vineyards and modest lemon and orange groves, presumably owned by the last of California's small-time farmers. Although most of these fields would disappear within a few years, in 1977 and 1978 you could still, while walking to the Circle K, cut across small lots of budding grapevines and lush citrus trees. In summer and fall the winds brought tumbleweeds to Cucamonga, which rolled through the town like something out of a movie western. Summer evenings were punctuated, especially in the foothills, by the mournful call of coyotes come to prey on house cats, small dogs, and unsecured garbage bins. Then there were the desert frogs. Thousands of them, crawling out from the fields at night and finding their way into backyard swimming pools.

The openness of the newly renamed Rancho Cucamonga, and all of its dusty, scrubby plots of dirt, was the key to Tom Fallon's plan. When he first moved to the area in 1974, settling in Alta Loma, Fallon saw the open land and salivated. At the time a local acre was selling for about ten thousand dollars. He knew it for what it was—a dirt-cheap opportunity—and he also saw that builders were increasingly becoming interested in the land. Lacking resources and credit to buy, however, Fallon could do nothing about it. He would have to bide his time. By 1978, with two sons having joined in the Cucamonga Hardware partnership, and another son working in the store hoping to become a partner, business was good. Now, at last, Fallon knew it was time to act. And it was also at this moment that Fallon and his business fell into some good fortune.

What happened was this: On the city block that occupied the corner of Archibald Avenue and Foothill Boulevard in Cucamonga, there existed an array of old low-slung shops and a mishmash of other buildings. In the 1960s the area had gained some underground notoriety for being the stomping grounds of musician Frank Zappa. In his early twenties at the time, Zappa had come to the area to work at Paul Buff's Pal Recording Studio, which was located on Archibald Avenue directly across the street from Cucamonga Hardware. The location would leave an impression on Zappa, and he would later describe the corner in his autobiography. "Cucamonga was a blotch on a map," he wrote. "On those four corners we had an Italian restaurant, an Irish pub, a malt shop and a gas station. North, up Archibald, were an electrician's shop, a hardware store and the recording studio. Across the street was a Holy Roller church, and up the block from that was the grammar school."[3]

In 1964 Paul Buff ran into financial trouble, and Zappa bought the studio, renaming it Studio Z, and promptly moved into the place. His life at the studio was a constant struggle, as Zappa, despite his genius, did not have much business savvy. He was rarely able to book recording sessions for other musicians, spending time instead recording his own music and eventually trying his hand at producing a cheap sci-fi movie.[4] In an effort to interest investors in his movie project, Zappa fatefully arranged to have the local paper, the *Cucamonga Daily Report*, run a feature story on Studio Z and his project. The fact that the story described Zappa hyperbolically as "the Movie King of Cucamonga" and attached a photo of the young impresario, convinced local law officials that the studio was likely producing pornography. When Zappa put out a casting call for locals to act in his movie, one of the auditioners was a member of the San Bernardino County vice squad, sent to try to entrap Zappa. "The local political subtext to all this," wrote Zappa later, "had something to do with an impending real estate development which required the removal of tenants before Archibald Avenue was widened." While the police officer did not get a part in the movie, he returned later and offered Zappa one hundred dollars to produce some entertainment for a stag party. When Zappa handed over the half-hour tape of goofy faked sexual acts to the officer, he was arrested. And though courts later determined Zappa had been entrapped, it was little solace. After serving a ten-day sentence on a reduced charge, Zappa tried to retrieve his tapes and other belongings, but was rebuffed. He was broke and had no way to make money. "I had to get the wire cutters and yank all my equipment out of there and evacuate 'Studio Z.'"[5] He promptly left Cucamonga and moved to a little apartment in Echo Park, never returning to the area.

Though many of the corner shops described by Zappa still existed in 1978, there were now, a decade-plus later, more businesses on and around the corner. Directly behind the store, for example, separated by a nicely paved parking lot, was a paint store, somewhat larger than the building that Fallon owned. On Foothill Boulevard, meanwhile, connected by more paved land (and a plot of dirt), stood a Yamaha shop, a building supply company, and, farther down, an auto repair shop. Fallon surveyed the scene and calculated. Because Cucamonga Hardware was doing brisk business, it was outgrowing its street-front space. In the back parts of the corner block, to the east and north behind his store, was land just waiting for some sort of development. In the more immediate vicinity, to the south and east, several of the shops looked a little worse for the wear, perhaps struggling to stay competitive in the wake of the 1973 recession. The building supply store, in particular, was beaten down, and the paint store was not doing much better. Fallon found this odd. Building was going on all over town, with new tracts of homes popping up, it seemed, almost every week. Business opportunities were everywhere for anyone willing to take them.

Tom Fallon had never been thought lacking in his gift of gab. It was one of his great strengths. Unlike most of his children, who favored the self-contained propriety of his Germanic wife, Katherine, old Tom was the proverbial congenial Irishman who could talk to pretty much anyone, anywhere, anytime. With his gift of gab working full force from the moment he bought into the hardware store, Tom Fallon learned that the owners of the auto supply shop were considering calling it quits. Fallon also learned the same was essentially true of a building supply yard that spread to Foothill Boulevard to the south. Finally, and here's where the plan really began to congeal, Tom learned that a group of local mover-shakers who owned large swaths of the local landscape, including the five-acre corner parcel of land on which Cucamonga Hardware, the auto supply shop, the building supply, and several other businesses were located, was interested in selling.

Even before the Dodgers lost the World Series to the Yankees in October 1977, Fallon had begun trying to convince his other three partners who owned Cucamonga Hardware—his sons Ken and Jim and accountant Nelson Hawley—that the key to success was expansion and growth. Now, with their environs booming, and with the recent merging of the three communities of Alta Loma, Cucamonga, and Etiwanda, Fallon knew it was a do-or-die situation.

Tom Fallon tried to convince his partners to make an offer on the land and the buildings. The cost to purchase all of this, of course, would be steep, but at the same time it would never be any cheaper than it was today. Financing would be tight, Nelson Hawley in particular pointed out, and making the mortgage payments would be dependent on growing the hardware store's business quite a bit. It was very possibly too much debt load, Hawley added. Fallon paused to consider the impossible numbers, then he realized something. Although the auto and building supply companies were looking to close, there were still other businesses that would remain on the land. He did some quick math, and the numbers fell in line. The rent that these businesses paid, along with the growing business of the hardware store, would make the mortgage payments affordable. So it was decided. In the spring of 1978 Fallon had an offer drawn up. The partnership collectively held its breath, its future in the balance as the region entered the warm part of the year.

Months later, in the late summer of 1978, after Cucamonga Hardware had established itself in its new, larger space and the partnership had opened a new garden center where the building supply store had been, the atmosphere of Southern California was growing uncertain, like much of the rest of the country. On the one hand, local anger about the times was evident in the taxpayer-driven move to limit property taxes once and for all. On the other hand, however, guilty remnants of the region's free-for-all hedonism and big-money daydreams struggled to come to terms with the era. The local dream purveyor, Hollywood, buoyed by its new blockbuster mentality, suddenly had regained its cultural and economic stature. Movies like *Star Wars* and *Jaws*, which had respectively become the number-one and -two box-office draws in 1977 and 1976, were at the center of the new activity. More than a year after *Star Wars*' release, in fact, Twentieth Century Fox was still capitalizing on the success of George Lucas's space adventure—so much so that in mid-July, the company announced a major "media blitz" ad campaign. "At the heart of this assault will be a television advertising schedule," wrote an entertainment reporter in June, "in which at least one *Star Wars* commercial will be seen on *every* prime time show on all three networks the nights of July 19, 20, and 21, as well as on every network children's program Saturday morning, July 22." The strategy, which was deemed "unusually audacious, even for the flamboyant movie industry," was meant to extend the buzz of the previous summer, when moviegoers made multiple cineplex visits to see the film. "It demonstrates the lengths to which film companies are prepared to go," the reporter continued, "in order to milk the maximum possible profit from what every movie mogul dreams of: a genuine blockbuster." As if to concur with this assessment, a movie executive was almost giddy about the campaign. "I know people who have seen it 70, 80 times," he said. "Figuratively, the country should OD on *Star Wars*."[6]

Of course, *Star Wars* wasn't the only Hollywood product that the country was OD-ing on in the summer of 1978. In December 1977 Paramount Pictures released a dance film loosely based on a 1976 *New York* article by Tom Wolfe's erstwhile colleague Nik Cohn.[7] Called "Tribal Rites of the New Saturday Night," the article purported to describe the working-class young people of wider New York City who were finding release in the city's developing disco subculture. Cohn wrote of his subjects:

> Kids of sixteen to twenty, full of energy, urgency, hunger. . . . They are not so chic, these kids. They don't haunt press receptions or opening nights; they don't pose as street punks in the style of Bruce Spring-

steen, or prate of rock & Rimbaud. Indeed, the cults of recent years seem to have passed them entirely. They know nothing flower power or meditation, pansexuality, or mind expansion. No waterbeds or Moroccan cushions, no hand thrown pottery for them. No hep jargon either, and no Pepsi revolutions. . . . Instead, this generation's real roots lie further back, in the fifties, the golden age of Saturday nights.[8]

Ironically, years later, despite the seeming *vérité*-like immersive style of his article, Cohn would admit that he had made up the entire thing. Having been given the juicy assignment to profile the burgeoning New York disco scene of the 1970s, Cohn, as a Brit, got bogged down in his attempts to understand the American working-class kids who frequented the nightclubs. To overcome the problem Cohn wrote a fictional account that was wholly based on "mod" club-goers he had known back in England in the 1960s. Despite this fact, the resulting film version of Cohn's story was a gritty, stylish melodrama called *Saturday Night Fever*. Adapted by screenwriter Norman Wexler and starring John Travolta, an actor who had made his first splash on an ABC TV sitcom called *Welcome Back, Kotter*, the film was a success for Paramount, earning nearly $250 million in both domestic and international ticket sales. Even more impressive, however, was the popularity of the film's official soundtrack album. The *Saturday Night Fever* original movie soundtrack featured music by many of the top disco acts of the era—K. C. and the Sunshine Band, Kool and the Gang, Yvonne Elliman, the Trammps, and, of course, the Bee Gees, whose songs were the most prominently featured. For much of 1978 the music from *Saturday Night Fever* was ubiquitous, blaring from car eight-track systems and on portable "boom box" tape decks, at nightclubs and roller rinks, and on radio stations and television. The album remained at the number-one spot on the U.S. *Billboard* charts for twenty-four straight weeks between January and July 1978, sold fifteen million copies in the United States alone (and more than twenty million copies overall), and won the Grammy Award for Best Album of the Year in 1979. It has been estimated that *Saturday Night Fever* ultimately generated, between box-office and album sales, more than $1.2 billion (in today's dollars).

All summer long, then, you couldn't avoid hearing the music from

Saturday Night Fever. And while the disco music fad would begin to fade after a seminal event that would take place at Comiskey Park on July 12, 1979, that was still a year away.[9] If you were in L.A., or elsewhere, in August 1978, you were hearing disco—with its falsetto and breathy singers, its "four-on-the-floor" beat and bouncy syncopated bass lines, and its soaring violins and synth sounds.

People across Los Angeles, and across the country, had distinctly different reactions to this lively background music, and the reactions both underscored and contradicted the prevailing mood of the time. For Tom Wolfe in New York, the music of the disco era must have hardly registered. Embroiled as he was in the scramble to finish his massive manuscript for *The Right Stuff*, not much of anything from the outside culture registered with Wolfe. He remained cloistered in his New York apartment, loath even to appear in public.

Tom Bradley, meanwhile, embattled in the continued negotiations over the Olympic Games, likely took solace from the music, realizing that life still existed beyond the frustrating walls of city hall—where the machinations and political games were pushing his dream to obtain the 1984 Olympics to the edge of a sharp precipice. The local political infighting, in fact, had begun to attract national attention. "Never have politics been played harder," suggested a national sportswriter at the time, "than they have been in the infighting over Los Angeles' bid for the Games of '84 . . . in *mano a mano* contests among petty bureaucrats. The participants include city councilmen who want to be mayor, a mayor who may want to be governor, a governor who may want to be President."[10]

Fortunately for Bradley, his decision to turn over the ongoing Olympics negotiations to others paid immediate dividends. "The seven-member citizens' committee was an important step back toward sanity and away from illusion," wrote William Johnson. "For the first time, there was true civic clout involved in the Los Angeles Olympic effort, for Bradley had selected powerful people from business and labor, both Republicans and Democrats. . . . As if by magic, a relative hush fell over city hall."[11]

As a result in late June several members of Bradley's citizens' committee flew to Montreal to meet with representatives of the IOC, certain that they had the framework for a compromise deal at last. At the meeting Bradley's citizens' committee promoted the idea that, in order to protect the city of Los Angeles from financial liability for the Games, cost-control oversight would be made the purview of a private group, the Los Angeles Olympic Organizing Committee. Unfortunately, the idea was met with skeptical silence from representatives of the IOC, and the group returned from Montreal no closer to an agreement. At this point, in late June, the situation around L.A.'s floundering Olympics bid seemed as dire as ever. And while Mayor Bradley, at a local press conference, vowed to keep fighting, his tone was one of resignation. Bradley's chief Olympics adviser, Anton Calleia, meanwhile, was even more gloomy than his boss. "I am paid to be an optimistic man," he said, "but in this matter I am most pessimistic. The bid is in trouble. What began as a wooing exercise from the City of Los Angeles toward the International Olympic Committee has turned into an adversary relationship. . . . The situation has polarized here and at IOC headquarters, . . . and all I see is conflict, constant conflict."[12]

A few days later, in a seeming last-ditch effort to rescue the bid, Mayor Bradley went public, making a speech about the importance of "saving" the Olympics from their own "excesses." He spoke about the "Spartan tradition" at the roots of the Olympics movement. But the words mostly fell on deaf ears. In mid-July the IOC countered Bradley's statements by expressing its "concern" that L.A.'s plan could end up "commercializing" the Games. A day later, with polls continuing to show weakening support from local voters, and with the IOC's drop-dead contract deadline of July 31 looming, Bradley decided to take charge with a final take-it-or-leave-it offer. Through his new secretary, Tom Sullivan, Mayor Bradley declared that if the IOC was unwilling to sign a contract with the LAOC, then the city would withdraw its bid for the Games. "If the I.O.C. does not accept the offer of the private Olympic committee," said Sullivan, "then as far as the city is concerned it's over. We will not pursue the Olympic Games any further." Sullivan continued by saying that, despite his hard stand, Mayor Bradley was hopeful that the IOC would accept this bid, which he thought was the best terms the IOC could reasonably expect from any city. "Los Angeles is not alone in its desire to protect taxpayers," Sullivan continued. "If Los Angeles cannot host the games and protect the taxpayers from a deficit, then I doubt there are many other cities that would want to put their taxpayers in that position. We feel it would be the I.O.C.'s own best interest to accept our offer at this point, in terms of carrying on the Olympic movement."[13]

Not surprisingly, on July 18 International Olympic Committee president Lord Killanin rejected Los Angeles's latest proposals, flatly stating that they "do not meet with the provisions of I.O.C. rules, particularly Rule 4," regarding the fiscal responsibility of the Games, "and do not comply with the resolution adopted by the I.O.C. at Athens provisionally awarding the 1984 Games to the city of Los Angeles."[14] As a result of the rejection Mayor Bradley grimly announced, later that same day, that he would immediately recommend that the city council withdraw the city's bid. As of July 18, after more than five years of trying, Bradley's lifelong Olympic dreams appeared, at long last, to be dead.

In the summer of 1978 in Los Angeles, with the jubilant music of the Bee Gees bumping up against the confusion of the times, Angelenos everywhere wondered exactly what defined their city. Unlike New York, which had been coping with debilitating brownouts and other visible signs of urban decay, the Son of Sam serial murder case, a controversial mayoral election—and a host of other systemic problems—Los Angeles had always boasted of its laid-back, sunshine-addled positivity, and endless optimism. Now, in 1978, as the city was coping with its own string of murders, a nasty political squabble over taxes, and the seeming loss of the Olympics (and widespread ambivalence about the Games), more and more people in Los Angeles were asking: *Are we as vital as we think?* On August 17, 1978, a *Los Angeles Times* article called "L.A.'s Vitality: Is the Force with Us?" pointed out how conflicted had become the former "hustling, boostering" home of the great California Dream. Calling the Los Angeles of 1978 a place where "no two people live in the same city," the story detailed the contradictory and confusing views people had of their home, of the times, and of the cultural and social issues of the later 1970s. Dave Smith, the article's author, wrote:

> In the early 1960s, the city of Los Angeles was zoned to accommodate an ultimate population of 10.5 millions people and could hardly wait until they were all present and accounted for. Old photographs . . . give the impression that local civic spirit reached a sort of apex in 1957 when the Dodgers forsook Brooklyn and moved to L.A. Photos of former Councilwoman Rosalind Wiener Wyman, youthful spark-plug of the drive to bring the Dodgers here, show her wearing an "L.A. Bums" cap, flashing a victory sign, clowning with then-Mayor Norris Poulson, being honored at a celebration dinner. Roses, roses, all the way, the photos seem to suggest, and one wonders what ever happened to that old spirit, the gangway-for-our-town feeling that brought the Dodgers here in the first place?[15]

Smith's interview of Rosalind Wyman was telling. Whereas that key figure of the effort to capture the Dodgers for Los Angeles spoke of the importance of shared sacrifice, Smith wondered in light of the city's failing Olympics bid if something essential had changed over the past twenty years. "On a deep level," replied Wyman to Smith's questioning, "there just isn't the energy that there used to be. People basically don't relate to the city as a whole. . . . They identify in terms of their neighborhoods, their immediate interests. We're into the 'Me Generation' now, and people don't have civic spirit when they're totally wrapped up in a philosophy of 'me, not us.' And Proposition 13 really sort of says it all. The masses are too busy trying to survive to have much booster spirit beyond their own immediate surroundings."[16]

Smith asked Mayor Bradley too about the seeming loss of grass-roots civic pride, especially in relation to the faltering Olympics bid, only to have the mayor shrug off the question. Bradley replied:

> Every survey shows that something like 80% of the people favor having the Olympics, provided that there is no cost to the taxpayer. As far as any spontaneous expression of feeling goes, I wouldn't expect any great emotional outpouring. We're still in the negotiations stage, and people just don't get all fired up when they know it's at that stage of development. We're talking about an event that is six years in the future. It's when we get closer to the event itself that Olympic fever will start to build. But not now. It's too early, and people are worried about their own pocketbooks. They are concerned about their own communities, all over the city.[17]

Despite the seeming ambivalence and loss of civic boosterism that had once characterized Los Angeles, there were of course still plenty of people seeking the California Dream. Though no one had any way of knowing, around that same time two figures were moving to California to start their own futures and realize their dreams. A young man name Larry Ellison, who had grown up an orphaned foster child in the Bronx and Chicago, moved to California in 1977, intending to use two thousand dollars of his own money to start a fledgling computer company. The company would later become the database company Oracle, and Ellison would become one of the richest men in the world. A year later, in 1978, California native Michael Milken moved back from New York City, where he had been at the investment firm Drexel Burnham Lambert, to work at the firm's branch office in Century City. In Los Angeles Milken would earn obscene amounts of money—that is, he would until he was indicted in 1989 on ninety-eight counts of racketeering and fraud—but that was in the future. In the troubled present, as the nation, and Californians increasingly, wallowed in an almost inexplicably intractable sense of self-pity, people on the make still knew that California was the place to come to make it big.

Well knowing this, Tom Fallon finally decided that he would take a big leap toward realizing his California Dream. Putting up every bit of collateral he and his partners had earned in Cucamonga Hardware, Fallon went to the bank and got approval for a mortgage. With the money he would buy the paint store, the business supply company, and much of the land on the corner block of Archibald Avenue and Foothill Boulevard. This included the Italian restaurant on the corner, a flower shop, and a bar, but there were also notable holdouts—in particular, the Yamaha store owner situated next to the building supply company, who simply didn't see the point in selling, as well as a small insurance company. The land altogether amounted to about five acres. With this purchase, which set back the partnership about $230,000 (the equivalent of about $840,000 in 2015 dollars), Fallon could move his hardware store to the larger space where the paint store had been. Fallon also planned to turn the building supply store, as well as much of the contiguous property between the two buildings, into his dream business—a garden center.

Most of the Cucamonga Hardware partners, caught up in Tom Fallon's enthusiasm, were excited about the move. One partner, however—Nelson Hawley, who had been in the partnership the longest—was not. Hawley was nervous enough about the overextended debt load that he asked the rest of the partners to buy him out. They did as he asked, and they wished him well in his retirement. Oddly, Hawley would fall sick and pass away less than a year later. But by then, by the time Hawley had passed away, Cucamonga Hardware would be rocked by another, altogether shocking, development—one that marked the end of an era in the Fallon family's personal history.

TWENTY-SIX

Clinching

The difference between the old ballplayer and the new ballplayer is the jersey. The old ballplayer cared about the name on the front. The new ballplayer cares about the name on the back.

—Steve Garvey

While baseball story lines had been mostly negative in Los Angeles over the long, hot summer of 1978, in September the tone of the season suddenly turned positive. Helping matters, beyond the Dodgers' suddenly sharp play, were several intriguing and somewhat uplifting stories that came to light during the last home stretch of the season.

Back in May a small item had appeared in local sports pages about the former Yankee pitcher, noted author, and erstwhile actor Jim Bouton. The story, which garnered little attention except among the most attentive baseball fans, described the pitcher's attempts to return to the Major Leagues in 1978 at the ripe old age of thirty-nine. Though Bouton had last pitched in the Majors in 1970, for the Houston Astros, he returned to baseball in 1975 as a knuckle-balling starter for the independent Class A Portland Mavericks. For Portland Bouton recorded a 2.20 ERA and won four out of five decisions. And then, despite this success, Bouton took the 1976 season off from baseball because suddenly he found himself working on and starring in a CBS TV sitcom inspired by *Ball Four*.[1]

When the television project was canceled in November 1976, after just five of its original seven episodes were aired, Bouton returned to the mound. In the spring of 1977 he was signed by Chicago White Sox owner Bill Veeck to pitch in the club's Minor League system. Bouton didn't do well for the Sox's Class AA team in Knoxville and was released, but rather than give up Bouton returned to the Portland Mavericks to finish the season. There, he won five of his last six decisions and kept alive the idea of making his way back to the Major Leagues.

In the winter of 1977–78 Bouton met media magnate Ted Turner, who was in New York to accept the Yachtsman of the Year Award for winning the America's Cup. Turner had recently bought the floundering Atlanta Braves baseball franchise, and immediately Bouton broached the subject of getting a shot to play for the Braves, to which Turner supposedly replied, "Sure, what the hell, why not?"[2] Which is how Jim Bouton got an invitation to pitch for the Braves during the spring exhibition season in March 1978.

Not everyone took the news about this late-life opportunity in stride. Much of the problem had to do with Bouton's status as a pariah in baseball circles—or "deviant," as he put it, based on some notions he had heard from a behavioral scientist. "In any human group, family, tribe, (or baseball team)," Bouton later wrote, "there are norms—shared expectations of behavior. Any member who deviates from these norms calls into question the basic values of the group. And groups don't like to have their basic values questioned." Whatever the reason, Bouton's writing career had marked him as a target, a "social leper" (as sportswriter Dick Young put it), and players avoided or derided him. (Pete Rose, famously, would shout "Fuck you, Shakespeare!" from the dugout whenever Bouton was pitching.) In 1978 player discomfort about the new era would fixate in a negative way on Bouton's comeback attempt. At Atlanta's spring camp, though Bouton pitched well, he was unpopular with the people who counted the most—particularly the team's farm director, Hank Aaron. "Henry hasn't been a fan of mine," said Bouton, "since we were on the Dick Cavett show together and he attacked my book and then admitted he hadn't read it."[3] At the end of spring training the Braves cut Bouton, but he didn't panic. When Aaron gave him the news he didn't argue or complain but told him that he respected his judgment. Bouton then flew directly to Atlanta to talk to Ted Turner in person, which is how he was given a modest shot to pitch batting practice with the Braves' Class AAA franchise in Richmond. Here, Bouton did not waste the opportunity.

After a stellar performance in May against the Major League club, Bouton was finally given a contract by the Braves to pitch for their AA farm team in Savannah. People around baseball were still skeptical and dismissive, suggesting he was too old to be a real Major League prospect, but Bouton would have none of it. "You don't pitch with your birth certificate," he said. Bouton pitched three intense months in Savannah, recording an 11-9 record with twelve complete games and a 2.82 ERA, and he served as something of a "guru" to the team's young squad. "I was the fountain of wisdom on everything from pitching and finances to careers and love lives," Bouton said. "I'd sit around my room at night with guys like Roger Alexander and Stu Livingstone, we'd make some popcorn on my hotplate, and have a few beers and shoot the bull. It was a kind of closeness which had been impossible for me to achieve years ago. At age 39 I was finally one of the boys."[4]

If Jim Bouton's comeback had stopped there, it would have been a remarkable-enough story. The veteran pitcher, who had last recorded a Major League win in July 1970 with the Houston Astros, had pitched, at age thirty-nine, a one-hit complete game, a two-hitter, and even a thirteen-inning shutout. And while these accomplishments had been at the AA level, Bouton had also survived the swampy, hundred-plus degree game-time temperatures of the Southern League and all-night bus rides across the countryside. But the story did not end there. Once the Savannah Braves' season ended in September, during the time that Major League teams expanded their rosters to call up prospects and other players they wanted to take a look at, the Atlanta Braves called Jim Bouton up to pitch. Bouton was once again a Major Leaguer. "I had made it to Emerald City," he said.[5]

Tom Fallon, had he known of Bouton's ups and downs in 1977 and '78, would likely have identified with the iconoclastic pitcher. Against the odds Fallon's hardware store was doing well—growing its customer base, becoming slowly more profitable since the move to the larger space and the opening of the garden center, turning a modest mom-and-pop shop into a sort of (real estate–based) business empire for the family. And the results of the recent June election in California had also given Fallon reason to hope for the future. That is, Fallon was pleased to see voters had overwhelmingly passed Proposition 13 in the June election. Limiting the seemingly ever-increasing amount of property taxes on local homes meant, Fallon knew, that wasteful state spending—on extravagant new freeway construction, bloated public employee rolls, and other unnecessary public works projects—would be curtailed, and small entrepreneurs and home owners like him and his family would find some relief. As a major real estate owner now, he was gratified that his instincts, which Nelson Hawley had feared, were correct: property was, he knew, the future in California, a ticket to security and wealth.

Among the growing coterie of customers that the newly relocated Cucamonga Hardware had attracted was an acknowledged local, and national, treasure—woodworker Sam Maloof, who lived just a few city blocks north of Tom Fallon on a five-acre lot in Alta Loma. Maloof, who was the son of Lebanese immigrants, had turned to woodworking in the 1950s without much credential other than his own hands. In time he became a leading figure in the international Crafts as Art movement of the 1970s. By 1978 Maloof had become a regular fixture at Cucamonga Hardware, often coming in to inquire about rare hand tools that the Fallons tried to find in their large store of hardware catalogs.

Still, despite the seeming outward success, there were signs that Fallon's empire was ultimately doomed. At the heart of the problem for the store were Fallon's sons. Though the three had been raised in the same household, and all had a certain "Fallon-ness" about them, in many ways they couldn't have been more different. Kenneth, the oldest of the three, and Tom's second child (after Thomas Jr.), was a deep and complicated personality, jovial at times and intense and competitive at others. In college, though Ken had a strong analytical and scientific bent, he had studied art and hoped to become an artist. However, as the family story goes, his wife, Sandra, ended those plans, telling him to study something more practical that would lead to a better future career. As a result Ken shifted his focus midway through college, graduating with a degree in mathematics. Meanwhile, James, Tom Fallon's third child, who was just a bit more than a year younger than Kenneth, couldn't be more different from his older brother. Though Jim was at times as focused and competitive as his brother, his personality was inward and sensitive. Though Ken and James attended college together, even rooming together in the same dorm at one point, James was uncertain what he wanted to do in life. He shifted his major numerous times, studying history at one point, then psychology, then animal science, and so on. It didn't help that midway through college James met a girl, Pamela Barnes of San Diego, and commenced a relationship that would lead, in short order, to pregnancy, a quick marriage, a birth, a year off from school to work, and a return to college on a part-time basis. James would graduate from school in 1969, seven years after he first enrolled, still unsure what he wanted to do (thus the detour with Tom Fallon to Barstow that summer after graduating). And finally there was Patrick, Tom Fallon's fifth of sixth children. Ever the witty comedian, Pat was liked by almost everyone who met him. Inwardly, however, he was less certain, comparing himself to his three older brothers. He had, after all, not gone to college as they had. Working at the store was a stopgap for Pat, something to do while he tried to figure out his life.

Patrick didn't let his uncertainly show around the store, choosing instead to remain jovial with his brothers and dad and other visiting family members. This was in sharp contrast to the chasm of difference that would develop between his two older brothers Jim and Ken. Jim, who was quiet and dedicated to his father and this enterprise, almost always worked well beyond what might be considered a regular schedule. This was particularly true after Nelson Hawley, who had been the accounting brains of the partnership, retired. Now that the account books were Jim's responsibility, scarcely a night passed now that he was not working until eight or nine in the evening, much to the frustration of his wife and three young boys at home. Ken, on the other hand, seemed less dedicated to the enterprise, less prone to work overtime, despite the fact that he had bought just as much of a financial stake in the store as his brother and father.

Tom Fallon, busy as he was hatching plans and hobnobbing with customers, seemed mostly unaware of, or unwilling to acknowledge, the tension between his sons. And with business doing well in the summer of 1978, Tom decided to do something special to break up the large and monotonous swath of asphalt that was the open yard of the garden center. It was an idea he had had after speaking with one of the store's best customers, woodworker Sam Maloof. They had been talking about woodworking techniques in general and in particular about the underrated technique of "clinching" off nails, or bending and hammering a protruding point of a nail back into the backside of a piece of wood so it cannot be removed. Good clinching, according to the self-taught Maloof, was a true sign of a good woodworker—and it created remarkably strong pieces. And that's when it struck Fallon: he would build a large structure that would model good woodworking, be a good conversation piece, and demonstrate what was possible to do with the tools that he sold at his store. Which is how, that summer, Tom Fallon set out to build a large wooden gazebo in the space between the hardware store and the garden center.

Back in New York City, far away from the dry-dusty stretches of suburban Southern California as the 1978 baseball season progressed, Tom Wolfe continued to struggle with his current book, *The Right Stuff*. Part of the problem was Wolfe was of two minds about the project. On the one hand, at moments when he felt confident and comfortable with himself, he was still convinced this was the book that put him on the map. He knew that the articles he had written on the space program for *Rolling Stone* in 1973 were among his best work, and he was sure that in his full-length book he'd take that a step further. He had plenty of good material, after all, as the outline for the book had spread to more than three hundred cross-indexed pages. Some large part of him couldn't wait to see how the book turned out. On the other hand, however, his progress on the book had slowed to a snail's pace, which was telling, considering how normally prolific he was as a self-supporting freelance writer. Two things seemed to be troubling him about *The Right Stuff*. First, despite his great ambitions for the book, and his faith in the quality of the story, he was also fully aware that no one in 1978 America was really clamoring for a comprehensive story about America's first astronauts. *That was then, and this is now* was a mantra of the age (and the title of a 1971 book about disillusioned middle-American youths by author S. E. Hinton, as Wolfe well knew). Further, because of the particular way he wanted to tell the early space program's story, Wolfe was finding it nearly impossible to juggle the tricky task of actually writing the damn thing. *The Right Stuff*, he learned, had no one single character to drive the narrative and connect the events in the story to the history of the time, as the character of Ken Kesey did for the '60s psychedelic era in *The Electric Kool-Aid Acid Test*. "With The Right Stuff," Wolfe told an interviewer a few years later, "you had to keep filling people in on world history."[6] And tying the astronauts' story in with the weighty history of an entire era seemed almost impossible to do in an interesting manner.

Still, by early 1978 Wolfe rededicated himself to writing the book. To give himself a further spur in the side, he called his agent, his book editor, and his editor at his publisher—Farrar, Straus, and Giroux—and scheduled meetings so he could let them know when they could expect his great masterpiece. There was no need to keep pussyfooting around, he thought. He had done the research, outlined the thing completely, and written large chunks in the form of magazine articles—now he just needed an intense six months to write the words. This meant he stopped taking calls (this was what he called his "period of stuffing telephones with cotton") and ceased all other work. During the four-plus years he had worked on *The Right Stuff* thus far, Wolfe had published three books, including two magazine article anthologies (*The New Journalists* and *Mauve Gloves and Madmen, Clutter, and Vine*) and a short and controversial volume on modern art (*The Painted Word*), and he had continued taking occasional other writing assignments. But no more! He would dedicate all his right stuff to *The Right Stuff*.

Wolfe's situation in 1978 was, of course, a classic writer's catch-22. "In order to write a long complicated nonfiction novel like *The Right Stuff*," said Wolfe, "I had to turn out three books of magazine pieces, some of them enlarged, just to maintain a cash flow."[7] He also took to wearing casual clothes that would force him to stay inside, as he would not dare be caught in them out on the street. "I can't go out into the street in khaki pants or jeans," Wolfe said. "So I put on a pair of khaki pants and a turtleneck sweater, a heavy sweater. . . . It's another way of boxing myself in." Thus steeled, Wolfe finally began to make significant progress. Following his standard practice, he set a daily quota of about ten pages (triple spaced) on his manual typewriter—or about two thousand words. His methods were particular to him and ultimately effective. "Any time I'm finished with that," he said, "I can quit. I will quit even in the middle of the sentence at the end of the tenth page." Still, Wolfe, admitted, maintaining the through line—that is, moving the narrative forward from one day to the next—was the trick. "The hardest thing is overcoming the inertia of beginning the next day," he said.[8]

Despite the long struggles of the past few years, through the winter and spring of 1978 *The Right Stuff* began to take shape. As the text developed Wolfe realized he was making a clear statement about something very purely American. "The exploration of space is merely the setting," he would say of his work some years later. "The real subject is status competition within the small, enclosed world of military flying. That is what drove the first seven astronauts and most of the first seventy-two astronauts." That is, Wolfe was getting at some deeper truth about Americans, about humanity, and about the urge to strive and achieve. And the story, while full of fabrication and speculation, was as true as he could make it. "To me, it's extremely important to be accurate," Wolfe said, "If people start to ask, 'I wonder if he makes up the parts in between that he doesn't know about,' that's when you're undercutting the whole enterprise if you indulge in it. . . . [Plus] there's a great satisfaction in taking the actual facts insofar as you can get them and turning this material into something that is as engrossing as fiction, and in some cases more so, when you succeed."[9]

While Wolfe moved his presumptive masterpiece to fruition in the summer of 1978, Mayor Bradley's dying Olympic dream, which he had all but pulled from life support on July 18, suddenly, against all odds, showed distinct signs of revival. A day after Tom Bradley had begrudgingly recommended that the city council withdraw the city's bid, Lord Killanin sent a note to Bradley, expressing the desire to renew the contract talks between the IOC and Los Angeles. Further, Killanin offered an olive branch by extending the previous contractual deadline of July 31 to August 21. He also suggested that Mayor Bradley and his negotiators come to Europe and meet with committee members to strike a deal.

Bradley's stance had worked. The idea that the city of Los Angeles was simply willing to walk away from the 1984 Games, even at this late a date, had resulted in two distinct outcomes among the members of the IOC. On the one hand, it shocked the committee into realizing what the real stakes were. And on the other hand, Bradley's announcement had the odd side effect of exposing the IOC's poor playing hand. That is, once it was clear that Los Angeles was recalling its bid for the 1984 Games, cities that the IOC had claimed were backup hosts now publicly backtracked. "If California, one of the richest states in the United States, cannot undertake the Olympics," said the Canadian sports minister at the time, "I feel it would be irresponsible for Canada to do so."[10] Similar sentiments came from Munich, in West Germany, and New York City. In effect, without Los Angeles, the IOC had to face the fact that there might be no Summer Olympic Games in 1984.

Although local opponents to the Games remained steadfastly opposed to reopening negotiations with the IOC, on July 21 Tom Bradley announced he was doing exactly that. From there an intense game of cat and mouse ensued. "Over the weeks of the deadline extension," write historians J. Gregory Payne and Scott Ratzan, "from July 31 to August 21, 1978, Bradley lobbied hard to change the financially important Rule 4. Throughout July, Bradley conducted intense telephone negotiations [centering on] . . . the liability to be assumed by the organizing committee and the U.S.O.C."[11] Finally, after some hard late-summer negotiating, it appeared that negotiators on both sides had agreed, at least in principle, on the framework of an agreement. And in late August the Los Angeles Olympic Organizing Committee submitted the city's final proposal to the executive board of the International Olympics Committee. Though all eyes expected that the board would endorse the proposal, Bradley had been on enough of a roller coaster over the past year to know not to count his chickens. At least not yet.

With all that was happening in Los Angeles in the summer of 1978, the Dodgers' push to the pennant came to seem, especially after the fireworks of August had simmered down, somewhat anticlimactic. Factoring in the Dodgers' pennant drive, however, were two of baseball's most intriguing characters. First, there was Steve Garvey, who in August reemerged, as Dodger fans by now had fairly come to expect, as a catalyst to the team's success. Fresh off the high of being named MVP of the 1978 All-Star Game and the low of his face-off with longtime clubhouse rival Don Sutton, Garvey came alive. During the week prior to his fight with Sutton, he hit .379, scored eleven runs, knocked in nine runs, and was named National League Player of the Week. Afterward, Garvey, embattled and somewhat ridiculed for his role in the fight, was undaunted. In September's stretch run he hit a torrid .392 and spearheaded the Dodger offense. In the first week of September, in key games against the Mets and Giants, Garvey collected ten hits (in twenty-nine at bats), with two doubles, a homer, and six RBIs. As a result the Dodgers won four of six games and pushed their lead to four games above the Giants. In the last week of September, Garvey went on an even greater tear, collecting thirteen hits in twenty-four at bats, knocking in eight runs, and lifting his seasonal average to .316, his highest average since 1975, the year after his MVP year.[12]

Garvey's biggest September game, however, would coincide with perhaps the biggest career game of the second of the late season's intriguing characters. Much to the consternation of a great many baseball people, including Dodger archrival Sparky Anderson (as well as many of the Dodgers themselves), Jim Bouton made a key start against the Dodgers in Atlanta on September 10, even as L.A. clung to a small lead in the West, just three games over the Giants and six and a half games over the Reds. It was Bouton's first Major League game in more than eight years, and he was ecstatic. "When I walked into Atlanta's Fulton County Stadium," he said, "I was floating as if in a dream. . . . When I got into my uniform with my old No. 56 on it and went out to the field, I could feel my heart pounding under my shirt. And what a feeling it was standing on the mound listening to the national anthem, waiting to pitch my first game. I felt like I was standing on top of Mount Everest. I thought to myself how lucky I was to experience this twice in the same lifetime." The first pitch Bouton threw was to the Dodgers' Dave Lopes, a called strike that brought cheers from the crowd. "Four pitches later," Bouton said, "Lopes struck out swinging on a dancing knuckler and the crowd roared. I felt like Rocky."[13]

After the first inning Bouton ran to the dugout with his arms raised in a victory salute. He would retire the sides in order in both the second and the third innings before the Dodgers finally caught up with his knuckler in the fourth with five runs off four hits, including a three-run homer by Monday. And while Bouton took the loss in the game, afterward he said he was entirely pleased with the outing. "I think I showed everyone that I was not awed pitching against the Dodgers and in the major leagues again," he said at the postgame press conference. "I showed I'm certainly competitive. If the fourth inning had happened in the first, it would have been semi disastrous, but I showed enough good stuff for batters to swing and miss." The day after the game Bouton was still gleeful about his good fortune, but others were not so pleased. Calling the game something of a "carnival atmosphere," many players on the Dodgers derided the aging pitcher. "We didn't feel he (Bouton) should have been out there," said Dodger captain Dave Lopes. "We thought it was a disgrace to the game having him pitch. He has no business out there on the mound. . . . It was a mental letdown to go to the plate against him."[14] Lopes pointed out that the team had been particularly annoyed when Bouton had thrown his hands up in the air. This was the reason both Monday and Lopes had taken extralong trips around the bases when they homered in the fourth and fifth innings, respectively. Reggie Smith added that "it was like batting against Bozo the Clown." Even the manager of the rival Reds, Sparky Anderson, suggested that he was going to call for an investigation by the commissioner. "We're in a pennant race," Anderson said. "Bouton should have to pitch against the Giants and Reds, too."[15]

Bouton, who had experienced his share of abuse from the baseball world, took the hubbub in stride. In his next game on September 14, Bouton won. "Bozo the Clown," he said years later, "beat the San Francisco Giants, 4–1." And while the Giant players were just as dismissive of Bouton, suggesting among other things that their children could have hit his pitching, Bouton could only laugh, saying he almost forgot who won the game. "Johnny Sain (the Braves' pitching coach) told me later I had revolutionized the sport," said Bouton. "Results in a game didn't count anymore. You just ask the opposition what they think."[16]

Later in the month Bouton gave Anderson his wish, squaring off against the Reds in a day game in Atlanta. "They did beat me," Bouton said. "But only 2–1. I allowed just five hits." After the game, to be fair, Anderson gave Bouton credit, which the pitcher always thought was remarkably gentlemanly. "He can pitch," Anderson said. "Nobody hit the ball hard off him. We got runs we shouldn't have got. Outstanding. He did a super job. He's a good pitcher."[17]

At the end of the season Bouton's record was mixed—two good outings, three not as good, a 1-3 record, and a 4.97 ERA. Still, considering that knuckleballers like Hoyt Wilhelm and Atlanta favorite Phil Niekro were known for their longevity, playing well into their forties in each case, some wondered if he might not give it another shot in 1979. Instead, Bouton decided to call it quits, leaving people in the media and around the league guessing at what could have been his motive for coming back in the first place.[18] "Some people said it was a publicity stunt," Bouton said afterward. "Publicity for what, they didn't say. . . . Other people said I was doing it to gather material for another book. Not a bad guess, although it would have to be a hellava book to justify the sacrifice in income. A few people said I just loved baseball and that certainly was true but that was only part of it. The ones who said I was crazy were probably the closest. Johnny Sain hit it right on the nose when he said I wanted to do something nobody had ever done before."[19]

After their game against Bouton the Dodgers continued winning and finally clinched the pennant on September 24 with a 4–0 win at home against the Padres. Key to the pennant-clinching win? Again, none other than the surging Steve Garvey, whose three hits and three RBIs were too much for San Diego to overcome. Rookie pitcher Bob Welch recorded the win, his seventh of the season (against four losses), in the team's last home game of the season in front of a near-sellout crowd of more than 50,000 fans. The final game's attendance gave the team an official season total in 1978 of 3,347,845 tickets sold, for an average of nearly 42,000 fans per game. The number not only crushed the Major League record that the Dodgers had set the previous season, but far surpassed the league's second-highest attendance, 2,583,389 by the Eastern Division champion Philadelphia Phillies.

TWENTY-SEVEN

The Inevitable Yankee Miracle

The majority of American males put themselves to sleep by striking out the batting order of the New York Yankees.

—James Thurber

After the Dodgers clinched a playoff appearance, the team retired to their home clubhouse to celebrate in the time-honored way—with beer and champagne showers. The antics, however, were much more subdued this year than in 1977. "We want to keep our emotions under control," Reggie Smith said afterward. "Last year we had a big celebration and everything was sort of anticlimactic after that. This year we want to let everything build. That's why I think we're going to be in the World Series and I think we have a great chance to win it." Center fielder Bill North echoed Smith's confidence. "We knew we were going to win the division," he said from the clubhouse. "That's why there was no sudden burst of accomplishment. We know we have to win seven more games (playoffs and Series) to make it right."[1]

Despite these explanations, there was another reason that the celebrations were toned down in 1978. Somewhat lost in the media and fan frenzy of the pennant race as it heated up in September was a team tragedy. On September 15, on the day that the Dodgers became the first team to pass the 3 million mark in attendance at home, and on the same day that Don Sutton blanked the Braves and tied Don Drysdale for another club record (forty-nine shutouts as a Dodger), first base coach Jim Gilliam collapsed at home and was rushed to the Daniel Freeman Hospital in Inglewood. At first it was thought Gilliam, who was still fairly young (age forty-nine) and in relatively good shape, had had a small stroke, but then, a little later, doctors discovered that he had actually suffered a cerebral hemorrhage. His condition became critical.

Gilliam, who had been in the Dodger organization continuously since his own playing days twenty-six seasons earlier, was a favorite among players and team management, highly respected for his dignified demeanor and his dedication to the team. "I wish number 19 was here," Bill North continued. "That kind of puts a governor on our elation. When someone . . . was in it with you, you want them to be able to enjoy in it with you, you want them to be able to enjoy the fruits of victory with you." Rick Monday agreed with North. "The last nine days [since Gilliam's sudden illness] have changed the feeling on the ballclub a great deal. There is a lot of mixed emotions. We're high after closing out our division and playing good baseball and being able to wrap it up at home in front of fans that have supported us like no other fans in baseball history. We're also low because in the clubhouse we did not have a guy who is loved by all taking part in the celebration." Even Tom Lasorda seemed down. "All of us have dedicated this pennant to a great human being," said Lasorda of the coach who had, just two years earlier, been mentioned as a top candidate for his job, "Jim Gilliam."[2]

Whatever his feelings, however, on September 25, with his team now officially crowned Western Division champions of the National League, Lasorda turned his focus to the tough battles that lay ahead. There were, of course, a couple of business items to attend to—one in-house and one outside the house. In-house, Lasorda needed to make sure his team's veteran lineup was healthy and well rested, and his pitching staff properly positioned, for the playoff run. On September 26, in a meaningless loss to the Cincinnati Reds, Lasorda sat his double-play combo, Bill Russell and Dave Lopes, for Teddy Martinez and Lee Lacy, respectively. He also pulled several other veterans—Cey, Smith, even Iron Man Steve Garvey—in later innings, and he inserted Tommy John, who had been nursing a calf injury, as a long reliever after the sixth inning just to get him some work. It was much the same story for the final five games of the season. In each game Lasorda alternated which regular would sit or leave the game early, though of course he was certain that his regular first baseman was always included on the lineup card. This was for two reasons: First, Garvey was dead set, as per usual, on reaching his season goal of two hundred hits—a feat that the first baseman did reach on September 28 in an 8–7 loss against the Reds. And second, Garvey was completing his third straight season of playing in every single game—a consecutive-game streak that extended now, at the end of 1978, to 508 games.

In addition to focusing on the well-being of his own team, Lasorda also turned his attention to what was happening around the rest of the league and who was likely to be the team's playoff opponent. The races around the league were shaping up intriguingly. In the National League playoffs, the Dodgers would have to face either the Phillies, who were currently in first place, or the Pirates, who were four games behind Philadelphia. Though the Dodgers had the same winning record—seven wins against five losses—against both teams, they had fared much better overall against the Pirates in 1978.[3] In addition, the Phillies seemed to harbor a lingering grudge against the Dodgers over their loss in the playoffs the year before. Adding to the sense of focus for the Phillies was the fact that Philadelphia's roster, save for a few small bit players, remained almost completely the same in 1978 as it was in 1977. To get to the Dodgers, however, they had to first get past a tough opponent in the Pirates.

On September 25 the Phillies, who clung to a four-game lead in the NL Eastern Division, won a tight twelve-inning game at home against the Expos. With the Pirates already having won at home against the Cubs, and the season on the line, Philadelphia had battled back in the bottom of the ninth against Montreal to score two runs and force extra innings. The Phillies then won in the bottom of the twelfth on an RBI single by shortstop Larry Bowa. As the Phillies were four games ahead of Pittsburgh with just seven games to play, the team's "magic number" was just four. But clinching would not come easy. After the Phillies split a doubleheader on September 26 against the Expos and the Pirates beat Chicago again, the magic number was three. And after both teams won on September 27, the Phillies' magic number had fallen to just two with only four games to play. Unfortunately for Phillies fans, however, those final four games would take place in the last place the Phillies could have hoped for—in Pittsburgh.

As the Phillies headed into the final weekend of the regular season, facing what was likely to be a vicious knockdown battle against the Pirates, the two races in the American League were wrapping up as well—one with little drama, and the other with enough drama to make up for the first. Going into the last weekend of September, the Kansas City Royals in the American League Western Division faced the Minnesota Twins, a fourth-place team that was nineteen games out of first place. The team from Kansas City had already clinched its third straight division title three days earlier on September 26, when they beat the Seattle Mariners at home. This Royals team was widely underrated, boasting a potent lineup that was spearheaded by a young and dynamic third baseman named George Brett and featured the lively bats of center fielder Amos Otis and designated hitter Hal McRae, speedy corner outfielders Al Cowens and Willie Wilson, a scrappy shortstop named Freddy Patek, and All-Star second baseman Frank White. The Royals also had a tough pitching staff led by ace Dennis Leonard, starters Paul Splittorff and Larry Gura, and closer Al "the Mad Hungarian" Hrabosky. That Kansas City was not given the respect it was due may have been because it could not seem to reach the World Series. For two straight years—in 1976 and 1977—the Royals had been beaten in the American League Championship Series by the New York Yankees.

As for those Yankees the 1978 season had progressed in many ways similarly to the season prior, with all the histrionics and infighting of a Billy Martin–led clubhouse. Yet in significant other ways the 1978 season was quite a different story for the Yankees. In both 1977 and 1978 the team was a strange conglomeration of fiery, explosively proud characters, whose dislike for each other was written large in events on and off the field and recorded for posterity in the daily newspapers. In both years too the team wallowed in its own inner turmoil, struggling, and failing, to find a regular formula for winning until the season ramped up in the home stretch of the late summer and fall. In both years the low point of the season occurred right around the All-Star break. In 1977, on July 17, the Yankees stood at 50-42, mired in third place behind the Red Sox and Orioles and its manager sagging under the weight of Yankee owner George Steinbrenner's constant meddling in team affairs. The low point of the season in 1977—the point when the "wheels came off," according to Jonathan Mahler—occurred on July 21, when the Yankees dropped a game against the Milwaukee Brewers, 5–4, after leading the game 4–0 in the bottom of the ninth. Steinbrenner came within a hair's breadth of firing Martin then, saying at one point, "When is somebody going to have enough intelligence to say . . . maybe the guy's in the wrong profession?"[4] What happened next, of course, is well documented. The Yankees got hot in late July and remained so all through August, winning twenty-nine of thirty-eight games between July 21 and September 1 to take command of their division. And they went 19-9 in September to win the East by two games over the Orioles and then beat the Royals in the playoffs and Dodgers in the World Series to emerge as world champions—all while being led by the guy who was maybe in the wrong profession.

If the Yankees were a team in turmoil in 1977, then in 1978 they were a disaster—or, more accurately, they were "the Bronx Zoo," as Sparky Lyle referred to the team in his diary-esque book (cowritten by Peter Golenbock) about the season. Despite the fact that the Yankees had won an unlikely world championship in 1977, and that Billy Martin had proved himself up to the task of leading his team to the highest achievement in the sport, the Yankee owner couldn't help but ride his manager, and his team, for much of the season. As a result the Yankees played middling baseball at best, even as their divisional competition had improved significantly. Just after the All-Star break, after a loss at home against the Royals, the Yankees were just 47-42 and stuck in fourth place behind the Orioles, Brewers, *and* Red Sox—a full fourteen games out of first. Just as in 1977 the clubhouse atmosphere was marked by contention, particularly between Martin and the Yankees' highest-paid player, Reggie Jackson. But unlike in 1977, at the All-Star break the Yankees' season seemed all but over.

For many of the Yankees, men who had spent much of their lives playing baseball and who prided themselves on being at the height of their difficult and challenging profession, the constant sparring between Martin and Jackson, and the near-constant meddling of their owner in the affairs of the team and decisions of the manager, grew exceedingly tedious during the 1978 season. In early July Lou

Piniella complained to the press about the bad atmosphere in the clubhouse, suggesting there were a number of players who simply didn't want to be there. Sparky Lyle agreed, saying both he and Piniella wanted to get out, and there were likely others. "George is pissing everyone off with all this crap between him and Billy," wrote Sparky Lyle about early July, "and Billy's pissing the players off, and those things alone are enough to destroy a ball club." Much of the tension was also likely unavoidable. "It's too bad that Reggie and Billy had to clash," said Lyle, "but the way both of them are, that's something that's going to go on forever. Neither one of them is going to let a dead dog die. No way, and neither one of them is gonna get any good out of it."[5]

Lyle's statements turned out to be prescient. As a result of the lingering feud between the two men, during the loss against the Royals on July 17, with the score tied 7–7 in the tenth, Reggie Jackson decided to publicly defy his manager. After a leadoff single by Thurman Munson, Jackson came up to bat. It was a critical moment in a critical game for a struggling team, and manager Martin, playing the odds as best he knew how, signaled for Jackson to bunt Munson into scoring position. After Jackson's first bunt attempt was a foul ball, Martin had second thoughts and signaled for him to swing away. But Jackson ignored this signal and attempted to bunt again, again to no avail. On the third pitch, with Martin now fuming from the dugout, Jackson attempted to bunt again on the third pitch, this time popping out to the catcher. Jackson's defiant act, which was in opposition to every notion of how the game is supposed to be played, was noted not only by Martin but also by his teammates. "Knowing how the game was played," said relief pitcher Sparky Lyle of the incident, "I knew Reggie wasn't bunting to move the runner. He was bunting to get back at Billy."[6]

Things exploded quickly after this latest affront by Jackson. Martin, furious with a player he thought overrated and overpaid, suggested to upper management that Jackson should be suspended for the remainder of the season. Upper management, however, settled on a five-game suspension for the outfielder, who not only was unapologetic about the incident but also played dumb as to what exactly he had done wrong. Martin grew only more furious at the slights, and, when a rumor began circulating that Steinbrenner was seeking to "trade" Martin to the White Sox in exchange for their manager, Bob Lemon, Martin lashed out at both the owner and his overpriced star, Jackson. "They deserve each other," Martin told a Chicago sportswriter. "One's a born liar, and the other's convicted."[7] A day later, as a result of the outburst, Steinbrenner sent his team president to Kansas City, where the Yankees were playing, to fire Martin, and, having caught wind of the impending move, Martin preempted Steinbrenner one last time by calling a press conference and announcing a tearful resignation.[8]

The gods of sports occasionally grant victory to the undeserving and unvirtuous. At least that's what long-suffering Red Sox fans had long told themselves as a kind of consolation for their years of futility. For much of the twentieth century, since their last World Series victory in 1918, Boston fans had endured a long stretch without a championship, punctuated by several heartbreakingly epic collapses and by the long stretches of dominance by their rivals the New York Yankees. But now, in July 1978, with the Yankees sputtering in fourth place, and the New York team's management and clubhouse in turmoil, Red Sox fans dared to hope that this might at last, after six long decades, be their year.

At the end of August the Red Sox remained in first place, now seven games ahead of the Yankees, who had moved into sole possession of second place. Despite Boston's strong lead in the division, there were some reasons for Red Sox fans to worry. First off, seven of Boston's final thirty games would be against the Yankees, leaving them vulnerable to a team that seemed to be surging at just the right time. Meanwhile, as fate would have it, the Red Sox's lineup was struggling with a devastating spate of injuries just as the pennant race was heating up. For instance, Boston's intense All-Star shortstop, Rick Burleson, strained ligaments in July and was out for about a month. Veteran outfielder–first baseman Carl Yastrzemski hurt his back in July and his wrist in August, while catcher Carlton Fisk suffered cracked ribs. Third baseman Butch Hobson had bone chips in his right elbow, as well as cartilage and ligament damage to both knees, and, on August 25, starting second baseman Jerry Remy chipped a bone in his left wrist when the Angels' Rick Miller slid hard into him during a steal attempt. Perhaps worst of all, steady outfielder Dwight Evans suffered a concussion on August 28 when he was hit in the head by a pitch. "And we didn't have a strong bench," said Red Sox pitcher Bob Stanley. "We got Frank Duffy to fill in for Burleson and he didn't do the job. . . . I remember Yaz coming in after one loss and saying, 'I've got a feeling we're going to blow this thing.' I think a lot of guys felt that." Stanley wasn't the only one who was concerned. "In 1975," Dwight Evans said, comparing the current season to the year Boston fell to the Big Red Machine in the World Series, "we were together. In 1978 we weren't together. We did not jell for some stupid, strange reason."[9]

Boston faced New York in a crucial series at home in September 1978. The results were such an unmitigated disaster for the team—especially in front of four sold-out crowds at their home park—that it quickly earned a pet name: the "Boston Massacre." The Red Sox's trouble began in the first inning of the first game, on September 7, when former Yankee pitcher Mike Torrez, whose record for Boston at the time was 15-8, gave up six hits and five runs. In the second inning Torrez was replaced by Andy Hassler, who promptly gave up seven hits and four runs in two innings, thus spotting the Yankees a seven-run lead after three innings. As if that weren't enough, the Yankees scored five more runs in the top of the fourth inning, and that was all she wrote—the Yankees took the game 15–3 on the strength of twenty-one hits and six innings of solid relief pitching by Ken Clay, who had come in to replace starter Catfish Hunter when he strained his groin in the fourth inning.

The next game, on September 8, was much the same story—the Yankees exploding for seventeen hits and thirteen runs in a 13–2 victory. The two-game devastation was almost unprecedented, akin to a mob-like revenge killing spree, and people around the league suddenly took note. "Boston's got the best record in baseball," said Yankees scout Clyde King at the time. "I could understand if an expansion team fell apart like this. It can't go on . . ." Even members of the Yankees were shocked at the turn of events. "We knew the Red Sox were hurting going into this Series," noted Sparky Lyle at the time, "but this is ridiculous. Evans was beaned last week, and he's still dizzy, and because of it he dropped a long fly ball that cost them, and he had to leave the game. Fisk has cracked ribs, and he made two throwing errors. Burleson booted one, and so did Scott, and Burgmeier threw one away too."[10]

Still, despite all the injuries, the sheer scope of the devastation—especially after the Yankees won the third game 7–0 on the strength of team ace Ron Guidry's two-hit pitching, and then won the fourth game 7–4—was mind-boggling. "How can a team get 30-something games over .500 in July," said Red Sox catcher Carlton Fisk, "and then in September see its pitching, hitting and fielding all fall apart at the same time?" And while the explanation provided by the Yankees' Reggie Jackson—"This team [the Yankees] is loaded with tough guys. This team is loaded with professionals"—was the sort of giddy one-upmanship that is often found in the thick of pennant races, especially between two rivals like New York and Boston, one thing was clear: now, on September 11, the two teams' fortunes had suddenly reversed.[11] Ever since July 24, the day after Yankees manager Billy Martin resigned, the Yankees had recorded a 39-14 record, while the Red Sox had gone 25-28. After the Yankees' "Boston Massacre" sweep at Fenway, the two teams had exactly the same record—86 wins against 56 losses—and were tied for the Eastern Division lead.

The Philadelphia Phillies came to Pittsburgh on September 29 for an evening doubleheader, needing just one win in four games to clinch the National League East crown. But the Pirates, clearly harboring their own aspirations for 1978, promptly won the first two games in dramatic fashion and closed within one and a half games of the division leaders. In the first game, with the score tied in the bottom of the ninth, the Pirates' leadoff batter, Ed Ott, tripled against pitcher Ron Reed and then came around to score on the play when outfielder Garry Maddox booted the ball. In the second (twilight) game, with the score tied 1–1 in the ninth, the Pirates rallied to load the bases with no outs. With Phil Garner coming to the plate, the Phillies brought in reliever Warren Brusstar, who had pitched well for the team all season, winning six games against three losses and recording a 2.33 ERA. Brusstar never got a chance to record an out, as, before he could retire Garner, he balked in the winning run.

Despite the disappointment of losing two close games, the Phillies regrouped and on September 30, the second-to-last day of the 1978 regular season, held on to win finally against the Pirates, 10–8. Interestingly, in the game Phillies starting pitcher Randy Lerch helped his own cause by slugging two solo home runs and holding on long enough—five innings—to get the win, thus clinching the team's third straight Eastern Division title.

In Los Angeles the Dodgers closed out the season in San Diego on Sunday, October 1, then hopped on a Monday-morning flight to Philadelphia in time for a Wednesday-night game at Veterans Stadium. In the American League, meanwhile, as of October 1 the Royals would have to wait to find out who would be their own playoff opponent. Having lost a fourteen-game lead over the Yankees as late as July 20, and then finding themselves two and a half games behind the Yankees on September 17, over the last two weeks or so of the regular season the Boston Red Sox had come roaring back. In the team's last thirteen regular-season games, the Red Sox went 11-2—including winning their last eight in a row—managing to tie the Yankees on the last day of the season when New York lost its final game at home against the lowly Cleveland Indians. The tie forced a one-game playoff to decide the final division champion; it was the first such one-game playoff in the American League since 1948, when the Cleveland Indians had faced the Red Sox after the two teams were tied at the end of the regular season.

"It was strange, but for a game that was so important to both teams," said Sparky Lyle, "there was very little tension. . . . The general consensus [among the Yankees] was 'We're going to win tomorrow.' We just knew we were going to win." And, true to Lyle's prediction, the Yankees did crush the Red Sox's hopes, though the tight 5–4 nail-biter was immediately deemed a classic by all who watched. "It was a tremendous day," Lyle continued. "I'll tell you, it really was like being in the seventh game of the World Series."[12] Though the Red Sox got to the seemingly invincible Ron Guidry, whose record to that point was an astounding 24-3, and led 2–0 after six, the Yankees fought back in the seventh inning off Mike Torrez. With two out and runners on first and second, the Yankees' number-nine hitter, the light-hitting shortstop, Bucky Dent, came up to bat. Dent, who had little power, was not the best option for the Yankees at this point in the game, but the team had no choice. An injury to Willie Randolph, the Yankees' usual second baseman, had left the team few infield options. Despite the less than optimal matchup, what happened next further burnished the Yankee legend. That is, in 1978, against their bitter rival the Boston Red Sox, New York experienced another Yankee miracle that put the team back in the playoffs against the Royals for the third straight year.

The moment couldn't have been any better scripted: It is a loud seventh inning in front of a tense Fenway crowd, and Torrez, who seemingly has his best stuff today, is pitching a gem. The diminutive Dent, meanwhile, seems overmatched and overwhelmed. Choking up on the bat, Dent is barely able to hold off on the first pitch, which is low and almost in the dirt. After hacking at the second pitch, a change-up that fooled him, Dent swings wildly at an inside and low fastball, sending the ball into his instep and bringing out the Yankees' trainer. A few moments later, after the application of some ethyl chloride to relieve the pain, and with a new bat brought to him by the batboy, Dent steps back in. A muted and tense wave of whistles and cheers spreads through the crowd. Torrez winds and delivers another fastball, this one right over the plate, and Dent slaps at the ball. "Deep to left," says Yankees television announcer Bill White, his voice rising as the ball sails over the Fenway Park short fence known as the "Green Monster." "Yastrzemski . . . will not get it! It's a home run! . . . A three-run home run for Bucky Dent! The Yankees now lead by a score of three to two."

The camera follows the unlikely hero, trotting around the bases with his head down, clapping once but seemingly fully aware of how unlikely was his contribution to the game. "And look at that Yankee bench, led by Bob Lemon," says White. "And a happy Bucky Dent. Yankees now lead three to two. Well, the last guy you expect to hit a home run just hit one in the screen. Bucky Dent!"

Though the Boston faithful took the loss hard—alternately seeing the tragedy as yet another instance of the "curse of the Bambino" or as the fault of the weak-hitting Yankee shortstop who would forever forward be known as "Bucky Fucking Dent"—the Yankees were pleasantly stunned that things went their way (even if they always seemed to do so). For New York it was a pleasant bit of vindication after such a long and tedious year of struggle and strife. After the game, as one sportswriter described, the Yankees sat in the subdued visitors' clubhouse, eschewing the traditional explosion of emotion and bubbly spirits, and together they just relished the moment. Players talked about whatever came to mind—"the sun, the Rocky Mountains, new and old managers, candy, God, revenge, and other pertinent topics"—anything but the ball game.[13]

They didn't need to talk about the ball game. After all, the Yankees had won and once again were the American League champs—and no one could take that away from them.

TWENTY-EIGHT

Chronic Hysteresis; or, Another Yankees-Dodgers Rematch

Father, friend, and locker room inspiration
that will never be forgotten.

—Davey Lopes, on the death of Jim Gilliam

It's hard to win a pennant, but it's harder losing one.

—Chuck Tanner

It was, as Yogi Berra might have said, *déjà vu all over again* in both the National League and the American League Championship Series. For the second straight year the NL West champion Dodgers faced the NL East champs, the Phillies, for the National League title. And in the American League the Yankees faced the Royals for the third straight year. In both cases as well, because of the history of the previous year, two teams—the Phillies and Royals—had something to prove against their rivals, the Dodgers and Yankees.

In the American League Championship Series, the Yankees, who hardly had time to catch their breath after their dramatic victory in Fenway Park on October 2, flew to Kansas City for the opening game. And they promptly continued their seasonal roll, beating the Royals 7–1 on the strength of a gutsy two-hit pitching performance by rookie starter Jim Beattie and second-year reliever Ken Clay. The sixteen hits that the Yankees' lineup recorded against the Royals' starter, Dennis Leonard—which included a double and home run by Reggie Jackson—of course helped as well. While the Royals came back to win the next day, 10–4, the series was never much in doubt once it returned to New York. On October 6 the Yankees won the third game of the series 6–5, coming back in the bottom of the eighth inning on a two-run home run by Thurman Munson that proved to be the difference in the game. In the fourth and final game, the Yankees turned to their ace, twenty-five-game winner Ron Guidry, to shut down the Royals. After giving up a single run in the first inning, Guidry settled down to lead the Yankees to another one-run win, 2–1.

After the game the Royals, who had now been knocked out of the playoffs by the Yankees three straight times, were understandably stunned—so much so that they seemed desperate for some sort of explanation for their plight. And in their desperation they fixed on a single play in Game Four that they decided made all the difference in the Series. In the fifth inning, with runners on first and second and just one out, and the game tied 1–1, the Royals rookie speedster Willie Wilson attempted to take matters into his own hands by stealing third base. It was a close play, but, as often seems to be the case at critical moments with the Yankees, third base umpire Lou DiMuro shattered Wilson's hopes. "I couldn't believe it when he called me out," said Wilson. "I thought I was in there standing up." And Wilson wasn't the only one who thought DiMuro missed the call. "I don't usually get on umpires," said Royals first baseman Pete LaCock, "but he didn't even wait. I saw it on instant replay and he was safe." Even the Royals' manager, Whitey Herzog, a veteran of nearly thirty baseball seasons, could not believe the call. "He was safe," said Herzog. "You could see that. All the world thought he was safe except for the man (umpire) at third. He had him (Wilson) out before he even got there."[1] Whatever the truth of the play, the call on the field turned out to make all the difference, as, one inning later, the Yankees went ahead for good.

After the game the Royals were crushed—the latest in a string of teams convinced that they were forever cursed to be play second fiddle to the franchise from the Bronx. "Things just don't look like they ever want to work out for us," said Kansas City shortstop Fred Patek.[2] To many it seemed like just another instance of the ball inexplicably bouncing in the direction of the Yankees, something the Dodgers no doubt recalled from their bad fortune in Game One of the 1977 World Series. Indeed, after the Yankees' amazing comeback in the American League East from fourteen games back—a distance that had been traveled by only one other team before, the 1914 Boston Braves, who came back to win the pennant after being fifteen games out of first place—the Yankees' ability to win the big games, over and over, had begun to seem somehow miraculous.

The Yankees' victims in the 1977 World Series, the Dodgers, meanwhile were performing seemingly preordained feats of their own against the frustrated Phillies. In the first two games of the series, at the Phillies' tough home ballpark—Veterans Park, where the home team had recorded a 54-28 record in 1978—the Dodgers barreled over Philadelphia to take a commanding 2-0 lead in the series. This was despite the pregame predictions of Phillies manager Danny Ozark that his team, which had ended the season on a high after vanquishing division rival Pittsburgh, would take the series in three straight games. In the first game L.A. came out swinging, collecting four home runs—including two by Steve Garvey, who also tripled—against a succession of Phillies pitchers. In the game every Dodger starter had recorded at least one hit by the sixth inning. It was, in a word, a complete shellacking. "Hell," said Phillies first baseman Richie Hebner after the game, "we play good baseball at home but we haven't won one (playoff) game here yet. I don't know why." Though the in-your-face comments of their opponent's manager may have rankled some in the Dodger clubhouse, after the game various Dodgers revealed they had been inspired by something else. In the Inglewood Hospital back home, Dodger coach Jim Gilliam, several weeks after having suffered a brain hemorrhage, was facing a grim prognosis. As the days wore on it seemed in fact that the Dodger coach was unlikely ever to recover, and so the Dodgers responded in the only way they knew how. "We dedicated the playoffs and Series to Jim Gilliam," said Dave Lopes after Game One of the National League Championship Series, "and that's all I could think about and that's why you saw me getting mentally ready and as psyched up as I could. Every time I went to the plate I thought about him, and I could hear the Devil (Gilliam's nickname) talking to me. . . . We're coming at them with everything we've got, and hopefully it will be enough."[3]

In Game Two, with Tommy John on the mound serving up his sinking fastball, the Phillies flailed away in frustration, recording just four hits and no runs in a 4–0 loss. Afterward, they had nothing but kind words for John's gutsy complete-game performance. "I had pitches to hit," said meaty Phillies outfielder Greg Luzinski, "but I hit 'em in the ground."[4] From there it was just a matter of time before the Dodgers clinched the series. In Game Three in Los Angeles, the Phillies did momentarily come to life, knocking Don Sutton out of the game in the sixth inning and handing the Dodger ace his first postseason loss of his career. Afterward, even though they still faced an uphill climb in needing to win two more games in L.A. to take the series, the Phillies were defiant. "Everybody said we were out of it," said Greg Luzinski. "But a lot of crazy things can happen." Luzinski, who had been quiet in the first two games of the Series, had recorded three hits in Game Three, including a home run. "We knew if we could beat Sutton and get a shot at (Doug) Rau," said Richie Hebner, "that there was a chance. . . . We've been fighting and scrapping all year."[5]

The Dodgers' Series-clinching victory, when it came, was the dramatic, unlikely sort of win that baseball fans live for. With Jim Gilliam still in the hospital, and still comatose, and with the hometown stadium filled to capacity, the Dodgers scrapped and fought and emerged victorious in a dramatic, back-and-forth ten-inning, one-run game. The hero of the game, unlikely as it seemed, was Bill Russell, while the goat was, just as unlikely, a usually sure-handed outfielder on the Phillies named Garry Maddox. Before the last out was recorded, the home crowd had had a lot to cheer for: Doug Rau's gutsy performance, pitching through trouble well enough to keep the game close for the Dodgers; Rick Rhoden's strong showing in long relief, giving up just one run on a home run by Garry Maddox; Dusty Baker's four-hit day, capped off by a clutch RBI against the Phillies' starter Randy Lerch; Steve Garvey's home run in the sixth, his fourth in the four-game Series; and so on. The winning rally came in the bottom of the tenth, after Dodger closer Terry Forster had clamped down on the Phillies in the top of the inning by recording two strikeouts against the heart of their order. With two outs against the tough Tug McGraw, Ron Cey started the Dodger rally with a walk. Then Baker, who had been unstoppable all evening, hit a hard line drive to center field. Even in the most ordinary of circumstances, against a barely adequate fielder, it was a routine play that should have ended the inning and extended the game. And in this case, setting up to catch the batted ball in "graceful, loping strides," was one of the best outfielders in the game—a multiple Gold Glove winner whose nickname, "the Secretary of Defense," said it all.[6] But Maddox missed the ball. When Bill Russell followed up with a bloop single up the middle, the fleet center fielder tried to make amends by turning a tough play, rushing in from his position as Cey rounded third and headed for home, but it wasn't to be. Maddox couldn't come up with the ball, and Cey scored, sending the Dodgers back to the World Series.

After the game Maddox couldn't explain what happened. "I don't think it was a tough play at all," he told reporters at his locker. "It was very routine. It was a line drive right at me that should have been caught. I missed it. Nothing distracted me. This is probably something I'll never forget the rest of my life."[7] And his teammates were just as stunned as Maddox. "If he has that play to make a million times," said Phillies third baseman Mike Schmidt, "he makes in 999,999 times." (The man who hit the ball, meanwhile, Dusty Baker, tried to defend his fellow outfielder after the game. "The toughest thing to catch in the outfield," Baker said, "is the low, sinking line drive that's scalded out there. It looks easy but it's the toughest play there is out there.") Even Danny Ozark couldn't seem to comprehend what happened. "It seems like all the bad things happen to the good guys," he said.[8] For the Dodgers, however, the victory was sweet, and the win led to an uncharacteristic outpouring of emotion—the Dodgers comporting themselves, according to one source, like "25 sailors on the first night of a 30-night leave."[9] After the requisite mob scene at home plate in the bottom of the tenth inning in Game Four, the Dodgers left the field, screaming profanity as they crossed through the stadium tunnel to the clubhouse. In the clubhouse, then, for nearly forty minutes, Lasorda loudly proclaimed his love for any and all players in his proximity, while Steve Yeager asked loudly over and over where the party would be. Young pitcher Lance Rautzhan, soaking up the scene despite his modest contributions on the season, held his four-year-old son as he spritzed Rick Rhoden with champagne. Even Steve Garvey, a noted nondrinker on a club of good-time players, sat drinking a beer while he was interviewed by two radio announcers about being named the Series MVP.

A day later, unfortunately, the inevitable news came. Jim Gilliam passed away in the hospital where he had been ever since collapsing nearly a month before. At a funeral held in the morning, in the off day before the first game of the World Series, his manager from his playing days Walt Alston spoke fondly of Gilliam. "The first ball that came to him, he dropped," Alston said of his introduction to Gilliam in Montreal in 1951. "It was the first time he had ever played the outfield. The next ball that came out there was over his head. He turned his back, ran out and caught it over his shoulder. I don't remember him ever dropping a ball again." Alston pointed out that he had seen Gilliam play for a total of sixteen seasons over his career—two at Montreal, and fourteen for the Dodgers. "I don't think he ever changed," said Alston. "He was the same the first time I saw him as the last—a quiet, hard-working ballplayer and a great guy. . . . He could do so many things that most people didn't know about. He could play pool, he could play bridge, and he could play baseball. But more important than all of that, he could relate to people so that he was just as good off the field as on it. In all the years we worked together, there wasn't a cross word ever between us. He was the ideal ballplayer and the ideal human being."[10] Officiating at the funeral was the Reverend Jesse Jackson, and pallbearers (both active and symbolic) included a host of former and past Dodger players and coaches, including Dave Lopes, Steve Garvey, Lee Lacy, Joe Black, Sandy Koufax, Don Drysdale, Duke Snider, Pee Wee Reese, and many others. Gilliam left behind his wife of many years, Edwina, and four children—two boys and two girls—as well as an entire team who admired him.

In 1978, then, the inevitable had occurred again. New York had somehow again won it all in the American League, and Los Angeles had beaten the powerful Phillies, setting up a rematch between the Yankees and Dodgers for another world championship showdown. It would be the tenth such meeting between the two teams in the World Series, going back to the days they both were in New York—the most of any two teams in the league—and it would be the third time the two teams had met in back-to-back World Series. And while fans of the also-rans across the country—in Kansas City, Boston, and

Philadelphia—could not be consoled after their teams' losses, much of the rest of the country looked forward to another matchup between the Boys in Blue and Mr. October and his Pinstriped Bombers.

From the get-go, something about the Dodgers-Yankees rematch felt familiar, close at hand. It wasn't a feeling of déjà vu, exactly, unlike with the League Championship Series. This was more the opposite: a realization that, although we knew the world had grown a year older, the 1978 World Series was the same as the year before. This was like a science fiction time loop—a.k.a. *chronic hysteresis*, as occurred in the popular 1977 young adult novel *I Am the Cheese* by Robert Cormier. In that story the lead character lives and relives the same experience over and over, like a long loop of film playing again and again. In the 1978 World Series, just as the year before, the Dodgers—who had essentially the same lineup as in 1977—came into the series in a confident mood. They were focused and intent on exploiting the weaknesses of an overpaid Yankees team. They seemed halfway assured of their inevitable victory. And looking over the teams' separate lineups, pundits generally agreed with the team from L.A.

Despite their comeback against the Red Sox, the Yankees' clubhouse, and particularly its pitching staff, had been torn apart by injuries this year. The team had lost so many starting pitchers in 1978—including Don Gullett, Andy Messersmith, and Ken Holzman—that manager Bob Lemon had been forced to go with a shaky four-man rotation throughout the playoffs that included one untested rookie, Jim Beattie, and one ailing veteran, Catfish Hunter, who was struggling with chronic shoulder soreness and other issues. Meanwhile, the Yankees had lost their starting second baseman, Willie Randolph, for the series. His place would be taken by an untested rookie, Brian Doyle, who had batted just .192 in a limited role on the season. Chris Chambliss was suffering through hamstring troubles. Mickey Rivers was ailing. And on and on. The Dodgers, meanwhile, were relatively healthy, boasting a pitching staff with a surfeit of starting pitchers—John, Sutton, the rookie Bob Welch, left-hander Rau, Hooton, Rick Rhoden—and several young live-armed relievers. Plus, the boys were loose and focused, dedicating what they expected to be their World Series run to "Devil" Gilliam. Even an editorial in the hometown paper seemed to confirm what everyone believed. "The Dodgers have learned a few things since last year's series, such as how to fight with each other in the locker room," suggested a cheeky editorial titled "Let's Get World Serious." "Like a lot of people we know, the Dodgers are older and meaner, and intent on achieving ultimate success before it's too late. There is no need for inspiration: the mere thought that winners make more money is sufficient. And, as a wise editor once told us, it does not matter how you play the game, so long as you win."

An additional boost to the Dodgers was the fact that, unlike in 1977, the World Series started in Los Angeles. The Series also, unlike the year previous, started with a convincing Dodger win. In Game One it was the Dave Lopes show. Wearing, like the rest of his teammates, a black patch on his right arm with a white "No. 19" embossed on it in tribute to his friend Jim Gilliam, the Dodgers' second baseman slugged two home runs and collected five RBIs in the Dodgers' convincing 12–5 win. Also contributing to the Dodgers fifteen-hit barrage were Dusty Baker, who homered in the second inning and collected three hits; Bill Russell, who had three hits and scored a run; and Steve Garvey, who had two hits and scored once. The Dodgers' starter, Tommy John, was solid enough to get the win, scattering eight hits and five runs by the Yankees over nearly eight innings of work. By the time he was removed with two outs in the eighth, one reporter noted, John had forced the Yankee battery to hit twenty ground balls.

After the game someone pointed out that the last time the team won the first game of a World Series was 1963, the year that the Dodgers famously swept the Mantle-Maris-Berra-era Yankees (and the only time the Yankees have ever been swept in a Series). Lasorda shouted that this was all dedicated to Gilliam. "We are determined to dedicate a world championship to him," Lasorda said. Lopes explained, meanwhile, that he was in a groove. "I've probably never been more relaxed," he said. "I'm relaxed because I'm very confident that we're the best team until the Yankees prove otherwise."[11] And in fact, in his behavior on the field in Game One, Lopes almost seemed to be challenging the Yankees to respond. After his second home run, for instance, Lopes thrust his fist in the air as he rounded the bases, coaxing the home-crowd fans to respond with a kind of "Dodger power" salute—even as his opponents watched and seethed.

Lopes had certainly come a long way from when Lasorda named him team captain back in spring training. In fact, Lopes's antics in the game had not gone without notice. Reggie Jackson, who had been the MVP of the previous World Series, seemed amused by the gestures. "I think the Dodgers were pretty sure they had us then," said Jackson years later, though he also suggested that he, for one, was hardly worried. "We felt we could beat anybody," said Jackson of the team after it emerged from the extra playoff game against Boston. "One way or another we were going to beat you." Others of the Yankees, however, were less diplomatic than Reggie in assessing the Dodgers' behavior. "The Dodgers really pissed us all off," Sparky Lyle wrote a year or so later. "Lopes was hitting these home runs and circling the bases with his finger pointing in the air, as if to say, 'We're number one.' How bush is that? Our guys kept saying, 'We don't want to just beat them. We want to really kick their ass.'"[12]

That ass kicking would have to wait, however, as the Dodgers had other plans in Game Two. With Burt Hooton up against the up-and-down Catfish Hunter, the Dodgers were confident—Hooton had been the Dodgers' most reliable pitcher over much of 1978. In the resulting pitchers' duel, the Yankees got the scoring started in the third inning by stringing together a couple of base hits in advance of a two-out, two-run double by Reggie Jackson. The Dodgers, however, responded with a run of their own in the bottom of the fourth when Ron Cey, batting with one out and runners on first and second, singled in Reggie Smith. And they went ahead in the sixth inning when Ron Cey struck again, this time with a two-out, three-run home run off Hunter that landed halfway up the bleacher pavilion in left-center field. It would be enough for the win, though the Yankees—and particularly Reggie Jackson—were not finished. The Yankees scraped together a run off reliever Forster in the top of the seventh on a couple of hits and an RBI grounder by Jackson. Then, with Forster entering his third inning of relief in the ninth, the Yankees threatened again. Bucky Dent led off with a single, and, one out later, Paul Blair walked to put the tying run in scoring position. Lasorda, coming to the mound, made a fateful decision. Determining that Forster had run out of steam, he signaled to the bullpen to send in the right-hander, his tall and lanky twenty-one-year-old rookie steam engine of a pitcher, Bob Welch.

After blowing a high fastball past Thurman Munson, Welch quickly got the Yankee captain to pop up, setting up a classic World Series moment. Afterward, some would deem it a showdown for the ages, the kind of tête-à-tête that could occur only in baseball. With two on, two outs in the ninth inning of a World Series Game Two, with everything on the line in a one-run battle, an untested rookie now faced the fearsome slugger who had all but demolished the Dodgers in the previous World Series (and was already responsible for driving in all three runs tonight)—Reggie Jackson. Many among the crew of esteemed national writers who were at the game—people like Roger Angell, Jim Murray, Phil Pepe, Dick Young, Dave Anderson—were, in the days and weeks that followed, effusive about the battle.[13] The showdown, they suggested, was exactly the sort of moment that made baseball so great.

With the entire season on the line for both teams, the at bat lasted nine pitches and more than seven high-pressure minutes. Adding to the tension was the fact that the entire stadium of fans—more than fifty-five thousand—were cheering, standing and stomping their feet, throughout the showdown. In the ABC TV broadcast booth, the announcers grew increasingly effusive. "You couldn't ask for a more dramatic moment for a young pitcher right here," said Tom Seaver from the booth, almost in awe from the start of the at bat. "You're getting it all here," said the homespun former catcher Joe Garagiola at the seven-pitch mark, with Jackson having fouled off four pitches and the count stuck at 2-2. "The kid against the veteran. The fast baller against the fastball hitter." Then, a few moments later, Garagiola effused even more. "I tell you, this kid, he doesn't have any shorts when it comes to that thing called guts. . . . He's just lookin' in, getting the sign, and firin'." And still the at bat continued.

Throughout the at bat Jackson looked agitated, nothing like himself in Game Six of the 1977 World Series. His swings were desperate, out of control, his body twisting and torquing, struggling to keep up with the young pitcher's speed. For his part, however, Bob Welch seemed preternaturally calm—calmer than anyone had a right to be under the circumstances. He looked like he was working on his car in the driveway, not throwing a small leather sphere at one of the most feared sluggers in the league in front of fifty-five thousand screaming people (and millions more watching television at home). Years later, in his as-told-to biography, Tom Lasorda took some amount of credit for setting up the showdown, as he had specifically chosen Welch to work in this situation for reasons that went beyond his talent as a pitcher. Certainly, Lasorda, like many in the Dodger organization, loved Welch's arm, the movement and velocity he got on the ball. But Lasorda had seen something in Welch during the season, something he thought more important. "Having dealt with many young players in both the major and minor leagues," Bill Plaschke wrote years later, "Lasorda recognized the look in Welch's eyes: the kid had no idea where he was, no clue about the importance of the situation. The kid was perfect." And how Lasorda treated Welch as the young pitcher took over the mound in the ninth inning was intended to assist him. "Instead of giving him a pep talk, he [Lasorda] handed him the ball, shrugged, and uttered two words: 'Throw strikes.'"[14]

Whatever the real situation the fact that the veteran seemed somehow less in control than the rookie only added more juice to the drama. In reality Welch was anything but blasé or overly confident, either in the World Series or as a ballplayer. In fact, he was the opposite, uncertain of his place on the team, of whether he would fit in and be able to stay up in the Major Leagues. In his own assessment of that first season, Welch was awkward with his teammates and the press, and he was never able to think of the right thing to say. "The press thought I was vague and distant," Welch would say in his own biography, "and I guess I was."[15] Originally from the Detroit area, from a family of hardworking, hard-drinking salt-of-the-earth types, Welch would later reveal another aspect of his personal makeup: he was an out-of-control alcoholic. But that wouldn't be an issue for a while yet, as he had yet, in his first season, to grow so erratic that he would require treatment to clean up. He was not drunk facing Jackson in 1978, nor was he hungover. He was just a cipher.

On the eighth pitch, Welch let the ball get away from him a little, tailing high and wide. The count was now full. Oddly, Jackson seemed stunned by the pitch, as if it had shown him something, some extra speed or movement that he'd not expected. Before the at bat, as Welch had warmed up on the mound, Jackson, who was careful in how he prepared for games, had spoken briefly to Graig Nettles about the kid. Jackson was hoping, in order to get a potential leg up, to learn one more bit of information about the rookie pitcher and what Jackson might expect to see from him if he happened to face him. Now, as the crowd ramped up the noise in anticipation of the payoff pitch, Jackson looked back and forth, to the screen and back at the pitcher, confused and disbelieving. And as he checked back into the batter's box, he gave his head a quick, private shake. Welch looked in and checked the sign from Yeager, though both of them knew what he was going to throw. Over in the dugouts, on both sides, the benches were alive with agitated movement. Coaches, players, batboys, attendants—everyone knew this was the ball game. It was the ninth pitch of the at bat. Either Jackson would now explode with a long hit—a bases-clearing double, or perhaps even a home run—or the Dodgers would prevail. In the Dodger dugout Lasorda sat amid a tangle of men, looking away from the field. He leaned forward, his elbows on his knees, almost as if in prayer. Welch set and delivered. It was his hardest fastball yet, a frozen rope of a pitch, a bit down and in. Jackson swung over the pitch, recoiling so hard after that he almost fell over. When he recovered his balance he exploded in frustration, slamming his bat down and barking like a drill sergeant. Jackson had been fooled. The kid had prevailed, and the Dodgers had gone up in the World Series, two games to none.

Baseball is a game of long history, but it is also, because of its particular stop-start rhythm, a game of emotional shifts, sometimes quick and subtle, sometimes jarring and devastating. In baseball one moment's euphoria can in the next instant become doom. A hitting streak is always in danger of becoming a game-ending double play, and a 0-21 slump can end with a game-winning home run. On October 11, 1978, the Dodgers were as high as they had been in October in many years. In the first two games of the Series, both at Dodger Stadium, the team had beaten their old rivals, and all was well. "It was unbelievable," said one man who was in a position to see events unfold, catcher Steve Yeager. "What a performance!" exclaimed Tom Lasorda. "That boy can pitch," said Bill North. It was the sort of performance, everyone understood, that could prefigure a glorious sweep to a championship. "All the Yankees seem to be swinging right now," wrote an L.A. sportswriter the day after Welch's dramatic performance against Jackson, "at the hard end of the Dodger rope."[16]

On October 12, as the team traveled to New York, players were at ease. It seemed, at last, the struggles and trials of the long and contentious season—of the past several seasons—were behind them. Winning does that, of course. Winning makes everything seem right. Except, as it happened, Welch's strikeout of Jackson turned out to be pretty much the last high note for the Dodgers for the rest of the Series. Lasorda and the Dodgers landed in New York, and almost immediately the team's mood dimmed. Perhaps they recalled their treatment at Yankee Stadium a year ago—when fans attacked the team bus, phoned death threats to several players in their hotel rooms, and showered the team with abuse and physical projectiles. Whatever the reason there's no explanation for what happened next: they lost three straight games to the Yankees. The first was a 5–1 loss to the dominating Ron Guidry in Game Three that amounted to the first World Series pitching loss of veteran Dodger pitcher Don Sutton's career. In the game, while the Yankees started their relentless attack in the first inning—when Roy White homered off Sutton—the Dodgers could manage only one extra-base hit.

In Game Four the Dodgers lost a heartbreaker that many believe should not have been a loss. It was, to many, a quintessential example of the ball breaking in the Yankees' direction. To Dodger players, staff, and supporters, the game was marred by what they saw as at worst blatant cheating, and at best a blown call. The play in question occurred in the sixth inning. At the time the Dodgers were holding on to a comfortable 3–0 lead. John had been baffling hitters as usual, recording nine ground outs in the first five innings. In the sixth, however, after rallying to load the bases with one out, the Yankees sent Lou Piniella up to face John. With two pitchers up in the bullpen, John treated Piniella carefully, pitching him low and on the outside part of the plate. On a 1-0 count Piniella connected on a John sinker and hit a soft, sinking line drive to Dodger shortstop Bill Russell that he seemed poised to catch. But the wily shortstop, seeing the runners frozen on the base paths, let the ball bounce off his glove, perhaps thinking he could end the inning in one easy play.

Scooping the ball up, Russell stepped on second base, forcing Jackson for the second out, and then threw toward first base to double-up Piniella. Unfortunately, the ball never reached first, instead striking Reggie Jackson and scuttling off into foul territory behind first base. Confusion followed, as Yankee base runners ran wildly around the bases while Dodger fielders gestured at Jackson. Lasorda, of course, rushed to the scene, loudly objecting that Jackson had interfered on the play and the batter should have been called out. "He got in the way of the ball," Lasorda shouted at first base umpire Frank Pulli. "He's gotta get out of the way. He got in the way of the ball. He's gotta get out of the way! . . . He was standing there, he made no attempt."[17] Despite Lasorda's vigorous protests, the home plate umpire, after a short huddle, called the ball dead but with no interference. Piniella was safe and awarded second base, and two runs were given to the Yankees. The Dodgers were deflated. Two innings later the Yankees tied the game, and in the bottom of the tenth they scored again for the 4–3 Series-tying win.

After the game, and for many years afterward, members of the Dodgers railed at the injustice of it all—especially after seeing the replays, which clearly showed that Jackson had leaned his hip into the ball—claiming these were "illegal tactics." Jackson, in the immediate aftermath, was wisely low-key in response to questions. "I didn't know where the hell to go," he said of the moment before he was struck by Russell's throw. "I just froze."[18] Years later, however, after the dust had settled, Reggie Jackson was far more candid about the play. "Did I mean to do it?" he asked rhetorically.

> Let's just say it was what Roger Angell called it, "an almost chance reaction." I had started to second, but I had no chance to get there before Russell did. I saw the ball coming toward me, and I thought, "I'm going to get hit in . . . a highly sensitive area." So I moved just a little. . . . I could've jumped all the way to one side or another. But I thought, "I'm in my right-of-way. I'm in the baseline. I'm going to be out anyway, so why not just stand there and play stupid?" I thought, "I'm out anyway, so it's not so bad if I stay here and let it hit me."[19]

Whatever Jackson's reasoning, or the nuances of the rule book, the effect of the play was it caused a sea change in the emotional narrative of the Series. The Dodgers, who had been within a hair of taking a 3–1 Series lead with two of the last three games to be played in Los Angeles, knew what they had lost. And when the team should have been focusing on the games yet to be played, now they were stuck in reviewing over and over what had happened. As a result the Dodgers could never really get back into the Series, losing a sloppy Game Five in New York, 12–2, to the rookie pitcher Jim Beattie, and then failing to rally in Game Six, despite being back at home with their own ace Sutton on the mound against the ailing Hunter. In the end it all proved too much for the deflated boys in blue. Once again, it was Reggie Jackson who crushed the Dodgers in the World Series, though this time he had done it with his hip, not with his bat.

Afterword

Leaving Babylon

Nobody is apt to look back on the 1970s as the good old days.

—*Time*, August 27, 1979

In the eighth inning of Game Six of the 1978 World Series, the Dodgers threatening with runners on first and third and one out, Bill Russell laced a sharp line drive down the third base line that looked, after it was struck, like a sure extra-base hit. Fans all around the city—working late in the office, at home in their TV rooms, listening in on the radio—momentarily leaped up in excitement, only to be immediately disappointed. People talk about the balance that exists in baseball between team effort and individual effort, how winning often depends on both well-coordinated teamwork and occasional game-changing individual performance. Russell's line drive could have been the individual effort that made the difference for the Dodgers, likely leading to two runs with the middle of the lineup due up and runners still on base. But it was instead a moment for another individual, Yankee third baseman Graig Nettles, to make the difference in the game. Taking a step to his right, Nettles cleanly fielded Russell's smash, smoothly threw the ball to second baseman Doyle, who stepped on second base for the force and threw on to first base to complete the double play and end the inning.

One inning later, after the last out was recorded in the 1978 World Series, a shell-shocked and disbelieving Tom Lasorda left the dugout at Dodger Stadium, entered the tunnel underneath the lower concourse, and walked to the home clubhouse. He lagged behind most of his players, his heart heavy in his chest. Later, he barely recalled entering the clubhouse and speaking to his players. He must've said encouraging words, but he couldn't swear to it afterward. After speaking, Lasorda left the clubhouse and walked to his office. There, he collapsed in his office chair and stared forward at nothing in particular. Members of the press came by, but for once he waved them away. His head hurt, his eyes were streaming tears, and he didn't want to talk. He couldn't believe it. His team, all his boys, had now lost it all two years running to the Yankees. He would never forget this moment, he told himself, never. He would carry this bitterness, this resentment—especially over that bastard Jackson—with him through life. It was just too much. He would never get over this, he told himself. Never.

Tom Lasorda was not the only person who struggled with disappointment and bitterness after the end of the 1978 World Series. For days afterward many Dodger players, staff, and team followers struggled to contain their bile toward the Yankees, their fans, stadium officials, Reggie Jackson, and the team's owner. Famous Dodger fan Lillian Carter, for example, was out to dinner with family friends on the night of Game Six, and when she heard the final score of the game she fell suddenly ill. Closer to home, meanwhile, Bill Russell told members of the press that a good part of the troubles of the Dodgers in the Series was because of the New York fans who, he said flatly, were "animals." Dave Lopes was even more blunt, suggesting that nothing could improve Yankee Stadium beyond a bomb blast. Adding fuel to the frustration of the Dodger camp was a newspaper commentary by writer Bruce Lowitt. Pointing out that New York was the more hardscrabble place, a city that had "the best and the worst but always the most" and was "facing bankruptcy and telling the rest of the country to buzz off," while Los Angeles was the "laid back land of the avocado, suntans, smog tans, easy living, starlets living in a dream world," Lowitt suggested that in the conflict of the two urban outlooks—as seen through the lens of a battle between their respective baseball teams—there was no contest. "Los Angeles is Tom Lasorda's love boat," wrote Lowitt, "cruising along like the Titanic, destined to run into that cold, hard, sharp, dealing thing called the Yankees, to get itself ripped to shreds . . . and to sink. New York is Dracula in pinstripes. Frankenstein in spikes. You can bet against it all you want, you can burn it, shoot it, rip it apart. But you can't kill it. And it'll getcha."[1]

The rhetoric got so heavy that on October 26, a full week and a half after the last game of the Series, Yankees owner George Steinbrenner suddenly demanded an apology from the Dodgers for their comments about Yankee fans. "If my fans want to pull up the grass after we win a championship," said Steinbrenner, "that's all right with me. I can pay for the grass. They can tear up all they want and if they want a hunk of it in their front lawn then I'm happy for them. If they want to throw toilet paper all over the place they can do that too, because we can clean it up. The fact is they didn't hurt anybody. They were just having fun. But you'd never know that from the remarks the Dodgers made."[2]

For any manager whose season ends in the ultimate disappointment, there is always the solace in the chance that next year could be *the year.* And certainly Lasorda had plenty of reason to be optimistic—his team still had a solid core of productive everyday players and a vaunted pitching staff. Despite the swirling frustration, a few days after the World Series Tom Lasorda had sorted his feelings out and returned to his usual bubbly self. "It's hard to believe it's all over and we weren't victorious," he said at a Chinese restaurant, fielding reporters' questions about the next season. "We're just going to see how the free agent draft goes. I'm sure Al (Campanis) will be doing all he can to improve the ball club. We'll be in constant touch and we'll both be going down to the Arizona Instructional League to look at the kids." Unfortunately for Lasorda, however, his dreams for 1979 began to come apart almost immediately after the end of the 1978 World Series. On October 18, the same day that Lasorda ate a double order of egg rolls in front of a gaggle of reporters, Tommy John, the Dodgers' stalwart left-hander who had won seventeen games and recorded an ERA of 3.30 in 1978, announced he was filing for free agency. At issue for John was the lingering resentment he felt at the Dodgers' lack of interest in signing the pitcher to a longer-term contract. "We repeatedly attempted to sit down with the Dodgers last winter," said John's agent, Bob Cohen. "We tried to say, 'Hey, Tommy's two-year contract is up this year, he can become a free agent when the season ends, he wants to sign here again, let's get a new contract out of the way so it's off everyone's mind. Nothing. April. May. June. They didn't really sit down with us until July. . . . Now, of course, what we want isn't what we wanted four or five months ago."[3]

The loss of John was a definite blow, but it wasn't the only change to the team. That is, plenty of the players who came to spring training full of hope in 1977 would be gone by the start of the 1979 season. Glenn Burke, who had been traded during the 1978 season, was now struggling on an eviscerated team in Oakland.[4] Left-handed reliever Lance Rautzhan, who had appeared briefly in each of the last two World Series against the Yankees, was not included on the team's extended forty-man roster in 1979, and his contract was purchased by the Brewers in May.[5] Pitcher Hank Webb, meanwhile, who had languished on the Dodgers' AAA team in Albuquerque in 1978, was released by the Dodgers after the season. Webb would pitch one more season, for the Class AAA Miami Amigos of the Inter-American League, before retiring to South Florida.[6] And the intriguing slugger Claude Westmoreland, who had continued to show power at the plate in 1978, unfortunately remained too much of a liability in the field for the Dodgers to find a place for him.[7] Though he would remain with Albuquerque for several more years, Westmoreland would never really come close to breaking into the Major Leagues.

A number of other Dodgers, middling and established veterans, would also see their Dodger careers end in 1979. Mike Garman, who had been traded by the Dodgers for a couple of low-level prospects to Montreal in mid-1978, was released by the Expos before the start of the 1979 season. Garman would kick around a couple of AAA teams in 1979 before retiring at the end of the season. Right-handed pitcher Rick Rhoden, meanwhile, whose star was once so ascendant that he had been named to the 1976 National League All-Star team, was traded in April 1979 for left-handed pitcher Jerry Reuss.[8] And finally, established left-handed starter Doug Rau, who barely missed earning a spot on the National League All-Star Game in 1978, would get shut down in the second half of 1979 after injuring his shoulder. After sitting out the second half of the season, Rau would be released by the Dodgers in 1980 and play one final season a year later with the California Angels.

All the injuries, trades, retirements, and poor performances[9] combined to doom Tom Lasorda's season in 1979. Rather than enacting his revenge against the Yankees in the World Series that year, the team instead suffered its first losing campaign in the past eleven seasons.

In 1979 the great Jamaican singer Bob Marley wrote a song that many would come to see as his greatest achievement, a work that spoke volumes about overcoming the fears and uncertainties of the era. At the time that Marley wrote "The Redemption Song," he was secretly suffering a great deal of pain and uncertainty from a recently diagnosed cancer. For Dodger watchers who were disappointed at two unjust losses to their bitter historic rival in 1978, redemption from the pain and frustration and uncertainty would certainly have been a welcome thing in 1979. But it was not to be.

In retrospect, however, it seems clear that the Dodgers' second straight World Series loss to the New York Yankees in 1978 was something of a watershed moment. Not only would the members of the losing team remember the loss with some bitterness for many years to come, but this Series would be a signal that the times had finally changed, that the age-old traditions of baseball had been replaced by a new reality. To many 1979 is now seen as the final year of baseball's "expansion era," which had started in 1961. In this era a number of vast, bewildering, and unsettling structural changes took place in the game, and the general behavioral patterns of ballplayers shifted.[10] Whereas the 1977 season had begun with an onslaught of worries over free agency, the 1979 season brought dawning acceptance of the changes to baseball, to its technologies and structures, and to the overall feel of the game. The designated-hitter rule, while still reviled by some throwback purists at the end of the decade, was accepted enough that several designated hitters were among the highest-paid players in baseball. The growing specialization of ballplayers—such as the pure closing reliever Bruce Sutter, who would save thirty-seven games in 1979, and Manny Mota, who would break the record for pinch hits in 1979—would scarcely be an issue. While some fans still recoiled at the replacement of age-old quaint urban ballparks with a wave of new spacious, bombastic space-age ballpark construction projects—the Astrodome in Houston (1964), Atlanta-Fulton County Stadium

(1965), Arlington Stadium (1965), Riverfront Stadium in Cincinnati (1970), Three Rivers Stadium in Pittsburgh (1970), Veterans Stadium in Philadelphia (1971), the Kingdome in Seattle (1976), and so on—the majority of fans hardly batted an eye. Even the imbalanced league structure—of fourteen teams in the American League and twelve in the National League, a result of the expansion in 1977—merely had the effect of increasing national interest in the sport, attendance at the ballparks, and league profits. Other changes deemed foul by traditionalists that were (mostly) accepted by 1979 were the deployment of lighter, harder bats that promoted more home run power; the use of batting gloves to aid in the gripping of these "whippier" bats; the tracking of pitch speed with newfangled radar guns; and the use of lighter but still durable catchers equipment that gave backstops more ease and mobility behind the plate. Then there were the lights. "Of prime importance," wrote David Q. Voigt, "was the almost total acceptance of night baseball games. [With the use of] such technology baseball now became a night-time spectacle."[11]

For the tradition-minded Dodgers the changes of the era had been somewhat hard to swallow. For the longest spell—starting with the collapse of the late 1960s all the way through their close-but-no-cigar championship drives of 1977 and 1978—the Dodgers sought to ignore the changing times, to turn their heads away from the increasingly flashy modern ballplayers and their odious multiyear contracts and focus simply on the Dodger Way. But Reggie Jackson and George Steinbrenner helped put an end to that sort of outmoded thinking, as did the team's collapse during the 1979 season. In 1979 the Dodgers fell to third place in the National League West, behind the resurgent Cincinnati Reds and the up-and-coming Houston Astros. The team's final record was 79-83, a kind of waking nightmare for Tom Lasorda. A few years after the season, he would tell a joke. "In 1979 two men met on the street," said Lasorda, "and the first guy asked, 'How are things?' 'Not so good,' the second guy answered. 'Business is just terrible. January was bad, February was awful, March was brutal.' 'You think you've got problems,' the first man said. 'My whole family was in a train wreck and they all got killed. What could be worse than that?' 'April.' That about sums up 1979." Not the funniest joke, to be sure, but a clear indication of the manager's state of mind during a long stretch of frustration. "Throughout the season," he continued, "every time I thought to myself, things could be worse, sure enough, they got worse."[12]

The *annus horribilis* that was 1979 did not affect the Los Angeles Dodgers alone. In 1979 recession returned with a vengeance to California and much of the rest of the country. With inflation climbing to 11.3 percent in 1979, several industries in the United States—primarily housing, steel, and the automotive industry—went into steep decline, dragging a number of associated industries with them. In 1979, in an effort to slow inflation, the Federal Reserve Board began clamping down on the money supply, causing interest rates to rise sharply.

In Cucamonga the rising interest rates of 1979 and steadily slowing sales put Tom Fallon's business suddenly at risk. Making matters worse, that year also saw the opening of an expansive new home improvement store called Builder's Emporium—a corporate-owned chain store that predated later, bigger stores like Home Depot—just a mile or so north of the spot where Cucamonga Hardware had quietly survived since the late 1800s. The decline in sales at Fallon's hardware store, which continued through the year and into 1980, presaged a likely default on the larger debt load on his recent land purchases. Realizing he would have to do something dramatic to rescue the partnership, Fallon proposed selling off the land they had purchased just a year or so before to developers who would turn the corner into a new and modern shopping center. With the profits from the sale they could find another location for their store and continue on as before. Complicating matters, unfortunately, was son Kenneth. In the spring of 1979 Ken, panicking at the downturn and spurred on by his wife, Sandy, asked to be bought out of the partnership, just as Nelson Hawley had been only a year before. Unfortunately for Tom and his remaining partner, son James, even as money had grown tighter for the business, Ken and Sandy argued that the increased value of the partnership's assets warranted a big payoff to leave the partnership. That is, they wanted a 100 percent return on their original investment in the partnership, fifty thousand dollars, and threatened to sue if they didn't get it.

As if the year wasn't tough enough for everyone, 1979 also saw the end of an era with the passing of movie icon John Wayne. On June 11, 1979, the seventy-two-year-old actor succumbed, at the UCLA Medical Center, to complications from the stomach cancer that had been discovered earlier in the year. Though Wayne's very Americanist, very patriarchal, and conservative swagger and life outlook put off a few members of the younger generation of the time—in 1982 a San Francisco–based punk band would release a song called "John Wayne Was a Nazi," which celebrated the death of a "great white hero" who "had lived much longer than he deserved"—to many others he was the great and rugged national hero of his time.[13] As the years passed, suggested the *New York Times* in its obituary, "Mr. Wayne was recognized as some sort of American natural resource, and his various critics . . . looked on him with more respect. Abbie Hoffman, the radical of the 1960's paid tribute to Mr. Wayne's singularity."[14] Wayne made his last public appearance in April 1979 at the Academy Awards, where he presented the Oscar for Best Picture and received an emotional standing ovation. "Thank you, ladies and gentleman," Wayne had said from the stage. "That's just about the only medicine a fella'd ever really need."

So, in 1979, times were up and down for many around Los Angeles. A small bit of good news for the city early in the year was the capture of one of the men who were suspected of perpetrating the Hillside Strangler murders of late 1977 and early 1978. Kenneth Bianchi, a troubled drifter, was arrested in January 1979 in Bellingham, Washington, where he had fled nearly a year earlier after he and his partner began to suspect that police were closing in on them. He had crudely murdered two young women in that city but left a host of clues that led to his apprehension and his connection to the murders in California. His Hillside accomplice, an older cousin named Angelo Buono, was apprehended in October.

Even better news in 1979 occurred when Tom Wolfe at last published his *big book*, which fully described the ineffable qualities of the American astronauts who innovated space travel for the country. The *New York Times* would give *The Right Stuff* an unequivocally glowing review, and it would become a best seller, be made into a well-received film that would garner eight Academy Award nominations (including for Best Picture), and would win four Oscars.

The success spurred Wolfe to plan future books on the same grand scale, and his efforts after the early 1980s, mostly fiction now, would become major literary events.

George Lucas would make several *Star Wars* sequels. In 1979 the first, called *The Empire Strikes Back*, would continue drawing millions of fans to movie theaters around the world. In time Lucas's ownership of Industrial Light and Magic, his stake in groundbreaking computer animation studio Pixar, and his ownership stake of the *Star Wars* franchise made Lucas one of the richest men in the world. After completing his presumed last *Star Wars* movie, *Episode III: Revenge of the Sith*, in 2005, a few years passed before the former auteur sold his entire company, Lucasfilms, to the Walt Disney Company for more than four billion dollars. Disney immediately began planning to produce another *Star Wars* movie.

Tom Bradley, meanwhile, would sign the final agreement with the International Olympics Committee in a ceremony at the White House on October 20, 1978, just two days after the Dodgers' loss at home against the Yankees. The compromise agreement that Bradley struck with the IOC put planning in the hands of a private organization, the Los Angeles Olympic Organizing Committee, and absolved the city of all liability for costs, just as Bradley intended all along. On March 26, 1979, the LAOC made a fateful hiring, choosing a forty-one-year-old business executive and entrepreneur named Peter Ueberroth to be the president and general manager of the committee. Ueberroth, essentially, would become the ultimate arbiter for every substantive decision made regarding the organization of the Los Angeles Games in 1984. And, despite the intrusion of Cold War politics, Ueberroth would perform this task splendidly. The L.A. Olympics in 1984 ultimately not only came off with hardly a hitch, but also earned a surplus for the city of nearly $250 million. After the Games Ueberroth was celebrated as a hero, receiving the Olympic Order, being named *Time*'s Man of the Year in 1984, and serving as the commissioner of baseball from 1985 to 1989. In time Tom Bradley's dream—the 1984 Summer Olympic Games—would be praised and celebrated for its obvious trappings of success. At the same time, however, some would claim the model that Ueberroth and Bradley promoted for the Olympics—of inviting a host of business interests to pay for the event through sponsorships—was the great death blow to the original idea of the Olympics. While Los Angeles may simply have saved the Olympics by bringing their excesses in line with modern realities, many around the world mourned the intrusion of corporate and industrial money in the great amateur ideal of the modern Olympics movement.

Despite the success of his Olympics dream, Tom Bradley's career would not progress beyond the mayoral level. Twice, in 1982 and 1986, Tom Bradley ran for governor of California against George Deukmejian. Bradley lost both times. In 1982 the margin was extremely close, and for a time it looked like Bradley would pull out the victory. In poll data conducted as late as the day of the election, Bradley was projected by various news organizations as the likely winner, but Bradley lost the election by about a hundred thousand votes (or 1.2 percent of those cast). The final results of the election would give rise to a new political term, the *Bradley effect*, which referred to the tendency of voters to misrepresent their true voting intention when it came to black candidates. Though Bradley would serve as mayor of Los Angeles until 1993, an unprecedented total of five terms, his legacy in that office would be somewhat tarnished by a fateful decision he had made back in 1978. His choice for chief of police, a tough, antigang hard-liner named Darryl Gates, would help create the conditions that led to the Rodney King beating in 1991 and subsequent riots in Los Angeles in 1992.

As for Tom Fallon, his fears of expensive family-rending litigation spurred him to urge that the Cucamonga partnership meet Kenneth Fallon's demands in 1978, and the two remaining members of the partnership took out a loan against their property to cover the costs. In 1979 the partners sold the land to developers, but because of various debts and the costs related to liquidating and relocating the business the two did not realize anything close to the profit that Tom Fallon had imagined. Tellingly, around this time half of Tom Fallon's six children would leave California. Tom's daughter Trish would be the first to leave, heading with her husband back to his roots in rural Delaware. Tom's two youngest sons, Patrick and Barry, would leave over the next few years, each escaping with their very young families to quiet rural spreads in the Pacific Northwest—Barry in Blue

River, Oregon, and Patrick in Sequim, Washington. What they fled was what increasing numbers of observers noted about the Southern Californian pattern of growth and its resulting congestion, urban sprawl, crime, and other gritty city problems.

In 1980 Fallon's hardware store moved thirteen miles down old Route 66 to a shopping center in LaVerne, and something about the location, or the community's drive-through quality, made it hard for the business to thrive as it had in Cucamonga. Though the partnership held on as long as it could, after several years the business became increasingly untenable. Seeing the writing on the wall—namely, that his father was struggling to hold on to his last major asset at an age when he should be thinking of retirement—son James Fallon walked away from the store, turning over all assets to his father, Tom, as a small nest egg.

For the Dodgers the year 1979 was best forgotten. Thing got so bad that, after the season, an L.A. paper conducted a December poll of its readers asking, "Should Lasorda manage the Dodgers next season?" "Gee, that's kind of tough," Lasorda said of the poll. "Two Western Division titles and two National League Championships in three years and this newspaper was wondering if I should be fired. Fortunately, I had learned early in my career that it is impossible to win an argument with anyone who buys ink by the gallon. So I ignored the poll." Besides, Lasorda added, "I won 5,822 votes to 2,123."[15]

Lasorda's Dodgers would eventually recover from the down year, rebuilding their pitching staff and getting healthy enough to tie for the Western Division title with Houston in 1980 before losing in a one-game tiebreaker playoff, 7–1. After the 1980 season, at a welcome-home luncheon, Lasorda promised the assembled crowd, as always, that the Dodgers would win the world championship in 1981. Yet the World Series almost didn't happen that year. A player strike in the middle of the season—primarily over the issue of compensation for teams that lose players to free agency—cut the season by more than a third. The Dodgers' eventual victory in the World Series, poetically enough over the New York Yankees in six games, came only after two unusual five-game playoff series—against the Astros, who had the best divisional record in the second half of the season, and the

Expos, who emerged victorious from the Eastern Division scrum. In both cases the Dodgers had to overcome losses in the first two games with dramatic, come-from-behind victories. Against the Expos, in fact, the final victory was secured by perhaps the most dramatic of all Dodger postseason home runs up to that point: a stunning ninth-inning shot by the team's starting right-fielder, Rick Monday. Yes, the embattled, often injured Rick Monday finally paid off for the Dodgers, some five years after coming to the team.

The championship that Tom Lasorda had long wanted to bring to Dodgerland would come just in time. In 1982 the team's core players would begin to scatter. An aging Dave Lopes would be traded to Oakland before the start of the 1982 season, replaced by a rookie named Steve Sax.[16] In 1983 Ron Cey would be traded to the Chicago Cubs for two prospects, making room for Pedro Guerrero to take over the position, and Steve Garvey would sign a free-agent contract with the Padres, making room for touted prospect Greg Brock.[17] Among the other Dodger players from 1977–78 who came up through the Minors with Tom Lasorda, few remained past the first years of the new decade. The injured Doug Rau was released outright by the Dodgers before the 1981 season, and Charlie Hough had been bought by the Texas Rangers midway through the 1980 season. Joe Ferguson was released by the Dodgers in August 1981. Steve Yeager would continue playing with the Dodgers through 1985 before being traded to the Seattle Mariners. Only quiet, unassuming Bill Russell would remain with the team into 1986, eventually retiring as a Dodger at season's end after an eighteen-year, 2,181-game career with the team.[18] Russell would become a Dodger coach under Lasorda in 1987 and later became manager during a tough transitional moment for the team in 1996–98.

Despite the crushing World Series losses in his first two seasons, Tom Lasorda would manage the Dodgers for twenty years, win two World Series titles (in 1981 and 1988),[19] and gain a spot in Baseball's Hall of Fame. The sport of baseball, meanwhile, from its point of crisis in the 1970s—with its labor struggles, changing character, attendant fan apathy (and antipathy)—would survive and thrive, regaining new fans even as the game continued to evolve. And while the strike in 1981 would cause a great deal of fan defection, and rampant drug use in the league would culminate in several sensational trials in the 1980s (and later performance-enhancing drug controversies in the 1990s and 2000s), baseball would survive its challenges as a pliable institution that could adapt and evolve with the times. As with America itself, baseball would repeat a cycle of decline, struggle, failure, redemption, and recovery over and over again, and the sport would prevail through it all.

NOTES

1. The Days of Bad Baseball

1. Born in 1928, Martin was part of the Silent Generation—those born between 1925 and 1945—who did not serve during World War II but came of age in the 1950s during the Korean crisis.

2. AP, "It All Started Very Innocently Tuesday," *Lethbridge (Alberta) Herald*, June 5, 1974.

3. Pete Spudich, "Dime Beer the Culprit," *Las Cruces (NM) Sun-News*, June 6, 1974.

4. Spudich, "Dime Beer the Culprit"; Kent Pulliam, "Do the Cleveland Fans Deserve a Team?," *Hutchinson (KS) News*, June 6, 1974; AP, "Fans Go Too Far," *Hutchinson (KS) News*, June 6, 1974; Spudich, "Dime Beer the Culprit."

5. United Press International (UPI), "Indians Protest Riot Forfeiture," *Owosso (MI) Argus-Press*, June 6, 1974.

6. Tom Wolfe, "The Me Decade and the Third Great Awakening," *New York*, August 23, 1976.

7. Tom Wolfe, *In Our Time* (New York: Farrar, Straus, and Giroux, 1980), 4, 7.

8. "To Set the Economy Right," *Time*, August 27, 1979.

9. Doug Brown, "Bottle Narrowly Misses Chylak after Close Call in Baltimore," *Sporting News*, May 28, 1966.

10. George Castle, *When the Game Changed: An Oral History of Baseball's True Golden Age, 1969–1979* (Guilford CT: Lyons Press, 2011), 313–14.

11. Castle, *When the Game Changed*, 7–8.

12. Whereas a strike had long been, by custom, any pitch located between a batter's knees and his midchest, in the 1960s strikes were now called anywhere between the knees and the shoulders.

13. "Charlie Finley: Baseball's Barnum," *Time*, August 18, 1975.

2. Where It Will Always Be 1955

1. Cucamonga had been made nationally famous as the strange-sounding punch line in a bit on the Jack Benny TV show. The strange sound of the town's name, *Cucamonga*, in fact, comes from the Native Tongva language. *Cuc* means to "come

from," *amo* means "water," and *nanga* means "village." So the name is said to mean "the village where water comes from," which was of course strange and ironic—since Cucamonga was bone-dry, even compared to the rest of Southern California.

2. Jimmy Carter, "Address to the National Press Club by Jimmy Carter Announcing His Candidacy for the 1976 Democratic Presidential Nomination," in *Jimmy Carter Presidential Campaign Announcement Speech Flyer* (December 12, 1974).

3. Castle, *When the Game Changed*, 33–34, 28.

4. Williams was eventually replaced, in time for the 10 Cent Beer Night riot, by another, lesser, 1950s-era luminary (and more successful manager)—Billy Martin.

5. Author James Michener called *The Boys of Summer* "America's finest book on sports." In 2002 *Sports Illustrated* selected Kahn's masterpiece as the best of all American books on baseball (and second-best sports book of all time). *The Boys of Summer* to date has been reprinted nearly ninety times and has sold more than three million copies.

6. Durocher led Brooklyn to a 1941 World Series appearance, its first in more than twenty years, where the team lost, for the first time, to the New York Yankees.

7. Branch Rickey, *Branch Rickey's Little Blue Book: Wit and Strategy from Baseball's Last Wise Man* (Toronto: Sport Classic Books, 1995), 17.

8. The year 1947 was also when Jackie Robinson would debut on the Dodgers' Major League squad.

9. Among the people whom Rickey would influence were Hall of Famers Walt Alston, Leo Durocher, Tom Lasorda, and Dick Williams, as well as Gene Mauch, Herman Franks, Don Zimmer, and Roger Craig—all of whom, after coming up through the Dodger system, went on to have successful careers as team leaders. So influential was Rickey that even rivals such as Sparky Anderson, manager of the Cincinnati Reds, were admirers. "Strictly for baseball fundamentals," wrote Anderson in his autobiography, "I believe the game peaked in the 1950s. That was primarily because of the genius of Branch Rickey. He was a baseball scientist. What Abner Doubleday invented, Mr. Rickey perfected. He was the greatest innovator this game has ever known. He had the sharpest baseball mind I ever saw." Sparky Anderson with Dan Ewald, *Sparky!* (New York: Prentice Hall, 1990), 91.

10. The Dodgers won 3,135 games during this stretch and the Yankees 3,185—a difference of *only* 50 games over thirty-five years. The only other team that came close to this level of success was the St. Louis Cardinals, who had won more than 100 fewer games—3,001—than the Dodgers.

11. Dan Epstein, *Big Hair and Plastic Grass: A Funky Ride through Baseball and America in the Swinging '70s* (New York: St. Martin's, 2010), 41.

12. This transaction, at the time widely derided, would eventually prove crucial to the Dodgers' fortunes, as it netted the Dodgers an important player in pitcher Tommy John.

13. Jim Murray, "On Dodgertown," *Schenectady (NY) Gazette*, April 4, 1977.

14. Walt Alston with Jack Tobin, *A Year at a Time* (New York: World Books, 1976), 194.

3. Detours along the Dodger Way

1. Tom Singer, "The Greatest Draft in Baseball History: Forty Years Ago, Dodgers Strike Gold with Their Picks," MLB.com, May 6, 2008.

2. Singer, "Greatest Draft."

3. Singer, "Greatest Draft."

4. Alston with Tobin, *Year at a Time*, 195.

5. "Game One, World Series Broadcast," ABC TV, October 11, 1977.

6. Halfway through 1976 the Dodgers, spurred by requests from several frustrated teammates, would trade Marshall to Atlanta.

7. Alston with Tobin, *Year at a Time*, 180; Anderson with Ewald, *Sparky!*, 92; Hank Hollingsworth, "Alston: The 'Quiet' Agitator," *Long Beach (CA) Independent Press Telegraph*, August 8, 1976.

8. For instance, outfielder Jimmy Wynn, who had disappointed in 1975, was traded along with several other players to the Braves for outfielder Dusty Baker; outfielder Willie Crawford was traded to St. Louis for infielder Ted Sizemore; catcher Joe Ferguson was traded to St. Louis for Reggie Smith; and Mike Marshall was traded to the Braves for reliever Elias Sosa.

9. Wire story, "Alston, Sportswriter Exchange Insults," *Hayward (CA) Daily Review*, August 23, 1976.

10. Ross Newhan, "If Fired, I Won't Cry," *Los Angeles Times*, September 19, 1976.

11. Newhan, "If Fired."

12. Ross Newhan, "Alston Retiring after Managing 23 Years," *Los Angeles Times*, September 28, 1978.

13. Newhan, "Alston Retiring."

14. Newhan, "Alston Retiring."

15. Ross Newhan, "Dodgers Get Their Man; It's Lasorda," *Los Angeles Times*, September 30, 1976.

16. Bill Plaschke with Tom Lasorda, *I Live for This* (New York: Houghton Mifflin, 2007), 117–18. Later, Lasorda also reportedly rebuffed a similar offer from the Atlanta Braves.

17. As it happens Lasorda's embrace of the "Dodger Blue" refrain was an example of his quintessential "company man" approach to the game. In 1977 Dodger administrators were looking at ways to build the team's already solid popularity when they struck on a simple notion. "I had always been impressed by the way the major colleges in this country have been able to develop a great spirit among their fans," wrote the team's vice president of marketing at the time, Fred Claire. "From Notre Dame football to Indiana basketball, there was a special flavor to these programs. And a central component of that flavor were colors, from the gold of the Fighting Irish's helmets to the bright red of the Hoosier's uniforms. So why not add a color to the Dodger identification, Dodger Blue? . . . I knew Tommy would be the perfect person to spread the blue all over town. It ended up being spread all over the world." Fred Claire with Steve Springer, *My Thirty Years in Dodger Blue* (New York: Sports, 2004), 39.

18. Plaschke with Lasorda, *I Live for This*, 63, 168.

19. UPI, "'Bums' Speak Up," *Pacific Stars and Stripes*, October 2, 1976.

20. Newhan, "Dodgers Get Their Man."

21. John Hall, "The New Man," *Los Angeles Times*, January 13, 1977.

22. Ross Newhan, "Now the Dodgers Know Where They Stand," *Los Angeles Times*, January 18, 1977.

23. Plaschke with Lasorda, *I Live for This*, 104.

24. Newhan, "Now the Dodgers Know."

25. UPI, "Dodgers Say Good-bye to Walt, but He Isn't Going Anywhere," *DeKalb (IL) Daily Chronicle*, December 9, 1976.

26. UPI, "Dodgers Say Good-bye."

4. Great Expectations, Everybody's Watching You

1. Buckner had 405 PAs in 1972, short of the 502 required to qualify for the batting title.

2. Ross Newhan, "Monday: The 4-Year Pitch," *Los Angeles Times*, January 12, 1977.

3. Ross Newhan, "Buckner on Trade: 'I Feel Like a Piece of Meat,'" *Los Angeles Times*, January 13, 1977.

4. Newhan, "Monday: The 4-Year Pitch."

5. Modern sabermetric thinking notwithstanding, fielding percentage was considered a vital stat in 1977. And while Dodger management was likely aware that other outfielders in the system were more talented in the field, the Dodgers hoped to find in Monday a balance between run production and power and decent-enough fielding.

6. Dave Distel, "It's 'Flag Day' as Cey Singles to Beat Cubs," *Los Angeles Times*, April 26, 1976.

7. Distel, "It's 'Flag Day.'"

8. Newhan, "Monday: The 4-Year Pitch."

9. In 1977 players and their families would stay in brand-new Spanish-style villas, which were situated around winding streets named after the Hall of Fame Dodger players of the past: Duke Snider Street, Jackie Robinson Avenue, Roy Campanella Boulevard, Sandy Koufax Lane. The wide array of features in the camp included the five-thousand-seat Holman Stadium, where the Dodgers played spring-training games; three additional full-size baseball fields, one of which had a battery of "Iron Mikes," or automatic pitching machines for players needing extra batting practice; a movie theater that showed a different film every night; an Olympic-size pool for players and their families; tennis and basketball courts; Ping-Pong and pool tables; a nine-hole golf course; and an eighteen-hole championship golf course called Dodger Pines. Despite the plentiful facilities at the Dodgers' camp, the location was still known for its intimacy. Orange groves, royal palm trees, and exotic species of flowering plants were a common feature of the landscaping. One *Sports Illustrated* writer called the place "a baseball training facility disguised as

an arboretum." According to another sportswriter from Pittsburgh who visited Vero Beach for the first time in 1977, the grounds were kept up as "meticulously as any condominium site in Florida." The writer was so taken by the Dodgers' camp that, despite his plans to tour all other training camps in Florida, he stayed in Vero Beach several additional days.

10. John Hall, "Spring Games," *Los Angeles Times*, March 18, 1977.

11. In 1976 the Dodgers had hit just 91 home runs, compared to the pennant-winning Cincinnati Reds' 141.

12. In 1976, for example, while playing with Class A Lodi, Westmoreland had committed nineteen errors in thirty-one games at third base.

13. Steve Brener, Fred Claire, and Bill Shumard, eds., *Dodgers '76 Media Guide* (Los Angeles: Los Angeles Dodgers, 1976).

14. George Vass, "These Rookies Are Tabbed 'Best Bets' of '77," *Baseball Digest*, March 1977.

15. Glenn Burke with Erik Sherman, *Out at Home: The Glenn Burke Story* (New York: Excel, 1995), 15.

5. The Land of Golden Dreams

1. "California: A State of Excitement," *Time*, November 7, 1969.

2. Tom Wolfe, *The Kandy-Kolored Tangerine-Flake Streamline Baby* (New York: Farrar, Straus, and Giroux, 1965), 88–89. Wolfe described how the challenge was thrown down in the California fashion, quoting one of the hot-rodders: "A guy goes up to another guy's car and looks it up and down like it has gangrene or something, and he says: 'You wanna go?' . . . Well, as soon as a few guys had challenged each other, everybody would ride out onto this stretch of Sepulveda Boulevard or the old divided highway, in Compton, and the guys would start dragging, one car on one side of the center line, the other car on the other. Go a quarter of a mile. It was wild. Some nights there'd be a thousand kids lining the road to watch, boys and girls, all sitting on the sides of their cars with the lights shining across the highway."

3. The pueblo's full name was el Pueblo de Nuestra Señora la Reina de los Ángeles del Río de Porciúncula (the Village of Our Lady, the Queen of the Angels of the Porziúncola River). It came from the name of the Italian city where Francis of Assisi established his Franciscan religious order.

4. The island of California was said to be populated only by Amazonian women who had "beautiful and robust bodies, and were brave and very strong" and whose weapons were golden "because there was no other metal in the island than gold." So when the Beach Boys, and Rivieras, and many other pop acts, sang relentlessly of the glowing golden sun over California and the bikini-clad girls who walked under the sun, they were merely continuing a centuries-long tradition.

5. *New York Times*, August 17, 1932. However, as C. Frank Zarnowski points out in his dissertation, "A Look at Olympic Costs" (Mount St. Mary's College [MD], 1982), the official report for the 1932 Olympics included "not one sentence" of financial information about the Games.

6. Also known as the Pasadena Freeway, or State Highway 110, the Arroyo Seco Parkway is still in use today, though it's considered outdated and somewhat dangerous.

7. One of them, a native of Harrisburg, Pennsylvania, named Bobby Troup, had had his songwriting career postponed for the duration while he served as the leader of the Marine Corps' Fifty-First Battalion Band. In 1946 Troup moved his family to California to pursue a songwriting and acting career. His first effort, a song called "(Get Your Kicks on) Route 66" that joyfully listed the place-names on the main highway that ran at the time from the Midwest to California, captured the imagination of a nation on the move.

8. Journalists and commentators praised the new California experience almost constantly in the postwar years with descriptions like "land of promise," a "unique" place, and a state where "old ways and traditions have their freest rein." Krise Granat May, *Golden State, Golden Youth* (Chapel Hill: University of North Carolina Press, 2002), 11.

9. May, *Golden State, Golden Youth*, 13.

10. Though family lore had long suggested that Tom's mother, Clara Farrington Fallon, had died after being beaten by her drunken husband, this central family tragedy actually had much deeper dimensions. That is, a recently discovered death certificate reveals that Clara died on August 20, 1926, at 10:30 p.m. of sepsis brought on by the self-induced abortion of what would have been the young woman's sixth child.

11. One of these families, who became friends with his own family, were Armenian immigrants named the Deukmejians. This family's oldest son, George, would, after finishing a law degree in 1952 and serving as an advocate in the army between 1953 and 1955, follow Fallon to California in 1955. Fallon remained friends with George Deukmejian as he began a career in California politics in the early 1960s and into the 1970s. Deukmejian would eventually become California's thirty-fifth governor, in 1983.

12. With an area of 20,105 square miles, San Bernardino County is the largest county by area in the contiguous United States.

13. Disney signed a contract with ABC TV to make use of the back catalog of his entertainment assets by airing a weekly Disney show. In return, ABC agreed to invest in Disney's park.

14. Morrison had been born in Utah in 1920 but moved to Southern California with his family when he was a teenager.

15. J. Gregory Payne and Scott C. Ratzan, *Tom Bradley, the Impossible Dream: A Biography* (Santa Monica CA: Roundtable, 1986), 4–5.

16. Bradley was one of only about a hundred black students at UCLA at the time, out of about seven thousand total students. A noted athlete who had grown up in Pasadena named Jackie Robinson would follow Bradley by enrolling at UCLA in 1940 and running track (as well as playing football, baseball, and basketball).

17. According to Bradley, Yorty was "no more than a part-time Mayor. Most of the time [he] wouldn't arrive until mid-morning, and then he was gone by mid-afternoon." Payne and Ratzan, *Tom Bradley*, 85.

18. Bernard Galm, "Interview of Thomas Bradley," UCLA Library Oral History Collection, September 6, 1978.

19. Payne and Ratzan, *Tom Bradley*, 111; Galm, "Interview of Thomas Bradley."

20. Galm, "Interview of Thomas Bradley."

6. We Were All Rookies Again

1. John Hall, "Still Bubbling," *Los Angeles Times*, April 3, 1977.

2. He would be released before the start of the regular season.

3. Hall, "Still Bubbling."

4. Newhan, "Now the Dodgers Know."

5. Newhan, "Now the Dodgers Know."

6. Newhan, "Now the Dodgers Know."

7. Burke had a hepatitis infection, and Rodriguez was struggling with a serious shoulder injury, from which he would not recover enough to play in the Major Leagues again.

8. Plaschke with Lasorda, *I Live for This*, 125.

9. Bill Shirley, "Everything's Jake," *Los Angeles Times*, March 6, 1977.

10. Bill Shirley, "Tom Lasorda Makes His First Cut—on Long Hair," *Los Angeles Times*, March 2, 1977.

11. Bill Shirley, "Is Tom Lasorda Contagious?," *Los Angeles Times*, March 10, 1977.

12. Don Merry, "Questions Surround Downing Signing," *Los Angeles Times*, March 15, 1977.

13. In 1976 a straight-up Sutton-for–Tom Seaver trade with the Mets had fallen through at the last minute.

14. Don Merry, "Unhappy? Sutton Won't Deny It," *Los Angeles Times*, March 17, 1977.

15. John Hall, "Silly Season," *Los Angeles Times*, March 22, 1977.

16. Merry, "Unhappy?"

17. In those five years, 1972 to 1976, Sutton had won 93 games, a total surpassed by only four other pitchers over the same period (Jim "Catfish" Hunter had 106 wins, Gaylord Perry 97, Luis Tiant 96, and Jim Palmer 94).

18. Garvey's six-year contract paid the first baseman $300,000 in 1977, the highest amount on the team, just above Sutton's $250,000 per year (for four years).

19. Don Merry, "Limp May Put Baker Out of Running," *Los Angeles Times*, March 19, 1977.

20. "Tommy John Is Ready to Play Out His Option," *Los Angeles Times*, March 2, 1977.

21. Don Sutton was set to earn $250,000 in 1977, while Charlie Hough was contracted for $80,000 in 1977, Doug Rau $125,000, and Tommy John $170,000.

7. The Game Has Gotten Worse

1. Hall, "Silly Season."

2. Glenn Miller, "125 Years: Spring Training Has Evolved from Drunk-Fest into Big Business," *Naples (FL) News*, February 10, 2013. Mack would go on to become a Hall of Fame manager-owner of the Philadelphia A's.

3. "John Hurls 6 Innings in 4–3 Dodger Loss," *Los Angeles Times*, March 22, 1977.

4. Charles Maher, "Kroc: Big Money Kills the Do-or-Die Spirit," *Los Angeles Times*, February 13, 1977.

5. Dave Distel, "Sparky on Baseball: Think of Loyalty, Fans," *Los Angeles Times*, February 10, 1977.

6. Hall, "Silly Season."

7. Free agency had been impossible in baseball for years because of a contract ploy, created by National League team executives in 1879, that was known as the "reserve clause." Because the biggest expense to ball teams in the struggling three-year-old National League at that time was player payroll, owners sought a way to keep player salaries from growing. The idea they hit on was to allow each team to "reserve" five players on its roster whom no other team could attempt to sign.

8. AP, "Silver Anniversary: Baseball Salaries Have Skyrocketed since 1975 Ruling," *Sports Illustrated*, December 23, 2000, http://sportsillustrated.cnn.com/baseball/mlb/news/2000/12/22/free_agency_ap/ (site discontinued).

9. Distel, "Sparky on Baseball."

10. Players didn't object to the new "reserve clause" at first. Because teams reserved their best five players, being chosen as such was thought to be a great honor. Gradually, owners expanded the reserve practice—raising the number of reserved players to eleven in 1883, twelve in 1886, and fourteen in 1887. Also in 1887 owners wrote the so-called reserve clause into the standard player contract for the first time. The clause stipulated, essentially, that all players were now bound to their team for their entire careers, unless the team decided otherwise. And thus, over just eight years, and before those affected could even react, the basic legal status of professional baseball players was completely transformed; owners had taken a fairly innocuous practice of "reserving" a few untouchable players on each team and, right under the noses of the players, created a system of lifetime indenture.

11. John Montgomery Ward, "Is the Base-Ball Player a Chattel?," *Lippincott's Monthly Magazine* 40, no. 21 (1887).

12. Other attempts to organize players in the first half of the twentieth century included the Players' Protective Association in 1900 and the Fraternity of Professional Baseball Players of America in 1912. In 1946 Robert F. Murphy formed the American Baseball Guild, the fourth attempt to establish a viable players union. Despite general support for the guild's goals, players remained reluctant to sign on. After an attempt to unionize all the players from one small-market, low-payroll team—the Pittsburgh Pirates—went nowhere, Murphy's guild folded after only one season.

13. Distel, "Sparky on Baseball."

14. What is often forgotten is that the case, *Flood v. Kuhn*, failed on appeal in the Supreme Court in 1972. The only direct result of the case and Flood's holdout was that it effectively ended the outfielder's playing career.

15. Jane Leavy, *Koufax: A Lefty's Legacy* (New York: Harper Perennial, 2003), 204.

16. The Dodgers' overall attendance in 1965, which was the best in the league at more than 2.5 million, would fall off by nearly 1 million fans (to about only 1.6 million) in 1967, the first year after Koufax's retirement.

17. Leavy, *Koufax: A Lefty's Legacy*, 205.

18. Dave McNally, an aging former Oriole pitcher who had been traded against his will to Montreal at the end of the 1974 season, was also included in the eventual appeal to the arbitration panel. McNally, knowing his arm was done, had no real intention of playing again, but the players association asked him to add his name to the grievance, and he agreed. He stayed with the grievance even after baseball owners offered him a bonus of twenty-five thousand dollars just to remove his name.

19. "Messersmith, McNally: Far Away from Free Agency's Beginnings," *The Sporting News*, February 9, 1987.

20. The owners, incensed, fired Seitz and then moved to appeal the decision in federal court. They hoped to wait out Messersmith and the players association, and the case dragged into the new year. On February 4, 1976, the Seitz decision was upheld in a federal district court, and the owners appealed to a federal appeals court in St. Louis. In the meantime, with players balking at signing a new collective-bargaining agreement, the owners ordered a player lockout on March 1, putting a stop to spring training before it could even begin. The lockout would last seventeen days. On March 10, 1976, the federal court in St. Louis upheld the Seitz decision, and, with owners deciding against further appeal, Messersmith and McNally were at last free to sign with whichever team they chose. On March 18 Kuhn ended the owners' lockout by ordering spring-training camps open.

21. Don Drysdale, the Dodgers' great ace before Sutton, held the team record for opening-day pitching starts, with seven between 1958 and 1969. Sutton, who would pitch his sixth in 1977, may well have had his eye on that record, as well as several others held by Drysdale (such as all-time Dodger leader in wins, career strikeouts, innings pitched, and shutouts). "They are not that important because they are records," Sutton said a day after being named opening-day starter, "but because of the man who holds them. When you think of Don Drysdale you think of endurance, longevity, intensity, and consistency. I'd like to be thought of along the same line." Don Merry, "Sutton's Place," *Los Angeles Times*, March 31, 1977.

8. But You Can Never Leave

1. California's El Dorado County today encompasses the "gold country" of the Sierra Nevada and its foothills. It is in this county where, at Sutter's Mill, gold was "discovered" in 1848.

2. Sherley Hunter, *Why Los Angeles Will Become the World's Greatest City* (Los Angeles: H. J. Mallen, 1923). Hunter was a prominent Los Angeles–based advertising copywriter.

3. Art Seidenbaum, "Implausible Dream—L.A.," *Los Angeles Times*, February 1, 1978.

4. Without the "warmth and the reliable sun," *L.A. Times* columnist Art Seidenbaum explained in 1978, "movies would never have come to settle their own fantasies here." Seidenbaum, "Implausible Dream—L.A."

5. Film director Roman Polanski, who came to the region in the late 1960s from his native Poland (via London), agreed with these notions. "Everything is easy here [in Los Angeles]," he said in an interview before 1969. "You want to learn karate, you can learn karate. You want to play chess, you can play chess. You want to drive racing cars, you can drive racing cars. Everything is accessible in this town."

6. Jack Slater, "Possessed by the Hollywood Dream," *Los Angeles Times*, June 20, 1976.

7. Harry Carr, *Los Angeles—City of Dreams* (New York: D. Appleton–Century, 1935), 264.

8. Seidenbaum, "Implausible Dream—L.A."

9. Erik Davis, *Visionary State: A Journey through California's Spiritual Landscape* (San Francisco: Chronicle, 2006), 8.

10. Sometimes the frustrated California dreamer became the tragic catalyst of disaster. Cultist Krishna Venta, who claimed he'd stepped off a rocket ship from an extinct planet called Neophrates, would end up killed in a 1958 bombing likely instigated by several former followers. In the 1960s and '70s various doomed militant groups and fringe factions thrived in California, including, most notoriously, the Weather Underground, the Symbionese Liberation Army, the Manson "Family," and Jim Jones's People Temple.

11. In 1969 *Time*, even in the midst of its long, glowing feature on the California lifestyle, presciently interviewed numerous people about the area's troublesome air quality. The reporter found one young woman who had set up a table at the Van Nuys Shopping Center with information about various clean-air advocacy groups: the Clean-Air Council, the Right to Clean Air, People Pledged to Clean Air, and Stamp Out Smog (SOS). "Right now," she told the *Time* reporter, "there are 10,000 people in the state getting petitions signed against smog. The people of Southern California are madder than hell." Meanwhile, just a few miles away in the San Fernando Valley, a woman named Joan Adkins had also been fighting smog for twelve years. "I have to put cream in my nasal passages, but sometimes my nose swells up anyway. . . . And I have to keep washing out my eyes. You know, they say that smog can affect your mental outlook, damage the brain." "Candide Camera: In Search of the Soul," *Time*, November 7, 1969.

12. A subject fictionalized in the 1974 film *Chinatown*, written by Los Angeles native Robert Towne and directed by Roman Polanski.

13. "Laboratory in the Sun: The Past as Future," *Time*, November 7, 1969.

14. Mike Davis, *City of Quartz* (New York: Verso, 1990), 131.

15. "Whatever Happened to California?," *Time*, July 18, 1977.

16. California's Family Law Act of 1969.

17. "Whatever Happened to California?"

18. Bernard Galm, "Interview of Thomas Bradley: Tape Number VI, Side Two," UCLA Oral History Collection, April 13, 1979.

19. Payne and Ratzan, *Tom Bradley*, 168. Of course, members of his press team found Bradley's low-key approach endlessly frustrating.

20. Two years later Phyllis Bradley would be arrested for possession of marijuana and amphetamines. Later charges would include shoplifting, more drug charges, and several felony crimes. In the 1980s, after a ten-year string of arrests, Phyllis finally underwent drug treatment and began to turn her life around.

21. Payne and Ratzan, *Tom Bradley*, 191.

9. Hollywood Stars and Blue Hard Hats

1. John Hall, "Curtain Up," *Los Angeles Times*, April 5, 1977.

2. Don Merry, "36,732 See Angels Lose to the Dodgers," *Los Angeles Times*, April 3, 1977.

3. Hall, "Still Bubbling."

4. Don Merry, "Lasorda's Dodgers Test the Count When It Counts," *Los Angeles Times*, April 7, 1977.

5. Don Merry, "The Dodger Image," *Los Angeles Times*, April 3, 1977.

6. In the team's early years in Los Angeles Walter O'Malley had hired a Hollywood producer, Mervyn LeRoy, during the team's push to get a ballpark built. Among other marketing tactics, LeRoy created a scale model of Dodger Stadium that showed the comfort and beauty of the place.

7. Jeane Hoffman, "Celebrities on Hand," *Los Angeles Times*, April 19, 1958.

8. When Koufax and Drysdale ended their holdout and returned to the team for the 1966 season, the film was made without either of the ballplayers.

9. *All That Glitters* was a satire that presented a world in which women ruled as the "stronger sex" and men were objectified. It starred Eileen Brennan, Chuck McCann, and Linda Gray, who played a transgender character named Linda Murkland, said to be the first such character to appear as a series regular on American television.

10. Charles Maher, "Acting Gets Rise Out of Ex-Dodger," *Los Angeles Times*, May 26, 1977. The show was panned by critics. *Time* called it "embarrassingly amateurish," with "flaccid" jokes, flat writing, "mediocre" acting, and "aimless" direction. It was canceled after only thirteen episodes. Parker would land a recurring role on the TV series *Police Woman* (1975–78) and appear in two TV movies and one feature movie—*Cry from the Mountain* (1985)—but that would be the bulk of his Hollywood career.

11. Plaschke with Lasorda, *I Live for This*, 129, 130.

12. The home opener at Dodger Stadium in 1977 was an afternoon game, which was something of an unusual occurrence in L.A. The last time the Dodgers' home opener had been an afternoon game was in 1962, the year of the first home opener ever held at the brand-new Dodger Stadium.

13. Dave Distel, "Sparky on Baseball: Think of Loyalty, Fans," *Los Angeles Times*, February 10, 1977; Merry, "Lasorda's Dodgers Test the Count."

14. Don Merry, "Cey Cheers His Manager," *Los Angeles Times*, April 8, 1977.

15. Don Merry, "Reggie Smith Turns a Nemesis into a Soft Touch," *Los Angeles Times*, April 16, 1977.

16. Don Merry, "Battery Sparks Dodgers' 5–0 Victory over Giants," *Los Angeles Times*, April 17, 1977.

17. Don Merry, "Even in Trouble, Dodgers Win," *Los Angeles Times*, April 21, 1977.

18. Anderson's bitterness came from an honest place. Having grown up in the Los Angeles area, he had been signed by the Dodgers and played in the team's farm system for nearly five seasons before being traded to Philadelphia at age twenty-four.

19. Don Merry, "Sutton Gives Lasorda an Opening, 5–1," *Los Angeles Times*, April 8, 1977; John Hall, "So Help Me," *Los Angeles Times*, April 11, 1977.

20. Ron Fimrite, "'God May Be a Football Fan,'" *Sports Illustrated*, July 12, 1982.

21. Plaschke with Lasorda, *I Live for This*, 125.

22. Larry Keith, "In L.A., It's Up, Up and Away with Cey," *Sports Illustrated*, May 16, 1977.

23. Cey's father owned several service stations in the Tacoma area.

24. Keith, "Away with Cey."

25. Keith, "Away with Cey."

26. "Can Dodgers Match Nickname?," *Los Angeles Times*, May 7, 1977. This letter appears to be the first time the nickname appeared in print. Interestingly, the nickname would fade a few years later and get picked up by another team, the New York Giants football teams that won Super Bowls in 1986 and 1990.

27. "Can Dodgers Match Nickname?"

10. A John Wayne Kind of Adventure

Epigraph: Peter Biskind, *Easy Riders, Raging Bulls: How the Sex-Drugs-and-Rock 'n Roll Generation Saved Hollywood* (New York: Simon & Schuster, 1998), 318.

1. "Ho, ho, ho" was Lasorda's response to the attack. John Hall, "The Brawlers," *Los Angeles Times*, March 27, 1977.

2. "Dodger Notes," *Los Angeles Times*, May 27, 1977.

3. Don Merry, "Dodgers Explode for 17 Hits and Rout Reds, 10–3," *Los Angeles Times*, May 28, 1977; Ross Newhan, "The Reds Having Second Thoughts," *Los Angeles Times*, May 28, 1977.

4. Merry, "Dodgers Explode."

5. Bean continued: "It was an honor to play for one of the all-time great baseball field generals . . . So it was with a lump in my throat that I knocked on his

office door inside the clubhouse in Pittsburgh after the big trade. 'Hello, Mr. Lasorda. I'm Billy Bean,' I declared with all the authority I could muster. Tommy may have achieved the status of a movie star, but he sure didn't look the part. A white-haired Italian, he was as bow-legged as an old cowboy. . . . 'How ya doin' kid?'" Billy Bean, *Going the Other Way: Lessons from a Life in and Out of Major League Baseball* (New York: Da Capo, 2004), 110–11.

6. Hall, "The Brawlers."

7. Don Merry, "Reds Win One, 6–3, and Hope It's a Start," *Los Angeles Times*, May 29, 1977; Don Merry, "Reds Want to Make It a Math Race," *Los Angeles Times*, May 30, 1977.

8. Don Merry, "Astros Deal Dodgers 4th Loss in a Row," *Los Angeles Times*, June 1, 1977; Don Merry, "Dodgers' Third Loss in Row No Problem—Lopes," *Los Angeles Times*, May 31, 1977.

9. Disappointed by the portrayal, Wayne wrote a letter to the film's star, a younger actor named Clint Eastwood. "That isn't what the West was all about," Wayne wrote. "That isn't the American people who settled this country." Peter Biskind, "Any Which Way He Can," *Premiere*, April 1993.

10. Wayne would succumb to illness in 1979, dying of stomach cancer at the UCLA Medical Center on June 11.

11. Patrick Goldstein, foreword to *Hollywood, Beverly Hills, and Other Perversities: Pop Culture of the 1970s and 1980s*, by George Rose (Berkeley CA: Ten Speed Press, 2008), 7; Biskind, *Easy Riders, Raging Bulls*, 22.

12. Paul Scanlon, "George Lucas: The Wizard of *Star Wars*," *Rolling Stone*, August 1977.

13. Scanlon, "George Lucas"; Michael Kaminski, *The Secret History of "Star Wars"* (Kingston ON: Legacy Books, 2008), 19. There were also practical reasons for Lucas to seek more general audiences for his film. "When I finished *American Graffiti*, again I was broke," Lucas said. "I had got paid twice what I made for THX—$20,000 for *Graffiti*—but it took me two years to do it. . . . So by the time I was finished, I was out of money again. . . . I said, 'I've got to get another picture going here—just to survive.' So that's when I decided that I wanted to do a children's film."

14. "I was writing the first Star Wars," Lucas said, "because it was soon after Nixon's presidency, and there was a point, right before he was thrown out of office, where he suggested that they change a constitutional amendment so that he could run for a third term. Even when he started getting into trouble, he was saying 'If the military will back me, I'll stay in office.' His idea was: 'To hell with Congress and potential impeachment. I'll go directly to the army, and between the army and myself, I'll continue to be president.' That is what happens here. An emergency in the Republic leads the Senate to make Palpatine, essentially, 'dictator for life.'" Kaminski, *Secret History of "Star Wars,"* 95.

15. Lucas's film changed drastically between the various draft versions. First there were too many characters, then too few. The plot was too simple, then too

complex. Princess Leia's role grew bigger, then smaller. Obi-Wan Kenobi and Darth Vader, initially one character, became two. The Force got a good side (originally called Ashla) and a bad side (Bogan). A character named Annikin Starkiller became Luke Skywalker. Kenobi began life as an elderly general, became an addled hermit, and then was an elderly general again. A "Kiber Crystal" appeared, then disappeared, and so on.

16. The shooting of *Star Wars* was as difficult as the writing. Production fell behind schedule due to freak rainstorms (in the Tunisian desert) and malfunctioning equipment. Lucas's waffling directorial style frustrated the cast and crew. "I had a terrible time; it was very unpleasant," Lucas said. "I spent all my time yelling and screaming at people, and I have never had to do that before." The project was so demanding that Lucas developed hypertension. When Lucas showed an early cut of the film to his filmmaker friends—Brian DePalma, Francis Ford Coppola, and Steven Spielberg, among others—most were not impressed. (Only Spielberg, reportedly, saw the potential of the film.) And there were more complications. By late 1976 hundreds of uncompleted special-effects scenes remained unfinished, a fact that forced a delay in the film's release. But Lucas never gave up on his film, and, finally, on May 25, 1977, *Star Wars* opened. Kaminski, *Secret History of "Star Wars,"* 137–38.

17. "Viewpoint: Letters," *Los Angeles Times*, June 4, 1977.

18. Don Merry, "The Man in Center," *Los Angeles Times*, March 24, 1977.

19. Don Merry, "Expos Have the Last Word, 6–2," *Los Angeles Times*, May 2, 1977.

20. Don Merry, "Lasorda Pep Talk Pays Off, Dodgers Win," *Los Angeles Times*, June 2, 1977.

21. Don Merry, "Home at the Top," *Los Angeles Times*, June 9, 1977.

22. Don Merry, "Buckner Takes Some of His Frustration Out on Dodgers," *Los Angeles Times*, June 7, 1977; Don Merry, "Cubs Beat Dodgers and Franks Tees Off," *Los Angeles Times*, June 8, 1977.

23. "Smith Nearly Goes Up the Wall," *Los Angeles Times*, June 9, 1977.

24. Don Merry, "Suddenly It's 7½; Lasorda 'Concerned,'" *Los Angeles Times*, June 13, 1977.

25. "Dodger Notes," *Los Angeles Times*, June 16, 1977.

26. Biskind, *Easy Riders, Raging Bulls*, 343.

27. As Lucas recalled *Star Wars*' opening weekend in a later magazine interview: "I was mixing sound [in Hollywood] on foreign versions of the film the day it opened here," he said. "I had been working so hard that, truthfully, I forgot the film was being released that day. My wife [and I] . . . ran off across the street from the Chinese Theatre—and there was a huge line around the block. I said, 'What's that?' I had forgotten completely, and I really couldn't believe it. But I had planned a vacation as soon as I finished, and I'm glad I did because I really didn't want to be around for all the craziness that happened after that." Kaminski, *Secret History of "Star Wars,"* 147–48.

28. Lee Grant, "'Star Wars' Out of This World," *Los Angeles Times*, June 4, 1977.

29. Roger Ebert, *The Great Movies* (New York: Broadway Books, 2002), 431.

30. Interestingly, this franchising bonanza came about nearly by accident. Initially, few toy companies saw the potential in turning the film's characters and visual elements into kids' toys. Only a small concern, Kenner Toys, took a chance at producing *Star Wars* figures after other toy companies passed on the opportunity. The three-and-three-quarter-inch plastic "action figures" that Kenner produced for *Star Wars* were not available in markets until well after Christmas 1977, but thanks to clever marketing presale buzz was widespread.

31. Biskind, *Easy Riders, Raging Bulls*, 316.

32. Don Merry, "Cey's Streak Ends but Not the Dodgers,'" *Los Angeles Times*, July 5, 1977.

11. Heroes and Villains

1. Widely quoted.

2. Because of the season's length Updike professed the belief that the intermittent individual heroics of players—the three-RBI game, the hitting streak, the ten-inning shutout, the game-winning grand slam—were of less importance ultimately than players dedicated to craft, "players who . . . care, that is to say, about themselves and their art." As an example, Updike held up the great Red Sox slugger Ted Williams. John Updike, "Hub Fans Bid Kid Adieu," *New Yorker*, October 22, 1960.

3. Widely quoted.

4. Jim Bouton, *Ball Four: The Final Pitch* (North Egremont MA: Bulldog, 2000), 406.

5. Merry, "Lasorda Pep Talk."

6. The Dodgers made room on their roster by placing veteran pitcher Al Downing on the disabled list. Downing, who had played with the Dodgers since 1971 and was perhaps best known for giving up Hank Aaron's 715th home run, was nursing a groin-pull injury at the time. His release on July 21 effectively ended the left-hander's pitching career. "If the Dodgers didn't feel I could help them," the thirty-six-year-old Downing said on hearing the news, "it's probably better for me I'm gone. . . . I've enjoyed my seven years here. It will continue to be my home. But life goes on. You turn the page and start and new chapter." "Dodger Notes," *Los Angeles Times*, July 22, 1977.

7. "Dodger Notes," *Los Angeles Times*, June 23, 1977.

8. Asked if Anderson's move was surprising, considering that the Reds' manager had often accused Sutton of cheating by doctoring the ball, Sutton said, "Not really. I think he respects me as a pitcher and I respect him as a manager. He has to protect his team. If I were him I'd do the same thing." "Dodger Notes," *Los Angeles Times*, July 14, 1977.

9. Charles Maher, "'I Wanted to Be Reggie Smith,'" *Los Angeles Times*, June 6, 1977; "Dodger Notes," *Los Angeles Times*, May 28, 1977; Maher, "'I Wanted to Be Reggie Smith.'"

10. UPI, "Dream Game Is a Dream Game for Don Sutton," *Los Angeles Times*, July 19, 1977; "Quotebook," *Los Angeles Times*, July 20, 1977.

11. The team's overall ERA on July 17, the Sunday before the All-Star Game, was a league-best 3.53, a fact that thus far had been mostly overlooked as fans and media fixated on the Dodgers' potent lineup.

12. Note that this was before the era of single-inning relief specialists.

13. "Viewpoint: Letters," *Los Angeles Times*, July 16, 1977.

14. Mal Florence, "Hough Takes Some Raps and the Rap," *Los Angeles Times*, July 11, 1977.

15. Garvey's 4,277,735 vote total was better than the next-highest vote getter, Joe Morgan, by nearly 1 million votes.

16. Jim Murray, "Garvey: Part Village Smithy, Popeye, Gehrig," *Los Angeles Times*, April 20, 1975.

17. Murray, "Garvey: Part Village Smithy."

18. Sportswriters sometimes called him "Popeye," and cartoons in the paper always accentuated the feature. "With those arms," said Sparky Anderson, "he doesn't even need a bat. He could 'fist' the ball off the wall on you." Murray, "Garvey: Part Village Smithy."

19. Roy Blount Jr., "Born to Be a Dodger," *Sports Illustrated*, April 7, 1975.

20. Garvey and Hamill were actually just a few years apart in age.

21. Cynthia Garvey with Andy Meisler, *The Secret Life of Cyndy Garvey* (New York: St. Martin's, 1989), 171.

22. Rick Reilly, "America's Sweetheart," *Sports Illustrated*, November 8, 1989.

23. Garvey with Meisler, *Secret Life of Cyndy Garvey*, 136.

24. Jim Murray, "Sour Smell of Success," *Los Angeles Times*, July 6, 1975.

25. Jeff Prugh, "Dodgers Win One and Deny Dissension," *Los Angeles Times*, July 1, 1975.

26. John Hall, "So Help Me," *Los Angeles Times*, July 6, 1977.

12. Dog Days in Dogtown

1. "Environment: The Great Western Drought of 1977," *Time*, March 7, 1977. According to the U.S. Geological Society, 1976–77 would end up as the driest two years in California's recorded history, though scientific records would show that much more severe drought had plagued the region in the distant past. Excerpt from R. W. Paulson et al., comps., "National Water Summary 1988–89—Hydrologic Events and Floods and Droughts: U.S. Geological Survey Water-Supply Paper 2375" (1989), 59, http://geochange.er.usgs.gov/sw/impacts/hydrology/state_fd/cawater1.html.

2. Ross Newhan, "In the Other Race, Cey Presses Garvey," *Los Angeles Times*, August 3, 1977.

3. Ross Newhan, "Garvey's Numbers Game Is 'Shocking,'" *Los Angeles Times*, August 24, 1977.

4. John Hall, "The Gallery," *Los Angeles Times*, August 16, 1977; Newhan, "Garvey's Numbers Game."

5. Newhan, "Garvey's Numbers Game."

6. Paul Dickson, *The Dickson Baseball Dictionary*, 3rd ed. (New York: W. W. Norton, 2011), 795.

7. Widely quoted.

8. Herman Weiskopf, "Baseball's Week," *Sports Illustrated*, June 19, 1967; "Insiders Say," *The Sporting News*, June 20, 1970.

9. *Talkin' Baseball: Baseball Quotes*, http://www.baseball-vault.com/baseball-quotes.shtml.

10. "Roller-Coaster to Nowhere," *Time*, August 29, 1977.

11. Jimmy Carter, "The President's Proposed Energy Policy, 18 April 1977," *Vital Speeches of the Day* 33, no. 14 (1977): 418–20.

12. The drought would not officially end until the following winter, when a series of monsoon-like storms inundated the region with water.

13. The Right Stuff

1. Ron Kantkowski, "Q+A Steve Yeager," *Las Vegas Sun*, April 6, 2006.

2. In 1973 Chuck Yeager had in fact come back in the public limelight, after a period of semiobscurity, for his myriad accomplishments in American aeronautics in the years leading up to the establishment of America's space program. This was thanks in part to articles that Tom Wolfe wrote on the program back in early 1973, over four issues of *Rolling Stone*. Titled collectively "Post-orbital Remorse," the first of four parts began with an examination of the conditions of the astronauts, and of the space program itself, during the launch of the final mission in the country's moon travel program, Apollo 17.

3. Yeager would, in fact, become famous several years later for appearing nude in *Playgirl*. His team nicknames would tell you all you need to know about Yeager: "Yang" and "Boomer."

4. The wedding was held there at the suggestion of Mayor Bradley's wife, Ethel, who was a huge Dodger fan. Kantkowski, "Q+A Steve Yeager."

5. Kantkowski, "Q+A Steve Yeager."

6. Widely quoted.

7. Allen E. Hye, *The Great God Baseball: Religion in Modern Baseball Fiction* (Macon GA: Mercer University Press, 2004), 6; Wayne Stewart and Roger Kahn, *The Gigantic Book of Baseball Quotations* (New York: Skyhorse, 2007), 34; Joe Garagiola, *Baseball Is a Funny Game* (Philadelphia: Lippincott, 2005); Jonathan Fraser, *Light: The Cultural Encyclopedia of Baseball*, 2nd ed. (Jefferson NC: McFarland, 2005), 149.

8. Tom Wolfe, "Post-orbital Remorse: The Brotherhood of the Right Stuff," *Rolling Stone*, January 4, 1973.

9. Tom Wolfe, "Post-orbital Remorse, Part Two: How the Astronauts Fell from Cowboy Heaven," *Rolling Stone*, January 18, 1973.

10. John Hall, "Spring Games," *Los Angeles Times*, March 18, 1977.

11. Ross Newhan, "Yeager 'Hit-No-Run' Victim in 2–1 Victory," *Los Angeles Times*, August 25, 1977.

12. Tom Lasorda with David Fisher, *The Artful Dodger* (New York: Avon, 1986), 268.

13. His record at the end of August was just 9-7.

14. Scott Ostler, "Garvey Comes Blasting Out of Slump," *Los Angeles Times*, August 29, 1977.

15. "Dodger Notes," *Los Angeles Times*, August 31, 1977.

16. That the request would go nowhere with the council did not detract from the support Bradley offered the Dodgers, reflecting the feelings of the majority of the citizens of Los Angeles.

17. "Morning Briefing," *Los Angeles Times*, September 10, 1977.

18. Ross Newhan, "John Clinches It with 19th Win," *Los Angeles Times*, September 21, 1977.

14. Gonna Fly Now

1. The modern World Series, a contest between the champions of the two modern Major Leagues—National and American—was first played in 1903. But the roots of this series go back to at least the 1880s, when a final "World Championship Series" was played between the National League champion and the American Association champion.

2. John Hall, "So Help Me," *Los Angeles Times*, October 3, 1977.

3. Tommy John with Dan Valenti, *My Twenty-Six Years in Baseball* (New York: Bantam, 1992), 214.

4. On September 26 John would get his twentieth win, the first time he had reached that milestone in his career. For the season he would finish second to Carlton in the Cy Young Award balloting.

5. Ross Newhan, "Dodgers Beaten; Sutton Likes Playoff Chances," *Los Angeles Times*, Sept. 24, 1977.

6. Starting in the mid-1940s Ozark had played eighteen years in the Dodgers' farm system, reaching the AAA level several times but never appearing in the Major Leagues. In 1956 he became a player-manager for the team's A team in Wichita Falls and worked his way to manage the AAA team in Spokane. From 1965 to 1972 Ozark was a coach under Walt Alston. He took over the managerial job of last-place Philadelphia in 1973, and, in 1976, he led the Phillies to their first playoff appearance in twenty-six years.

7. Don Merry, "Phils Glad—Won't See Reds," *Los Angeles Times*, October 2, 1977.

8. Charles Maher, "Russell Makes No Alibis for His Key Errors," *Los Angeles Times*, October 5, 1977.

9. The Phillies' home record in 1977 was 60-21.

10. Don Merry, "Cey's Home Run Shakes but Doesn't Rattle Phils," *Los Angeles Times*, October 5, 1977.

11. Maher, "Russell Makes No Alibis."

12. John Hall, "The Leader," *Los Angeles Times*, October 6, 1977.

13. Hall, "The Leader."

14. John with Valenti, *My Twenty-Six Years*, 215.

15. Charles Maher, "Lasorda Lays It On, Slice by Slice," *Los Angeles Times*, October 6, 1977.

16. Mitchell Nathanson, *The Fall of the 1977 Phillies* (Jefferson NC: McFarland, 2008), 198.

17. Charles Maher, "Lasorda Doesn't Sound Like a Happy Winner," *Los Angeles Times*, October 9, 1977.

18. Maher, "Lasorda Doesn't Sound."

19. Jackson, years later in his account of the 1977–78 seasons, had a lot to say about being benched by Martin in Game Five of the American League Championship Series. "He told the press it was because I didn't hit Paul Splittorff. . . . It was true I didn't have a great season against him. He was a good left-hander, a mainstay of their staff, great control. Counting the first game of the playoffs, that year I was 2–12 against him, although I hit a double and home run as a Yankee against him, in Kansas City. But he pitched all of us tough. That year he was 3–0 against us. . . . I honestly didn't know what Billy thought he was trying to do. I don't know if he was trying to make a statement, show he could win it all without me. . . . What was Billy thinking? I don't know. At this point, I didn't know, and I didn't care why." Reggie Jackson with Kevin Baker, *Becoming Mr. October* (New York: Doubleday, 2013), 147.

20. William Mead, *The Official New York Yankees Hater's Handbook* (New York: Putnam, 1983), 9.

21. Michael Shapiro, *Bottom of the Ninth: Branch Rickey, Casey Stengel, and the Daring Scheme to Save Baseball from Itself* (New York: St. Martin's Griffin, 2010), 83. The A's general manager, Parke Carroll, was in on the take. Carroll had once worked for the Yankees and once suggested it didn't matter that his A's were forever abysmal—as long as the Yankees won.

22. Roy Terrell, "Yankee Secrets," *Sports Illustrated*, June 22, 1957.

23. Baseball's commissioner Ford Frick, as *Sports Illustrated* explained, testified before the congressional committee, suggesting that collusion did not exist in this case. "Whether the committee was satisfied, no one is exactly sure," the magazine reported. "After listening to Mr. Frick's testimony, they just looked blank." Terrell, "Yankee Secrets."

24. Shapiro, *Bottom of the Ninth*, 66.

25. Both widely quoted.

26. Robert W. Creamer, *Babe: The Legend Comes to Life* (New York: Simon and Schuster, 1974), 270.

27. Widely quoted.

28. Jimmy Breslin, *Can't Anybody Here Play This Game? The Improbable Saga of the Mets' First Year* (Chicago: Ivan R. Dee, 2002), 80.

29. All of this is chronicled in Jonathan Mahler's 2005 book, *Ladies and Gentlemen, the Bronx Is Burning: 1977, Baseball, Politics, and the Battle for the Soul of a City* (New York: Farrar, Straus, and Giroux, 2005).

30. No facial hair except mustaches and no hair below the collar.

15. Klieg Lights, Smoke Bombs, and Three Massive Bombshells

1. Jim Murray, "Dodgers Face Baseball's Version of Krupp Works," *Los Angeles Times*, October 11, 1977.

2. Mike Downey, "The Stories Never Stopped, but Neither Did the Abuse," *Los Angeles Times*, June 9, 1995. Mantle's account is a rollicking one, but it seems somewhat exaggerated. According to official records, the game in question, an 8–5 Yankee win, occurred on May 21, 1956. There is no record of an actual fight, however, or of Lasorda knocking down Martin. According to an account by Peter Golenbock, "Martin was involved in a shouting match on the field in Kansas City. Yankee pitcher Don Larson [had] brushed back outfield Harry Simpson of the A's. In the eighth inning A's pitcher Tom Lasorda brushed back Hank Bauer. The next pitch went at Bauer's head. Martin started to run from the dugout onto the field when three Yankees held him back. Martin was swearing at Lasorda, threatening him. With Mantle at bat, Martin made another threat, Lasorda walked over to the Yankee dugout, 'Come on,' Lasorda yelled at Martin. The umpires kept them apart." When Lasorda faced Martin in the top half of the ninth inning, Martin was called out on strikes. Peter Golenbock, *Wild, High and Tight* (New York: St. Martin's, 1994), 108.

3. Ross Newhan, "Series: Once More with Feeling," *Los Angeles Times*, October 11, 1977.

4. Newhan, "Series: Once More."

5. Murray, "Dodgers Face Krupp Works."

6. Charles Maher, "Ump Was Out of Position to Make the Call—Garvey," *Los Angeles Times*, October 12, 1977.

7. Maher, "Ump Out of Position."

8. Interestingly, Nestor Chylak was the home plate umpire in that series, in the town where he would nearly get brained by a bottle thrower just a few years later.

9. Charles Maher, "The Bleachers' Heavy Artillery Was on Target," *Los Angeles Times*, October 13, 1977.

10. Ross Newhan, "Should Billy Have Let the Cat Out?," *Los Angeles Times*, October 13, 1977; Ross Newhan, "Martin Says He'll Manage without Jackson's Help," *Los Angeles Times*, October 14, 1977.

11. Newhan, "Martin Says He'll Manage."

12. "Morning Briefing," *Los Angeles Times*, October 15, 1977.

13. Charles Maher, "Baker: 'We Ain't Losing . . . We're Just Behind," *Los Angeles Times*, October 15, 1977.

14. "Color Their Mood Blue . . . as in Dodger Blue," *Los Angeles Times*, October 16, 1977.

15. Charles Maher, "Lasorda's Talk Lifts Dodgers," *Los Angeles Times*, October 17, 1977.

16. "Color Their Mood Blue," *Los Angeles Times*.

17. Bill Shirley, "The Dodgers Win Another Night in the Bronx," *Los Angeles Times*, October 17, 1977.

18. Don Merry, "Sutton Thinks It Will Go Seven," *Los Angeles Times*, October 17, 1977.

19. UPI, "Callers Threaten Garvey, Lopes," *Los Angeles Times*, October 19, 1977.

20. Jackson with Baker, *Becoming Mr. October*, 181.

Interlude

1. Jackson's three-homer game was not the first in World Series history. "Babe Ruth had hit three home runs in a single World Series game," Jonathan Mahler pointed out in his book *Ladies and Gentlemen*, 337. In fact, Ruth had done it twice. Still, Jackson's feat was unique in that he did it on three consecutive pitches.

2. Mahler, *Ladies and Gentlemen*, 337; Mike Gonring, "Jackson's Incredible Show Ends Series," *Milwaukee Journal*, October 19, 1977.

3. Chuck Perazich, "It'll Be Reggie, Reggie, Reggie on the Label, Label, Label," *Youngstown (OH) Vindicator*, October 23, 1977.

4. Mahler, *Ladies and Gentlemen*, 338.

5. Dave Anderson, "Column," *Miami News*, February 6, 1978.

6. Jackson with Baker, *Becoming Mr. October*, 36–37.

7. Jackson with Baker, *Becoming Mr. October*, 37. While the Dodgers did put in a bid for Jackson in the free-agent "draft" that year, they never made an actual offer. "They laid back," Jackson said. "I never did find out why."

8. This disdain reached a head on June 18 of the year, during a nationally televised Saturday-afternoon game against the Boston Red Sox, when Martin, incensed that Jackson seemingly had loafed on a play, removed the outfielder midinning for bench player Paul Blair. When Jackson tried to confront Martin in the dugout, the two nearly came to blows.

9. This included bench coach Elston Howard, the catcher-outfielder who broke the Yankees' color barrier as a rookie in 1955. According to Howard's friend Yogi Berra, he was so put off by Jackson's habit of calling attention to himself that, when Jackson asked Howard one day how he would have fared on the great Yankees teams of the 1950s and '60s, Howard immediately deadpanned (much to Berra's delight): "Fifth outfielder." Harvey Araton, *Driving Mr. Yogi* (New York: Houghton Mifflin Harcourt, 2012), 33.

10. Jackson with Baker, *Becoming Mr. October*, 167.

11. John Hall, "Dodgers Explain Defeat with One Word—Reggie," *Los Angeles Times*, October 19, 1977.

12. Ken Rappoport, AP wire report, October 19, 1977; Hall, "Dodgers Explain Defeat."

13. Ross Newhan, "Lasorda: Yanks Champs but Dodgers Are Better," *Los Angeles Times*, October 20, 1977.

14. Robert J. Banning, "Letter to the Editor," *Los Angeles Times*, October 28, 1977; Ron Hart, "Reggie Jackson and Tom Lasorda Get Ugly in Fox Broadcast Booth," *Yahoo Contributor Network*, June 26, 2010, http://voices.yahoo.com/reggie-jackson-tommy-lasorda-6292096.htm (site discontinued).

15. "As soon as the word was out that you were going *up*, even before any official announcement, your life changed. You were no longer just another officer candidate. That was what an astronaut who had never been up really was: not an astronaut but an officer candidate. As soon as you were chosen you were a new person around the Manned Space Center and around Clear Lake. It was like election, salvation. You had just been certified by the powers that be as someone who officially possessed The Right Stuff." Tom Wolfe, "Post-orbital Remorse, Part Three: The Dark Night of the Ego," *Rolling Stone*, February 15, 1973.

16. Wolfe, "Post-orbital Remorse, Part Two."

17. Rappoport, AP wire report.

18. Cyndy Garvey claimed that there was a hidden spout on the bottom edge of the case.

19. Garvey with Meisler, *Secret Life of Cyndy Garvey*, 211–12.

20. Wolfe, "Post-orbital Remorse, Part Three."

21. Wolfe, "Post-orbital Remorse, Part Three."

22. Payne and Ratzan, *Tom Bradley*, 212–13.

16. Rediscovering Baseball

1. Roger Angell, "The Sporting Scene with Sudden Endings," *New Yorker*, November 14, 1977.

2. The mark shattered the previous league record of 2,755,184 fans, set by the Los Angeles Dodgers in 1962.

3. Baseball's following had risen 3 percent since 1974, while NFL Football, struggling with a lack of offensive scoring in its games and dominated in the 1970s by small-market teams like the Steelers, had fallen 3 percent over the same time period.

4. The only clear exception to the rule—the one team whose tickets sales had declined—were the Oakland A's, who found themselves with an owner who was, after selling off all of his star players, seeking to liquidate the franchise.

5. Charles Maher, "News of Baseball's Demise Is Greatly Exaggerated," *Los Angeles Times*, September 27, 1977.

6. Gordon Verrell, "Unity a Dodger Plus, Says Cey," *The Sporting News*, January 14, 1978.

7. Maher, "News of Baseball's Demise."

8. John with Valenti, *My Twenty-Six Years*, 221.

9. Verrell, "Unity a Dodger Plus." Cey had reason to be magnanimous. A few days after the interview, on January 15, his wife, Fran, would give birth to their second child, Amanda Beth Cey.

10. Verrell, "Unity a Dodger Plus."

11. Ross Newhan, "The Good Scout," *Los Angeles Times*, January 17, 1978.

12. Another version of Lasorda's ailment suggested he actually had contracted a case of food poisoning during his stay in Santo Domingo, where he was a celebrity at the local restaurants and cafés. *The Sporting News*, January 21, 1978.

13. Lasorda had to turn down an invitation to a White House prayer breakfast, though he did accept an invitation from Frank Sinatra to spend four days as his Palm Springs houseguest.

14. Newhan, "The Good Scout."

15. Newhan, "The Good Scout."

16. Newhan, "The Good Scout."

17. The other players offered for the megastar in addition to Rhoden were Lee Lacy, Rick Sutcliffe, and Rafael Landestoy.

18. Crawford batted .333 against the A's in that series, slugging one home run and one RBI in six plate appearances over three games.

19. Bob Oates, "Monday Is Aching to Get Back to Work," *Los Angeles Times*, February 12, 1978.

20. Oates, "Monday Is Aching."

21. Oates, "Monday Is Aching."

22. The amount of average annual rainfall in Los Angeles is just under fifteen inches.

23. Skip Bayless, "Mr. Garvey Replaces Mr. Lincoln," *Los Angeles Times*, February 26, 1978.

24. Ross Newhan, "Lasorda Says NL Champions Can Be Even More Productive This Season," *Los Angeles Times*, February 26, 1978.

25. "Dodger Notes," *Los Angeles Times*, March 2, 1978; Ross Newhan, "Lasorda Names Lopes Captain," *Los Angeles Times*, March 2, 1978.

26. Newhan, "Lasorda Names Lopes Captain."

27. Newhan, "Lasorda Names Lopes Captain."

28. Ross Newhan, "Yeager Has Bigger Year in Sight," *Los Angeles Times*, March 3, 1978.

29. Ross Newhan, "Spring Hopes Eternal for Pair," *Los Angeles Times*, March 12, 1978; "Insiders Say," *The Sporting News*, February 11, 1978; Newhan, "Spring Hopes Eternal."

30. Ross Newhan, "No. 1 Reggie? Just Ask Smith," *Los Angeles Times*, March 22, 1978.

31. Newhan, "Spring Hopes Eternal."

32. Ross Newhan, "Their Days as Dodger Players Are Numbered," *Los Angeles Times*, March 4, 1978.

17. Paradise Defiled

1. "Whatever Happened to California?"; Michael Davie, *California: The Vanishing Dream* (New York: Dodd, Mead, 1972), 250.

2. "Whatever Happened to California?"

3. His mother had been taken to Auschwitz and died there.

4. Charles "Tex" Watson and Chaplain Ray, *Will You Die for Me? The Man Who Killed for Manson Tells His Own Story* (Grand Rapids MI: Fleming H. Revell, 1978), 136.

5. Marina Zenovich, dir., *Roman Polanski: Wanted and Desired* (Antidote Films, 2008).

6. Joan Didion, *The White Album* (New York: Simon & Schuster, 1979), 42.

7. According to the Public Policy Institute of California, Los Angeles's crime rates closely mirrored overall state statistics in the 1960s. The rate of violent crime more than doubled between 1960 and 1970—from 239 incidents to 475 incidents, respectively, per one hundred thousand residents. Most other sorts of crimes—including rape, murder, robbery, assault, against property, and so on—followed the same pattern over the decade. "California Crime Rates, 1960–2012," Disaster Center, 2014, http://www.disastercenter.com/crime/cacrime.htm.

8. Payne and Ratzan, *Tom Bradley*, 205.

9. Payne and Ratzan, *Tom Bradley*, 205.

10. Payne and Ratzan, *Tom Bradley*, 206.

11. Famously, while in office Bradley reserved only three days a year for his wife—her birthday, his birthday, and the Academy Awards.

12. Payne and Ratzan, *Tom Bradley*, 215.

13. Payne and Ratzan, *Tom Bradley*, 215.

18. The Redemption of Rick Monday

1. Ross Newhan, "Dodgers Use Jayvees and Twins Don't Like It," *Los Angeles Times*, March 14, 1978.

2. Newhan, "No. 1 Reggie?" The Dodgers would release the thirty-one-year-old Crawford at the end of the spring training after he hit just .192 in twenty-six at bats.

3. Ross Newhan, "Monday Leaves Troubles behind Him," *Los Angeles Times*, March 15, 1978.

4. Ross Newhan, "OK, Anderson Tells the Dodgers, Let's See You Do It Again," *Los Angeles Times*, March 21, 1978. Rose, helpfully enough, assessed each member of the Dodgers' lineup, somewhat echoing the concerns of the Dodgers' own management. "We know about Steve Garvey's consistency. We know Ron Cey is among the top five in RBI consistency. What we don't know is if people like Dusty Baker and Reggie Smith and Steve Yeager can repeat the years they had in 1977."

5. Ross Newhan, "Campanis Says Pitching Gives Dodgers Edge," *Los Angeles Times*, March 27, 1978.

6. Ross Newhan, "The 'Voice' of Baseball Coming in Loud and Clear," *Los Angeles Times*, March 26, 1978.

7. Newhan, "Pitching Gives Dodgers Edge."

8. Ross Newhan, "Reggie Smith Upset, Hurt; Game Rained Out," *Los Angeles Times*, April 1, 1978.

9. Newhan, "Reggie Smith Upset."

10. Ross Newhan, "Dodger Mood: Color It Blue," *Los Angeles Times*, April 6, 1978.

11. Newhan, "Dodger Mood Blue"; "Dodger Notes," *Los Angeles Times*, April 7, 1978.

12. Ross Newhan, "Little D Starts Measuring Up to Big D Tonight," *Los Angeles Times*, April 7, 1978.

13. Ross Newhan, "Dodgers Unload Their Monday Punch, 13–4," *Los Angeles Times*, April 8, 1978.

14. "Dodger Notes," *Los Angeles Times*, April 8, 1978.

15. Ross Newhan, "Dodgers Hit by Everything but the Dome," *Los Angeles Times*, April 13, 1978.

19. Every Day We Pay the Price

1. Ross Newhan, "Dodgers Blast Both Seaver and Morgan," *Los Angeles Times*, April 27, 1978.

2. Newhan, "Dodgers Blast Seaver and Morgan."

3. Ross Newhan, "A Win over Dodgers Eases Buckner's Pain," *Los Angeles Times*, May 3, 1978. Buckner added, "Nothing against the L.A. Fans, but these people [in Chicago] are terrific. We don't draw the numbers they do in L.A., but . . . they've really made me feel at home and they've sent a thousand suggestions as to what I should do for the ankle, everything from magic lotions to diet. You name it and I've tried it."

4. "Dodger Notes," *Los Angeles Times*, May 4, 1978; Ross Newhan, "Garvey Stops Hitting; Dodgers Stop Losing," *Los Angeles Times*, May 4, 1978.

5. Years later Lasorda would downplay his manner of speaking as a manager. "Hey, I know," he told a reporter, "when I'm in the clubhouse or on the field, I'm bad. I know that." Tom Hoffarth, "Q&A: Tommy Lasorda Talks Food, Baseball and Motivation, as Only Mr. Dodger Can," *L.A. Daily News*, July 15, 2013, http://www.dailynews.com/general-news/20130715/qa-tommy-lasorda-talks-food-baseball-and-motivation-as-only-mr-dodger-can.

6. Newhan, "Garvey Stops Hitting."

7. The Twins had shipped Blyleven to Texas in June 1976, and the Rangers then moved the pitcher to Pittsburgh in a four-way trade also involving the Braves and Mets in December 1977.

8. Ross Newhan, "Pirates Steal One from John, Dodgers, 6–4," *Los Angeles Times*, May 8, 1978; Ross Newhan, "Garvey Strategy: Return to Home, Collect 200 Hits," *Los Angeles Times*, May 9, 1978.

9. Newhan, "Garvey Strategy."

10. Elected as prime minister of the country in 1972, Manley had at the beginning pursued a socialist agenda, primarily by nationalizing the local export industries and by attempting to more equitably distribute wealth among Jamaica's poor. As a result of his policies American investment in the country slowed, and the local economy suffered. In 1974 Seaga rose to lead the conservative Jamaica Labour Party and oppose Manley. Both politicians, unfortunately, paid gangsters to help them hold power over local regions, which created the internecine violence that inspired the One Love Peace Concert.

11. The song's lyrics were pointedly appropriate for the occasion.

12. This belief was due to the fact that Montreal faced massive financial losses of up to two billion dollars after hosting the 1976 Summer Games, while Munich was traumatized by terrorist attacks at the 1972 Munich Olympics. (The so-called Munich Massacre by the Palestinian-based Black September group led to the murder of eleven members of the Israeli Olympic team.) In fact, the recent realities of the Olympic Games likely were why no city other than Los Angeles had submitted a final bid for the 1984 Games.

13. Kenneth Reich, "Olympics Won't Be Negotiated in Media—Bradley," *Los Angeles Times*, April 4, 1978.

14. Kenneth Reich, "Olympics Talks End on Note of Confusion," *Los Angeles Times*, April 12, 1978.

15. Kenneth Reich, "Bradley Says L.A. Can Veto Costs of Olympics," *Los Angeles Times*, April 13, 1978.

16. Ross Newhan, "Kingman's 3rd Homer Beats Dodgers in 15," *Los Angeles Times*, May 15, 1978.

20. The Ballad of Glenn and Spunky

1. Plaschke with Lasorda, *I Live for This*, 144.

2. Plaschke with Lasorda, *I Live for This*, 126.

3. Plaschke with Lasorda, *I Live for This*, 144, 191.

4. Marshall Berges, "Ernestine & Reggie Smith," *Los Angeles Times*, August 13, 1978.

5. He was drafted out of high school by the Minnesota Twins in 1963 and made his Major League debut with the Red Sox in 1966.

6. Howard Bryant, *Shut Out: A Story of Race and Baseball in Boston* (Boston: Beacon, 2003), 90.

7. Berges, "Ernestine & Reggie Smith."

8. Jeff Angus, "Reggie Smith," *SABR Baseball Biography Project*, 2014, http://sabr.org/bioproj/person/29bb796b.

9. Bob Oates, "Davey Lopes, the Quiet Man," *Los Angeles Times*, May 10, 1978.

10. Ross Newhan, "Smith Wins It in 9th on 4th Hit," *Los Angeles Times*, May 16, 1978.

11. He had just four doubles in sixty-five plate appearances for a paltry .288 slugging percentage.

12. Glenn Burke with Erik Sherman, *Out at Home: The Glenn Burke Story* (New York: Excel, 1995), 46; Jerry Bias and John Siple, "Letters," *Los Angeles Times*, March 11, 1978; Doug Harris and Sean Madison, *Out: The Glenn Burke Story* (Comcast Sportsnet Production, 2010).

13. Ross Newhan, "Dodgers Add Win and Bill North," *Los Angeles Times*, May 17, 1978.

14. Charges were eventually dropped in the case.

15. Ross Newhan, "A Clean Start," *Los Angeles Times*, May 18, 1978.

16. Ross Newhan, "Burke Trade Stops the Music," *Los Angeles Times*, May 21, 1978.

17. Harris and Madison, *Out*.

18. According to accounts, Glenn Burke was on deck in the game when Dusty Baker reached a key seasonal milestone—his thirtieth home run—in the sixth inning of the last game of the season on October 2, 1977. After Baker reached home Glenn greeted him with an upraised open hand, and Baker slapped it—and the high five was born. Interestingly, Baker's home run meant the Dodgers had four such players who reached the milestone in 1977, a league record. Also, Burke followed Baker's blast with one of his own—his first, and one of only two he would hit in his career.

19. Newhan, "Burke Trade."

20. To confuse matters Campanis has tended to deny the story (or refuse to speak of the matter), and Burke has given several different reports regarding his response to Campanis—that he either angrily dismissed the suggestion or retorted wryly, "I guess you mean to a woman?"

21. Harris and Madison, *Out*.

22. Burke with Sherman, *Out at Home*, 29. "After the experience," Burke said, "I cried for four hours. I was practically hyperventilating. The tears weren't from guilt, they were from relief. I was relieved because for the first time I was sure of who I was." Burke with Sherman, *Out at Home*, 36.

23. Burke with Sherman, *Out at Home*, 37, 39.

24. Burke with Sherman, *Out at Home*, 8, 9.

25. Jennifer Frey, "A Boy of Summer's Long Chilly Winter; Once a Promising Ballplayer, Glenn Burke Is Dying of AIDS," *New York Times*, October 18, 1994.

26. Harris and Madison, *Out*.

27. Burke with Sherman, *Out at Home*, 46.

28. Peter Richmond, "Tangled Up in Blue: The Brief Life and Complicated Death of Tommy Lasorda's Gay Son," GQ, October 1992.

29. Burke with Sherman, *Out at Home*, 18.

30. Richmond, "Tangled Up in Blue"; Burke with Sherman, *Out at Home*, 46.

31. Burke with Sherman, *Out at Home*, 20.

32. Burke with Sherman, *Out at Home*, 6, 46.

33. Burke with Sherman, *Out at Home*, 71.

34. Burke with Sherman, *Out at Home*, 18.

21. Ain't Talkin' 'bout Love

Epigraph: Tom Nolan, "California Dreamin' with the Eagles," *Phonograph Record* (June 1975).

1. The title of the first episode, "A Man about the House," was a nod to the BBC sitcom *Man about the House* (1973–76) on which *Three's Company* was based.

2. David Frum, *How We Got Here: The Seventies, the Decade That Brought You Modern Life—for Better or Worse* (New York: Basic, 2000), 191.

3. Edward Berkowitz, *Something Happened: A Political and Social Overview of the Seventies* (New York: Columbia University Press, 2006), 198, 210–11.

4. Wolfe, "Me Decade."

5. Born John Paul Rosenberg in Philadelphia in the 1930s, Erhard come west in the early 1960s. Eventually settling in Los Angeles in 1963, Erhard became heavily involved in the various self-help philosophies and programs of the time—including Dale Carnegie's training course, encounter psychotherapy, L. Ron Hubbard's Scientology, and Alexander Everett's Mind Dynamics—all of which were quite active in Southern California and had devoted followings. Erhard eventually became an instructor of Mind Dynamics seminars and took over the Los Angeles–area instruction, but he had bigger ideas.

6. Wolfe, "Me Decade."

7. Wolfe, "Me Decade."

8. Barney Hoskyns, *Hotel California* (Hoboken NJ: John Wiley & Sons, 2006), 20–22, 23. The Los Angeles music scene involved, at one time or another, such acts as the Mamas & the Papas; Crosby, Stills, Nash, and Young; Joni Mitchell; Frank Zappa; the Monkees; the Doors; Buffalo Springfield; the Byrds; Donovan; Fleetwood Mac; Jackson Browne; the Eagles; the Beach Boys; and many other bands and figures—all of whom had houses up in Laurel Canyon, where they often mixed and mingled with each other and with the squadron of groupies who frequented the area.

9. Hoskyns, *Hotel California*, 23, 137, 138.

10. Beyond these well-known incidents at the Roxy Theater, the nightclub was host to a number of groundbreaking performances throughout the 1970s and into the 1980s, many of which were recorded or broadcast on local television. Among the performances were ones by Frank Zappa & the Mothers of Invention, Bob Marley and the Wailers, Van Morrison, George Benson, Bruce Springsteen & the E Street Band, and so on.

11. Eckland, in many ways, epitomized the high-end aspect of the rock-and-roll social scene of L.A. in the 1970s. Having famously dated Rod Stewart, in 1979 she hooked up with, and became engaged to (but never married), Phil Lewis, who later became the front man of one of Los Angeles's highly sexualized, hair-centered glam rock bands of the era, L.A. Guns.

12. Paul Ciotti, "Lite Romance: Men Love to Love Women, but Why Don't More Men Love Them Forever?," *Los Angeles Times*, June 14, 1987.

13. Ciotti, "Lite Romance."

14. Davie, *California: The Vanishing Dream*, 174.

15. "The Porno Plague," *Time*, April 5, 1976.

16. While videotape recorders had existed since the 1950s, early devices were too expensive for home use, and the formats were so diverse that no single economy of scale existed for the production of commercially taped videos to thrive. However, it was the porn industry that almost single-handedly made the VHS tape commercially viable. "The fledgling home video industry wasn't yet big enough for

the major studios to release their titles on tape; pornography led the way. According to *Video* magazine, a pioneer publication in this new market, almost 70% of pre-recorded tapes sold in 1977–78 were X-rated." David Jennings, *Skinflicks: The Inside Story of the X-Rated Video Industry* (Bloomington IN: First Books Library, 2000), 53.

17. Holmes, who had been born in Ohio but moved to Los Angeles in the later 1960s after a stint in the U.S. Army, grew to become something of a household name. "He was simply the King," said adult filmmaker Bob Chinn. Coco Kiyonaga and Michael Copner, "The Boogie Days and Nights of Bob Chinn," *Cult Movies*, no. 24 (1997).

18. "Valley Retrospective: The 1970s," *Los Angeles Daily News*, January 20, 2011, http://www.dailynews.com/20110131/valley-retrospective-the-1970s.

19. Bobby Bouton and Nancy Marshall, *Home Games: Two Baseball Wives Speak Out* (New York: St. Martin's, 1983), 138. This book was about the trials of baseball wives.

20. Fimrite, "God a Football Fan."

21. Baker and Harriet divorced in 1987, right at the end of Baker's playing career, and he remarried in 1994.

22. He and Gloria later divorced.

23. "Playboy Interview: Steve Garvey; A Candid Conversation with the Squeaky-Clean, All-American Baseball Star," *Playboy*, June 1981.

22. Untaxing the Golden Cow

1. It was widely reported at the time that the last "profitable" Olympic Games were those held in Los Angeles in 1932.

2. While team President Peter O'Malley said in early 1978 he was confident that the Dodgers could work out a schedule with Olympics planners, in the end the idea fell through, and an open-air Olympic Swim Stadium was built, with the financial backing of the McDonald's Corporation, on the campus of the University of Southern California.

3. Payne and Ratzan, *Tom Bradley*, 216.

4. Payne and Ratzan, *Tom Bradley*, 216.

5. Frances Savitch, who at the time was an aid to Mayor Bradley.

6. Zev Yaroslavsky, "L.A. Needs Saving from Its Inferiority Complex," *Los Angeles Times*, April 9, 1978. Yaroslavsky expressed even deeper fears—that the city would overextend itself, that the Olympic Games would be a great disappointment because they won't do "for us what we think they can," that the city's lack of resolve in its response to the IOC regarding controlling costs would put it in an untenable position, and that the IOC's eventual demands would lead Los Angeles into a "financial quagmire." "What city in its right mind would want to salvage our bid?" he asked. "The fact remains that if the IOC refuses to play by our rules, the 1984 Olympics could become a refuge that no country would be willing to grant an entry visa."

7. Payne and Ratzan, *Tom Bradley*, 217; Kenneth Reich, "L.A.'s Olympic Bid Not Acceptable, IOC Indicates," *Los Angeles Times*, May 9, 1978.

8. "Maniac or Messiah," *Time*, June 19, 1978.

9. Howard Jarvis with Robert Pack, *I'm Mad as Hell* (New York: Times Books, 1979), 277, 278.

10. Jarvis with Pack, *I'm Mad as Hell*, 280.

11. Jarvis with Pack, *I'm Mad as Hell*, 16.

12. Jarvis with Pack, *I'm Mad as Hell*, 21; "Sound and Fury over Taxes," *Time*, June 19, 1978.

13. Jarvis with Pack, *I'm Mad as Hell*, 17.

14. Jarvis with Pack, *I'm Mad as Hell*, 19, 20, 21.

15. Jarvis with Pack, *I'm Mad as Hell*, 7.

16. Jarvis with Pack, *I'm Mad as Hell*, 24–25, 41.

17. William Endicott, "Property Tax Fighter's Goal: Get Some Political Muscle," *Los Angeles Times*, June 7, 1970.

18. Payne and Ratzan, *Tom Bradley*, 193.

19. Jarvis with Pack, *I'm Mad as Hell*, 38. In actuality, Jarvis would later learn, either through trickery or "sheer incompetence" the politicians mistakenly disqualified the organization's petition. "We filed more than 650,000 signatures before the deadline," wrote Jarvis, "but then more than 200,000 of them were arbitrarily discarded by temporary help: boobs who were hired off the streets by county registrars' offices throughout the state. More than 100,000 signatures were thrown out in Los Angeles County alone, and about three-quarters of them should have been allowed. . . . [Governor Jerry] Brown wouldn't extend our deadline and give us a chance to submit more signatures. . . . Nevertheless, we made a great showing that year and came close to getting on the ballot."

20. Jarvis with Pack, *I'm Mad as Hell*, 39.

21. William Oscar Johnson, "A Flaming Olympian Mess," *Sports Illustrated*, June 26, 1978.

22. Kenneth Reich, "L.A. Officials Conditionally Give in to IOC," *Los Angeles Times*, May 17, 1978.

23. Johnson, "A Flaming Olympian Mess."

24. Johnson, "A Flaming Olympian Mess." In effect, Proposition 13 set property-tax assessment levels back to their 1975 value and limited increases to future property taxes to a maximum of 2 percent per year. Additionally, the proposition prohibited any reassessment of a new base year value (that is, due to an increased property value) except in cases of a change in ownership or the completion of new construction.

25. Kevin Mattson, *What the Heck Are You Up to, Mr. President? Jimmy Carter, America's "Malaise," and the Speech That Should Have Changed the Country* (New York: Bloomsbury, 2010), 176.

26. Bernard Galm, "Interview of Thomas Bradley: Tape Number VI, Side Two," UCLA Oral History Collection, April 13, 1979.

27. Johnson, "A Flaming Olympian Mess."
28. Johnson, "A Flaming Olympian Mess."
29. Johnson, "A Flaming Olympian Mess."

23. Nothing Is Clicking Right Now

1. Gerry Hannahs and Larry Landreth; neither would ever establish themselves in the Majors.

2. He would retire for good from baseball after the 1979 season.

3. Mark Purdy, "Lacy and Cey Go Long Way to Help Hooton," *Los Angeles Times*, May 22, 1978.

4. "Notes," *Los Angeles Times*, May 24, 1978; "Letters: Fans on Dodgers," *Los Angeles Times*, May 27, 1978.

5. Ross Newhan, "Dodgers Quiet Down Giants' Batters, Fans," *Los Angeles Times*, May 28, 1978.

6. "Letters: 'A Poor Loser,'" *Los Angeles Times*, June 3, 1978.

7. Ross Newhan, "Dodgers Hold a Pair of N.Y. Rap Sessions," *Los Angeles Times*, June 7, 1978.

8. Marty Bell, "Don Sutton Does Not Bleed Dodger Blue," *Sport*, June 1978.

9. Ross Newhan, "Welch Takes Reds in Stride, 4–3," *Los Angeles Times*, June 25, 1978. Sutton would break both of Drysdale's Los Angeles Dodger pitching records—lifetime wins and strikeouts—in his next start, on June 29.

10. Ross Newhan, "Dodgers Turn This Chinker into 5–4 Win," *Los Angeles Times*, June 11, 1978.

11. Bob Welch with George Vecsey, *Five O'Clock Comes Early: A Cy Young Award-Winner Recounts His Greatest Victory* (New York: Simon and Schuster, 1991), 87; Ross Newhan, "Dodgers Are High on Welch's Fastball," *Los Angeles Times*, June 29, 1978.

12. Newhan, "Dodgers High on Welch."

13. Ross Newhan, "Reggie Smith's Status Clouds Dodger Future," *Los Angeles Times*, June 11, 1978.

14. Tom Hamilton, "Dodger Pitching Rapped by Dodger Pitcher," *Los Angeles Times*, June 15, 1978.

15. "Dodger Notes," *Los Angeles Times*, June 18, 1978.

16. The Minor Leaguers turned out to be Rafael Landestoy and future All-Star Jeff Leonard.

17. Ross Newhan, "Ferguson Is Back as Backup Man for the Dodgers," *Los Angeles Times*, July 2, 1978.

18. Hamilton, "Dodger Pitching Rapped."

19. Scott Ostler, "Dr. Marshall Wields Scalpel," *Los Angeles Times*, July 2, 1978. Marshall went on to say that while he liked playing for Walt Alston, his manager during his years with the Dodgers, eventually the front-office restrictions on Alston were, according to Marshall, a problem. This was apparently particularly true when it came to how to the manager used Marshall. "Walt Alston was

super," said Marshall. "But they really didn't let him manage after May of 1976." Eventually, when the iconoclastic pitcher ran up against some legal troubles (for trespassing at a facility at Michigan State University, his alma mater), Marshall was traded by the Dodgers to the Braves without Alston's approval. "The team is not noted for its compassion. Instead of saying, 'What can we do to help a teammate get through a tough period?" they think, 'Oh, my word, how will this affect the team?'"

20. Ross Newhan, "Dodgers Let 8–0 Lead Vanish," *Los Angeles Times*, July 6, 1978.

21. Newhan, "Dodgers Give Astros a Win."

22. Newhan, "Dodgers Give Astros a Win."

23. Lasorda said, on the off day before the All-Star Game, that he was writing personal letters to several National League players—including Garry Maddox of the Phillies, Ken Griffey and Dan Driessen of the Reds, and Bill Madlock of the Cubs—for being unable to add them to the team. (Both he and Billy Martin, the AL manager, expressed the opinion that the roster should be expanded from twenty-eight players to thirty.) "All-Star Notes," *Los Angeles Times*, July 11, 1978.

24. Dave Distel, "MVP: 'I Don't Hit with My Chin,'" *Los Angeles Times*, July 12, 1978.

24. The Grapple in the Apple

1. Rich Roberts, "Lasorda Tape: A Bleeping Mess," *Los Angeles Times*, August 10, 1978; Scott Ostler, "Fight Banded Dodgers Together," *Los Angeles Times*, October 13, 1978.

2. "Dodger Notes," *Los Angeles Times*, August 13, 1978; Scott Ostler, "Monday Resurfaces; So Do Dodgers, 5–4," *Los Angeles Times*, August 16, 1978.

3. Scott Ostler, "Dodgers vs. Giants: Born Again," *Los Angeles Times*, August 10, 1978.

4. Scott Ostler, "Temper, Temper . . . Mets Beat Dodgers," *Los Angeles Times*, August 20, 1978.

5. Fimrite, "God a Football Fan."

6. Fimrite, "God a Football Fan."

7. Thomas Boswell, "As Smith Goes, So Go Dodgers, 5–4 over Phils," *Washington Post*, August 16, 1978.

8. Boswell, "As Smith Goes."

9. Boswell, "As Smith Goes."

10. Boswell, "As Smith Goes."

11. Plaschke with Lasorda, *I Live for This*, 127.

12. Milton Richman, "Dodgers Garvey, Sutton Have Fight," *Milwaukee Journal*, August 21, 1978.

13. According to Tommy John, the teammates were Lopes, Smith, Russell, and Monday. John with Valenti, *My Twenty-Six Years*, 224.

14. Fimrite, "God a Football Fan."

15. Plaschke with Lasorda, *I Live for This*, 128; Fimrite, "God a Football Fan."

16. Plaschke with Lasorda, *I Live for This*, 127–28.

17. John with Valenti, *My Twenty-Six Years*, 224.

18. John with Valenti, *My Twenty-Six Years*, 224; Ostler, "Fight Banded Dodgers Together."

25. Is the Force with Us?

1. Lynne Bronstein, "Underwhelmed by the Word, 'Awesome,'" letter to the editor of the *Los Angeles Times*, April 30, 1977.

2. Despite the struggles of the decade, in 1976 the economy had grown by an unremarkable, but still solid, 5 percent and had followed up with similar numbers through 1977 and 1978. The jobless rate, which had peaked at 9 percent midway through 1975, declined to 7.5 percent by January 1977 and then to 5.9 percent in August 1978. Real median household income grew by 5 percent between 1976 and 1978, and all sorts of industries and businesses reported steady growth, even if it was generally mitigated by the high inflation of the era. (In 1978 inflation reportedly was 7.65 percent.)

3. Frank Zappa with Peter Occhiogrosso, *The Real Frank Zappa* (New York: Touchstone. 1990), 42. The Pal studio was known among music aficionados of the time for having one of the few available multitrack tape recorders, which Buff had built himself. In 1962, for example, a then unknown band of young musicians had driven from its home base in Glendora to record two songs at Pal—a droll number called "Surfer Joe" and a secondary tune meant to be its B side called "Wipe Out." In May 1963 the B side reached number two on the national *Billboard* charts. Pal also was the locus for a number of other regional and national hits: "Memories of the El Monte" by the Penguins (1963), the original demo of "Pipeline" by the Chantays (1963), "Tijuana Surf" and "Grunion Run" by the Hollywood Persuaders (1963), and so on.

4. Zappa had written a movie script called *Captain Beefheart vs. the Grunt People*, which was loosely based on the life of the parents of Zappa's friend Don Vliet, who performed as a musician under the name Captain Beefheart.

5. Zappa with Occhiogrosso, *The Real Frank Zappa*, 55, 60.

6. Martin Rossman, "Recall the 'Star Wars' Hype? You Ain't Seen Nothin' Yet," *Los Angeles Times*, June 18, 1978.

7. Cohn, a British-born transplant to New York who was often called the "English Tom Wolfe," would later joke that he had "hated" Wolfe at the time of his arrival. Neil Spencer, "Arts: Mr. Saturday Night," *Independent*, May 19, 1998.

8. Nik Cohn, "Tribal Rites of the New Saturday Night," *New York*, June 7, 1976.

9. On July 12, 1979—a.k.a., "the day disco died"—promoters with the Chicago White Sox held an event called Disco Demolition Night. Scheduled to take place between a doubleheader against the Detroit Tigers, the event asked fans to bring their disco records and pile them in center field, where they would then be exploded. Meant to attract young fans of rock music, the event ended with a major

riot, during which the raucous crowd tore out seats and pieces of turf and caused other damage. The White Sox, like the Indians before them on 10 Cent Beer Night, were forced to forfeit the second game to the Tigers.

10. Johnson, "A Flaming Olympian Mess."

11. Johnson, "A Flaming Olympian Mess."

12. Johnson, "A Flaming Olympian Mess."

13. Johnson, "A Flaming Olympian Mess"; Kenneth Reich, "Bradley Set to Drop Olympic Bid If Offer Is Rejected," *Los Angeles Times*, July 17, 1978.

14. Kenneth Reich, "Olympics Tell L.A. 'No,'" *Los Angeles Times*, July 18, 1978.

15. Dave Smith, "L.A.'s Vitality: Is the Force with Us?," *Los Angeles Times*, August 17, 1978.

16. Smith, "L.A.'s Vitality."

17. Smith, "L.A.'s Vitality."

26. Clinching

1. Called *Ball Four*, the show was meant to be a fictionalized version of his famous, tell-all book of the same name. "We wanted 'Ball Four,' the TV show, to be like 'M.A.S.H.,'" said Bouton some years later. "Instead it turned out more like 'Gilligan's Island' in baseball suits." Jim Bouton, "Ten Years Later. . . . Ball Five," in *Ball Four*, 412.

2. Bouton, "Ten Years Later," 435.

3. Bouton, "Ten Years Later," 415, 437.

4. "Morning Briefing," *Los Angeles Times*, May 28, 1978; Bouton, "Ten Years Later," 441.

5. Bouton, "Ten Years Later," 442.

6. Joshua Gilder, "Creators on Creating: Tom Wolfe," *Saturday Review*, April 1981.

7. Carole Iannone, "A Critic in Full: A Conversation with Tom Wolfe," National Association of Scholars website, August 11, 2008, https://www.nas.org/articles/A_Critic_in_Full_A_Conversation_with_Tom_Wolfe.

8. Gilder, "Creators on Creating."

9. Iannone, "Critic in Full"; Gilder, "Creators on Creating."

10. Kenneth Reich, "IOC Willing to Renew Talks, Bradley Told," *Los Angeles Times*, July 20, 1978.

11. Payne and Ratzan, *Tom Bradley*, 222–23.

11. With his late-season heroics, Garvey began to be mentioned in discussions regarding the 1978 season's MVP voting, a fact that was inconceivable as late as early August. Garvey would eventually finish second, behind Dave Parker of the Pirates.

13. Bouton, "Ten Years Later," 442.

14. Scott Ostler, "Bat Day for Angels, Dodgers," *Los Angeles Times*, September 11, 1978.

15. Bouton, "Ten Years Later," 443.

16. Bouton, "Ten Years Later," 443.

17. "Morning Briefing," *Los Angeles Times*, September 28, 1978.

18. Interestingly, during his comeback attempt while playing with the Portland Mavericks a few years earlier, the ever-resourceful Bouton had been involved in the invention, along with a teammate named Rob Nelson, of a brand-new product. One day, while sitting in the bullpen and passing time by "drowning bugs in tobacco juice," Nelson told Bouton that there should be a suitable substitute for chewing tobacco that would allow ballplayers to keep their swarthy image while remaining relatively healthy. The two sent away for some gum base, mixed up some recipes, and shredded it like chaw. In time a division of Wrigley bought the idea, reformulated the gum, and eventually released it as Big League Chew—giving the world yet another novel reason to appreciate Jim Bouton.

19. Bouton, "Ten Years Later," 445.

27. The Inevitable Yankee Miracle

1. Scott Ostler, "A Happy Day for Dodgers Is Also a Sad Day," *Los Angeles Times*, September 25, 1978.

2. Ostler, "Happy Day for Dodgers."

3. The Dodgers had scored sixty-one runs against Pittsburgh and given up just forty-four runs, while the Phillies had actually outscored them, 48–55.

4. Mahler, *Ladies and Gentlemen*, 243.

5. Sparky Lyle and Peter Golenbock, *The Bronx Zoo: The Astonishing Inside Story of the 1978 World Champion New York Yankees* (Chicago: Triumph, 1979), 156, 170.

6. Lyle and Golenbock, *Bronx Zoo*, 169.

7. Kayla Webley, "Hiring and Firing Billy Martin—Top 10 George Steinbrenner Moments," *Time*, July 13, 2010. Martin was referring to Steinbrenner's conviction in 1974 for making illegal donations to Richard Nixon's 1972 reelection campaign.

8. Though Steinbrenner did replace Martin with Bob Lemon, less than a week later, oddly enough, the Yankees' owner, perhaps influenced by the sentiment of Yankees fans, announced that Martin would remain on salary with the team as an "adviser" and, oddly, that he would become the team's manager again in 1980, when Bob Lemon would be moved to the front office.

9. Richard L. Shook, "Memories of '78 Red Sox Collapse Hang Heavily over Boston," *Los Angeles Times*, July 20, 1986.

10. Mark Newman, "'78 'Boston Massacre' Revisited," mlb.com, August 21, 2006, http://m.mlb.com/news/article/1621531/; Lyle and Golenbock, *Bronx Zoo*, 216.

11. Newman, "'78 'Boston Massacre' Revisited."

12. Lyle and Golenbock, *Bronx Zoo*, 243–44.

13. Scott Ostler, "New York Claims a Home Away from Home in Boston," *Los Angeles Times*, October 3, 1978.

28. Chronic Hysteresis; or, Another Yankee-Dodgers Rematch

1. "Royals Blame Third-Base Umpire," *Los Angeles Times*, October 8, 1978. Whitey Herzog had been signed as a high school ballplayer in 1949 by, of all teams, the New York Yankees, and he had had a relatively undistinguished, journeyman eight-year career as a ballplayer before becoming a scout and coach for the Kansas City A's.

2. "Royals Blame Umpire."

3. Don Merry, "The Fall Guys of the Fall Are Now 1–7 in Playoffs," *Los Angeles Times*, October 5, 1978; Scott Ostler, "Dodgers Are Up . . . Phillies Go Down, 9–5," *Los Angeles Times*, October 5, 1978.

4. Don Merry, "Phils Become a Bunch of Carpet Beaters," *Los Angeles Times*, October 6, 1978.

5. Don Merry, "That Playoff Grave Remains UnPhilled," *Los Angeles Times*, October 7, 1978.

6. Don Merry, "'I Missed It . . . It Was Right at Me'—Maddox," *Los Angeles Times*, October 8, 1978.

7. Merry, "'I Missed It."

8. Jim Murray, "The Day Garry Maddox Dropped a Pennant," *Los Angeles Times*, October 8, 1978.

9. Earl Gustkey, "Sadness amid Dodger Cheer: Jim Gilliam," *Los Angeles Times*, October 8, 1978.

10. Milton Richman, "Alston: Gilliam Was THE Ideal," *Los Angeles Times*, October 9, 1978.

11. Scott Ostler, "'Never More Relaxed'—Lopes," *Los Angeles Times*, October 11, 1978.

12. Jackson with Baker, *Becoming Mr. October*, 279; Lyle and Golenbock, *Bronx Zoo*, 248.

13. The next day in many papers across the country, there even appeared a poem commemorating the event—written by some nameless AP reporter who likely dare not sign his name. It was, of course, a takeoff on "Casey at the Bat." "The outlook wasn't brilliant for the Yankees in LA / The score stood 4–3, two out, one inning left to play" began the poem, just to give an idea of its quality.

14. Plaschke with Lasorda, *I Live for This*, 137.

15. Welch and Vecsey, *Five O'Clock Comes Early*, 102.

16. Scott Ostler, "Dodgers Lose Their Cool over the Iceman," *Los Angeles Times*, October 12, 1978; John Hall, "Series Diary," *Los Angeles Times*, October 12, 1978.

17. "Game Four, World Series Broadcast," ABC TV, October 14, 1978.

18. "Game Four, World Series Broadcast."

19. Jackson with Baker, *Becoming Mr. October*, 281.

29. Afterword

1. Bruce Lowitt, "Tale of Two Cities, One Overmatched," *Los Angeles Times*, October 20, 1978.

2. UPI, "Steinbrenner Wants the Dodgers to Apologize," *Los Angeles Times*, October 27, 1978.

3. Scott Ostler, "For Lasorda, It's Sweet and Sour," *Los Angeles Times*, October 19, 1978; Ross Newhan, "John Says He'll Go Free Today," *Los Angeles Times*, October 19, 1978.

4. Under manager Jim Marshall in 1979, the A's would record a miserable, Major League–worst 54-108 record. Burke, meanwhile, continued to struggle against Major League pitching, batting just .213 with virtually no power in ninety-four plate appearances. In 1980, with the team's reins in the hands of the nomadic, homophobic Billy Martin, Burke would become even more discouraged. After a half season on the A's AAA team in Ogden, still reeling from slights and insults from Martin and his staff, Burke quit baseball for good.

5. Rautzhan would appear in three games as a reliever for the Brewers in 1979, recording a 9.00 ERA. After spending one more season pitching for Milwaukee's AAA team in Vancouver in 1980, Rautzhan would retire at age twenty-seven and return home to Pennsylvania.

6. Having appeared in fifty-three Major League games with only middling success, Webb's more enduring impact on the Major Leagues may have been his son, Ryan Webb, who credits his career as a professional ballplayer to his father. "He's awesome to talk to about baseball," said Ryan Webb. "I call him every day and tell him what I'm doing. Since high school we would go out after the games and talk baseball. He's the reason why I'm here." Juan C. Rodriguez, "Ex–Major Leaguer Hank Webb Still Catches Heat from Son, Ryan," *Fort Lauderdale (FL) Sun Sentinel*, February 23, 2011, http://articles.sun-sentinel.com/2011-02-23/sports/fl-marlins-0224-20110223_1_scott-hairston-deal-padres-major-league.

7. After committing an astounding fifty-three errors at third base in 1977, Westmoreland split time in the outfield and first base for Albuquerque in 1978, where he continued to struggle. In fifty-three games as an outfielder, for example, he committed eleven errors, for a dismal .911 fielding percentage.

8. Rhoden's and Reuss's careers mirrored each other's in many ways. Having both been All-Stars as younger men, in 1979 they were deemed damaged goods by their teams. After the swap each would struggle in 1979—Reuss recording a 7-14 win-loss record for the Dodgers and Rhoden appearing in only one game for the Pirates in 1979 due to injury—but they both would eventually return to form and pitch well throughout much of the 1980s.

9. Don Sutton, for instance, recorded his first losing season in a decade in 1979, and his ERA of 3.82 was above the league average.

10. "Compared with their immediate predecessors of the Postwar Age," wrote one commenter, "the mod new breed differed in many ways. In social background, looks, dress, language, personality modes, attitudes, aspirations, affluence, playing style and performances, the new breed stood apart from past generations of players." David Q. Voigt, "A New Breed of Baseball Players," *Baseball Research Journal*, SABR online (undated), http://research.sabr.org/journals/new-breed-of-baseball-players.

11. Voigt, "New Breed of Baseball Players."

12. Lasorda with Fisher, *The Artful Dodger*, 266.

13. Wayne was well aware of how polarizing he could be and later acknowledged that much of his image—the swagger, the manner of speech, the way he held himself on camera—was a conscious creation. "When I started, I knew I was no actor and I went to work on this Wayne thing," he recalled. "It was as deliberate a projection as you'll ever see. I figured I needed a gimmick, so I dreamed up the drawl, the squint and a way of moving meant to suggest that I wasn't looking for trouble but would just as soon throw a bottle at your head as not." Richard Shephard, "'Duke,' an American Hero," *New York Times*, June 12, 1979.

14. Shephard, "'Duke,' an American Hero."

15. Lasorda with Fisher, *The Artful Dodger*, 269.

16. Sax would be named to the All-Star team in 1982, win the Rookie of the Year Award, and play fourteen years in the big leagues.

17. In 1982 Brock had hit forty-four home runs at Albuquerque, while batting .310 and recording an outstanding on-base percentage of .432; he wouldn't come close to matching these numbers in the Major Leagues.

18. Only one only other player, Zack Wheat, would play in more games as a Dodger, in Brooklyn; Russell's mark would be the most games played by a Dodger in Los Angeles.

19. Interestingly, the second of these titles also almost never happened. According to a story told by Fred Claire, a few years after his World Series triumph in 1981 Lasorda, frustrated at the money he was earning, decided to issue an ultimatum. "It was just after the conclusion of the 1983 season," wrote Claire years later. "The Dodgers had reached the playoffs only to be eliminated in the National League Championship Series by the Philadelphia Phillies, who knocked them out by winning the best-of-five series in four games." Lasorda, realizing that he was one of the most popular sports figures in Los Angeles, and the country, wanted to be rewarded for that. "He was appreciative of the opportunity to manage a high-profile team," Claire continued, "but business was business and he felt he was making a large contribution to the Dodger business." When negotiations reached an impasse, Lasorda, in essence, walked away from the job. (Rumors were rampant that the New York Yankees had dangled a five-year contract to Lasorda.) Peter O'Malley, the team's president and owner, asked his management staff for recommendations for a replacement, and, eventually, one name rose to the top. "I had given some thought to the subject," said Claire, "because I knew it was a possibility for discussion, so I wasted no time in offering my candidate—Joe Morgan." Morgan had just completed his twenty-first year in the Majors with the Philadelphia Phillies and was known to be considering retirement. "I received a second on my suggestion of Morgan . . . and approval from Peter. Al went along." A call was made (to the Phillies' owner) to get permission to speak to Joe, and the team was one step away from making a move when, fatefully, Tommy Lasorda called back to announce he had reconsidered and would accept the team's final offer if it still stood. "Tommy came upstairs, signed the contract and remained the Dodger manager for another 13 seasons." Claire with Springer, *My Thirty Years in Dodger Blue*, 82–86.

INDEX